The law and elder

There are more than 9 million people over pensionable age in England and Wales and this number is increasing in relation to the rest of the population. *The Law and Elderly People* was the first text to provide easily accessible information in a systematic and comprehensive way for those involved in advice-giving and service provision in this rapidly developing field.

This second edition has been fully revised and completely updated to reflect the major legal and social changes which have occurred since publication of the first edition in 1990. Concerned for the independence and autonomy of both the young elderly and the old elderly, the new text includes detailed discussion of important changes in the fields of occupational and state pensions, as well as other state benefits; housing tenure as it affects older people; community and residential care following the implementation of the NHS and the Community Care Act 1990; the restructuring of health care; and personal and family matters such as the effects of divorce in old age and the rights of grandparents.

By contextualising legal issues within the framework of social policy and social change the editors and contributors demonstrate an interdisciplinary approach which will be of practical help to all those concerned with the welfare of the elderly and to undergraduates and lecturers in social work, law and gerontology.

Aled Griffiths is Principal Lecturer and Head of the Department of Business and Social Administration at Coleg Normal and Visiting Lecturer at the University of Wales, both in Bangor. **Gwyneth Roberts** is Senior Lecturer in Social Policy at the University of Wales, Bangor.

The law and elderly people
Second Edition

Edited by Aled Griffiths and
Gwyneth Roberts

London and New York

First edition published by Routledge in hardback 1990

© 1990 Aled Griffiths, Richard H. Grimes and Gwyneth Roberts

Second edition published 1995
by Routledge
11 New Fetter Lane, London EC4P 4EE

Simultaneously published in the USA and Canada
by Routledge
29 West 35th Street, New York, NY 10001

© 1995 Selection and editorial matter, Aled Griffiths and Gwyneth Roberts;
individual chapters, the contributors.

Typeset in Times by
Florencetype Ltd, Kewstoke, Avon

Printed and bound in Great Britain by
Mackays of Chatham PLC, Chatham, Kent

British Library Cataloguing in Publication Data
A catalogue record for this book is available from the British Library

Library of Congress Cataloging in Publication Data
A catalogue record for this book has been requested

ISBN 0-415-12044-6 (hbk)
ISBN 0-415-11324-5 (pbk)

In memory of
Stewart Pritchard
a much missed colleague and friend

Contents

4 Residential and nursing care   140
Lynda Bransbury

Contributors

Aled Griffiths Principal Lecturer at Y Coleg Normal, Bangor and Visiting Lecturer at University College of North Wales, Bangor.

Gwyneth Roberts Senior Lecturer at the School of Social Policy and Sociology, University College of North Wales, Bangor.

Hugh Howard Solicitor, and part-time Chairman of a Social Security Appeal Tribunal, a Disability Appeal Tribunal and a Child Support Appeal Tribunal.

Rebecca Jordan Solicitor, specialising in housing and matrimonial law.

Jeff Harrison Housing Adviser for a firm of solicitors; has worked as a housing adviser for local tenants' associations and a local authority Housing Aid Centre.

Lynda Bransbury Parliamentary and legal officer for the Local Government Information Unit, specialising in community care and local government finance.

Table of cases

Table of statutes

Table of statutory instruments

Preface

The purpose of this book is to examine aspects of the law which may be of particular significance in the lives of older people. The six main subject areas discussed here are: employment and income; accommodation and housing; community care; residential care; health provision and its delivery; and family and personal matters.

Many important changes have taken place in these areas of the law since the first edition of this book in 1990, not least the coming into force of the NHS and Community Care Act 1990, and the introduction of the internal market in the health service. Important changes have also taken place in the field of income support and housing. All in all, this has meant a major up-dating of the text.

Our hope is that the text provides a useful guide to some of the more important legal issues, and will contribute, in some small way, towards enabling older people to enjoy, for as long as possible, independent, self-fulfilling and autonomous lives.

Acknowledgements

We are most grateful for the help we have received from a number of people in preparing this edition of *The Law and Elderly People*. We would like, in particular, to thank John Borland, Jaswant Chanay, Brian Jones, Rachel Forrester-Jones, John Keady, Mike Nolan and Jan Luba for their helpful advice and suggestions. We would also like to thank the Library staff at the University of Wales, Bangor and Deborah Bird for word processing Chapter 2. Last but not least, we once more owe very special thanks to Geraldine Roberts for her commitment and skill in producing various versions of this book, including the final one. Unfortunately, Angela Rowlands, who contributed so much to the production of the first edition, was unable, because of ill health, to work with us on this occasion.

Responsibility for the final text remains with us. We have tried to state the law as it stood in England and Wales as at the end of March 1994. However, it should be noted (in relation to Chapter 6) that the report of the Review Committee on NHS complaints procedures was published by the Department of Health in May 1994, under the title 'Being heard'; and (in relation to Chapter 5) that draft guidance was issued by the Department of Health and the Welsh Office, in August 1994, which is aimed at clarifying NHS responsibility for meeting long-term health care needs.

Aled Griffiths
Gwyneth Roberts

List of abbreviations

AA   Attendance Allowance
ABU   Agencies Benefits Unit
AMA   Ajudicating Medical Authority
AO   Ajudicating Officer
APP   Appropriate Personal Pension
ASW   Approved Social Worker
CAA   Constant Attendance Allowance
CABx   Citizens' Advice Bureaux
CCG   Community Care Grant
CGT   Capital Gains Tax
CHC   Community Health Council
CHS   Community Health Services
CLN   Community Liaison Nurse
CPN   Community Psychiatric Nurse
CRAG   Charging for Residential Accommodation Guide
CTB   Community Tax Benefit
CTT   Capital Transfer Tax
DAT   Disability Appeal Tribunal
DGM   District General Manager
DH   Department of Health (after July 1988)
DHA   District Health Authority
DHSS   Department of Health and Social Security (up to July 1988)
DLA   Disability Living Allowance
DMU   Directly Managed Unit
DN   District Nurse
DPB   Dental Practice Board
DSS   Department of Social Security (after July 1988)
DWA   Disability Working Allowance
EAT   Employment Appeal Tribunal

EC	European Community
ECT	Electro-Convulsive Therapy
EPA	Enduring Power of Attorney
EU	European Union
FC	Family Credit
FHS	Family Health Services
FHSA	Family Health Services Authority
FP	Family Premium
FPS	Family Practitioner Services
FSAVC	Free Standing Additional Voluntary Contributions
GMC	General Medical Council
GMP	Guaranteed Minimum Pension
GMS	General Medical Services
GOS	General Opthalmic Services
GP	General Practitioner
GPFH	General Practitioner Fund Holder
HAS	Health Advisory Service
HB	Housing Benefit
HC	Health Committee
HM	Hospital Manager
HP	Hire Purchase
HPP	Higher Pensioner Premium
HRP	Home Responsibility Protection
HSC	Health Service Commissioner
HV	Health Visitor
IBIP	Invalidity Benefit/Invalidity Pension
ICA	Invalid Care Allowance
IHT	Inheritance Tax
IS	Income Support
LMC	Local Medical Committee
MHAC	Mental Health Act Commission
MHRT	Mental Health Review Tribunal
MO(C)	Medical Officer (Complaints)
MSC	Medical Services Committee
NAHA	National Association of Health Authorities
NHS	National Health Service
NI	National Insurance
OPAS	Occupational Pensions Advisory Service
OPB	Occupational Pensions Board
OPCS	Office of Population and Census Studies
PAYE	Pay As You Earn
PCC	Professional Conduct Committee

PO	Pensions Ombudsman
PP	Pensioner Premium
PPC	Preliminary Proceedings Committee
PPG	Patient Participation Group
PVS	Persistent Vegetative State
RADAR	Royal Association for Disability and Rehabilitation
RCGP	Royal College of General Practitioners
RCNHS	Royal Commission on the National Health Service
RGN	Registered General Nurse
RHA	Regional Health Authority
RMO	Regional Medical Officer
SDA	Severe Disability Allowance
SDB	Severe Disability Benefit
SDP	Severe Disability Premium
SEN	State Enrolled Nurse
SERPS	State Earnings-Related Pension Scheme
SFMFG	Social Fund Maternity and Funeral Payments Guide
SFO	Social Fund Officer
SHA	Special Health Authority
SIB	Securities Investment Board
SSAFA	Soldiers, Sailors and Airmen's Families Association
SSAT	Social Security Appeal Tribunal
SSC	Social Services Commissioner
SSD	Social Security Department
SSI	Social Services Inspectorate
UGM	Unit General Manager
UK	United Kingdom
UKCC	United Kingdom Central Council
WO	Welsh Office

1 Employment, income and retirement

Aled Griffiths and Hugh Howard

1.1.1 During the course of the century there has been a considerable decline in the number of those of retirement age still at work. At the turn of the century more than two-thirds of men aged sixty-five and over were in the labour force, but by 1989 only 9 per cent were so employed (Walker and Taylor 1992). In contrast, the proportion of economically active women has slightly increased in very recent years. For instance, the economic activity rate for women aged sixty to sixty-four rose from 19 per cent in 1987 to 23 per cent in 1992 (OPCS 1992). One explanation for the different trend is that women are much more likely than men to work part-time (Dibden and Hibbett 1993).

1.1.2 Recent research into the effect of age on performance suggests that age is not a sensible basis on which to judge the ability to learn or work, save where muscular strength is the primary requirement (Trinder *et al.* 1992). Similarly, evidence exists to show that older workers' supposed inability to cope with technological changes has been overstated; most can cope with the changes demanded of them (Trinder 1990).

1.1.3 Nevertheless, the trend towards earlier retirement for men seems set to continue. Initially the prerogative of managers and white-collar workers, early retirement has spread to wider sections of the work-force and has generally been seen by managers and trade unions as an uncontentious way of achieving 'headcount reduction' (Cliff 1991). In fact, the economic activity rate for men aged sixty to sixty-four dropped from 55 per cent in 1987 to 53 per cent in 1992 (OPCS 1992). Thus, almost half the male population is economically inactive at sixty years of age. An OPCS retirement survey found a desire among older workers for gradual retirement, with the option of part-time work being available. Men, however, usually retire abruptly and part-time work is likely to involve a change of employer and occupational downgrading (Casey *et al.* 1991). In short, particular work and retirement patterns are being forced on older people as a result of age discrimination, and inflexible personal and pension policies (Trinder *et al.* 1992). Many non-working older people want to work (CBI 1989).

1.1.4 This is not to argue that retirement age should be raised for everyone. Research findings suggest that for some people retirement improves health. According to American literature, studies carried out in the 1960s, which suggested that imposed retirement had a negative effect on self-image, gave grossly exaggerated results. Loss of work may not be nearly as devastating to the individual as was once assumed (Ekerdt 1983). The status of older people may also be enhanced by the legitimisation of leisure (Pampel 1981). The argument here is simply that individuals should be allowed greater choice whether or not they continue to work beyond pensionable age.

1.1.5 The Employment Department has recognised the need for a change in attitude and has set up an Advisory Group. The long-term aim is to encourage employers to make the most of older workers' expertise and abandon age discrimination in all their personnel policies, including recruitment and training policies (*Employment Gazette*: March 1993). It would, however, be wrong to be over-optimistic about the outcome. Only a few years ago, the government of the day elected not to support a Private Member's Bill entitled the Employment Upper Age in Advertisement Bill 1990. The Bill would have made it an offence to refer to an upper age limit in advertisements. It appears that the government's view was that ageism could not be successfully defeated by law, though Employment Department local centres were instructed to dissuade employers from putting upper age limits in advertisements (*Eagle* 1991). In the meantime, between a quarter and a third of all advertisements contain age restrictions. Moreover, age is included in only a third of employers' equal opportunities policies and not all employers have such policies (Dibden and Hibbett 1993).

The Social Chapter signed by all member states of the European Union stresses the importance of combating every form of discrimination, but makes no specific reference to age discrimination. Numerous EC directives, which have the force of law, exist to combat discrimination based on gender and their impact has been significant, particularly in relation to pension and retirement schemes (see below at paras. 1.6.4 and 1.9.2). In addition, it is open to individuals who have suffered age discrimination in employment to petition the European Parliament. Indeed, an EU pressure group, Eurolink–Age, has initiated a campaign to encourage aggrieved individuals to do so, and a draft form of Petition is available (*Eagle* 1990).

1.1.6 Research also shows little evidence of employers helping employees to prepare for retirement (Trinder *et al.* 1992). This is to be regretted for, as others have stressed, improvement in the standard of living for many individuals will come only via a long-term process of argument and negotiation with a range of organisations and institutions within each community (Laczko and Phillipson 1991). This chapter will hopefully assist those engaged in the process.

1.2.1 EMPLOYMENT PROTECTION

In Great Britain about two-thirds of elderly people, 5.7 million, live on the margins of poverty, as defined by the state, compared with around one-fifth of the non-elderly. Even those in employment are often on low incomes (Walker 1991). Employment protection and wage protection are therefore of crucial importance.

1.2.2 THE CONTRACT OF EMPLOYMENT

Where a dispute arises over the terms of a contract, particularly in relation to rights arising on its termination, it is usually important for the employee to be able to ascertain its contents. It is still common practice for many contracts of employment to be entered into orally, or both orally and in writing. In accordance with s.1 of the Employment Protection (Consolidation) Act 1978 (EP(C)A 1978), most employees who work for more than eight hours a week are entitled to receive a written statement from their employer setting out the terms of the contract not later than two months after commencement of employment. The existence of the contract will not, however, be affected should a statement not be issued. In such circumstances, the terms of the contract will be deduced from custom, practice or by implication. The statutory statement itself is not conclusive evidence of the terms of the contract, although it can help to establish what those terms are.

The statement must include information on the scale and rate of enumeration, terms and conditions relating to hours of work, entitlement to holidays and holiday pay, incapacity for work due to sickness or injury, sick pay, pensions and pension schemes, the length of required notice (employee and employer), job title, place or places of work, and any relevant collective agreements. Individuals employed by organisations who employ twenty employees or more are also entitled to receive information relating to any disciplinary procedures adopted by the employer. Should no written statement be provided, or should the one which has been provided be incomplete, an employee can ask an industrial tribunal to determine what should be included in it.

1.2.3 WAGES PROTECTION

Section 35 of the Trade Union Reform and Employment Rights Act 1993 (TURERA 1993) abolished Wages Councils. Over 2.5 million workers in a number of industries, including retail, hotel and catering, hairdressing and clothing manufacturing, lost their right to receive legal minimum rates of pay. However, those engaged in the relevant industries prior to the legislative change will probably retain some protection against employers who subsequently attempt to reduce wages. An action for breach of contract based on an implied term that such employees be paid not less than the legal minimum rate may possibly be recognised by the courts (Hunt and Miller 1994).

The EP(C)A 1978 (ss.8–10) provides most employees with a right to an itemised pay statement. Provided that the employee works for eight hours or more (or sixteen if the employer employs less than twenty employees), he/she has the right to particulars of the gross amount of wages or salary and the amount of any variable or fixed deductions.

1.3.1 DISABLED EMPLOYEES

Employment opportunities for disabled people are in principle assisted by the Quota Scheme introduced by the Disabled Persons (Employment) Acts 1944 and 1958 (DP(E)A 1944 and 1958) which provide that 3 per cent of employees in firms with more than twenty employees should be registered as disabled.

Although the duty is not binding on the Crown, government departments have nevertheless agreed to accept the same responsibilities as other employers (*Employment Gazette*, April 1993). The National

Health Service and Community Care Act 1990 (NHSCCA 1990) has also removed Crown immunity from NHS employers. To register, a person must be substantially handicapped in obtaining or keeping employment. Particular jobs, such as car-park attendant, are designated as suitable for disabled persons and they must be employed in preference to able-bodied persons. Some hazardous industries are, however, exempted. It is also possible to apply for a special permit if the full quota cannot be filled, either because of the lack of a suitable candidate or the unsuitability of the work.

1.3.2 It is an offence to disregard the statutory provisions, but prosecutions are rare. Three-quarters of employers fail to meet the quotas, but since 1944 there have only been some ten prosecutions under the legislation (Employment Policy Institute 1992). Nevertheless, registration as a disabled person should not be regarded as futile, since a degree of protection has been established at common law. In *Kerr v. Atkinson's Vehicles Ltd (1974)*, it was held that an employer should not expect a normal standard of work or output from a disabled person. Dismissal would be fair only if it could be shown that the standard of a person's work was below that which could reasonably be expected from him/her. An employer would also need to show the case had been given special consideration and that the needs of the business made dismissal necessary (*Pascoe v. Hallen and Medway (1975)*).

1.3.3 The Employment Service (an Executive Agency of the Employment Department) has published a Code of Good Practice on the employment of people with disabilities. Although compliance with the guidance is voluntary, its contents will be taken into account when deciding whether a dismissal is fair or not (Robertson 1993).

1.3.4 Companies which employ more than 250 employees have, also, in their Annual Reports, to outline their policies on the recruitment, training and career development of workers with disabilities (Companies (Directors' Report) (Employment of Disabled Persons) Regulations 1980).

1.4.1 MINIMUM NOTICE PERIODS

Except where there is serious misconduct, a person is entitled to be given notice for the period set out in his/her contract of employment. A contract for a fixed term does not require notice since it is brought to an end automatically by passage of time (*Labour Party v. Oakley (1987)*). Failure to renew a fixed-term contract may, however, amount to an unfair dismissal (*Terry v. East Sussex County Council (1977)*; *Johnstone v. BBC Enterprises Ltd (1993)*). Where there is no express provision for notice in the contract, reasonable notice must be given. What is regarded as reasonable will vary, depending upon the position held by the employee. It has been held that a senior engineer was entitled to more that a month's notice, and that reasonable notice in such circumstances could have been anything between six months and one year (*Hill v. C. A. Parsons & Co. Ltd (1971)*). Whatever the contract provides, the length of notice cannot be shorter than the minimum required by statute. This varies according to length of service. After four weeks, an employee is entitled to one week's notice, until he/she has been engaged for up to two years. The employee is then entitled to one week's notice for each completed year of service up to a maximum of twelve weeks (EP(C)A 1978, s.49(1)). A person employed for seven years or over, for example, would be entitled to seven weeks' notice.

Where an employee is given notice, but is asked to work until the notice has expired, dismissal will not be effective until the end of that period. In effect, should an employee leave sooner, he/she will be regarded as having brought the employment to an end, rather than having been dismissed (*Walker v. Cotswold Chine Home School (1977)*).

1.4.2 An employee must give a minimum of one week's notice of termination of employment, but the contract of employment can stipulate a longer period (EP(C)A 1978 s.49(2)). In theory, an employee who failed to work out his/her period of notice could be sued for breach of contract. This is unlikely in practice.

1.5.1 FRUSTRATION OF THE CONTRACT

Where performance of a contract of employment is rendered impossible by some intervening event, it will be brought to an end automatically by operation of law. In legal terms, the contract is said to have been 'frustrated'. The most common causes of frustration are probably sickness or injury. An accident may be so serious that it is apparent that the employee is no longer able to perform his/her part of the contract.

Prolonged periods of sickness could also result in the employer claiming the contract of employment no longer exists. Relevant considerations are the length of employment; how long it could have been expected to continue were it not for the illness or injury; the nature of the work; the type of employment and the employer's need to have the work done; the terms of the contract, including the provision of sick pay; and whether, in all the circumstances, a reasonable employer could be expected to give the employee more time to return to work (*Egg Stores (Stamford Hill) Ltd v. Leibovici (1977)*).

Where an occupational sick-pay scheme exists, the contract will normally continue until such time as payment under the scheme comes to an end, but this is not always the case. The contract may come to an end earlier where sickness or injury is so serious that there is no prospect, in the foreseeable future, of the employee returning to work. It should be stressed, however, that absence from work, even for a long period of time, does not necessarily mean that the contract has been frustrated. In *Maxwell v. Walter Howard Designs Ltd (1975)*, the employee had been sick for nearly two years. It was held that the post did not need a permanent replacement and that the contract of employment had not, therefore, been frustrated. Where the contract has been frustrated, the employer need not dismiss the employee, but could do so, and claim the dismissal to have been fair.

1.6.1 UNFAIR AND WRONGFUL DISMISSAL

Under the EP(C)A 1978, protection against unfair dismissal extends to most employees who can show they have been in continuous employment for two years and for not less than sixteen hours per week (or for not less than eight hours per week after five years of employment) (EP(C)A 1978, s.64 as amended). A person of normal retiring age is outside this protection. In occupations where there is no established age for retiring, the normal retirement age will be sixty-five for both men and women. Where dismissal is on the grounds of an employee's membership of a trade union (or his/her intention to join one), it is not necessary to show that there has been continuous employment for the requisite period. The same rule applies where a person has been dismissed because of refusal to join a trade union.

1.6.2 A person who does not have a sufficient period of continuous employment, or is past normal retiring age (see para. 1.6.3 below), or is over sixty-five years of age, may be able to bring a claim for breach of contract based on wrongful dismissal (*Age Concern*

Scotland v. Hines (1983)). An action for wrongful dismissal would also be the appropriate course of action in the case of a highly paid employee. The maximum compensatory award for unfair dismissal is currently £11,000, plus an appropriate basic award. Substantially higher damages may be obtainable in appropriate cases for actions brought on the basis of a common law action for wrongful dismissal. Compensation for wrongful dismissal must be paid without deduction of any payments due to the employee from an occupational pension scheme (*NORCROS PLC v. Hopkins (1993)*).

1.6.3 UNFAIR DISMISSAL AND NORMAL RETIRING AGE

'Normal retiring age' is not necessarily identical with 'pensionable age'. 'Pensionable age' is simply the age at which an employee is entitled to retire on a pension but not necessarily obliged to do so. It would be an example of unfair dismissal, therefore, compulsorily to retire an individual who had not yet reached normal retiring age, but who was beyond pensionable age. Although those over sixty-five are excluded from the terms of the EP(C)A 1978, this does not bar the making of a claim for unfair dismissal on the basis that a person could have continued to work after sixty-five. In *Wood v. Louis Edwards & Sons Ltd (1972)*, a 62-year-old manager was awarded compensation on the grounds that he would not have retired until he was seventy. Anticipated overtime earnings can be taken into account when assessing a compensatory award.

Normal retiring age is not necessarily the retirement age specified in the contract of employment either, although there is a strong legal presumption that the two are identical. The presumption can be rebutted, however, if there is some other age at which employees are regularly retired. If the contractual retiring age has been abandoned, so that employees retire at a variety of ages, then there is no retiring age and the exclusion, at the age of sixty-five, operates. In *Waite v. GCHA (1983)*, the House of Lords indicated that in cases of dispute, the primary question was the employee's reasonable expectation at the relevant time. This test was also applied in *Whittle v. Manpower Services Commission (1987)*, a case which concerned a civil servant who had been dismissed when he was sixty-three. The contractual age for retirement was sixty, although, in practice, most employees worked beyond that age, about half of them working until they were sixty-five. As a result of cutbacks it was decided, in 1984, to retire all those aged sixty-four. Twelve months later, this age was reduced to sixty-two, and a Circular to that effect was issued. The applicant became compulsorily retired under the new policy and then claimed he had been unfairly dismissed. He failed at the initial tribunal hearing and also on appeal. The Employment Appeal Tribunal (EAT) held that the Circular had the effect of altering the reasonable expectation of those in the applicant's position so that they would normally expect to retire at sixty-two. Sixty-two, therefore, became the normal retiring age and since the applicant was beyond that age when dismissed, he was not entitled to bring an action for unfair dismissal. On the evidence available, the fact that some of the applicant's colleagues had continued in employment after the age of sixty-two, so as to accumulate full pension rights, was abnormal, and did not affect normal retiring age.

An employer, in the absence of a normal retiring age, can introduce a new retiring age so long as there is no breach of the employee's contract, or any suggestion that the arrangement is a sham. A properly communicated decision can take effect immediately, even if it is at odds with a previous expectation of being retained in employment until an older age (*Brooks v. British Telecommunications PLC (1992)*).

1.6.4 NORMAL RETIREMENT AND GENDER

As indicated above at para. 1.6.1, the age limit of sixty-five applies to all employees in the absence of a normal retiring age. The principle of equality will apply if the contractual retiring age attempts to discriminate between men and women. The decision of the European Court in *Marshall v. Southampton and South West Hampshire Area Health Authority (1986)*, and the subsequent enactment of the Sex Discrimination Act 1986 (SDA 1986), has provided women aged sixty or over with the opportunity to bring an action for unfair dismissal. It should be noted, however, that it is possible for an employer to have a variety of retiring ages for different jobs provided there is no direct or indirect discrimination based on gender (*Bullock v. Alice Ottley School (1993)*). Mrs B was a part-time pantry assistant at the school. She was dismissed at the age of sixty when she reached the school retirement age, although male staff (gardeners) were allowed to retire at sixty-five. The EAT accepted the employers' argument that the different retirement ages could be justified – gardeners and maintenance men required special skills and there were difficulties in recruiting them, which explained and justified their later retiring age.

1.6.5 FAIR DISMISSAL ON GROUNDS OF INCAPACITY

Section 57 of the EP(C)A 1978 sets out the grounds upon which dismissal is fair. These include the employee's conduct and capability. 'Capability' includes skill, aptitude, health or other physical or mental quality. Dismissal on grounds of sickness might, therefore, be fair. It is for the employer to show that he/she acted reasonably. An important, though not necessarily crucial, consideration in this context, is whether or not the employer has consulted the employee about his/her state of health and future work prospects. In *Polkey v. A. E. Deyton Services Ltd (1987)*, the House of Lords held that where consultation had not taken place, and where this was not the result of obdurate behaviour on the employee's part, there would be a prima facie case for holding the dismissal unfair. Other factors would need to be taken into consideration, however, in determining whether the employer's action was reasonable, including the business needs of the firm. Risk of future illness cannot be used as grounds for fair dismissal unless the employment is of such a nature that the risk makes it unsafe for the employee to continue in the post. In *Converform (Darwen) Limited v. Bell (1981)*, the applicant was a works director who had been absent from work as the result of a heart attack. He recovered, but his employers refused to allow him to return to his post because they thought there was risk of another attack. It was held that his dismissal had been unfair. It should also be noted that dismissal for gross misconduct of an apparently mentally ill employee can be unfair. The company's procedure for dealing with incapacity due to ill health should be used instead (*James Halstead Ltd v. Curtis (1994)*).

It is possible, however, for dismissal to be fair even where the period of sickness was brief. The approach taken in earlier cases which suggested that an employer needed to warn an employee was clearly erroneous, for an employee cannot be warned against being in poor health. Employers are, however, required to treat their employees with sympathetic consideration, and make all necessary enquiries (Selwyn 1993). Indeed, in cases of absence due to an industrial injury, such consultation is probably essential (*Wright v. Eclipse Blinds (1990)*).

1.6.6 Dismissal can be treated as retirement. In *Harris v. Lord Shuttleworth and Others (Trustees of the National & Provincial Building Society Pension Fund) (1993)*, the Court of Appeal decided that termination of employment by dismissal could still constitute 'retirement from the service by reason of incapacity'. The plaintiff was employed by a building society for ten years before being dismissed at the age of forty-five, following long absences on grounds of illness. Under the rules of the pension fund she was entitled to a deferred pension on reaching sixty, but she claimed that the dismisal amounted to retirement by reason of incapacity and that she was, therefore, entitled to a full pension payable immediately in accordance with the rules of the pension fund. The Trustees had concluded that the medical evidence did not support her claim to be so 'incapacitated' as to justify full retirement from work, and that, in any case, termination of employment by way of dismissal did not constitute 'retirement'. The Court of Appeal rejected the Trustees' argument and concluded that the fact that the building society had dismissed her rather than her giving notice of an intention to retire, did not preclude such termination amounting to 'retirement by reason of incapacity'.

1.6.7 REINSTATEMENT AND RE-ENGAGEMENT

Where an industrial tribunal decides that an employee was unfairly dismissed, it has discretionary powers to order reinstatement or re-engagement. If the order is for *reinstatement*, the employer must treat the employee, in all respects, as if he/she had not been dismissed. The tribunal can specify the arrears of pay due to the employee, for example, and any other rights or privileges, including rights of seniority and pension. In a recent decision, the Court of Appeal suggested that there were two stages at which an industrial tribunal could decide whether reinstatement was practical; first, before making an order, on the evidence before the tribunal; and second, if an order is made but not complied with. Problems at stage two might affect the size of the compensation paid (*Port of London Authority v. Payne and Others (1993)*). If the order is for *re-engagement* the employer is required to re-engage the employee in a post comparable to that from which he/she was dismissed. Tribunals often deem it impracticable to make such orders, and the aggrieved employees simply receive compensation.

1.7.1 REDUNDANCY

For the purposes of s.81(2) of the EP(C)A 1978, an employee is dismissed by reason of redundancy if dismissal can be attributed wholly or mainly to:

(a) the fact that the employer has ceased, or intends to cease, to carry on the business for the purposes for which the employee was employed by him/her, or has ceased, or intends to cease, to carry on that business in the place where the employee was so employed, or

(b) the fact that the requirements of that business for employees to carry out work of a particular kind, or for employees to carry out work of a particular kind in the place where he/she was so employed, have ceased or diminished or are expected to cease or diminish.

Redundancy can, therefore, arise in two principal circumstances, that is, where the whole business closes down; or where the business carries on, but the need for the services of a particular employee ceases or diminishes. Where the change in an employee's work situation is sufficient to change the nature of the employment, an employee who is unwilling or unable to perform the new function could claim that he/she has been made redundant.

1.7.2 Three issues, in particular, warrant consideration here. First, to what extent is an employee obliged to move location with his/her firm? A person approaching retirement might not wish to be uprooted and might prefer to be treated as redundant. An employee's obligations will depend upon the nature of his/her contract of employment. The question of law is whether or not the employer has authority, under the terms of the contract, to order the move, so that the words 'in the place where the employee was so employed' can be said to include the place where he/she could be obliged to work under the terms of the contract of employment. It is, therefore, a question of construction in each case. Where a contract contains a specific term to that effect, legal authority to require a move to another location exists (*Rank Xerox v. Churchill (1988)*). A term in the contract which merely allows the employer to require the employee to travel will not necessarily satisfy this legal requirement (*Litster v. Fran Gerrard (1973)*). In the absence of an express term, the circumstances will have to be examined so as to determine whether or not a term can be implied into the contract (*O'Brien v. Associated Fire Alarms Ltd (1969)*). The question whether an employee can be required to move will depend, therefore, upon the terms of the contract. Even where there is no express or implied contractual term, the employee may be obliged to accept any suitable alternative employment offered by the employer. The fact that the alternative employment is at a different location does not necessarily render it unsuitable. Even where an offer of work elsewhere is regarded as 'suitable', however, an employee will not lose his/her right to redundancy payment if refusal to move can be seen as 'reasonable'. The suitability of the offer of alternative employment must be assessed objectively, but the reasonableness or otherwise of an employee's refusal will depend on subjective factors such as health, family commitments, or retirement plans. Such factors may make it reasonable to refuse what, at first sight, might have appeared suitable alternative employment (*Paton Calvert and Co Ltd v. Westerside (1979)*).

1.7.3 Second, what is the basis upon which an employee can properly be selected for redundancy? Unfair selection for redundancy could amount to unfair dismissal. Where a particular selection is contrary to an agreed procedure, or to customary arrangements, and no special reasons exist justifying departure from that agreement or arrangement, dismissal will be unfair. In *Suflex v. Thomas (1987)*, it was held that the phrase 'last in, first out, subject to exceptions' was sufficiently certain to constitute a 'customary arrangement'. In another case, it was held that customary arrangements on the basis of 'last in, first out', without further specification, referred to continuous, not cumulative, service (*Crump v. Chubb & Sons Lock & Safe Co Limited (1975)*). An employee who has longer continuous service should, therefore, usually be given preference over an employee with more overall service, but shorter continuous service. Selection on the basis of 'last in, first out' usually discriminates in favour of older workers, but indirectly discriminates against women, and could be contrary to the provisions of the Sex Discrimination Act 1975 (SDA 1975). In situations which are unfair to women, the employer would need to satisfy a tribunal that the selection arrangements were necessary.

1.7.4 Third, what are the legal consequences of volunteering for redundancy? Should that happen, those involved may still qualify for redundancy payments (*Burton Allton and Johnson Ltd v. Peck (1975)*). This situation can be compared with that in which the employer and employee come to a mutual agreement to part company, because, for example, of the possibility of redundancies at a future date (*Morton Sundour Fabrics v. Shaw (1966)*). In such situations, employees are not deemed to have been dismissed by reason of redundancy. The essential question, therefore, is by whom was the contract of employment brought to an end? (*Martin v. MBS Fastenings (Glynwed) Distribution Ltd (1983)*)

Harsh decisions are still made, however. In the case of *Scott v. Coalite Fuels and Chemicals (1988)*, the employees were given notice of redundancy. During the period of their notice, they were offered, and subsequently accepted, early retirement as an alternative. On leaving employment, they received lump sums under the pension scheme and reduced pensions. In deciding to accept this offer, the employees were influenced by the fact that if, according to rules of the pension scheme, they had accepted redundancy and a frozen pension, there would have been no survivor's benefit if they died before reaching the age of sixty-five. The question at issue, therefore, was whether the employees had converted their prospective redundancy dismissals into termination of the contract by mutual consent. The EAT upheld the decision of the tribunal that the contracts had been terminated by mutual agreement. It has been argued elsewhere (Bourn 1988) that this decision seems at odds with the approach adopted in the earlier case of *McAlwane v. Broughton Estates Ltd (1973)*. In that case, it was suggested that a situation such as this would give rise to termination by consent on rare occasions only. Sir John Donaldson said:

> it would be a very rare case indeed in which we properly found that the employer and the employee had got together and, notwithstanding that there was a current notice of termination of the employment, agreed mutually to terminate the contract, particularly when one realises the financial consequences to the employee involved in such an agreement.

According to this judgement, consensual termination should rarely be an issue.

1.7.5 The qualifying conditions are the same as those that apply to unfair dismissal. Men and women above the normal retiring age or over sixty-five years of age are excluded.

1.8.1 TRANSFER OF UNDERTAKINGS

The Transfer of Undertakings (Protection of Employment) Regulations 1981 came into operation as a result of an earlier EC Directive 2(77/187/EEC) and are designed to protect the right of workers who work for businesses that are sold or transferred to another employer. For instance, an employee's right of action for unfair dismissal is one of the liabilities that can pass to the new employer. In *Green-Wheeler v. Onyx (UK) Ltd (1993)*, the appellant, a dustman, was made redundant by the council shortly before refuse collection was transferred, with all other relevant workers, to a contractor, Onyx. He was re-employed by Onyx, but dismissed seven weeks later. The EAT held that he had continuous employment. In another case, it was decided that the new employers will be required to provide an equivalent pension scheme to that of the vendor company where there is a transfer of an undertaking. In *Perry v. Inter Colleges Ltd Bristol IT (1993)*, the claimant, Mr P, was previously employed by the YMCA and had been a member of their superannuation scheme. The new employer's scheme was less generous, but the Tribunal decided that:

> any contract of employment transferred by virtue of the relevant regulations (reg. 5) shall be deemed to include such rights as are necessary to protect the interests of the employee in respect of rights conferring on him immediate or prospective entitlement to old age benefits, including survivors benefits under supplementary pension schemes.

In the more recent case, however, of *Walden Engineering Co. Ltd v. Warrener (1993)*, the EAT declined to follow the suggestions contained in the *Perry v. Inter Colleges Ltd* case. It can only be hoped that the higher courts will adopt the more radical approach taken in Perry.

1.9.1 OCCUPATIONAL PENSIONS

Occupational pension schemes can be provided by employers to give pension and life assurance benefits to employees, quite separate from the benefits provided by the state. An occupational pension is payable, therefore, regardless of entitlement to a state pension. Nevertheless, eligibility for an occupational pension can affect entitlement to state benefits.

Some 11 million British employees benefit from occupational pension schemes (Pension Law Review Committee, 1993), or put another way, occupational pension schemes cover about half the employee population (Davies 1993). They mainly provide benefits based on a member's own earnings at, or near his/her retirement, although a minority provide benefits on a money purchase basis and, for the latter schemes, some of the comments made in respect to personal pensions will be relevant. Full-time employees contemplating a reduction in working hours towards the end of their working life should give careful consideration to the possible implications of doing so.

Some employers make no provision for occupational pensions whilst others exclude certain types of employee, for example, part-time or temporary workers and those who cannot join until they have completed a defined period of employment (Davies 1993). A research report (McGoldrick 1984), based on a sample of one hundred schemes, found that part-timers were entirely excluded from 62 per cent of the schemes, and that, in a further 15 per cent, only those who worked for a stated minimum number of hours were eligible to join.

Another problem is that many people change their job several times and a change in employment might ultimately have a significant effect on the value of their pension. For instance, one estimate suggests that an individual on average pay who belongs to a typical scheme might expect to have a replacement ratio, taking state benefits into account, of 90 per cent or more whereas with three changes of employment, the replacement ratio could fall to some 70 per cent (Davies 1993). The Pension Schemes Act 1993 (PSA 1993), ss.69–86, not yet in force, seeks, *inter alia*, to better preserve benefits under occupation schemes, but only time will tell whether the problem will be reduced.

1.9.2 European Directive 56/613/EEC requires that there be no discrimination between men and women in access to, and benefits from, occupational pension schemes. The Social Security Act 1989 (SSA 1989) was enacted to implement the Directive, but a number of problems have risen as a result of the decision in *Barber v. Guardian Royal Exchange Assurance Group (1990)* (see para. 1.10.5 below).

Where inequality of access persists, a complaint can be made to an industrial tribunal. On receiving a complaint, the tribunal can order an employer to stop discriminating against an employee, and to back-date membership in the scheme for a period of up to two years. Schemes imposing special conditions on part-time workers might give rise to a complaint of discrimination under the SDA 1975, s.1. The employer would be in breach of the Act unless it could be established that such conditions were justified by reasons other than sex. More importantly, it would seem that in the light of the EC Directive on Equal Treatment and the decision of the European Court of Justice in *Barber v. Guardian Royal Exchange Assurance*

Group (1990) that policies which exclude part-timers, or ignore part-time service, are unlawful. Indeed, it has been tentatively suggested elsewhere that provision in UK law which requires a person to be working for more than sixteen hours per week before he/she can have access to certain statutory benefits, might be held to be unlawful (Selwyn 1993). This may be the implication of the House of Lords decision in *R v. Secretary of State for Employment, ex parte Equal Opportunities Commission and Another (1994)*.

1.9.3 Some schemes make provision for part-time employees. Their terms and conditions will vary but might include provision for doubling part-time hours for the purposes of calculating pension rights. Free, independent and confidential advice on such matters is available for older people from the Occupational Pensions Advisory Service (OPAS) (see para. 1.9.13 below). Assistance may also be available from the Occupational Pensions Board (OPB), set up under the Social Security Act 1973 (SSA 1973), which is responsible for advising the Secretary of State on occupational pension matters. One of the Board's responsibilities is to ensure that pension schemes meet the statutory requirements, such as providing equal access to men and women, as well as the preservation of pension benefits for those leaving particular employment. Although the OPB can advise, it will not intervene in a particular dispute. Disputes can be resolved only by the members and the trustees of the scheme in question. A member of a pension scheme is entitled to receive information about it from the trustees, and if information is withheld, can request the OPB to make representations on his/her behalf. Alternatively, a member can apply to the county court for an order directing the trustees to provide the information which has been requested. The rules relating to entitlement to information are set out in the Occupational Pension Scheme (Disclosure of Information) Regulations 1986. Under the regulations, the rights of pension scheme members, and other specified parties, are not limited to receiving basic information only. They are also entitled, on making a written request, to an actuarial valua-tion and statement, for which a reasonable charge may be made. The Occupational and Personal Pension Schemes (Miscellaneous Amendments) Regulations 1992, also require trustees and managers to include information about OPAS and the Pensions Ombudsman (PO) in the basic information they provide. Section 113 of the PSA 1993, when in force, will also allow the Secretary of State to extend the disclosure requirements to prospective members and spouses.

1.9.4 Although equal access is now a legal requirement, it does not always give protection against discrimination in respect of the terms of the pension scheme. As indicated above, research shows that occupational pension schemes often discriminated between men and women as to the terms and conditions upon which benefits were offered, and as to the amount provided. Attempts at remedying injustices through the European Court of Justice have proved to be only partially successful. In the recent case of *Ten Oever v. Stichting Bedrijfspensioenfonds voor het Glazenwassers en Schoonmaakbedrijf (1993)*, it was confirmed that equality of treatment between men and women in occupational pensions may be claimed only for benefits payable for periods of employment after 17 May 1990, the date of the judgment in *Barber v. Guardian Royal Exchange Assurance Group*.

The Social Security Act 1986 (SSA 1986), however, provides equality of treatment in one instance. Under s.9(3), contracted-out occupational schemes must provide benefits for widowers on the same basis as benefits for widows, except where a wife had died before 6 April 1989.

1.9.5 Another important change introduced by the SSA 1986 is the requirement that, after two years' membership, all schemes must preserve a member's benefits rather than refunding the contributions made (s.10). Previously, this rule applied only where membership had lasted for five years. The most controversial change, however, is that an occupational pension scheme can be administered on a money purchase basis as well as on a final salary basis. Final salary occupational pension schemes provide the employee with a pension based on a percentage of his/her final salary. A lump sum is often payable as well. Usually the employer and the employee both pay an agreed proportion of the employee's salary into the pension fund. The pension is normally protected against inflation under the terms of the Pensions (Increase) Act 1971 (P(I)A 1971), as amended. Final salary schemes are also required to provide guaranteed minimum pensions (GMPs) for members and surviving spouses (SSA 1986, s.6).

In contrast, money purchase schemes do not guarantee the level of the final pension. Employer and employee contributions are paid into a fund which, on retirement, is used to purchase a pension. The level of the pension will depend entirely upon the size of that fund. Some protection exists, however, in that money purchase schemes must be approved by the OPB. Minimum contributions are also required as a pre-condition of contracting-out of the state scheme. Members of both types of occupational pension have a statutory right to pay additional, voluntary contributions so as to increase their pension entitlement on retirement (SSA 1986, s.10).

1.9.6 Employers can no longer insist upon employees becoming members of an occupational pension scheme. Employees have the right to opt out and may, instead, choose to take out a personal pension, or participate in the state earnings-related pension scheme (SERPS) (see para. 1.19.1 below). Deciding upon the best course of action can be difficult.

1.9.7 More than 30,000 pensioners were left without immediate protection after auditors discovered that some £400 million was missing from a total of £695 million in pension schemes controlled by the late Robert Maxwell (*Financial Times*, 2 June 1992). Earlier examples of pension fraud existed (*The Times*, 24 December 1991), but the scale of the Maxwell fraud has alerted the public to the vested interests which have blocked reform of occupational pensions (Raphael 1992). The Pensions Law Review Committee (1993) (Goode Committee), set up in the wake of the Maxwell scandal, made a number of recommendations aimed at increased regulation of occupational pension schemes. The Committee succinctly described current pensions legislation as being 'masterly in its conciseness and almost wholly unintelligible'. Ironically, however, given the controversial background of the Report, the Committee concluded that existing pensions law is over-prescriptive. Indeed, the Committee rejected the suggestion put to them in the course of consultations that there was a need to codify trust law and the role of trustees. More surprising is that stiffer recommendations were not made in relation to fund custody arrangements. The Committee concluded that it would not be right to 'require trustees to place pension fund assets with independent custodians'. The Committee, however, did recommend that there should be a minimum solvency standard and that compensation be available for losses arising from fraud, theft or misappropriation. The appointment of a Pensions Regulator was also recommended. The Regulator would be responsible for monitoring and enforcing standards and empowered to carry out spot checks independently of complaints. In addition, the Regulator would be expected to lay down a Code of Practice relating to the exercise of control over occupational pension funds. The Committee, however, provides no explanation for why it should believe that a Code of

Practice would work when it also paradoxically concluded that the trust law duties of trustees are too complex and highly developed to be codified in regulations. It is unclear whether the government intends to legislate on the basis of the proposals contained in the Report.

In the meantime, it is clear that trustees have an implied legal duty of good faith (*Imperial Group Pension Trust Ltd (UK) v. Imperial Tobacco (1991)*). The court held that in every contract of employment there was an implied obligation of good faith on the part of the employer, and that managers of a company's pension scheme were subject to the same implied obligation.

1.9.8 PERSONAL PENSIONS

There are two types of personal pensions. First, appropriate personal pensions (APPs), which individuals use to contract out of SERPS and simply substitute for the state scheme (see para. 1.19.1 below). Second, there are ordinary personal pensions, taken out to provide benefits additional to either the APP or SERPS.

It is estimated that about 5 million personal pensions have been taken out since they were introduced in 1988 (Davies 1993). With the exception of married women, and widows paying National Insurance contributions at a reduced rate, employees have the right under s.1 of the Social Security Act 1986 (SSA 1986) to choose a personal pension in preference to membership of an occupational pension scheme. Since their introduction, personal pensions are the only new pension schemes available to the self-employed. Those contributing to retirement anuity contracts at the time of the change were allowed to continue with their existing arrangements, but differences between the two types of policy are important since the percentage of the funds that can be taken tax-free varies as does the age at which retirement can be taken (Reardon 1988).

1.9.9 A personal pension scheme is defined in s.18 of the Finance (No.2) Act 1987 as a scheme whose sole purpose is the provision of annuities or lump sums under arrangements made by individuals in accordance with the scheme. As with occupational pensions, personal pension schemes must be approved by the OPB. A Memorandum containing guidance notes on the social security and contracting-out requirements is available. Approved personal pension schemes can vary between issue of an insurance policy, or annuity contract; a unit trust scheme set up solely for the purpose of providing personal pensions; or an investment of contributions in shares or deposits with a building society or an interest account with a bank (OPB 1988). Personal pensions are thus provided by insurance companies, unit trusts, building societies or banks.

1.9.10 As an inducement to invest in a personal pension scheme, employees can exercise a 'contracting-out' option. This is available only for those paying Class One National Insurance contributions (see para. 1.11.2 below) and does not apply to the self-employed. 'Contracting-out' of the state scheme is possible, however, only if a minimum number of contributions are made to the personal pension scheme. This is then paid over by the Department of Social Security (DSS) to the body providing the personal pension. From 1988 to 1993, this payment was increased by a bonus from the state representing 2 per cent of the employee's earnings used to calculate the SERPS element, or £1 per week, whichever was the greater (Personal and Occupational Pension Schemes (Miscellaneous Amendments) Regulations 1992).

Persons over thirty years of age who opt out of the State Earnings Related Benefit in favour of a personal pension scheme will receive an additional 1 per cent annual rebate from their National Insurance contributions. Age-related rebates are to continue for a further five years.

Employees can decide to pay contributions into a pension plan which is entirely separate from any occupational pension scheme. Payments of this kind are known as 'free standing additional voluntary contributions' (FSAVC). Contracting-out may also be possible in such circumstances if the additional voluntary contributions provide a sufficiently substantial pension.

1.9.11 Concern has been expressed that a spouse's financial situation could be unfairly prejudiced if an employee elected for a personal pension. During the Act's Parliamentary stages, the Opposition unsuccessfully sought to amend the Bill so as to ensure that such decisions would need confirmation by the spouse. It also sought to have a provision inserted for a 'cooling-off period' which would allow the employee to change his/her mind. The right to cancel membership within twenty-one days and have contributions (if any) returned, has been provided for in certain schemes, and in other schemes may be protected by the terms of the Financial Services Act 1986 (FSA 1986) (OPB 1988). Regulations also require personal pension schemes to make provision for 'qualifying' widows and widowers. Under the Personal Pensions Schemes (Personal Pension Protected Rights Premiums) Regulations 1987 (reg. 3(2)) and the Personal and Occupational Schemes (Protected Rights) Regulations 1987 (reg. 10(1), a widow or widower must either be forty-five years of age or over, or caring for a child under eighteen in circumstances which are specified. A pension will be paid until a widow or widower dies, or remarries while under pensionable age. In certain circumstances, a pension can be paid after the death of the widow or widower (reg. 10).

Regulations also require personal pension scheme rules to specify that the rate of payment will be determined without regard to the sex or marital status of the member (reg. 4(2)).

1.9.12 Personal pensions are sold as individual policies. Thus they have to carry the high cost of marketing and selling such contracts. As a result, much of the money paid into such arrangements is consumed by expenses, certainly far higher than the equivalent proportion in occupational schemes or the state scheme (Davies 1993). Measures in the SSA 1986 would have allowed the government to put a ceiling on the commissions and charges which make the sale of personal pensions attractive to life companies and their salesmen. No action was taken with the then Secretary of State apparently preferring to rely on competition and on disclosure rules rather than on statutory regulation (Hughes and Hunter 1993). Be that as it may, it is clear that additional regulation is required. The recent interim report commissioned by the Securities Investment Board (SIB) found that four out of every five of 500,000 pension transfers had been sold incorrectly. Overall, only sixty-six out of 753 files showed an acceptable level of advice. Of the rest, 396 were unsatisfactory, 59 were suspect, and 214 were both. More than three-quarters of brokers and agents had not obtained sufficient details of the occupational scheme from which they were advising customers to transfer. It is also clear that hundreds of thousands of people, mostly in their forties, who have contracted out of the SERPS, would be better off moving back into the state scheme (McConnell 1993).

Financial service firms are being told by their regulators not to destroy any files relating to personal pension plans sold to people transferring from or opting out of occupational pension schemes. Compensation could run into millions, perhaps billions of pounds. The National and Provincial Building Society, for instance, the UK's eighth largest, had made provisions of about £2 million to meet its potential liabilities in respect of 850 personal pensions it sold to people transferring out of employers' schemes. If that level of provision was reflected across the whole financial service sector, the total set aside for an estimated 500,000 pensioner transfers would be more than £1 billion (Smith 1994).

1.9.13 THE OCCUPATIONAL PENSIONS ADVISORY BOARD SCHEME (OPAS)

The Occupational Pensions Advisory Board Scheme (OPAS) is available to give free help and advice to individuals who have a problem concerning either an occupational or personal pension. Advice is available to anyone who has pension rights, which includes working members of pension schemes, pensioners, those with deferred pensions from previous employment, and dependants.

There are essentially four ways in which OPAS can assist. First, advisers can translate jargon and explain the effect of various provisions. Second, OPAS, on receipt of the appropriate consents, can approach the scheme's authorities on behalf of the enquirer. Third, OPAS can respond to general enquiries on a pension matter and fourth, it can explain how and when other complaints authorities, such as the Pensions Ombudsman and the Insurance Ombudsman, can help.

1.9.14 THE PENSIONS OMBUDSMAN (PO)

The Pensions Ombudsman (PO) was established under the Social Security Act 1990 (SSA 1990)) and can investigate complaints of injustice caused by maladministration by the trustees or managers of an occupational or personal pension scheme, or by the employer.

A complaint must be made in writing within three years of the complaint becoming known. The PO has no right to investigate a complaint or dispute about a state social security benefit, a complaint or dispute already the subject of court proceedings, a dispute on a point of fact or law about any of the public service pension schemes except the National Health Service Superannuation scheme of England and Wales, and a complaint or dispute about an armed forces pension. The PO can, however, investigate *maladministration* concerning a public service pension scheme, and the explanation for the existing bar on investigating disputes, concerning fact or law, is that public service schemes incorporate their own appeals procedure.

The Goode Committee, however, has recommended that the PO's role be extended to cover all aspects of public service pension schemes. A person complaining about an armed forces pension has a right to go to the Defence Council. The total number of complaints and disputes received in the year 1992–3 was 2,166; the vast majority were complaints of maladministration rather than disputes of fact or law (Pensions Ombudsman 1993).

1.10.1 EQUALITY OF TREATMENT AND DISCRIMINATION

The impetus for equal treatment is largely the result of the UK's accession to the European Community in 1972. Any common law or statutory rule which is contrary to European law is void, and if there is any conflict between European law and British law, the former must be applied. Article 119 of the Treaty of Rome, for instance, requires member states to ensure and maintain the application of the principle that men and women should receive equal pay for equal work. An Article is directly applicable, and provides members with no discretion as to its implementation. A Directive, in contrast, is binding only as to the result to be achieved, so member states are free to choose how to implement the policy. There are a number of Directives in force which are relevant on the employment/ retirement rights of older workers, including Directive 75/117/EEC on Equal Pay; Directive 76/207/EEC on Equal Treatment; Directive 77/187/EEC on acquired rights as to the transfer of undertakings; Directive 79/7/EEC on Equal Treatment in Social Security Matters; and Directive 86/613/EEC which requires equal treatment in Occupational Pension Schemes.

1.10.2 In strict legal theory, a Directive is not enforceable against a non-state body or a private individual. It should be noted, however, that a state is widely defined to include any body which emanates from the state and which provides public services (*Foster v. British Gas (1991); Doughty v. Rolls Royce PLC (1992)*).

1.10.3 The Sex Discrimination Acts of 1975 and 1986 (SDA 1975 and 1986) were enacted to comply with the equal treatment Directive. Section 2 of the SDA 1986 makes provisions relating to retirement unlawful if they involve discrimination against a woman in relation to a job offer, or the way she is afforded access to opportunities for promotion, transfer or training, or in relation to dismissal or demotion. Dismissing a woman on grounds of age, when a man in a comparable position would not be dismissed, is unlawful. It would, for example, be unlawful to make a woman over sixty ineligible for promotion if a similar rule relating to men referred to sixty-five as the relevant age. The SDA 1986 applies to those engaged in partnerships as well as to those who are employees.

Section 2 was introduced following the decision of the European Court of Justice in *Marshall v. Southampton and South West Hampshire Area Health Authority (1986)*. It was decided that the dismissal of a woman solely on the grounds that she had attained the qualifying age for a state pension, when that age was different for men and women under national legislation, constituted discrimination on the ground of sex, contrary to article 5(1) of the Equal Treatment Directive No. 76/207. Since this Directive applied directly to state, but not to private, employees, the major practical effect of s.2, therefore, was to extend protection to those employed other than by the 'state'.

1.10.4 More recently, the same plaintiff has succeeded in removing the statutory compensation limits for employees discriminated against in the public sector, which throws into question the statutory limits for compensation for employees in the private sector (*Marshall v. Southampton and South West Hampshire Area Health Authority (1993)*). Substantial compensation is therefore possible. The Sex Discrimination and Equal Pay (Remedies) Regulations 1993 give effect to the decision by removing the limit on awards for sex discrimination and enables industrial tribunals to add interest to such awards. The new regulations have been in force since 22 November 1993.

1.10.5 The SDA 1986 did not affect the rules on eligibility for a state pension since, by virtue of Article 7 of the EC Directive on Social Security, member states of the European Community were free to decide for themselves at what age state pensions became payable. The same had been thought to be true in respect to occupational pensions, but the European Court of Justice in *Barber v. Guardian Royal Exchange Assurance Group (1990)* decided that a pension paid to an employee under a contracted-out private pension scheme constituted 'pay' and, therefore, fell within the scope of Article 119. Accordingly, if such a scheme had differential age qualifications for the eligibility of male and female employees to a pension on redundancy, it offends against the Article. As a result of the Barber case, occupational pension schemes are required to have equal pension ages in respect of pensionable service since 17 May 1990. Moreover, equal treatment for men and women must be applied to survivors' pensions for widowers and widows (*Ten Oever v. Stichting (1993)*).

It would appear, however, that not all occupational pensions are subject to the Barber precedent. In *Griffin v. London Pension Fund Authority (1993)*, the appellant belonged to a local government pension scheme. It was a compulsory scheme to which both the employer and the employee were required to contribute. A statutory provision had the effect of reducing G's pension on the day of her sixtieth birthday. Her appeal was dismissed on the basis that the applicant's scheme was a statutory one governed by exhaustive rules leaving the employer no discretion. As such, the scheme could be distinguished from normal contracted-out schemes.

1.10.6 Similarly, a bridging loan pension paid to women and men between the ages of sixty and sixty-five is not discriminatory (*Birds Eye Walls v. Roberts (1994)*). Mrs Roberts brought proceedings against her former employers claiming that the calculation of her bridging loan was contrary to the EC law. The bridging pension was paid to employees who, like her, had to take early retirement prior to reaching the statutory retirement age. From the age of sixty, the amount of the bridging pension, paid to a woman, was reduced on the grounds that she was in receipt of a state pension. She alleged that this was discriminatory as a man's bridging pension was not reduced until five years later. She was in receipt of a widow's pension. The European Court of Justice held that it was not contrary to Article 119 to take account of entitlement to state pension.

1.10.7 Directive 79/7/EEC (1979) aims at ensuring equal treatment for men and women in the area of social security, but as indicated above, Article 7 allows states to exlude matters relating to the determination of pensionable age for the granting of old-age and retirement pensions and the possible consequences thereof on other benefits. However, the European Court of Justice in *Secretary of State for Social Security v. Thomas (1993)* decided that discriminatory eligibility criteria for SDA and ICA are in breach of EC Directive 79/7. Social Security (Severe Disablement Allowance) Amendment Regulations 1993 implement the Directive by extending entitlement to SDA to married women who failed to qualify for non-contributory invalidity pension. The European Court's judgment in Thomas does not specifically deal with discrimination in contributory benefits, but the decision could have an effect on benefits such as unemployment benefit, sickness benefit and invalidity benefit, since they are also linked to pensionable age and are covered by the Directive. Although the link between invalidity benefit and pensionable age has knock-on effects to income support (IS) and housing benefit (HB), with the result that men have greater access to higher premiums between sixty-five and seventy than women, such inequalities cannot be challenged under the Directive (*R v. Secretary of State for Social Security, ex parte Smithson (1992)*). A detailed discussion of the Thomas case is to be found elsewhere (Sohrab 1993).

1.10.8 EQUALITY AND STATE PENSION AGE

The decision in Barber and subsequent cases is one of the justifications used by the government for proposing to equalise state pensions at sixty-five for both men and women (HMSO 1993). The new scheme will not start until 2010 and women's pension age will then be raised gradually to reach sixty-five by 2020. No woman aged forty-four or over in December 1993 will be affected by the change. Those between thirty-eight and forty-three will receive their pensions at ages between sixty and sixty-five. Only those aged thirty-eight or under will have to wait until they are sixty-five.

There is considerable opposition to the government's proposals, with numerous organisations (such as State Pensions at Sixty Alliance) campaigning for state pensions for all at sixty.

1.10.9 WAR PENSIONS

The title 'war pension' is extremely misleading, giving the false impression that only those injured on active service may claim. This is not the case, but the misunderstanding is probably the reason why many fail to claim a benefit to which they are entitled. One estimate suggests that there could be as many as 120,000 eligible people who have not claimed (Blanchfield 1992). Fortunately, there is no time limit for claiming and all a claimant needs to show is that he or she was on duty, or on direct route to or from duty, when injury occurred. Among the questions claimants need to consider are the following. First, were they injured, taken ill or did they suffer from any condition during their service years? Second, has any pre-service injury or condition been made worse by the service experience? Third, has the injury or condition left the person concerned with a permanent loss or limitation of faculty. Some SSAFA branches, such as Anglesey, have actually been campaigning to try to ensure better take up, with some encouraging results (Ade 1992). War pensions are non-taxable and will not affect service pensions, and only impact on IS, HB and CT. Awards can amount to lump sums or weekly pensions. A detailed explanation of their scope and potential is to be found elsewhere (Saxton 1993).

1.11.1 STATE WELFARE BENEFITS

There are a number of state welfare benefits to which an elderly person may be entitled. It is important to understand the basis on which the different benefits are paid. Some depend upon whether a person has paid, or been credited with, National Insurance contributions. These are known as contributory benefits. None of the contributory benefits is means-tested. People are entitled to the benefit because of their contributions, not because they have little or no resources. Entitlement depends on contributions or credits. Generally the system of crediting contributions aims to assist those established in the scheme who, for reasons beyond their control, were unable to make the necessary contributions.

Other benefits are non-contributory. This means that people are entitled to them because of their needs, whether financial or because of disability, and it does not matter that the claimant has not paid into the National Insurance fund. Some of these benefits are means-tested which means that a claimant's income and resources are taken into account in deciding how much, if any, benefit is payable. Other benefits are known as overlapping benefits. That means that a claimant can only claim one of the benefits which is designated as overlapping.

Some benefits are taxable, others are not. It can be important, depending on a person's other income, to consider which benefit to claim because of tax implications. Some benefits entitle a claimant to claim additional amounts for dependants. Child Benefit is not dealt with in this chapter, although some people of pensionable age do claim it because they look after, for example, grandchildren. Indeed, it should be noted that a person having the child living with him/her is given priority as a claimant of the benefit. Some grandparents, therefore, who have children living with them, will have every right to claim Child Benefit (Sched. 10, para. 1(2), Social Security Contributions and Benefits Act 1992 (SSCBA 1992)).

All benefits have to be 'claimed'; they are not paid automatically, except for cold weather payments (see para. 1.38.1 below). There are different time limits and rules for claiming the respective benefits. For some benefits a late claim may be accepted. For others no extension of time is allowed. In the event that a late claim is disallowed, the decision may be challenged in a number of different ways (see para. 1.42.1 below).

The importance of claiming cannot be over-emphasised. Some 700,000 'missing' people may have lost their right to old age pensions or be receiving less than they should. An auditor's report warned ten years ago that a quarter of the addresses of people paying NI contributions towards pensions were out of date. The Ministry acknowledged that the investigation showed many had emigrated or died. The National Audit Office estimates that some 163,000 people aged sixty-five to eighty are not receiving a full pension; 130,000 are losing more than £5 per week. Some 40 per cent of the potential claimants are women who worked part-time and may not realise that they are entitled to pensions (National Audit Office 1991).

1.11.2 CONTRIBUTIONS

National Insurance contributions are usually collected for the DSS by the Inland Revenue when it collects PAYE or self-employed person's tax. The DSS section which deals with a person's contribution record is known as the Contributions Agency. The Contributions Agency should have a complete record of a person's contributions to the National Insurance fund. These will include the old way of collecting contributions which was by purchasing a stamp and submitting completed cards at the end of each year.

There are five different classes of contributions, and liability to pay depends upon whether the individual concerned is an employee, self-employed or a voluntary contributor. The class determines the contribution conditions and the benefits. Persons over pensionable age are exempt from paying into the contribution scheme (Social Security Act 1975, (SSA 1975) s.4).

Class 1 contributions are paid by employers and employees. They are paid as a fixed percentage of earnings. Those who contract out of SERPS pay a lesser amount. Class 1 contributions entitle a person to all the contributory benefits. Class 2 contributions are paid by self-employed earners and entitle them to all contributory benefits except unemployment benefit. Class 3 contributions are voluntary flat-rate contributions paid by those who wish to keep up a contribution record. They entitle persons to widow's benefit and retirement pension. Class 4 contributions are additional contributions paid by the self-employed based on a percentage of their profits. They confer no additional benefits over those already paid for by Class 2 contributions.

1.11.3 The distinction between being employed and self-employed is usually clear, but in practice the line sometimes proves difficult to draw. The judiciary over a number of years has developed a number of tests aimed at clarifying this distinction (*Ready Mixed Concrete (South East) Ltd v. Minister of Pensions and National Insurance (1968)*), and the law is well discussed elsewhere (Selwyn 1993). In the context of social security certain groups are deemed to be employed earners while others are deemed to be self-employed (Social Security (Categorisation of Earners) Regulations 1978, Sched. 1, paras 1–6).

1.11.4 As indicated above, requirements as to contributions vary depending upon the benefit which is being claimed. Some general points must initially be made. First, married women who, before 1977, chose to pay reduced contributions into the National Insurance scheme fall into a special category with limited entitlement to long-term benefits. Second, between 1961 and 5 April 1975, persons paying Class 1 contributions paid an additional graduated contribution giving entitlement to a graduated pension. Third, before 5 July 1948 there was another contributory scheme which may still entitle a person to an enhanced pension. Fourth, a claimant may be entitled to more than one benefit. If benefits overlap, the usual rule is that the claimant is entitled to receive the benefit which is paid at the highest rate. Fifth, claimants may only be entitled to benefit at a reduced rate where the contributions record falls short of the full requirement. A person may be credited with Class 1 contributions even when he/she may not have been paid. Finally, claims must be made within specified time limits which are strictly adhered to, and which will be extended only where good cause can be shown.

1.12.1 CREDIT AND HOME RESPONSIBILITY PROTECTION

Class 1 contributions can be credited in a number of circumstances. A comprehensive account is to be found elsewhere (Poynter and Martin 1993). These circumstances include where an employer has failed to hand the money over to the Inland Revenue; a person is sick or unemployed; a person is receiving ICA to look after someone, or would be in receipt of ICA but because of overlapping prefers to claim widow's benefit; a widow is not receiving widowed mother's allowance or widow's pension at the full rate; a person is on jury service; and a man over sixty takes early retirement. The latter will be credited with contributions until he is sixty-five so as to entitle him to a full state pension at that age.

Credits are not available for any tax year in which the claimant is abroad for more than 182 days. Until the law is changed, women are not required, or entitled, to pay contributions once they are sixty years of age or over. In contrast, men between sixty and sixty-five years of age must continue to pay contributions as required, even if their contribution record is already sufficient to qualify them for a full Category A retirement pension. As suggested elsewhere (Poynter and Martin 1993), this provision discriminates against men on grounds of sex, but is not contrary to European law because it is a necessary consequence of having a differential retirement age. Benefits which arise from the determination of pensionable age are excluded from the relevant Directives (Directive 79/7/EEC (Equal Treatment in Social Security Matters) Article 7). However, the relevant Directive requires member states to examine periodically matters excluded in the light of social developments, to ascertain whether there is justification for maintaining the exclusion.

1.12.2 The most important contribution credit arrangement, designed to compensate carers, is home responsibility protection (HRP). The right of those not paying NI contributions are sometimes protected if they are caring for another person. The number of years during which this task is carried out is deducted from the number of years during which a carer would otherwise have had to make contributions (Social Security Pensions (Home Responsibilities and Miscellaneous Amendment) Regulations 1978). Protection relates both to retirement pension and to widow's pension. Home responsibility protection is available if, during a complete tax year, child benefit has been received in respect of a child under sixteen; or IS has been received without the person being required to be available for work since he/she is looking after an invalid person, or spends at least thirty-five hours a week looking after someone receiving attendance allowance (AA) or constant attendance allowance (CAA) (under the Industrial Injuries or War Pensions schemes), or the higher or middle rates of DLA care component (reg. 2(2)).

A person could qualify for home responsibility protection if he/she has not paid sufficient NI contributions for retirement pension purposes in a particular tax year. Married women and widows who had originally elected to pay NI contributions at a reduced rate, can benefit from the home responsibility protection scheme should they elect to pay contributions in full. Those likely to spend more than two years out of employment would be well advised to elect to do so since the right to pay reduced contributions terminates at the end of the second year. Other married women may also benefit from paying full Class 1 NI contributions. This issue is discussed more fully elsewhere (Poynter and Martin 1993).

The government's proposals if implemented would equalise the maximum number of years of home responsibility protection (HRP) for a full basic pension to twenty-two (DSS 1993a). This increase of three years for women, together with the automatic award of NI Credits for women aged sixty to sixty-four, would help more women qualify for a basic pension. It is also intended to extend HRP to SERPS, allowing those with caring responsibilities to obtain a full SERPS pension on the basis of twenty years' earnings.

1.13.1 TIME LIMITS AND BACK-DATING

Most benefits can be claimed up to three months before entitlement and claims for retirement pensions are actually accepted up to four months in advance. A claim outside the time limit will succeed if there has been 'good cause'. However, late claims are only allowed in relation to unemployment benefit, sickness benefit, invalidity benefit, severe disablement allowance and industrial injury benefits.

1.13.2 Ignorance of the law is not of itself a good cause for delay, but, in C1/147/1986, it was recognised that the complexity of the law could excuse delay. The Social Security Commissioner suggested that the crucial question was whether the person concerned had done, or omitted to do, that which could reasonably be expected, having regard to rights and duties under the social security scheme. Relying on advice from social security officials was held to be a sufficiently good cause. By contrast, relying on independent professional advice may not be, although this may result in a claim against the adviser on the basis of his/her negligence (R(U)9(1974)). Regulations now give the Secretary of State discretion to treat any letter, or even a claim for another benefit, as a valid claim. This discretion applies to all NI benefits (Social Security (Claims and Payments) Regulations 1987). Even where an earlier communication is not treated as a valid claim, or where 'good cause' cannot be shown, the right to benefit is not necessarily lost permanently. A claim might still succeed, although the claimant will usually lose out because there is only a limited right to receive back-dated benefit. The time limit for retirement pensions, widow's benefits and invalid care allowance is twelve months.

Unemployment benefit in contrast must be claimed on the very day for which the claim is made, unless instructions have been received to claim on another day. In practice, after the initial claim, the claimant will usually be told to claim fortnightly. Sickness or invalidity benefit need to be claimed within one month. It should also be noted that time limits also apply to non-contributory benefits. For instance, funeral expenses need to be claimed within three months from the date of the funeral.

1.13.3 Claimants who fall foul of the time limit back-dating rules may be able to persuade the DSS to meet its moral obligations and make an *ex-gratia* payment. Such payments are at the discretion of the Department and the intervention of an MP and/or the Parliamentary Ombudsman may help in such circumstances (Poynter and Martin 1993). For instance, in C15/650/91, a case concerning the back-dating of a late award of AA, the Ombudsman suggested that the Secretary of State might wish to award an *ex-gratia* payment for the person in question.

1.14.1 STATE PENSIONS AND PENSION LEVELS

By far the largest expenditure on contributory benefits is on retirement pensions. State pensions were received by 9.9 million people in 1992–3 and cost £26.9 million, an increase of around 35 per cent in real terms since 1976–7 (CSO 1994). Only three people in ten, however, believe the state pension alone will be enough to support them in old age, according to a national opinion poll survey (*Guardian* 1993). Indeed, a recent report claims that the UK devotes only 6.9 per cent of the gross national product to state pensions protection, with only Ireland of the twelve member states of the EU being less generous (Centre for Policy on Ageing 1994).

The government clearly believes such comparisons to be misleading, suggesting that they fail to take account of other state benefits such as free prescriptions (Widdecombe 1993). Be that as it may, the de-indexing of basic pensions from average earnings since 1980 has resulted in a steady decline in pensioners' living standards relative to wage-earners (Walker 1991). Older people are heavily dependent upon the state for financial support; around 90 per cent of them receive some form of social security benefit and three-fifths derive at least three-quarters of their income from state benefits (Walker 1993).

1.14.2 It should also be noted that there is some evidence to suggest that the pessimists have got their sums wrong and that Britain could afford more (*The Economist* 1993). Indeed, even the official statistics suggest that the costs of providing benefit for older people have been overestimated. Spending on retirement pensions between 1994 and 1995 is forecast to cost £750 million less than anticipated because of a downward revision in pensioner numbers following the 1991 Census (DSS 1993b).

1.14.3 A Private Member's Bill, entitled the Elimination of Poverty in Retirement Bill, has been proposed on some seven occasions, but has not received government support. Among the measures contained in the Bill was the restoration of the link between state pensions and average earnings, the creation of a Minister for Pensioners, the requirement that health and local authorities should produce annual reports on available facilities, the abolition of standard charges for services such as gas and electricity, and the provision of free television licences.

1.15.1 CATEGORIES OF STATE PENSION

There are eight separate pension schemes operated by the DSS. Category A pensions are paid on the basis of the claimant's contribution record. Category B pensions are paid on the basis of the claimant's spouse's contribution record. There are three types of Category B pension depending on whether the claimant is a married woman, widow or widower. Category C pensions are paid to men over 109 and women over 104 who are married to (or in some cases, divorced from) a man who is at least 109 years old, or who are widows and whose husband would now be at least 109 years old if he had lived. Widows who married older husbands may, therefore, benefit under this provision. Category D pensions are paid to persons over eighty and are non-contributory. Graduated retirement benefit is an additional amount paid on the basis of contributions paid between 1961 and 1975. SERPS are earnings-related pensions paid to those who have paid contributions in excess of the minimum required for entitlement to a basic retirement pension.

1.15.2 PENSIONABLE AGE AND RETIREMENT

Entitlement to the two contributory pensions (Categories A and B) depends upon the claimant having attained 'pensionable age' which is sixty-five for men and sixty for women (SSCBA 1992, s.122(1)). This discriminatory provision is not contrary to EU law.

The requirement as to age has given rise, in some circumstances, to the problem of proving the claimant has reached the requisite age. Where no birth certificate is available, other evidence may suffice. In R(P)1/75, which concerned an immigrant from a district of Pakistan where there was no register of births, medical evidence was held to be admissible.

1.15.3 Entitlement no longer depends upon an 'act of retirement'; it is no longer necessary formally to retire. It is sufficient to have reached pensionable age. It is possible for a person to claim a retirement pension whilst continuing work. The pension will, however, be added to income for the purposes of taxation. A person may not claim any addition for his/her spouse if the spouse is working.

The fact that a pension is taxable may be crucial in deciding whether to claim it. A person who is in receipt of severe disablement allowance (SDA) or IB/IP is not taxed on those benefits, so that if a person is in receipt of either of those benefits at the time of retirement, he/she may be well advised not to retire. The advantage of deferment would be that these benefits are not taxable and recipients also receive a higher rate of IS and other means-tested benefit than most retired persons.

1.16.1 THE EARNINGS RULE

The earnings of an individual over pensionable age, but below retiring age, can affect entitlement to a pension. This used to be of great significance, but now only affects increases in pension paid for dependants. If the claimant lives with a dependant and that dependant has earnings presently in excess of £45.45 per week (1994–5), no increase in a Category A or B pension can be paid in respect of the dependant. For those who have been receiving an increased pension since 14 September 1985, more generous rules apply and earnings of up to £45 (1993–4) are disregarded with a reduction of 5 pence for each 10 pence up to £49.05 and for each 5 pence earned thereafter (Social Security Benefit (Dependency) Regulations 1977).

1.16.2   The decision of the Court of Appeal in the case of *Cottingham and Geary v. Chief Adjudication Officer and the Secretary of State for Social Security (1992)* may mean that the earnings rule in relation to dependants has been entirely without legal foundation since 16 September 1985. It may mean that many pensioners who have been refused increases of benefit for adult dependants will be entitled to substantial arrears.

1.17.1 DEFERRED RETIREMENT

Schedule 1 of the SSA 1975 has the effect of increasing the rate at which Categories A or B retirement pensions are paid where retirement has been deferred by a person who has attained pensionable age. The increase is assessed by reference both to the basic and to the SERPS component of the pension (see para. 1.19.1 below). A widow will benefit from her late husband's deferred retirement providing she does not re-marry before reaching pensionable age, that is, sixty. A widower is similarly entitled to any increase based upon his late wife's deferred pension, provided he is over pensionable age, that is, sixty-five or over, at the time of her death. Where a person defers his/her pension for the maximum period of five years, he/she will receive an increase in pension of some 37 per cent per week (Poynter and Martin 1993).

These rules are a throw-back to the days when retirement pensions were subject to an earnings rule which meant that people over pensionable age who decided to remain in employment would generally derive no benefit from claiming. Nowadays, unless the individual concerned is claiming IB/IP or SDA (in which case, there may be advantages in not claiming the retirement pension), he/she will usually be well advised to claim the pension immediately. First, the sum could be better invested (Poynter 1992; Dibben 1991). Entitlement to means-tested benefits will not be affected unless the total capital sum exceeds £3,000. Another reason for taking the money immediately is that the right to the pension dies with the individual. You cannot bequeath a pension as you can investments. Only the spouse could benefit in circumstances where the individual died before making a claim, and even then only in certain circumstances. In contrast, Poynter and Martin (1993) suggest one tragic situation where it might be advantageous to defer. In the case of a terminally ill married man whose wife is sixty or over, deferment would provide the widow on his death with the right to claim a lump sum £1,000 widow's payment. Even in these circumstances, deferment may not be a sensible option as more may be lost in pension payments than is actually gained.

The government has recently proposed some radical changes intended to encourage deferment (DSS 1993a). Fewer than 2 per cent take up this option, but, from 2010, it is hoped to increase the deferment rate to 10 per cent a year, and the five-year limit on the number of years deferment is being abolished. This will provide a more attractive inducement for individuals to continue to work beyond retirement age.

1.17.2 Failure to claim retirement pension is treated as a deferment.

1.18.1 DE-RETIREMENT

Once a pension has been claimed, it is possible for the claimant to 'de-retire'. The effect of this is to defer pension entitlement as described above. In the event of such, formal notice must be given. This can be contrasted with the situation where no notice is required, that is, where a person has not yet made any claim for a pension. The decision to de-retire can only be made once (Social Security (Widows Benefit and Retirement Pensions) Regulations 1979).

A man whose wife is entitled to a Category B retirement pension by virtue of his contributions cannot elect to cancel retirement unless his wife consents, or withholds her consent unreasonably. In R6/60(P), it was held that it is for the husband to show his wife has acted unreasonably. Examples of unreasonable behaviour would be pique, or spite, or a desire to stand in the husband's way. On the facts, it was held that the wife had acted reasonably; she had refused consent because cancelling retirement would have resulted in substantial loss.

1.19.1 THE STATE EARNINGS-RELATED PENSIONS SCHEME (SERPS)

Participation in SERPS depends upon whether the employee pays Class 1 NI contributions and is not contracted-out of SERPS. Contracting-out of SERPS is possible where the employee opts for an occupational pension or an approved personal pension. Where contracting-out has occurred, the employer and employee pay reduced NI contributions and contribute instead to the cost of alternative provision.

1.19.2 The rules for calculating SERPS are complicated, but depend, basically, upon the claimant or his/her spouses's 'earnings factor' in the 'relevant' years. Widows and widowers can receive two additional pensions, one based upon their own contributions, and another based on the contributions of the deceased spouse. A useful example of the way in which these are calculated is available elsewhere (Poynter and Martin 1993). Those who wish to plan ahead can enquire of the Contributions Agency how much additional pension they are likely to receive. A special form for doing so is available (NP 38).

1.19.3 The provisions of the SSA 1986 changed the method of calculating SERPS, but will not affect persons reaching pensionable age before 6 April 1999. The intention and net effect of these provisions will be to reduce the cost of the scheme from an estimated £25.5 billion in the year 2033 to around £15 billion. Section 18 makes such savings possible by basing the calculation on average life earnings, rather than on the basis of earnings for the best twenty years, as in the past. Another reduction in cost has been achieved since 1988–9 by calculating the SERPS element on 20 per cent rather than 25 per cent of earnings, as previously. Some transitional protection is provided, however, for those reaching pensionable age between 6 April 1999 and 5 April 2009, when the basic percentage will be increased by 0.5 per cent for each complete tax year in which the claimant has reached pensionable age before the tax year 2009–10. Section 19 also amends existing legislation so that where a husband dies after 5 April 2000, the widow will be entitled to only half the amount of the spouse's pension, rather than to the whole of it as at present.

1.19.4 An explanation of the method of calculating additional pensions from 1999 is contained in DSS leaflet NP 46.

1.20.1 GRADUATED PENSIONS

Those paying Class 1 NI contributions between April 1961 and April 1975 contributed to a graduated pension scheme. These participants are entitled to a pension supplement calculated on the number of graduated pension units purchased during the period of the scheme's operation. A widow is entitled to half the graduated pension earned by her late husband, as well as to any graduated pension earned on her own contributions. The additional pension can be paid to someone not entitled to the basic retirement pension. It is increased if retirement is deferred. The contribution conditions discriminate against women. For every £7.50 contributed by a man during the relevant years, but £9 contributed by a woman, that individual is now entitled to £7.09 a week (National Insurance Act 1965 (NIA 1965) s.36; Social Security (Graduated Retirement Benefit) (No.2) Regulations 1978). Moreover, it has been suggested elsewhere that these discriminating provisions may be unlawful and open to challenge because they contravene European Equal Treatment Directives (Poynter and Martin 1993).

1.21.1 CHOICE OF PENSIONS

Legislative changes have been introduced which aim at encouraging individuals to turn either to occupational pension schemes or to personal pension schemes in preference to remaining in SERPS. Over 50 per cent of employees are already members of occupational pension schemes with a large majority of these in contracted-out schemes. Given the reduction in entitlement to SERPS, referred to above, the only practical choice for those already in an occupational scheme is between remaining in membership or opting for a personal pension scheme. The government has promoted personal pensions by giving bonus incentives, but only those who have been in occupational pension schemes for less than two years will qualify. There are other reasons for suggesting that, as a general rule, those who are members of occupational schemes would be well advised to remain in them, rather than take out a personal pension scheme (Bolver 1991).

First, under an occupational pension scheme, the employer is obliged to contribute towards the pension. On average, an employee pays about 5 per cent of his/her earnings into an occupational pension scheme with the employer paying between 5 and 20 per cent. By comparison, there is no requirement for an employer to make any contribution to a personal pension scheme, and evidence suggests most employers are reluctant to do so (Bourke 1988). Second, occupational pensions usually provide a degree of financial security for the families of those employees who die, or who are forced to retire from work early because of ill health. The benefit payable from a personal pension scheme, however, will depend upon the size of the fund accumulated at time of death, or forced retirement (Chatterton 1988). Financial security for the families of those in personal pension schemes may need to be safeguarded by arranging additional assurance, at extra expense. Third, occupational pension schemes are usually 'final salary' schemes in comparison with personal pension schemes which are of the money purchase type and therefore vulnerable to stock market fluctuations. Fourth, the administrative costs of personal pension schemes are likely to be higher, whereas the collective nature of occupational schemes provides scope for discount.

There are arguments on the other side which would favour personal pension schemes, but they do not seem particularly convincing. It has been suggested, for instance, that personal pensions facilitate employment mobility, and that members of occupational pension schemes could be discouraged from changing employment since frequent changes might adversely affect pension rights. The difficulty of transferring between occupational pension schemes may, however, be exaggerated. Legislative changes include provision for ensuring easier transfer of accrued pension rights and benefit entitlement under occupational pension schemes (Health and Social Services and Social Security Adjudication Act 1983 (HSSSSAA 1983), s.19 as amended). Those adversely affected by a change in employment could, in any case, top up their occupational pension entitlement by contributing to a FSAVC scheme. Another argument in favour of personal pension schemes is that they are more tax efficient since, as previously mentioned, they provide greater tax relief, especially for older contributors. There may be little by way of financial advantage to the employee, however, since the employer need make no contribution to the cost of a personal pension. The situation would be considerably different should the employer agree to contribute to the costs of providing a pension. Personal pensions also allow members to draw a pension at fifty, without necessarily giving up work. Some investment schemes offer to re-invest money released from a pension fund, but those contemplating such action may be in danger of not making proper provision for their retirement. It may also be the case that better financial returns can be achieved by leaving a personal pension undisturbed (Wright 1988).

Where no occupational scheme exists, employees are faced with one choice only, whether to remain in SERPS or take out a personal pension scheme. A universal state scheme is acknowledged to be relatively cheap to run, even with a complicated benefit structure. Indeed, it is estimated that only about 5 per cent of the NI contributions paid by the state are consumed in expenses. The low level of cost reflects the fact that the scheme is compulsory with associated economies of scale (Davies 1993).

In spite of the incentive bonus which is available for those taking out personal pension schemes, it would seem that men between forty and forty-five, and women between thirty-five and forty would, usually, do better to remain within the state scheme since the cost of providing equivalent benefits in a private pension scheme are higher at these age levels (Walkington and Scott 1993; Hunter 1992). Indeed, The Prudential in 1993 was advising men over forty-nine and women aged forty-two with earnings in excess of £8,500 to return to SERPS (McConnell 1993). With a competitive commercial market now offering pension and assurance cover, independent expert advice is often essential. The Occupational Pensions Advisory Service (OPAS) may be able to assist.

Employees face having to make crucial decisions over pensions. Changes to the relevant legislation will mean lower pensions for those relying upon SERPS. Those most affected will be the ones least able to afford an additional personal pension. They include individuals disabled during their working lives, women, employees with fluctuating earnings, and those suffering long spells of unemployment.

1.22.1 PENSIONS – WORKING ABROAD

Some countries, such as Italy, have very generous state pension schemes, with the result that company schemes are less common. In other EU countries, such as Germany, company schemes are more common, but early leavers are treated differently from those in the UK. Personal pension plans are rare outside the UK. Where an employee contributes to a state pension scheme in another EU country, he/she will usually receive a pension from that scheme, whether or not the individual remains there or retires to the UK (Pridham 1993). However, where an individual was required to pay old age insurance contributions to two member states for one and the same period, aggregation of the two pensions is lawful (*Larsy v. Institut National D'Assurances Sociales pour Travailleurs Independants (INASTI) (1993)*).

1.22.2 Working outside the EU for a foreign employer can sometimes endanger 'pension rights' of UK citizens. In some cases, the contributions paid into another country's social security system will not plug the gap in the UK National Insurance record, with the result that the claimant will only be entitled to a reduced pension. Moreover, the individual concerned may not qualify for a state pension in the country concerned. Entitlement will depend on the existence or otherwise of a reciprocal agreement between the state in question and the UK. Other individuals who join overseas private pension schemes are at risk of seeing their benefits dwindle through currency fluctuations, or disappear through take-overs (Davenport 1992). To protect a UK state pension, anyone going abroad to work can now pay Class 3 contributions in the UK.

1.23.1 RETIREMENT ABROAD

Retirement and widow's benefit are payable irrespective of the length of stay abroad. If it is intended to be away for six months or longer, it is advisable to inform the DSS which in turn can make arrangements for paying the pension abroad. If residing in an EU country, the recipient will receive the annual benefit increases as if resident in the UK. The same does not apply in a country outside the EU, unless there exists a reciprocal agreement which refers to the payment of annual increases.

1.24.1 EARLY RETIREMENT

Those who leave employment 'voluntarily' and 'without just cause' may be disqualified from unemployment benefit for a period up to twenty-six weeks (SSCBA 1992, s.28). If they are compulsorily retired, or take voluntary redundancy, they cannot be disqualified, however, although it remains important for employees to be dismissed and not simply to resign or retire (R(U) 3/91). The onus for showing just cause is on the claimant, and the 'just cause' must relate to his/her personal circumstances. In R(U)2/81, a school teacher was encouraged to take early retirement, but failed in his attempt to show 'just cause' for leaving the employment. His unsuccessful submission to the tribunal was that the public interest would be served by the savings accruing to the education budget, and by his making way for younger members of the profession. Among the submissions which have succeeded have been loss of confidence by the claimant in his/her mental or physical ability to perform essential duties, and pressing domestic or personal circumstances (Poynter and Martin 1993).

A person who gives up work to look after a sick relative would probably have good 'cause', but may, nevertheless, be refused benefit because he/she is not available for work. Persons facing such a dilemma might consider claiming ICA and IS.

1.24.2 Since redundancy payments are a form of compensation for the loss of a job, they do not affect a person's right to unemployment benefit. Employees sometimes receive an additional lump sum payment as an incentive for them to retire from employment early. The effect of such payments upon an individual's entitlement to unemployment benefit will depend upon whether the sum represents compensation for loss of job, or compensation for loss of earnings. If the former, entitlement to benefit will not be affected. If the latter, entitlement will be temporarily lost. Consequently, a lump sum which includes payment in lieu of notice, disqualifies a claimant from entitlement to unemployment benefit for the period during which he/she is deemed not to be unemployed (*Chief Adjudication Officer v. Brunt (1988)*). It is advisable, therefore, to ensure that payments of this kind should not be directly referable to rates of pay, or period of notice. This is best achieved by the payment being rounded up, and presented as an *ex-gratia* payment.

1.24.3 Men retiring at sixty can be credited with Class 1 NI contributions so as to satisfy contribution conditions for receipt of a retirement pension (Social Security (Credits) Regulations 1975). Thus, a male employee retiring at sixty can be credited with full contributions for the five years preceding pensionable age. Credits are not available for women wishing to retire five years before attaining pensionable age, that is, at fifty-five rather than at sixty. Women who choose to continue working after the age of sixty, however, need not pay NI contributions.

1.25.1 ADMISSION INTO HOSPITAL

The effect of admission into hospital on entitlement to retirement pension and other benefits, such as sickness or invalidity benefits, severe disablement allowance and widow's benefit, depends upon two factors: the length of stay; and the existence or otherwise of a dependent relative. A dependant is defined in the regulations to include, *inter alia*, the other spouse when the couple are retired pensioners who normally live alone. Where there are no dependent relatives, the pension will be reduced by £23 per week after six weeks in hospital. Only half this amount is deducted when there are dependent relatives. When a person becomes a long-stay patient, that is, remains in hospital for longer than fifty-two weeks, a further reduction is made. If there are no dependent relatives, the pension is reduced to £11.50 per week, but where there is a dependent relative, the pension is reduced by £23 per week. The patient who has a dependant is entitled to receive directly only the same amount as patients with no dependants, that is, £11.50 per week. The remainder of the pension, together with any increase for a dependant to which entitlement exists, is paid to the dependant. Provision is more generous for those receiving a war pension or war widow's pensions. A war pension is not reduced on admission to hospital. It will be increased, in fact, if treatment is for a war injury (see DSS leaflet MPL 153). A war widow's pension is paid at the full rate for the first fifty-two weeks and is reduced only subsequently.

A long-term patient may lose entitlement even to a reduced pension (or have it further reduced) if he/she is unable to act for him/herself and the pension is paid directly to the hospital authorities. The medical officer in charge of the patient must certify that he/she is not capable of appreciating the money or the comfort that could be bought with it. Entitlement is, therefore, at the medical officer's discretion. Where a patient spends days outside hospital, he/she is then entitled to have the pension fully restored on a pro-rata basis. It is also worth noting that, for this purpose, hospital admission and discharge days are regarded as 'home' days. Indeed, where persons regularly spend weekends with carers, the latter might be entitled to the full rate of ICA, since that is a 'weekly benefit' and not one paid on a daily basis. It also needs stressing that only a full 'day' in hospital gives rise to a reduction in entitlement. Where a patient spends part of the day in hospital and part of it away, the pension should be restored in full for that day. A patient spending part of a day attending a social services day centre as a prelude to discharge, for example, should have the pension restored for those days. As suggested elsewhere, where a person is not receiving the weekly allowance, either directly or in the form of comforts, the matter should be raised with the community health council (CHC) (Robertson 1993).

1.26.1 SEVERE DISABLEMENT ALLOWANCE

Severe disablement allowance (SDA) is paid to people who are unfit for work on a long-term or permanent basis because of a medical condition. The medical condition may be one that has occurred in a person's youth or it may be congenital. It may have arisen at any time during a person's life. For these reasons the benefit is non-contributory. It is also non-taxable. A person who is in receipt of SDA, but who in addition requires IS, will receive a higher amount than is normal. It can be paid beyond pensionable age. For tax, contribution and IS reasons, it may be more advantageous to claim SDA than pension. Advice should be taken.

To qualify for SDA, a person must satisfy all the following conditions: he/she must be incapable of work and have been so for 196 days; the incapacity must have arisen before he/she was twenty years old or, if after that age, the person must be 80 per cent disabled; in general terms he/she must reside in Great Britain; the person must not be over pensionable age, but it will continue to be paid if the person was in receipt of it before attaining pensionable age. It will continue to be paid after pensionable age even though the person may cease to be incapable of work or ceases to be disabled. It needs to be stressed, however, that in the light of the Thomas case (see para. 1.10.7 above), any woman who first meets the conditions for SDA between the ages of sixty and sixty-five will also qualify for the benefit.

A person may also qualify if he/she has a 'passport' to SDA because he/she has been in receipt of another non-contributory invalidity pension such as AA, mobility allowance, or is registered blind.

Disablement of 80 per cent is assessed by reference to Prescribed Degrees of Disablement under the industrial injuries schemes. For example, amputaton at the hip is 90 per cent disablement. Where the disability relates to a personality disorder, the position is more complicated. In R(5) 4/89, the claimant had been involved in two traffic accidents and made a claim for SDA. The Adjudicating Medical Authority (AMA) assessed the degree of disablement at 63 per cent. In arriving at the figure the AMA had taken four medical conditions into account, but the claimant identified twelve 'areas' in which he had suffered a loss of faculty resulting in severe disability. The Commissioner suggested that the appropriate way would be either to make separate assessment of the various disabilities and aggregate them, or simply to look at the matter in the round. The Commissioner also confirmed that a Tribunal could inquire into the claimant's personality change in order to assess the extent of disablement.

Incapacity for work has a special meaning. The claimant must satisfy one of two tests. First, that the claimant is incapable of work, meaning work which he/she can reasonably be expected to do by reason of some specific disease or bodily or mental disability. Alternatively, the claimant must be under medical observation because he/she has an infectious disease; or the claimant must have a certificate from his/her GP stating that for convalescent or precautionary reasons he/she should not work and is under medical treatment, and is not working; or that the work being undertaken is therapeutic.

The 'incapacity for work' requirement gives rise to most appeals for SDA. In simple terms, not only has a person to be incapable of work by virtue of a medical condition, but also is unable to do any work which it is reasonable for him/her to do. Work means work which an employer would be prepared to pay for. What is reasonable to expect a person to do depends on his/her age, education, experience, state of health and other personal factors. The government has announced a review of the incapacity test and the rules are almost certain to change with effect from April 1995. The test of what is reasonable to expect a person to do is likely to disappear so that incapacity will be determined solely on medical criteria. The proposed test will assess the individual's ability to carry out a range of work-related activities, such as walking and bending, and other mental and sensory as well as physical activities.

1.27.1 MOBILITY ALLOWANCE

Since April 1992, mobility allowance has been replaced by the mobility component of Disability Living Allowance (DLA). However, some old claims may still be going through the system. The test for mobility allowance is the same as for the higher rate of the mobility component of DLA (see para. 1.29.1 below). Entitlement to DLA had to occur before the claimant's sixty-fifth birthday, but the claimant had a year's grace in which to claim before his sixty-sixth birthday. The award lasts until the claimant's eightieth birthday.

1.28.1 ATTENDANCE ALLOWANCE

This too has been replaced by the care component of DLA for those who claim before their sixty-fifth birthday. Attendance allowance (AA) is still available for those who become entitled after their sixty-fifth birthday on the same basis as for the middle and highest rates of the care component of DLA (see para. 1.29.1 below). The benefit, assuming the qualifying conditions are satisfied, is only payable from the date of claim. There is no provision for back-dating. The case law remains unaffected by changes in the system. However, the new adjudication and assessment arrangements that apply to DLA will also apply to AA.

There are no upper age restrictions upon claiming AA, nor is it necessary for the claimant to have satisfied the qualifying conditions before attaining the age of sixty-five. Most applicants are successful; between May and December 1992 there were no less than 502,000 claims and a success rate of 78 per cent (HL 1993). The allowance is a weekly benefit paid to those who need a legally prescribed level of care and attention from someone else. Unless terminally ill, they must also have been in need of care for at least six months. The allowance is not necessarily paid to the carer. Indeed, it is not strictly necessary for the person to be receiving care. The only requirement is that the claimant is in need of attendance.

The allowance is paid at two rates: a lower rate when the care is required either during the day, or during the night; and a higher rate when attendance is required during both day and night. Persons who qualify on the basis of a terminal illness will automatically qualify for the higher rate. The conditions relating to eligibility for the allowance differ significantly, according to whether the claim is for day-time or night-time attendance.

1.28.2 The legal requirements for claiming attendance allowance are set out in the SSCBA 1992, s.64:

A person shall be entitled to an attendance allowance if he/she is aged sixty-five or over, ... and the prescribed conditions to residence and presence in Great Britain are satisfied, and either

(a) he/she is so severely disabled physically or mentally that, by day, he/she requires from another person either –

   (i) frequent attention throughout the day in connection with his bodily functions, or
   (ii) continual supervision throughout the day in order to avoid substantial danger to him/herself or others; or

(b) he/she is so severely disabled physically or mentally that, at night –

   (i) he/she requires from another person prolonged or repeated attention in connection with his/her bodily functions, or
   (ii) in order to avoid substantial danger to him/herself or others he/she requires another person to be awake for a prolonged period or at frequent intervals for the purpose of watching over him/her; or

(c) he/she is terminally ill.

1.28.3 In spite of the fact that 'residence' or 'presence' in Great Britain is required, AA continues to be payable where the resident is temporarily abroad for up to six months. The allowance, however, is not exportable on a permanent basis and it appears that it is necessary to qualify for the benefit before moving abroad (CA/516/1991). Presence in an EU country may help bypass the requirement. Persons who meet one of the 'day' conditions and one of the 'night' conditions will qualify for the higher allowance. Under earlier legislative provisions, there was no need for the claimant to show that he/she required 'another person to be awake for a prolonged period or at frequent intervals for the purpose of watching over him/her'. It merely required 'continual supervision throughout the night'. It was held in the Moran case (see R(A)1/88), which concerned a person suffering from epilepsy, that the requirement for continual supervision could be satisfied if a person's need for supervision was unpredictable, and where the consequence of having no supervision would be grave. It confirmed that a person standing by to intervene if necessary, was exercising supervision. This could be adequately achieved even if, for some of the time, the supervisor was asleep. The case was regarded as having established a particularly useful precedent which could apply to people who were mentally alert but nevertheless vulnerable during 'attacks'. The purpose of the recent legislative change was to close the door on this development. The Benefits Agency usually regards twenty minutes of attention as 'prolonged', and 'repeated attention' simply means twice or more. Moreover, it is not necessary for the attention to be required every night, or even most nights, provided it is a fairly regular feature (Poynter and Martin 1993).

1.28.4 It needs stressing that the new provision applies to night-time attendance only. The Moran case remains good law for those requiring continual supervision throughout the day. The meaning of 'throughout the day' was explained in CA/1140/1985. The claimant had total visual handicap and needed help with bathing and laying out his clothes, and in cutting up his food at mealtimes. He also needed help in walking up stairs and in walking outside his home. The claim was rejected on the basis that the claimant's need for attention in connection with bodily functions were confined 'in the main' to the beginning and the end of each day and that he did not satisfy the requirement for frequent attention throughout the day. The Chief Commissioner reversed the decision, stressing that refusal of the claim could not be justified on the basis that there were gaps in the supervision. The evidence relating to the day must be looked at as a whole, where the need for care was naturally connected. It is also clear from CA/97/1987 that the scope of the precedent established in Moran is not limited to 'mental attacks'. The claimant suffered from multiple myelomatosis (that is, thinning of the bones which makes them liable to fracture with minimal pressure) and successfully appealed against the decision. The Social Security Commissioner concluded that the requirement for continual supervision had to be considered in the context of the supervision needed by a person who, by a simple movement, could cause him/herself a spontaneous fracture. It would be surprising if a similar argument could not be put in respect of those suffering from other physical complaints. Indeed, in R(A)4/92 the Commissioner held that the lack of a warning of an epileptic attack did not in itself mean that the claimant did not require supervision. If the presence of another person could reduce the danger, that could be sufficient to establish entitlement to attendance allowance.

1.28.5 Although the night supervision test is harder to satisfy, it should be remembered that in *R v. Social Security Commissioners, ex parte Connolly (1986)* the Court of Appeal suggested that in determining a person's need for attention, the essential consideration was what he/she 'reasonably required' and not what was 'medically required'. The significance of the distinction is illustrated by R(A) 3/86. The claimant had a mental handicap and suffered from grand mal epilepsy. She was incontinent at night and received attention for fifteen minutes twice per night in order to change night clothes and sheets. The DMP considered that, if adequate padding were used, there would be no medical need for repeatedly changing the bed. It was held that, since that decision was based upon medical considerations only, it was erroneous in law.

1.28.6 A new assessment and decision-making structure was introduced in April 1992. The new system is largely based on self-assessment, with all decisions taken by Adjudication Officers (AOs), that is, by lay people rather than medical professionals. In cases of dispute the claimant can ask for a review within three months of the decision. The case will then be reviewed by another AO. A further right of appeal exists to an independent tribunal – usually the Disability Appeal Tribunal (DAT). However, it appears that the new system is proving difficult to administer with claimants waiting five to eight months for AA reviews (*Welfare Rights Bulletin* 1992). The targets for clearing claims have been established, for example 60 per cent within thirty-five days and 95 per cent within sixty days. One welcome innovation, however, is that a claim can be made on behalf of a person who is terminally ill without the ill person's knowledge or authority. These 'special rules' even allow for an appeal in such circumstances.

1.28.7 The regulations allow for flexibility where a person's condition improves but deteriorates again later. In such circumstances, the claimant need not satisfy the six months qualifying period for a second occasion. AA may be awarded for life, or for a shorter fixed period.

1.28.8 For elderly people, the financial significance of receiving AA cannot be overstated. First, it can be paid to each member of a family who qualifies for it. Second, it is not taxable. Third, it can be paid in addition to other NI benefits such as IB/PA, SDA, and the mobility component of DLA. Fourth, it is usually ignored for the purposes of assessing IS and HB. Entitlement to AA is also one of the ways of qualifying automatically for the higher pensioner premiums under the IS scheme.

1.29.1 DISABILITY LIVING ALLOWANCE

There are two components of disability living allowance (DLA), the mobility component and the care component. Each is paid at different rates. A claimant may qualify for either component or for both at the same time. Each component may be awarded at a different level. An important feature of DLA is that it can be awarded for life, or for a fixed term as appropriate. For example, the mobility component might be awarded for life in the case of a double amputee, but the care component might only be awarded for five years. If both components are awarded for a fixed rather than a life term they must be for the same length of time.

A person must satisfy the conditions before his/her sixty-fifth birthday and claim before his/her sixty-sixth birthday. The government at the outset conceded that older people would not benefit under the new changes, justifying their exclusion on two grounds. First, that an increasing number of pensioners now have the benefit of occupational pension schemes and, second, by implying that older people would be the prime beneficiaries of the government's community care reforms (DSS 1990). Even if the government's controvertible assertions could be justified (Edwards 1992), the fact remains that existing policies unfairly discriminate against older people. Moreover, the new changes add to the discrimination in one important way.

A new lower rate care component has been introduced which has no equivalent under AA provisions. A claimant who does not qualify for either the higher or middle rates of the care component (identical to 'day' and 'night' conditions under AA) may qualify for the lower rate if he/she:

(a) requires, in connection with his/her bodily functions, attention from another person for a significant portion of the day (whether during a single period or a number of periods); or
(b) cannot prepare a cooked main meal for him/herself if he/she has the ingredients.

Several important questions arise, including what is meant by 'significant portion of the day' or how the 'cooking test' can be satisfied. The most important point to grasp, however, is that claimants will lose the right to the lower rate at sixty-five and be placed in the absurd position of either losing out financially or claiming that their circumstances have deteriorated overnight, thus allowing them to qualify for the middle or highest rate of benefit. The rule is, therefore, yet another example of an ageist and stigmatising policy.

A new lower mobility component has also been introduced. A claimant for the lower rate need not show that he/she is unable to walk, but rather be

> so severely disabled physically or mentally that, disregarding any ability he/she may have to use routes which are familiar to him/her on his/her own, he/she cannot take advantage of the facility out of doors without guidance or supervision from another person most of the time.

As the Disability Alliance conclude, the recognition that mobility restrictions are not always physical in origin is an important breakthrough (Disability Alliance 1992). The eligibility rules can also, arguably, be regarded as more rational for the perverse reason that there is no mobility benefit entitlement whatsoever for people who first need help with mobility after reaching the age of sixty-five. A person in receipt of a mobility component before reaching sixty-five will continue to receive it provided the relevant criteria are satisfied. The rules have been designed to ensure that DLA recipients who are over sixty-five are treated no differently from other pensioners (Wikeley 1992). So, for example, it will not be possible for a person receiving the lower rate mobility component to be up-graded to the higher component after reaching sixty-five.

A person is only entitled to mobility benefit if his/her condition is such that he/she will be able to take advantage of the benefit. This is designed to prevent claims from persons who, for example, are totally paralysed and confined to bed and for whom no amount of financial assistance will make them mobile. A person must have satisfied the conditions for three months prior to the date of the award and also be likely to satisfy them for six months following the award.

The claim form is lengthy. However, the forms are issued following a request and the claim will be treated as being made from the date the form was posted to the claimant provided it was filled in and returned within the time limit which is six weeks or such other time as the DSS thinks reasonable. This gives sufficient time to complete the form properly. As in the case of AA, the claim form is a self-assessment form. It must be counter-signed by someone who knows the claimant, and by the claimant's doctor. The DSS may ask for further information.

Experience to date suggest that claimants may not be very expert at filling in the forms and certainly a significantly lower percentage of claims for DLA have been successful than for AA – only 58 per cent (*Welfare Rights Bulletin* 1992). A number of explanations can be given. First, the form is very long and a number of people give up before reaching the end, or their answers may become less accurate. Second, questions are very personal, relating to help to go to the toilet, etc., and some people may not wish to be embarrassed by answering the forms correctly, whereas others may not wish to admit to a need for help and understate their problems. They seem very optimistic, or are poor judges of time and distance. Some people overstate their problems, or their symptoms and needs, and do not seem to be consistent with the medical diagnosis. They do not accurately assess how long it takes them to go to the toilet, or how far they can walk. Some people do not know the difference between 100 feet, 100 yards or 100 metres.

One of the most absurd restrictions has been removed. The previous upper age limit of eighty years for mobility allowance has been abolished.

Case law decided in relation to mobility allowance will be relevant in relation to issues concerning the mobility component of DLA.

1.30.1 INVALID CARE ALLOWANCE

In contrast to AA, invalid care allowance (ICA) is payable to the carer and not to the disabled person. It is relevant to the financial and social well-being of elderly people for three distinct reasons. First, it may encourage and enable individuals to provide elderly people with the support and the care which they need. Second, as providers of care, they will themselves sometimes qualify for the allowance, although, as a general rule, those over sixty-five years of age will have no entitlement. Claimants entitled to the allowance immediately before reaching sixty-five years of age, or who would have been except for overlapping benefit provisions, retain their entitlement providing they continue to satisfy all the qualifying conditions. Third, the rules provide for those receiving the allowance when they reached retiring age to continue receiving it, even if they are no longer caring for another person. In effect, it becomes a non-contributory pension. Women are now entitled to make their first claim after reaching sixty years of age (*Secretary of State for Social Security v. Thomas (1993)*).

1.30.2 Invalid care allowance is taxable except for increases for children. The decision of a married couple whether to claim ICA can depend on their tax situation. If a married woman looks after her husband, her husband cannot claim an increase on her account. This could be significant where the claimant is receiving IB/IP in respect of a spouse since the increase is not taxable. Conversely, the ICA is characterised by a more generous earnings rule.

A person who claims ICA is entitled to be credited with Class 1 National Insurance contributions which will obviously have an effect on the benefits a person may wish to claim as a result of those contributions. A dependant is not entitled to be credited with contributions just because he/she is a dependant.

1.30.3 Section 37 of the SSA 1975 sets out the qualifying condition for the receipt of ICA. The section provides that an individual will be entitled to ICA if he/she is regularly, and substantially, engaged in caring for a severely disabled person, and is not in gainful employment. It is not necessary, however, to have given up gainful employment in order to become the carer, nor need the claimant have ever been in gainful employment. Although the legislation refers only to women, it is presumed that men too would be entitled to the allowance.

1.30.4   An operational definition of the phrase 'regular and substantial care' is given in the regulations. A person will be deemed to have satisfied the requirement if he/she provides, 'or is likely' to provide care for at least thirty-five hours a week. A person who provides less than thirty-five hours regular care can never be deemed to be providing 'substantial' care. The act of 'caring' is nowhere defined in the legislation or regulations. The probable legal effect of including the phrase 'is likely to be ... engaged' in the regulations is to allow for temporary absences by the carer over and above the period of absence allowed for in the regulations.

The regulations allow for absences of up to a total of four weeks in every twenty-six-week period, without any loss of entitlement. As with attendance allowance, the claimant does not necessarily lose entitlement on going abroad, but for ICA there is usually a limit of four weeks. The four-week limit will not apply, however, if the claimant continues in the caring role.

Should the claimant go away unaccompanied, he/she can continue to receive ICA but the person providing substitute care during that time will receive no additional payment. Even under normal circumstances, only one person is entitled to ICA. Where two people are involved as carers, one of them may be entitled to home responsibility protection (see para. 1.12.2).

1.30.5   In the context of claiming ICA, a 'severely disabled person' is a person in receipt of either the middle or higher rate of the care component of DLA or their equivalent rate of AA with respect to industrial or war disablement. A person is not to be treated as 'gainfully employed' unless his/her earnings exceed £50 per week (1994–5 figures).

1.30.6   The financial impact of ICA is not as great as that of other benefits referred to above. This is because of the rules relating to overlapping benefits.

1.31.1   INCOME SUPPORT

Income Support (IS) replaced supplementary benefit/pensions in April 1988. It is intended as a safety net for those whose income falls below a level prescribed by Parliament. It is a means-tested benefit so that a claimant's resources are taken into account. Because it is non-contributory, the claimant need not have paid NI contributions. Entitlement to IS can act as a passport to other benefits. Most of the benefits in question are available to older people, irrespective of IS entitlement. Some important exceptions exist, however, such as entitlement to community care grants. Often it pays to claim IS even though the weekly income from benefit is hardly improved (see Appendix I).

1.31.2 A common complaint is that IS is not adequate. Evidence suggests that some two-thirds of the budgets of pension householders are consumed by food and clothing. The Breadline Britain survey found that some 73 per cent of pensioners on low income 'choose' to go without three or more necessities compared to 9 per cent of younger people (Mack and Lansley 1985). Items such as bus fares, fuel bills, extra laundry bills are not provided for directly under IS. Loans or grants from the Social Fund may be an option in some circumstances.

1.31.3 Where a claim for IS is made, it can be made by an individual on his/her own behalf and on behalf of other 'family' members, including a husband, wife, cohabitee, or child where the unit lives together (SSCBA 1992, s.124; Income Support (General) Regulations 1987).

1.31.4 There are five qualifying conditions of particular relevance to older applicants. First, neither the claimant nor his/her partner can be in full-time work (sixteen hours per week or more). The regulations provide, however, that persons are not to be treated as if engaged in paid work where, *inter alia*, they are engaged in voluntary work for a charity or voluntary body; or as a childminder in their own home; or as carers for a person who receives, or has applied for, AA or DLA; or if earning capacity has been reduced by physical or mental disability to 75 per cent or less than they would otherwise be capable of earning.

Second, the claimant must be available for work or exempted from this requirement. Persons aged sixty and over are exempt and those aged between fifty and fifty-nine may be exempted. The latter exemption applies to those who have no prospect of getting full-time employment. To qualify, the claimant must show that he/she has not had a full-time job for the last ten years, and that he/she has not been required to sign on the unemployment register during that time. The rule in the main is aimed at women who are widowed or divorced and whose children have grown up (Webster and Wood 1993). Third, the claimant must be resident in Britain, but persons who do go abroad temporarily can continue to receive the benefit for up to four weeks. A short holiday in the sun would not therefore bar a claim. Fourth, a claimant must have less than £8,000 in capital.

Fifth, a claimant's income must be less than his/her 'applicable amount'. The applicable amount consists of three elements: first, a personal allowance for each member of the family unit; second, a premium for any special needs; and third, in certain cases some housing costs. The personal allowances are reviewed annually and are set out elsewhere (Webster *et al.* 1994). The premiums are allowable for certain specific needs and recognise the additional expense caused by old age, disability or bringing up children. The significant premiums for elderly people include disability and severe disability premium, carers premiums and the pensioner premiums. A claimant who is, or who has within the family unit, a person with a need covered by the premiums is entitled to add the amount of the premium to the personal allowance in determining the extent of the applicable amount.

1.31.5   PREMIUMS

A claimant may qualify for more than one premium; but, in general, he/she will be entitled to one only, that is, the premium which gives the highest benefit. There are three exceptions to this rule, two of which are of particular importance here. The first exception is that a family premium (FP) can be paid in addition to any other premium which the claimant is receiving. An FP is payable to claimants who are responsible for children who live within the same household. Second, the severe disability premium (SDP) can be paid at the same time as the disability premium (DP) or higher pensioner premium (HPP).

A pensioner premium (PP) is payable to a claimant who is, or whose partner is, sixty years of age. It is paid at two rates according to age – a lower rate for those aged sixty to seventy-four and a higher rate for those between seventy-five and seventy-nine. Couples will be entitled to the enhanced rate provided that one partner fulfils the age requirement.

To qualify for HPP, the claimant must satisfy one of three conditions. First, either the claimant or his/her partner must be aged eighty or more. Second, the claimant was receiving DP as an element of IS, HB or council tax benefit (CTB) before reaching sixty years of age. Eligibility also depends on receipt of DP at some point during the eight week period leading up to the claimant's sixtieth birthday.

Third, the claimant or his/her partner are aged between sixty and seventy-nine and either receive a qualifying benefit, are registered blind, or have an NHS trike or a private car allowance. A qualifying benefit includes an AA (or an equivalent benefit paid as a result of an industrial or war injury), DLA, disability working allowance (DWA), mobility supplement, IB/IP or SDA.

The eight-week limiting rules are arbitrary. Individuals can be unlucky and lose entitlement to HPP simply because they failed to qualify for IS during the eight weeks preceding their sixtieth birthday. A bequest or other capital gift received during this critical period could deprive the claimant of entitlement to HPP until he/she reaches eighty, unless he/she could claim a disability benefit and so qualify along that route.

The number qualifying for SDP is likely to be small since the eligibility criteria are very difficult to satisfy. To qualify for SDP the claimant must be receiving AA or the higher or middle rate of the care component of DLA. Where the claimant is one of a couple both must be receiving it. The implicit assumption, therefore, is that a partner should accept responsibility for caring for the disabled person, unless he/she is also disabled. Second, there must be no adult non-dependants aged eighteen or over, residing with the claimant. Certain co-residents, such as boarders or temporary visitors, are disregarded. Third, no one should be receiving ICA for caring for the claimant. Where both partners are receiving AA, the right to SDP will be preserved where ICA is paid to a carer in respect of only one of them. Where no one is receiving ICA with respect to either claimant, both will be entitled to the premium. A carer cannot be forced to claim ICA. Conversely, neither can a carer be prevented from making a claim. Where no claim for ICA is made, however, and the carer him/herself is receiving IS, or some other similar state benefit, the risk exists that he/she may be credited with notional income, equivalent to the amount of ICA which would be available. Finally, a carer premium can be allowed if the claimant or his/her partner receives ICA or would get ICA were it not for the rule on overlapping benefits.

Entitlement to carer's premium depends on the claimant or his/her partner receiving ICA or being entitled to ICA were it not for the overlapping benefit rules. A double carer's pension is available where both claimant and partner satisfy the relevant conditions.

1.31.6 HOUSING COSTS

Housing costs, as an element of the 'applicable amount', have now been largely superseded by the housing benefit scheme, but in certain instances these are allowable where they consist of mortgage interest repayments, interest on a loan taken out for certain repairs and improvements to a home (rented or owner occupied), ground rent and certain service and co-ownership charges. In all instances the property must be the home that the claimant (and family) normally lives in and the claimant must be responsible for the actual cost involved.

In C15 760/92, the claimant applied for IS following the death of her daughter with whom she lived and who, prior to her death, had held a mortgage on the property. It was decided that housing cost in respect of the mortgage could be met as the person who was liable could not meet the cost.

Limitations exist on the amount of mortgage interest repayments in that most claimants only receive 50 per cent of the amount for the first sixteen weeks of the claim. Those over sixty are exempted from this restriction.

Interest on second mortgages is also available on condition that the loan is taken out for home improvements or repairs. Claimants, however, cannot receive interest on a new loan for repairs and improvements taken out whilst receiving IS, unless a loan is taken out to meet service charges for which the claimants are liable. If a person is considering taking out a home loan for improvements he/she should check with the DSS that the particular improvements are approved for this purpose. There are a lot of 'Care and Repair' schemes around the country offering cheap home improvements for the elderly. Most are reputable but some have resulted in pensioners taking on loans which they find IS will not pay for because the repairs are not allowed under the regulations.

Reasonable improvements can, however, include improvements carried out on land not owned or occupied by the claimant. In C15/129/93, the claimant acquired a loan to renovate her property and to build an access road in order to carry out the required work. Each case depends on its facts and it is clear that subjective considerations can be of importance. In C15/278/92, the claimant borrowed a substantial amount of money from a building society to improve his house in order to accommodate his disabled son. The claimant success-fully appealed against refusal of the claim and the Commissioner in question concluded that 'other improvements which are reasonable in the circumstances should be interpreted subjectively to include all the relevant circumstances'.

Other costs allowed include interest on hire purchase (HP) agree-ment to buy a home (these are not common but there are some areas of the country where people are buying their homes on HP); rent or ground rent in respect of a long lease of more than twenty-one years; payments as part of a shared ownership scheme; some service charges if they are imposed as a condition of occupation of the home (C15/616/92); and site fees for caravans and mooring fees for boats. In contrast no housing costs will be allowed in respect of non-qualifying loans for home improvements, water and sewerage charges, and payment for fuel and cooking. Similarly, rent or board and lodging and hostel payments are usually paid by HB which is a separate benefit administered by local housing authorities (see para. 1.34.1 below).

1.31.7 RESOURCES

Having assessed the correct 'applicable amount', it is the resources of the claimant that are next taken into account in making the calculation of entitlement to IS. Resources consist of both capital and income. Where capital totals more than £8,000, there is no right to IS. Capital not exceeding £3,000 is disregarded in its entirety. Some capital assets, notably the value of a dwelling occupied as a home, and personal possessions (other than those acquired with the intention of reducing capital in order to secure entitlement) are disregarded. A list of disregarded capital assets is set out in the regulations (Income Support (General) Regulations 1987). Capital includes not only savings, but also certain insurance policies and items that are in the nature of an investment (for example stocks and shares). Capital between £3,000 and £8,000 is treated as producing a notional 'tariff' income. Each block of £250 (or part thereof) is deemed to produce a weekly income of £1. Assessing a person's capital resources can give rise to complex legal problems. It is first necessary to establish that the capital belongs to the claimant. In R(SB)49/83, for instance, the claimant had bought a house, but argued it had been bought on behalf of his son, who was repaying the loan. The Social Security Commissioner held that it was possible, in such circumstances, to regard the claimant as holding the property on a resulting trust for the benefit of a third party. Where it can be established that the claimant is a trustee, the asset cannot be regarded as forming part of the claimant's capital resources.

It should be noted that any attempt to deprive oneself of capital (or income) with a view to claiming benefit will attract the 'notional' resources rules. The Benefits Agency will treat the claimant as still having the resource in such instances. It is not therefore advisable for a prospective claimant to dispose of capital to, say, other family members to avoid the consequences outlined above. However, not all transfers of ownership will fall foul of the rules. In C15/621/91 the claimant and his wife (who received IS) were in arrears with their mortgage and the building society was pressing for possession. They had a daughter living with them and the claimant wanted to solve his debt problem without making his daughter homeless. The house was transferred to the daughter who took over the mortgage and the claimant and his wife were rehoused by the local authority. This course of action was decided upon despite warnings from the Benefits Agency that the transfer would be regarded by them as a deprivation of capital. The claimant successfully appealed against refusal of his claim for IS. Somewhat ironically, the fact that a warning had been given was held to be in his favour – his purpose in making the tranfer could not have been to secure continued entitlement to IS.

Income resources are also relevant, but not all income is counted either in full or part. The income of all members of the claimant's family unit are aggregated (save for certain limited exceptions), but included in those ignored entirely are: any care components of DLA and AA (other than for a claimant in a private residential or nursing home since 1 April 1993); pensioners' Christmas bonus; mobility allowance and DLA mobility component; social fund payments; payments of HB and CTB; and any transitional payments due as a result of the benefit changes in 1988.

Some income is ignored in part and this includes the first £15 of earnings for anyone qualifying for certain premiums, for example disability premium or higher pensioner premium, and the first £10 of certain war pension payments. Also included in the definition of income will be any tariff income generated by capital.

1.32.1 TRUST PROPERTY

The treatment of capital and income to which a person is entitled under a trust fund, should also be noted. Where a person's interest is 'reversionary' (that is, arising only when some specified event occurs, such as the death of another person) the capital value must be disregarded (Income Support (General) Regulations 1987). Similarly, where a person's interest in a trust fund, or property held on trust, constitutes a life interest under which he/she is entitled to income, then the capital value of the interest is ignored. It may be different, however, where the terms of the trust enable the trustees to encroach on capital. In R(SB)13/87, the claimant had a life interest in her husband's residuary estate. The terms of the trust gave the trustees a discretionary power to make use of capital if the income was insufficient for the claimant's suitable maintenance. The Social Security Commissioner confirmed the need to consider the value of the claimant's interest in the capital of her husband's estate, because of the trustee's power to use the capital for the claimant's benefit.

1.33.1 A DWELLING

The most frequent problems relating to resources generally are probably those which arise over the treatment of a dwelling as a capital asset. As indicated above, the value of a dwelling occupied as the claimant's home is disregarded. Nevertheless, problems can arise on purchase or sale of premises, or where the claimant leaves his/her former home to stay with relatives, for instance, or to enter a residential home. The capital disregard, which applies to one dwelling only, can relate to premises acquired for occupation which the claimant intends to occupy as a dwelling within twenty-six weeks of acquisition, or such longer period as is reasonable in the circumstances. This also applies to proceeds held as a result of the sale of premises where it is intended to use the capital for the purchase of other premises to be occupied within a similar period of time (Income Support (General) Regulations 1987). The effect of leaving a dwelling in order to live with relatives, or to enter a residential home, depends upon four factors. First, whether a partner or relative continues to occupy the premises; second, the intention of the claimant; third, the availability of the premises; and fourth, the period of absence from the premises.

The regulations provide for the value of premises to be disregarded if they are occupied, in whole or in part, by a partner or relative of any member of the family who is aged sixty or over or is incapacitated, or the former partner of a claimant where the claimant is not to be treated as occupying a dwelling as a home (that is, where the claimant has been away from home for at least fifty-two weeks), but this provision shall not apply where the former partner is a person from whom the claimant is estranged or divorced.

A 'partner' includes the other member of an unmarried couple. The statutory definition of a family also takes account of unmarried couples. A 'relative' need not, therefore, be related to the claimant; but, unlike a partner, a relative must be over sixty years of age, or incapacitated.

Where neither a partner, nor a relative, remains in occupation, the dwelling will be treated as capital unless it is the claimant's intention to return. The regulations provide that a person shall be treated as occupying a dwelling as his/her home for a period not exceeding fifty-two weeks. In exceptional circumstances (for example, where the person is in hospital or otherwise has no control over the length of his/ her absence), the period can be extended, but there must be an intention to return (Income Support (General) Regulations 1987 Sched. 3, para. 4(8)). Where the intention is to give up the home permanently, the disregard does not apply.

1.34.1 HOUSING BENEFIT

Housing benefit (HB) is a means-tested benefit which assists people on low income with payment of rent. The scheme is administered by local housing authorities and the benefit is calculated in a similar, though not identical, manner to IS. Those receiving IS are not subject to a further means-test on making a claim for HB, although a formal claim must, nevertheless, be made. A claim may be back-dated for up to a year in certain circumstances. Only the more important differences between IS and HB are discussed here.

This benefit is restricted to those claimants who are responsible for the payment of rent, either in the private sector or to the local authority. The capital limit is, in this case, presently £16,000, but the tariff rules apply to capital in excess of £3,000. Otherwise, the same figures as for IS are used to calculate whether a claimant's resources exceed or fall short of the applicable amount. Providing the rent level is not deemed to be excessive, a claimant's rent should be met in full by HB. For those not receiving IS the calculation referred to above is required.

If a claimant's income does not exceed the applicable amount, HB of an amount equal to that of the eligible rent should be payable. If the claimant's income exceeds the applicable amount, then HB is the amount of the eligible rent less 65 per cent of the difference between the applicable amount and the claimant's income. This deduction from what would otherwise be the full amount of HB is known as a taper.

In calculating the eligible rent certain items are deducted, such as fuel charges, water rates, and the cost of meals if provided for the tenant by the landlord. If a non-dependant shares the accommodation, set amounts are deductible. The rules for HB are to be found in the SSCBA 1992 (s.130) and related delegated legislation (Housing Benefit (General) Regulations 1987). Special provisions exist for those claimants who are in residential homes. Except in limited circumstances, those living in residential and nursing homes are ineligible for HB. Before January 1991, residents who did not qualify for IS could apply for HB. Only those who were entitled to HB before 30 October 1990 continue to receive it.

Before April 1993, some claimants received HB because they lived in a home with less than four residents, or were in full-time work, or paid a commercial rent to a close relative. They can continue to claim (even if they move accommodation) providing they continue to be financially eligible (Webster and Wood 1993). (Financial support and residential care are discussed in Chapter 4).

Once a claim has been made and the claimant has supplied all the necessary information, the authority must determine the claim within fourteen days or, if this is not reasonably practicable, as soon as possible after that (Housing Benefit (General) Regulations 1987 reg. 76(3)).

Where it is impracticable for the authority to determine a claim for a rent allowance within fourteen days of the claim being made, the authority has a legal duty to make an immediate payment on account based on a reasonable estimate of entitlement to benefit – unless the delay in processing the claim arises out of the claimant's failure, without good cause, to provide any evidence which the authority reasonbly requires and which has already been specifically requested (reg. 91(1)).

1.34.2 Despite the very specific nature of the above rules, concern has been growing over delays in processing claims and the failure of most local authorities to make obligatory payments to private tenants (*Welfare Rights Bulletin* 1993). Claimants who have lost accommodation because of an authority's failure to make payments on account may have a case for initiating a civil action for damages. It should also be noted that a Housing Benefit Review Board should apply its own judgment to the merits of an appeal and not simply rely on the local authority's consideration of whether the statutory tests were satisfied. In addition, the review board must also give reasons for its conclusions (*R v. Housing Benefit Review Board, ex parte Gibson (1993)*).

1.34.3 As with IS, case law is developing. In one interesting case of concern to elderly people in mining and ex-mining communities, it was decided that the receipt of free coal amounted to income for HB purposes. The applicant was the widow of a miner who used to receive 9 tons of free coal a year. The court held that as such arrangements reflected good personnel practice on behalf of British

Coal and had come about as part of national agreements, and the coal could not be regarded as voluntary payments. In the case in question, the widow concerned had converted to gas and received an annual cost payment in lieu of coal. It is pointless to speculate, but perhaps the case might have been stronger had the complainant continued to burn coal. In another case, charges made by a landlord for counselling or support services for the mentally ill in rented accommodation were not ineligible service charges to be excluded from housing benefit, even if the landlord did not spend most of his time providing such services (*R v. North Cornwall DC, ex parte Singer (1994)*).

1.35.1   COUNCIL TAX BENEFIT

The council tax (CT) replaced the poll tax in April 1993. It is the tax paid to local authorities to help pay for the services they provide. One difference between council tax benefit (CTB) and the former poll tax benefit is that the new benefit can cover up to 100 per cent of the council tax bill. Under the former arrangements, everyone had to pay 20 per cent of their poll tax. The main difference, however, is that the new tax is primarily a tax on domestic property, not persons. There is a personal element but essentially CT is a charge made by local housing authorities on certain individuals based on the banded value of the home in which they live or which they own (Local Government Finance Act 1992 (LGFA 1992) ss.1–9). Properties are allocated to one of eight bands, the lowest being band A and the highest band H. Each authority sets its own rate of CT. There will be one bill for each self-contained dwelling. An appeal procedure exists to challenge the banding valuation. Most of the concessions are aimed at disabled persons and carers (Bransbury 1993).

Liability for the tax usually falls on those aged eighteen or over and who are resident in the property. If there is more than one person who is resident, there is a priority order to decide who will be liable. Liability depends on status, ranging from a resident freeholder, lease holder, tenant, licensee, to other people such as squatters. In some circumstances, a non-resident owner will be liable. The owners of residential and nursing homes are liable for the tax, but can pass this on to the residents, for instance, as part of their accommodation charges.

1.35.2 The amount of tax can be reduced by certain allowances. These are disability reductions, discounts and transitional relief. If a person who is liable for the tax is disabled and the home in which he/she lives has been specially adapted, a reduction is given in the form of a lowering of that property banding by one band. In other words, a property banded C would be treated as D for the purposes of the tax. Only certain adaptations apply (Council Tax (Reductions for Disabilities) Regulations 1992, reg.3). Discounts are given in certain cases, for example, where the property is occupied by a single person or is empty. Certain occupants are disregarded entirely for the purposes of the tax, for example the severely mentally impaired, patients in hospital, and carers who live with a person who receives DLA care component or AA paid at the higher rate. Finally, transitional relief can be given to a person who is paying more under the council tax scheme than under the poll tax system.

1.35.3 There are two types of benefit: main CTB and alternative maximum CTB. The latter is usually referred to as second adult rebate. To claim main CTB, the claimant's income must be low enough and his/her capital must be below £16,000. There is no capital resource ceiling for the alternative benefit which is aimed to help persons who have adults in their home that do not pay rent or share liability for CT. It is not possible to receive both benefits, but a local authority should assess entitlement to both types of benefit and pay whichever is the higher. The benefit to elderly people could be significant, particularly since many live on their own and are clearly liable to pay CT. The local authority has the responsibility to ensure that the correct calculation of tax is made (including the giving of discounts), but the onus lies upon the individual to apply for CTB or the alternative benefit.

1.36.1 THE SOCIAL FUND

The Social Fund replaced the system of single payments, most urgent needs payments, as well as maternity and death grants available under the old supplementary benefits scheme. It was established to help people with exceptional needs which are difficult to meet from regular income and falls into two parts, the regulated fund and the discretionary fund. The former provides for non-discretionary grants (not repayable), whereas discretionary grants and loans are repayable.

There are three types of discretionary award: community care grants (CCGs), budgeting loans and crisis loans. Each of the discretionary awards is determined by a Social Fund Officer (SFO) according to directions and guidance issued by the Secretary of State under s.32 of the Social Security Act 1986 (SSA 1986). Under s.33(10) of the Act, directions are legally binding upon an SFO. Claims for mandatory awards from the 'regulated fund' are subject to review and appeal to a Social Security Appeals Tribunal (SSAT).

The discretionary fund, in contrast, is budget limited. There is no right of appeal against a decision to the SSAT, although there is an internal review and a right to a further review by a Social Fund inspector. The budget limited nature of the fund means that each DSS office has a budget for the year. The amended legislation provides the Secretary of State with explicit power to issue directions regulating budgetary allocation (SSCBA 1992, s.140(3)). The evidence suggests that some offices are as much as 30 per cent overspent on social fund budgets and are resorting to harsh policy guidelines in order to balance the books (*Welfare Rights Bulletin* 1992b).

1.37.1 FUNERAL EXPENSES

A person can claim funeral expenses from the social fund if he/she is in receipt of one of the qualifying benefits, which are income support (IS), family credit (FC), disability working allowance (DWA), housing benefit (HB), or council tax benefit (CTB).

1.37.2 The funeral must take place in the UK. This limitation is currently being challenged on the basis of the Race Relations Act 1976 (Webster *et al.* 1994). Funeral means burial or cremation. Thus a 'funeral' is not a service which blesses or otherwise remembers the deceased before his/her body is flown abroad for burial. The claimant cannot even claim the costs of taking the body to the airport since the burial or cremation is taking place abroad. The claimant's resources must be within the capital limit which in this case means that any capital in excess of £500, or £1,000 if the claimant or his/her spouse is over sixty, has to be taken into account in making the funeral expenses payment.

More than one person might be considered responsible for the funeral. It is not uncommon for the relative in receipt of one of the 'passport' benefits to make the application, thus relieving other relatives who may be in poor financial circumstances, but not themselves in receipt of a 'passport' benefit. The Benefits Agency should accept that the claimant is responsible for the costs if the person concerned has obtained a funeral director's estimate (*The Social Fund Maternity and Funeral Payments Guide* (SFMFG)). However, the person making the claim need not be a relative of the deceased, or have arranged the funeral.

1.37.3 The Social Fund will pay for the necessary documentation, a coffin and (in the case of a cremation) an urn, the cost of a hearse and one following car, the reasonable cost of flowers, undertaker's fees and other necessary fees and the costs of one return journey for the claimant within the UK.

Again there have been numerous reported decisions. In IS/SB 11/91, the Commissioner was required to decide on the meaning of the words 'deceased's home'. A claim for funeral expenses included the cost of transporting the deceased from Cheltenham, England to Wislow, Scotland. The deceased had lived in England for nine years but had originally come from Scotland and his widow arranged for him to be buried there. The Commissioner held that the arrangements were not commensurate with a simple funeral and disallowed the extra expense incurred. In RI5 14/92, however, the claimant succeeded in justifying additional costs associated with arranging a Jewish burial.

1.38.1 COLD WEATHER PAYMENTS

The cold weather payments system is supposed to be, and for the most part is, automatic, so that a separate claim does not need to be made. In the event that a person does not receive a payment to which he/she thinks he/she is entitled, he/she should enquire of the DSS and, if not satisfied, should appeal to the SSAT. The DSS usually place advertisements in the local press advising if an area qualifies for a payment. The requisite conditions trigger automatic payment.

First, a period of cold weather must have been forecast or recorded in the area in which the claimant lives. A period of cold weather is one which in seven consecutive days the mean (that is, average) temperature has not exceeded 0 degrees Celsius. The country is divided into sixty-three separate areas, each of which has a weather station. Each of the sixty-three areas covers a number of postcode areas. Second, a person must have been in receipt of IS for at least one of those days. Third, older claimants must, in addition, have been awarded a pensioner, higher pensioner, disability or severe disability premium.

The current cold weather payment (1994–5) is £7 per cold weather week. The intention is to raise the payment to £7.50 in future.

1.39.1 COMMUNITY CARE GRANTS

Community care grants are discretionary but directions have been issued by the Secretary of State which are fully binding. Thus, a Social Fund payment may be awarded to promote community care where such assistance will help an applicant to re-establish him/herself, or a member of his/her family, in the community following a stay in institutional or residential care. The rules have given rise to considerable confusion and litigation. In *R v. Social Fund Inspector, ex parte Mohammed (1992)*, the focus was on the meaning of the word 'community'. The applicant had come to the UK as a refugee from Ethiopia and had been placed in temporary hostel accommodation. She subsequently found a flat, but was refused a grant towards the cost of furniture on the basis that she could not be re-established into a community to which she had never belonged. The word 'family' appears four times in the relevant rules, but is not defined, and Decision E (1993) focused on the definition. A single man was attempting to make suitable arrangements so he could accommodate his mother whose long-standing marital problems had affected her mental and physical state of health over the years. The Social Fund Inspector overturned the original decision and conceded that the term could include such an arrangement. *The Social Fund Guide* specifies certain groups as having priority for certain grants. Elderly people are included in the priority list, particularly if they have restricted mobility, or difficulty in performing personal tasks.

1.40.1 BUDGETING LOANS

Budgeting loans are available for people who need to buy items which they cannot easily finance out of their IS. These might include essential items of household equipment or home repairs, fuel meter installation charges, etc. The loans are repaid out of IS at prescribed rates, usually over a period not more than one and a half to two years. Crisis loans are designed to meet one-off disaster-type situations. They might be used to help with the consequences of a fire or flood. A person's means and resources are taken into account, but a loan will be paid if they are insufficient to meet the need. There is a defined list of income and resources which will be taken into account and excluded.

1.41.1 HELP WITH VAT ON DOMESTIC FUEL

Fifteen million people will gain extra help to meet the cost of VAT on fuel. Help will be available to all those receiving income-related benefits, all pensioners, widows (including war widows), the long-term sick receiving IB/IP and SDA, and people receiving ICA.

1.42.1 REVIEWS, APPEALS AND REDRESS OF GRIEVANCES

The final section in this chapter concerns the processes by which aggrieved parties can challenge a decision of another, be that an ex-employer, a pensions company or the DSS.

Complaints arising from alleged discrimination in the search for work, or conditions at work, lie to an industrial tribunal. Likewise a person who qualifies for protection against unfair dismissal or compensation in the event of redundancy may use the same process (the Industrial Tribunal's jurisdiction can be found in the EP(C)A 1978 ss.128–31). The Industrial Tribunal is also the forum for cases alleging unauthorised deductions from wages (Wages Act 1986 (WA 1986) s.8, but see *Delaney v. Staples (1992)*).

Cases other than those above that involve claims against an employer should be brought before the civil courts. This will normally be the county court. Disputes that stem from an alleged breach of contract (for example, a dispute over a private pension scheme) will in principle fall to be decided by reference to the civil courts unless the contract contains the means for dispute resolution, in particular arbitration. One important development in this field has been the introduction of the Occupational Pensions Ombudsman.

1.42.2 Social security benefits are subject to a special set of administrative and procedural rules. A claimant who wishes to challenge the decision of the Benefits Agency or the Employment Department must first receive or insist upon that decision in writing. This will normally follow from a formal claim for benefit. By law, the adjudication officer (AO), who makes initial decisions, must provide such a decision within fourteen days of the date of application and the claimant is entitled to written reasons for that decision (SSCBA 1992 s.21). Certain matters are the exclusive preserve of the Secretary of State or the Social Security Commissioner (SSC) and are subject to different rules (Poynter and Martin 1993).

Presuming that the decision is made by the AO, the claimant has two options open to him/her. First, the claimant can seek a review of the decision. It is also open to the AO to review a decision if this is felt necessary. Reviews for DLA or AA can be on any ground, but otherwise there must be particular grounds, for example the decision was made in ignorance of, or mistake as to, a material fact (Poynter and Martin 1993).

Whether the decision is reviewed or not, the claimant can take the second course of action, that is, to lodge an appeal. This must normally be in writing and within three months of the original decision. The effect of lodging the appeal is to activate a review of the case. The appeal can proceed if the claimant does not accept the outcome of the review. Appeals are heard by the appropriate tribunal (Social Security Appeal, Medical Appeal or Disability Appeal) and a further appeal lies within six weeks on a point of law to the SSC. Leave of either the appeal tribunal or the Commissioner is required. Further appeals on law lie to the Court of Appeal and House of Lords and eventually to the European Court of Justice.

1.42.3 It is also possible to complain to the Parliamentary Commissioner for Administration (the Parliamentary Ombudsman), but this must be channelled through an MP. The DSS have agreed a formula for the payment of compensation in certain cases (Poynter and Martin 1993).

1.42.4 Finally, it may be possible to pursue a complaint by seeking a judicial review of a decision-making process. The procedure is discussed in relation to other matter in Chapters 3, 4 and 6.

2 Living in the community

Rebecca Jordan and Jeff Harrison

2.1.1 ACCOMMODATION AND THE ELDERLY

The vast majority of people over pensionable age live in non-institutional accommodation. Elderly people are represented across all housing tenures. Over half are owner occupiers, two-fifths rent from a local authority, and one in ten rent privately. What is particularly striking is the number of owner occupiers who own their properties outright – over 90 per cent. The proportion of owner occupiers is, however, less among the older elderly, and those living alone, with a corresponding increase in the proportion renting (McGlone 1992). This chapter looks mainly at the legal considerations relevant to those living in owner-occupied property, or holding tenancies in the public and private sectors. Reference is also made, however, to those who for a variety of reasons find themselves homeless in old age. Issues related to moving in with relatives and friends are discussed in Chapter 7 at 7.18.2.

2.2.1 HOMELESSNESS

Homelessness is a growing problem affecting the elderly as well as the young. A recent Age Concern Greater London report estimated that approximately 30 per cent of the total number of homeless people in London are over fifty (Morton 1992).

The 'homeless' as such have no legal right to accommodation of any kind. In some circumstances, however, the Housing Act 1985 (HA 1985) Part III places a duty upon local housing authorities (that is, District Councils and, in London, the Borough Councils) to provide or arrange accommodation for certain categories of homeless people.

The definition of 'homeless' under Part III includes being in accommodation that it is unreasonable to continue to occupy (HA 1985, s.58(2A)) and emergency temporary accommodation. People living in night shelters, hostels and other temporary accommodation can, therefore, be considered homeless. Those whose accommodation is clearly unsuitable can also apply as homeless, for instance, disabled or elderly people living in accommodation where they cannot get upstairs to a bedroom or bathroom. A person can also be homeless if he/she has no accommodation in which he/she can live with a carer with whom he/she normally lives (Widdowfield and Coles 1994).

2.2.2 Section 14 of the Housing and Planning Act 1986 (HPA 1986), which amends the Housing Act 1985 (HA 1985), deals with the suitability of accommodation offered by a housing authority in discharging its duties towards a homeless person. The HPA 1986 specifies that in deciding what is suitable, the authority must have regard to other provisions in the HA 1985 relating to slum clearance (Part IX), to overcrowding (Part IV), and to houses in multiple occupation (Part XI). The HPA 1986 also provides that a person is not to be treated as having accommodation unless it is such as would be reasonable for him/her to continue to occupy. In other words, it may now be easier for a person to be deemed homeless when he/she has inadequate accommodation. In determining what is reasonable, however, the general situation relating to housing in the district may be taken into account, and the legal definition of 'reasonable' may be somewhat narrower than that which is acceptable to the applicant. In addition, only homeless people who are in a priority need group and are not intentionally homeless will have a right to be provided with permanent accommodation under the HA 1985, s.59.

Elderly people considered to be 'vulnerable' have priority need. Vulnerability is not defined in the Act, but the Code of Guidance (DoE 1992b) which accompanies it, suggests that authorities should look not just at whether people are old, but at the extent to which their age has made it hard for them to fend for themselves. All applications from people aged sixty or over should be considered carefully, especially where the applicant is leaving tied accommodation. A flexible and pragmatic approach should always be adopted in assessing the needs of the elderly (para. 6.9). In *R v. Lambeth London Borough Council, ex parte Carroll (1987)*, the Court was required to consider the meaning of the term 'vulnerable' for the purpose of the Act and to consider the extent of the local authority's duty to enquire into the circumstances of an applicant. The facts reveal that only the evidence from the medical officer had been considered and it was held that the local authority had therefore failed in its duty to consider the case on its merits. The judge remarked that there were occasions when a medical report would constitute sufficient evidence. In some circumstances, however, additional evidence might be required.

Even where people over sixty are in good health, it is good practice to take into account other factors which make the elderly less able to fend for themselves, for example reduced income, inability to secure mortgages as well as the possibility of deterioration of health if they are allowed to remain homeless. Whilst some local authorities have a policy of considering all people over the age of sixty to be vulnerable, a combination of factors such as advancing age and ill health may combine to make a person vulnerable, even if the person is still under sixty (Moroney and Goodwin 1992).

The duty to provide accommodation extends also to those who might reasonably be expected to live with the person to whom the duty is owed. In *R v. Lambeth London Borough, ex parte Ly (1987)*, the applicant was a 74-year-old refugee who had fled from Vietnam with her son and daughter-in-law. The housing authority offered her and her four elder grandchildren a four-bedroomed flat, 2 miles away from the hotel where the rest of the family was accommodated. It was unsuccessfully argued that the authority was under a duty to offer accommodation which was large enough to house the whole family. It was held to be a question of fact for the authority to determine who might reasonably be expected to live with the applicant. It was relevant, in coming to a decision, for the authority to consider the nature and extent of the family unit, as well as the practicability of providing accommodation for such a large group.

2.2.3 A recent House of Lords decision may have serious consequences for applications by elderly people for housing under Part III of the HA 1985. It was held that an application for priority need housing, under s.62 of the HA 1985, cannot be made on behalf of a potential applicant who is unable through lack of capacity, either to make, or consent to, the making of the application (*R v. Oldham Metropolitan Borough Council, ex parte Garlick and other appeals (1993)*). While this case concerned dependent children, and a person with learning disability, it raises concerns over the further treatment of elderly people suffering from mental frailty or illness, such as Alzheimer's disease, who may be regarded as lacking the necessary capacity.

2.2.4 The duty to rehouse is qualified in several important ways. As indicated above, it is necessary to show homelessness and a priority need. In addition, it is necessary to show that the applicant is not intentionally homeless; in other words, the homeless person's own acts or omissions did not cause him/her to become homeless. The applicant must also establish a local connection with the authority, otherwise the receiving authority can refer the applicant to an authority where he/she may have a local connection.

If a person who is unintentionally homeless and in priority need has no local connection with the area of any housing authority in Great Britain then the duty to secure accommodation for him/her rests with the authority to which he/she applies (Code of Practice, para. 8.5). Authorities cannot refuse to rehouse a family because they are immigrants. Everyone admitted to Britain is entitled to equal treatment under the law. Persons with limited leave to remain here, however, may prejudice their immigration status by making an application under the Act (para. 4.12).

A temporary duty to house is placed on the authority whilst it investigates the reasons for the homelessness, or if priority need has been established but intentional homelessness is also found. Where temporary accommodation is provided the housing authority may levy a charge for providing it (HA 1985, s.69(2)). A council need only provide the accommodation for long enough to give the person a reasonable opportunity to make other arrangements. This will depend on the time-scale involved in the authority completing its investigations.

The Act is silent as to the type of accommodation to be provided (s.69(1)). Either public or private housing can be used, including housing association stock. The Code of Guidance to the Act suggests, *inter alia*, that if an elderly person qualifies for accommodation under the 1985 Act and also needs care and attention, the offer of Part III accommodation under the National Assistance Act 1948 (NAA 1948) (see Chapter 4 at para. 4.5.1) or other appropriate care would be sufficient to satisfy the duty under the 1985 Act. This is not to imply that a housing authority can avoid its duties to homeless people by simply redirecting applicants to social service authorities.

Given these rules, the right to accommodation is limited and often depends more upon the policy of the local housing authority than on legal entitlement (Luba 1988). Ways of challenging local authority decisions are not readily available, unless by way of judicial review.

An applicant cannot become intentionally homeless if he/she leaves accommodation which it would not be reasonable for him/her to continue to occupy. In *R v. Tower Hamlets LBC, ex parte Hoque (1993)*, the applicant, who was disabled, was a joint owner of his parents' two-bedroomed flat. The flat was occupied by the applicant, his parents, his wife and his wife's children. The council decided that, although there was overcrowding, because the applicant was co-owner, and because the overcrowding was caused by his own action in increasing the size of his family, it was reasonable for him to continue to occupy the flat. It was held that the decision-making process had been tainted by the value judgements of the council's officer and ran counter to the Code of Guidance. The decision was quashed (Luba and Madge 1993a).

Once accommodation has been acquired certain rights and responsibilities come into existence. The different types of accommodation and the obligations and entitlements which attach to each are examined below.

2.3.1 COUNCIL RENTED ACCOMMODATION

Council housing offers greater security of tenure and lower rents than private rented housing and is therefore often the preferred choice of those in the rented sector. Twenty per cent of the nation's housing stock is owned by local authorities, but the number of properties in this sector is declining rapidly.

British local authorities built less than 9,000 new dwellings in 1990, compared to over 16,000 in 1988 and 65,000 in 1979. The biggest slump in local authority housebuilding was in Yorkshire and Humberside, where the number of new dwellings built in 1990 was less than a third of the 1988 figure. There was also a drop of 60 per cent or more in London, the North West of England and in Wales. In Scotland, the number of new dwellings built by local authorities in 1990 was only 16 per cent lower than in 1988. Over the same period, the number of new dwellings built by housing associations has grown by about 20 per cent. But despite this increased level of housing association provision, the public sector as a whole produced fewer newly built dwellings in 1990 than in 1988 (*Roof*: November 1991).

Since 1992, the London boroughs and the metropolitan districts have been required to prepare unitary development plans, and authorities in non-metropolitan areas are required to prepare local plans. The Secretary of State's advice is that unitary development plans should address a range of topics, including new housing and figures for housing provision in each district. Planning policy guidance stresses that authorities should consider the likely impact of planning policies and proposals on different groups in the population, including elderly and disabled people. It also stresses that social considerations are relevant in looking at the need for affordable housing. As a result, local planning authorities will be able, in future, to require an element of affordable housing in new developments in the private sector (Shiner 1993).

2.3.2   APPLYING FOR COUNCIL HOUSING

Local authorities do not have a general duty to provide council housing. At a time when housing stock is declining, applicants for council housing will usually face a long wait for an offer. Obtaining a tenancy depends on personal circumstances, the local housing situation and the allocation policies of the local authority. Local authorities have a duty to publish details of their allocation policies and must not act in clear contravention of these (HA 1985, s.106). Those applying will usually join a waiting list and may be required to re-apply each year. Many authorities use a points system 'which assesses housing need by awarding points for factors such as overcrowding, poor health and lack of amenities' (Goodwin 1992).

2.3.3   SECURITY OF TENURE

'Secure tenancies' were first introduced into the public sector by the Housing Act 1980 (HA 1980) to give tenants security of tenure similar to that enjoyed by tenants in the private sector under the Rent Act 1977 (RA 1977) (see para. 2.5.2 below). The provisions of the HA 1980 have subsequently been consolidated into the HA 1985 and further amended by the HPA 1986.

2.3.4   A secure tenancy arises whenever a landlord is a prescribed public body, that is, either a local authority, an urban development corporation, the Development Board for Rural Wales, the housing corporation, a housing trust which is a charity or an unregistered housing co-operative (HA 1985, s.80). Most tenants of registered housing associations prior to 15 January 1993 when the Housing Act 1988 (HA 1988) came into effect had secure tenancies. Tenancies granted after that date are assured tenancies (see para. 2.5.5 below). As a result, most, if not all, elderly people living in council property are secure tenants. The HA 1985 excluded some tenancies from complete security of tenure, but few of the exceptions are relevant here (HA 1985 s.79(2) Sched.I). Those relevant to some elderly people include tenancies held in connection with employment, accommodation for homeless persons (HA 1985 Sched.I, para.4) and tenancies of almshouses. Full security may be lost where a secure tenant assigns the tenancy or sublets the whole property (see below at paras. 2.5.12). Legal proceedings must be brought before possession can be gained, however, and before legal proceedings can be commenced an effective notice of intention to seek possession must be served on the tenants.

2.3.5 GROUNDS FOR POSSESSION

Where a tenancy is secure, the onus is upon the landlord to show that granting termination of the tenancy would be justified on one or more of the seventeen statutory grounds for possession (1–16 + 10A) set out in the HA 1985 (as amended) (HA 1985, Sched.II, Parts I–III). Grounds 1–7 relate to a tenant's conduct and include non-payment of rent, breach of the tenancy agreement, committing a nuisance, allowing deterioration to the premises or fittings, or making false statements. Ground 8 applies to any arrangement whereby a dwelling has been made temporarily available to a secure tenant while repair work is carried out on the original dwelling. Where proceedings for possession are based on grounds 1–8 the court must also be satisfied that it will be reasonable for the order to be granted. Thus, where possession against a secure tenant is sought on the basis of rent arrears, it might be deemed unreasonable to grant the order if rent had been withheld (and retained) because of refusal by the landlord to carry out proper repairs. Similarly, where possession is sought on the basis of ground 8, it might be successfully resisted if completion of repair work at the original dwelling had taken a considerable time and the tenant was fully settled at the temporary dwelling (Luba *et al.* 1992).

Grounds 9–11 provide for possession to be granted because the dwelling is overcrowded, needed for reconstruction or development (added by s.9 of the HPA 1986), or, where the landlord is a charity, the tenant's continued occupation would conflict with the objects of the charity. In such cases, possession will be granted only if the court is satisfied that suitable alternative accommodation will be made available. Where the landlord is not a housing authority, that obligation will be satisfied if the local housing authority produces a certificate confirming that suitable accommodation will be made available by the authority. Where no certificate is issued, or if the landlord is a housing authority, the suitability criteria set out in the Act come into play (HA 1985, Sched.2, Part IV, paras. 1 and 2). The list of factors necessary to meet the suitability requirement is not exhaustive (*Enfield LBC v. French (1984)*). Among them is the distance between the alternative home and a member of the tenant's family where proximity is essential for the well-being of the family member or of the tenant. The term 'family' is defined broadly (s.113) (Luba *et al.* 1992).

A court cannot grant an order on grounds 12–16 unless it believes that it is reasonable to make an order, and it is satisfied that suitable alternative accommodation is available. Ground 12 relates to tied accommodation, that is, to a tenancy in property occupied only on the basis of particular employment, whereas grounds 13–15 relate to accommodation for persons with special needs. Ground 13 concerns the possession of properties designed specifically for the needs of disabled people and containing features 'substantially different' from those of the ordinary dwellings. To be '*substantially* different' the dwelling must have been designed for the special needs of the physically disabled. In *Freeman v. Wandsbeck (1983)*, it was held that adding a ground floor toilet was not, in itself, sufficient to fulfil this requirement. Possession will be granted on the basis of ground 13 only if it can be shown that no disabled person continues to live in the dwelling, and that it is required for another disabled person. Similar conditions must exist for possession to be granted under grounds 14 and 15. Ground 14 applies to dwellings provided by housing associations or housing trusts for persons whose circumstances make it especially difficult to satisfy their housing needs. Ground 15 applies where:

The dwelling house is one of a group of dwelling houses which it is the practice of the landlord to let for occupation by the persons with special needs and:

(a) a social service or special facility is provided in close proximity to the group of dwelling houses in order to assist persons with those special needs,

(b) there is no longer a person with those special needs residing in the dwelling house, and

(c) the landlord requires the dwelling house for occupation (whether alone or with members of his/her family) by a person who has those special needs.

Each of these criteria needs to be satisfied before possession can be granted. It is assumed that if a warden service provided for a sheltered housing complex is discontinued, an application for possession under ground 15 might not be successful.

Ground 16 provides for possession to be granted where the tenant is occupying accommodation which is more extensive than he/she reasonably requires. This right applies only where the tenant has 'succeeded' to the tenancy (see para. 2.5.9 below), but not where the 'successor' to the tenancy is the former tenant's spouse. It does not, therefore, apply to a widow/er of the deceased tenant who is under-occupying (Luba *et al.* 1992). Further, the statute specifically requires the court to take the tenant's age into account in determining whether an order is reasonable under ground 16. Two other factors must also be taken into account in deciding on the reasonableness of possession procedures. These include the period for which the tenant has occupied the dwelling, and any financial or other support given to the previous tenant by the current tenant of the premises.

As indicated above, the burden of proof throughout is on the landlord who must show that, on the balance of probabilities, at least one of the grounds has been made out. In contrast to the situation in the private sector, no mandatory ground for possession exists here. Except in relation to grounds 9–11, a court has power to stay or suspend execution as long as it thinks fit (HA 1985, s.85(2)).

2.3.6 SUCCEEDING TO A SECURE TENANCY

Under the provisions of the HA 1985, the spouse of a deceased tenant, or another member of his/her family, (including a cohabitee) is entitled to succeed to a tenancy where certain conditions are met. To be entitled, a person must have been occupying the dwelling as his/her principal, or only, home at the time of the tenant's death. Where the would-be successor is not a spouse, he/she must have lived with the former tenant for a period of twelve months preceding his/her death (HA 1985, s.87). This may sometimes apply to elderly widow/ers who share council premises with a brother or sister. In *Waltham Forest London Borough Council v. Thomas (1992)*, it was held that whilst a successor must have resided with the deceased tenant during the period of twelve months ending with the tenant's death, the residence did not have to be for the whole twelve months in the house to which the succession was claimed.

The statutory provisions allow for one succession only. Where the tenant's spouse has succeeded to the tenancy, a child living in the dwelling will have no further right of succession (HA 1985, s.87, s.89(2)(a)).

2.3.7 ASSIGNMENT

Since the aim of public housing provision is to meet social need, the general rule is that the tenant cannot assign, that is, transfer the tenancy to another person (HA 1985, s.91).

Except in three prescribed cases, the secure tenancy is not capable of assignment, namely: assignment by way of mutual exchange, assignment pursuant to a property transfer order made under the Matrimonial Causes Act 1973 (MCA 1973) s.24, and assignment to a person who would have been qualified to succeed to the tenancy if the tenant had died immediately before the assignment. Where assignment takes place in any of these circumstances, the assignee is entitled to full security even where the tenancy agreement contains a prohibition on assignments; but if the landlord's authority is not obtained, the assignee may be vulnerable to an action for possession for breach of a term of the tenancy. In *Peabody Donation Fund (Governors) v. Higgins (1983)*, the tenancy agreement contained an absolute prohibition on assignments. The tenant wished to retire to Ireland and to transfer the tenancy to a daughter who lived with him. He executed an assignment to her by deed. The Court of Appeal held that the secure tenancy had been validly assigned to the daughter, but it was suggested that she might be vulnerable to an action for possession for breach of a term of the tenancy. Even so, a landlord could only succeed if it could be shown that she had acted reasonably in seeking possession. Assignments made by way of exchange require the landlord's written consent (HA 1985, Sched. 3, s.92). Where an assignment benefits a person who would be entitled to succeed to the tenancy on the death of the secure tenant, the assignee need not be the preferred successor. It is sufficient that the assignment is made to a person *qualified to succeed*. This provision could be used to avoid the 'spouse preference rule', and so ensure that a child of the family, for example, succeeded to the secure tenancy. Such a step might be contemplated by an ageing parent anxious to provide security for a disabled adult son or daughter living in the household. This provision might be more commonly used, however, by a tenant wishing to prevent a dispute between one of two potential successors, or in order to transfer the tenancy prior to retirement elsewhere.

2.3.8   SUB-LETTING AND LODGERS

Secure tenants may take in lodgers without a landlord's consent, but sub-letting the property requires agreement in writing (HA 1985, s.93(1)(b)). Failure to obtain consent will not affect the existence of the sub-tenancy, but could make the main tenant liable to possession proceedings under ground 1. The HA 1985 states that the landlord's consent to a sub-letting must not be withheld unreasonably (HA 1985, s.94).

In law, a lodger is deemed to be a licensee. The distinction between a lodger and sub-tenant is, therefore, crucial in determining an individual's right to possession. If a tenant sub-lets the whole of the property, his/her security will be affected (HA 1985, s.93(2)). It will not, however, bring the tenancy to an end automatically. To recover possession, the land-lord will need to bring the tenancy to an end by giving notice to quit (Luba 1993). Where the occupier is fully integrated into the tenant's household, the likelihood is that he/she is a lodger. The usual test is whether or not the occupier has control over the whole of the property, although the intention of the parties is also important.

It is unlikely, therefore, that an elderly person who has been 'boarded-out' under a local authority scheme (see Chapter 3 at para. 3.4.1) who moves to live with a person who is a tenant, will thereby become a sub-tenant. Where an elderly person is anxious to ensure optimum autonomy, however, a sub-let should be considered.

2.3.9 THE TERMS OF THE TENANCY

Landlords must provide their tenants with information which explains the terms of the tenancy and the provisions of Part IV and V of the Housing Act 1985 in clear and simple language (HA 1985, s.104). The terms will usually continue unaltered until the tenancy is brought to an end in one of the ways described. They can be altered, however, by agreement or by 'Notice of Variation' served on the tenant by the landlord who must also invite the tenant's comments (HA 1985, s.102 and s.103). This provision ensures that a degree of prior consultation takes place before Notice of Variation can be served. The prior consultation is not, however, required if the variation applies simply to the rent or to payment made in respect of services or facilities provided by the landlord, or to payment in respect of rates (HA 1985, s.103(3)). In such cases, the terms can be varied by giving one month's notice to the tenant. The only sanction then available to a tenant is to give Notice to Quit (Mitchell 1987). Where prior consultation is required, however, failure to take a tenant's comments into account would invalidate any variation in the terms of the tenancy. Tenants also have a statutory right to be consulted on matters of housing management, either individually or collectively, through a tenants' association (HA 1985, s.105).

2.3.10 A tenancy remains secure until possession is granted by a court, or until it is surrendered by the tenant or notice to quit is given by the tenant (HA 1985, s.82).

2.3.11 The rules relating to the repair and improvement of property which apply in both the public and private sectors are discussed below at para. 2.6.1. Some, however, apply specifically to secure tenancies and are therefore discussed here. A secure tenant may only carry out improvements with the landlord's written consent (HA 1985, s.97(1)) which cannot be unreasonably withheld. The term 'improvement' is defined widely in this context so as to include any alteration or addition such as putting up a television aerial or decorating the exterior (HA 1985, s.97(2)). A landlord may not increase the rent because of improvements to the property made by the tenant (HA 1985, s.101(10)). At the end of the tenancy, the tenant may be reimbursed for any authorised improvements provided the effect is to increase the property's notional market price, or to raise the level of rent at which it can then be let (HA 1985, s.100). Reimbursement is limited, however, to the cost of improvement offset by any grants received by the tenant.

As long as they comply with certain procedural requirements, secure tenants have been entitled, since January 1986, to recover from their landlords the cost of 'qualifying repairs' (Secure Tenancies (Right to Repair Scheme) Regulations 1985). This procedure is hardly used in practice, its scope being limited to repair work in the range of £20 to £200. It also requires the service of a multiplicity of forms and counter notices, involves the tenant in discharging the responsibilities of the landlord, and provides no compensation for disrepair, or the fact that the tenant had to use these remedies. It is in almost all respects a less satisfactory remedy for tenants than the use of legal proceedings (Luba 1991).

The system has been recast by the Leasehold Reform, Housing and Urban Development Act 1993 (LRHUDA 1993). The Commencement and Transitional Provision No. 3 Order 1993 brought s.121 (right to have repairs carried out) into force on 1 December 1993 and s.122 (right to compensation for improvements) on 1 February 1994. The procedure to be followed is set out in the Secure Tenants of Local Housing Authorities (Compensation for Improvements) Regulations 1994 (draft) and the Secure Tenants of Local Housing Authorities (Right to Repair) Regulations 1994 (draft), which came into force on 1 April 1994.

The compensation system will apply to improvements begun after 1 April 1994 and any compensation will be payable at the end of the tenancy. Compensation will be limited to 'eligible improvements'. Tenants exercising their Right to Buy, or purchasing under the new Rents to Mortgage Scheme (see para. 2.4.4 below) will have no right to compensation.

The improved Right to Repair scheme is a Citizen's Charter initiative. It aims to ensure that secure local housing authority tenants have a simple and reliable way of getting urgent repairs carried out. The scheme covers repairs costing up to £250 which, if not carried out within a specified period, are likely to jeopardise the health, safety and security of the tenant. If a repair is not completed within a prescribed time, the tenant will be entitled to require the council to appoint a second contractor. If the repair is not completed by the end of the second prescribed period, the tenant will be entitled to compensation of £10, plus £2 a day for every day the repair remains uncompleted, up to a maximum of £50.

2.4.1 THE RIGHT TO BUY

Council tenants and most secure tenants of non-charitable housing associations are entitled to purchase their homes from the council under the 'Right to Buy' scheme, provided they have been tenants for at least two years (HA 1985, s.119).

The right to buy has had the single most devastating effect on local authority housing stock. Since the enactment of the HA 1980, nearly 1 million properties have been sold in England alone. In Scotland, over 140,000 have been sold off in the last ten years.

This sell-off has come at a time when the capacity for local authorities to build or acquire new dwellings to compensate for the loss has been severely curtailed by capital spending restrictions.

The right to buy has taken a greater proportion of Welsh council housing stock than in any other locality. Right to buy sales in Wales accounted for over a quarter of the 1980 stock. As the increasing number of right to buy sales are not being met by other forms of social housing, new build, affordable housing in Wales looks like becoming scarcer. In England, right to buy sales account for nearly a fifth of the 1980 stock. There are considerable variations within this figure. The North West has the lowest figure of 13 per cent and the South West the highest with 25 per cent. Right to buy hasn't been as significant in Scotland as it has in England and Wales. Scottish sales account for only 13 per cent of the 1980 stock (*Roof*: November 1991).

The right to buy option has already been exercised by many elderly people. However, according to the 1991 *General Household Survey*, a larger proportion of owner occupiers and local authority tenants had heads of household aged seventy-five or over than did local authority accommodation bought under the right to buy provisions.

It is suggested that those aged seventy-five or over were less likely to have bought because they were retired, or were about to retire, when the legislation came into force.

A right to buy was introduced for tenants in the public sector by the HA 1980. The provisions are now to be found in Part V of the HA 1985, as amended by the HPA 1986 and LRHUDA 1993. The right is preserved upon the disposal of the dwelling by a public land-lord authority to a private sector landlord (s.171A, inserted by s.8 of the HPA 1986)). The Housing (Extension of Right to Buy) Order 1987 also confers a right to buy the freehold of a house upon secure tenants who have an intermediate public sector landlord and a public sector freeholder.

2.4.2 Where tenancies are expressly excluded from the provisions of the HA 1985, Part V, the statutory right to buy will not arise. Those expressly excluded are tenancies granted by charitable housing trusts, charitable housing associations, housing co-operatives (that is, housing associations registered or deemed to be registered under the Industrial and Providence Society Act 1965 (IPSA 1965) and housing associations which never received public housing funds. Certain types of dwellings, listed in Sched. 5 of the HA 1985, are automatically excluded. They include specially designed dwellings for the physically disabled (paras. 6–8), group dwellings for persons who are mentally disordered (para. 9), group sheltered housing for persons of pension-able age where social services or special facilities are provided (para. 10). Single dwellings can also be excluded under paras. 6–8 of the Schedule. Paragraph 8 applies when one or more of the three specific alterations have been carried out by the landlord. These are the provision of not less than 7.5 square metres of additional floor space, the provision of an additional bathroom or shower room and the installation of a vertical lift.

Other dwelling houses which are particularly suitable for occupation by elderly persons age sixty or more may also be excluded from the provisions governing the right to buy. However, the circumstances in which these houses are excluded have been restricted since 1 January 1990 as it was felt that the rules unfairly prejudiced elderly people. Dwellings first let on or after 1 January 1990 cannot now be excluded from the right to buy provisions as being particularly suitable for elderly people. In addition, property which is particularly suitable for elderly people and was let for occupation by a physically disabled person below pensionable age cannot be excluded from the right to buy. Where property was let before 1 January 1990 and is considered particularly suitable for elderly people, the tenant must apply to the Secretary of State to determine whether the dwelling may be sold. Before he/she makes a determination, the Secretary of State will have to be satisfied that the dwelling is particularly suitable for persons of pensionable age having regard for its location, size, design, heating system and other features, and that it was let to the tenant or a predecessor for occupation by a person aged sixty or more. If no such application is made by the tenant, the question shall be deemed to have been determined in favour of the landlord (LRHUDA 1993, s.106).

2.4.3 Where there is a right to buy, two kinds of entitlement arise. First, a secure tenant may purchase the freehold from the landlord authority at a notional market value (HA 1985, s.127). In effect, the purchase price is calculated on the basis of what the dwelling would fetch if sold by a willing vendor. The market value is set by the landlord authority, but an appeal against it can be made to the District Valuer (HA 1985, s.128).

Second, the secure tenant is entitled to a discount which will vary according to the length of time he/she has occupied the dwelling as a public sector tenant. The minimum discount, where the dwelling is a house, is 32 per cent, plus 1 per cent for every complete year by which the qualifying period exceeds two years. The maximum discount entitlement for a house is 60 per cent, but is more generous for a flat, at 70 per cent. The way in which the discount is calculated also differs. In the case of a flat, the minimum discount is 42 per cent plus a 2 per cent addition for each complete year by which the period of the qualifying tenancy exceeds two years (HA 1985, s.129, Sched. 4 as amended by the HPA 1986, s.2). On divorce from a secure tenant, or upon his/her death, the ex-spouse or widow/er may be able to take the time spent occupying the property with a secure tenant into account (HA 1985, Sched. 4).

2.4.4 The right to a mortgage, to defer completion and to a shared ownership lease have been abolished by the LRHUDA 1993. The Act, however, has introduced the right to acquire homes on rent-to-mortgage terms (a new s.96). The government aims to encourage 1.5 million council housing association tenants to buy their homes through this scheme. Tenants who have been receiving housing benefit (HB) for the last twelve months will not be eligible (LRHUDA 1993, s.143A). The scheme gives tenants the right to acquire their home by making an initial payment which can be financed by a mortgage with repayments equivalent to their current rent. The initial payment will attract discount at the tenant's 'Right to Buy' discount rate. The proportion of the 'Right to Buy' purchase price which is not met by the initial payment is known as the 'landlord's share'. Redemption of the landlord's share is secured by a mortgage on the property. The landlord's share must normally be redeemed in full by making a final payment on disposal of the property or one year after the death of the purchaser or the survivor of joint purchasers. Purchasers can also make voluntary payments at any time to redeem the landlord's share in full, or in part. There will normally be a discount of 20 per cent on these further payments (Manning and Susan 1993).

Private financial arrangements can be made to raise the necessary capital with a bank or building society. Many building societies are prepared to consider giving elderly people interest-only mortgages with the capital being repaid when the property is eventually sold. Some societies apparently require applicants for interest-only schemes to be at least sixty years of age. Others are more flexible, especially where the applicant is already retired (Bookbinder 1987).

2.4.5 A purchaser may nominate up to a maximum of three family members to share the right to buy. To qualify automatically, an individual must either have been living with the secure tenant as his/her spouse, or must have been living in the dwelling for at least twelve months before the right to buy is exercised. In all other circumstances, the right to nominate additional joint purchasers can be exercised only with the landlord's consent. If the power to nominate 'deemed joint tenants' is exercised, however, but the parties are subsequently in dispute, the additional purchasers may be unable to demand the property be sold (HA 1985, s.123).

2.4.6 The social and financial implications of buying a home should be carefully considered. Housing benefit (HB) will no longer be available, although those on income support (IS) may qualify for assistance with mortgage interest payments and certain service charges. The charges made for services provided by an outside authority, and not the landlord, which are not connected 'with the provision of adequate accommodation' do not come within the meaning of service charges. Therefore, charges for water and sewage services are not covered. Housing costs will not be met in full if there are non-dependent grown-up children living in the house and if the housing costs are deemed to be excessive (Income Support (General)

Regulations 1987 Sched. 2, para. 10(3)) (see Chapter 1 at para. 1.31.1). Those not entitled to IS should establish whether the service charges will be payable after purchase. In *Sutton (Hastoe) Housing Association v. Williams (1988)*, it was decided that landlords have a right to levy service charges (which include elements for both improvement and repair) where the purchaser has been expressly notified that such expenditure would be necessary.

2.4.7 Any discount received by the purchaser under the right to buy provisions is not repayable on his/her death. A subsequent disposal by his/her dependants could, however, bring the repayment provisions into operation, since the discount is normally repayable in whole or in part if the property is sold within three years of the purchase (HA 1985, s.155(2), as amended by HPA 1986, s.2(3)).

2.4.8 Tying up savings in property can lead to financial hardship. Several schemes have been devised to assist owner occupiers with cashflow problems which are most likely to arise where maintenance costs are high (see para. 2.8.3 below). It should be noted that some 84 per cent of local authority housing is in need of renovation at an average cost of £4,900 per dwelling (CSO 1988).

Those contemplating exercising the right to buy should be advised that becoming a home owner is likely to lessen their chance of being accepted on a waiting list for public sector rented accommodation in the future (Bookbinder 1987). However, elderly people who have exercised their right to buy and get into difficulties will not be excluded from making applications under Part III of the HA 1985 (see para. 2.2.1 above). Advice should also be taken as to the implications of accepting financial help from a relative (Bookbinder 1991).

2.5.1 PRIVATELY RENTED ACCOMMODATION

Around 6 per cent of the population now live in privately rented accommodation. However, older people, particularly those aged seventy or over, elderly women and those who live alone, are more likely to rent accommodation privately (Smythe and Browne 1992). Older people living alone are also more likely to live in purpose-built flats or maisonettes.

Elderly people are more likely to live in older housing which is likely to be in poorer condition, lacking in amenities and with sub-standard heating. Privately rented accommodation is particularly subject to these deficiencies (DoE 1988).

2.5.2 SECURITY OF TENURE

The tenant of a house let as a separate dwelling who neither shares
accommodation with the landlord nor pays for board or attendance is
normally protected under the Rent Act 1977 (RA 1977) as a *protected*
tenant or, under the Housing Act 1988 (HA 1988), as an *assured*
tenant. There are some exceptions, however, including tenancies at low
rents, holiday lettings and assured shorthold tenancies, that is, certain
tenancies for fixed periods of six months or more. Licences are
excluded from full Rent Act or Housing Act protection, but the use of
this statutory loophole has been largely closed by the courts and few
agreements these days are treated as licences (*Street v. Mountford
(1985)*).

The HA 1988 introduced fundamental changes to private security
of tenure. In effect, there are now two separate regimes governing
security of tenure, and accordingly possession proceedings, depending upon the date when a particular tenancy was created. Tenancies
created before January 1989 will have full Rent Act security of tenure
and the benefit of rent regulation. Some tenancies created on or after
15 January 1989 are less secure and are subject to minimum rent
control.

Almost all new residential tenancies created on or after 15 January
1989 are *assured* tenancies or *assured shorthold* tenancies governed
by the provisions of the HA 1988. *Assured shorthold* tenancies
provide no long-term security of tenure and are subject to minimal
rent control. This lack of security means that 'the adjective "assured"
is something of a misnomer' (Luba *et al.* 1992). The main exceptions
are new tenancies granted by the same landlords to existing Rent Act
protected tenants (HA 1988, s.34). However, many elderly tenants
will have pre-January 1989 tenancies and will still be covered by the
Rent Act.

2.5.3 RENT ACT TENANCIES

The statutory grounds upon which a Rent Act tenancy can be
re-possessed are listed in Sched. 15 to the RA 1977 and Sched. 2 to
the HA 1988. In some cases, the court has *discretion* whether or not
to grant possession, whereas in other circumstances, the grant is
mandatory.

In relation to protected tenants, the *discretionary* grounds 1–10 set
out in the RA 1977 closely resemble grounds 1–8 under the HA 1985
although differences also exist. The inclusion of alternative suitable

accommodation, for example, effectively amounts to an additional discretionary ground (Luba *et al.* 1992). Another difference is that Case 9 has no parallel in provisions under the HA 1985. This allows a landlord to recover possession under the RA 1977 where the dwelling is reasonably required for the occupation by him/herself or certain members of his/her family. He/she must show that the need is genuine. It would not be sufficient for instance, for it to be needed simply as temporary accommodation whilst repairs are being carried out at the home of a landlord or a relative. It is not possible either to rely upon Case 9 if a landlord purchased the dwelling after a protected tenant came into possession of it. This restriction does not apply where the landlord inherited the dwelling or acquired it through a family settlement. A protected tenant has a complete defence to possession proceedings brought under this Case if it can be shown that he/she would suffer greater hardship if a possession order was granted than would be caused to the landlord if it were refused. A point taken into account when assessing the extent of hardship is the health of the parties and their physical proximity to relatives (*Thomas v. Fryer (1970)*).

2.5.4 The grounds for *mandatory* possession under the RA 1977 may be more relevant to elderly people as landlords than as tenants. Case 11 as amended by the Rent (Amendment) Act 1985 (R(A)A 1985) provides for possession by owner occupiers who have let their property during a period of absence. It also provides, *inter alia*, for possession where the owner has died and a member of the family residing with him/her at the time of death requires the house as a residence. Case 12 may have an even greater relevance since it allows possession to be granted to an owner who requires the premises as a retirement home. It is not necessary for the landlord to have resided in the dwelling.

A landlord must give a tenant written notice that possession is recoverable on one of the mandatory grounds. Schedule 15, however, provides that this requirement can be dispensed with if the court thinks it justifiable to grant a possession order.

2.5.5 ASSURED TENANCIES

In relation to *assured* tenancies, the discretionary grounds 9–16 set out in the HA 1988 are similar to those under the Rent Acts. In addition to ground 10 governing rent arrears, there is a further discretionary ground based on persistent delay in paying rent. Ground 11 provides that, even if no arrears exist on the date when possession proceedings are issued, persistent delay in paying rent that is due, is a ground for possession. Possibly the most significant difference is the inclusion for the first time, at ground 8, of a mandatory ground for possession on the basis of at least three months' rent arrears. Mandatory ground 6 provides for possession if the landlord wishes to demolish or reconstruct the property and cannot do so with the tenant there. As under the Rent Acts, owner occupiers have a mandatory ground for possession under the HA 1988 and the provision is much wider in ambit than its Rent Act equivalent (Luba *et al.* 1992).

2.5.6 SHORTHOLD TENANCIES

A further *mandatory* ground exists in relation to *assured shorthold* tenancies which were created by the HA 1988 to give landlords power to grant new types of tenancies for a minimum period of six months. Again, prior notice must be served in the prescribed form which states that the tenancy is to be an *assured shorthold* tenancy. The tenancy cannot be determined within the fixed period by the landlord other than on the grounds of forfeiture. There are two kinds of notice seeking possession. The first kind, served either during the fixed term, or on the last day, must give the tenant a minimum of two months' notice. The second kind, served after the end of the fixed term, must give the tenant a minimum of two months' notice and must state that the property is required under the provisions of s.21 of the HA 1988.

2.5.7 POSSESSION PROCEDURES

Even where valid grounds for possession exist, a Rent Act tenancy must normally be terminated only by service of a notice to quit in the prescribed form. When a protected tenancy comes to an end, it becomes a statutory tenancy providing similar protection to a Rent Act tenancy as long as the tenant does not give up possession. In the case of tenancies under the HA 1988, a notice seeking possession is required. Section 5 of the Protection from Eviction Act 1977 (PfEA 1977) (as amended by the HA 1988) requires that at least four weeks' notice be given for a Rent Act protected tenancy. For tenancies under the HA 1988, the notice required varies between two weeks and two months depending on the grounds for possession. Where the Rent Act tenancy has become a statutory tenancy, however, a landlord is not obliged to provide Notice to Quit before possession proceedings are brought. A statutory tenant will, nevertheless, remain liable for rent until the statutory tenancy comes to an end. It can be terminated either by the granting of a possession order or through a voluntary agreement between the landlord and tenant, or by the tenant serving notice to quit (RA 1977, s.2 and s.3).

2.5.8 If the court is satisfied that one of the *mandatory* grounds for possession applies, it has power to adjourn, stay or suspend an order for possession for fourteen days only, unless exceptional hardship would be caused, in which case possession may be deferred for up to six weeks (HA 1980, s.89(1)). If a *discretionary* ground is proved, the court has discretion to adjourn the proceedings, stay or suspend the execution of any order or postpone the date of possession for such period or periods as the court thinks fit, although when doing so, the court must impose conditions relating to the payment of rent or rent arrears (HA 1988, s.9).

A tenant wishing to oppose a claim must file a defence and the judge will consider if a full hearing is necessary (County Court (Amendment 3) Rules 1993).

2.5.9 SUCCEEDING TO A TENANCY

When a Rent Act *protected* tenant dies, a surviving spouse who is living with the tenant at the time of his/her death or, if there is no such spouse, a member of the tenant's family who had been living with the tenant for two years immediately before his/her death has a right to have the tenancy transmitted to him/her. The spouse provisions have been extended by the HA 1988 to include a person who has been living with the original tenant as his/her wife/husband.

The surviving spouse and the other members of the tenant's family must show that they resided with the tenant at the time of death (RA 1977, Sched. 2, paras. 2 and 7). From the decision in *Foreman v. Beagley (1969)* it would seem, however, that the courts may be prepared to extend the definition of 'residing with' to include situations where family members were not in fact residing with one another at the time of death, for example where the tenant was in hospital when he/she died. In that case, a widow had succeeded to the tenancy of a flat upon the death of her husband, from 1965 until her own death in 1968 when she was in hospital. In 1967, her son moved into the flat and lived there until his mother's death. Evidence was presented to show that he would have stayed there to look after his mother had she been able to return from hospital. The court held, however, that there had been no 'factual community of living', nor any agreement to establish such community during the relevant period. It took the view that throughout the son had been in a position of caretaker. A similar decision was reached in *Swanbrae Limited v. Elliott (1987)* where a daughter who retained another residence spent three or four nights a week with her mother during the latter's terminal illness. It was held that she was not residing with her mother.

Not all those who are related to the tenant are to be treated as members of his/her family. The courts have applied the common sense test of what an ordinary person would say when asked whether or not the individual was a member of the tenant's family. This is known as the 'family nexus' test (Mitchell 1987). The conduct of the parties can also be taken into account and the more remote the relationship, the more important that is likely to be. In *Langdon v. Horton (1951)*, the court held that two sisters who had gone to live with their widowed cousin, and remained with her until she died twenty-nine years later, did not qualify as members of her family. They had simply shared the flat with their cousin for their own convenience, but in *Jones v. Whitehill (1950)*, it was held that a niece who moved to look after her elderly aunt and uncle was a member of their family.

2.5.10 Where a relative was qualified to succeed, two transmissions of the statutory tenancy were possible until the HA 1988 came into force. Since 15 January 1989 only one statutory succession is possible irrespective of whether or not there was a succession prior to the implementation of the Act (*Dyson Holdings Limited v. Fox (1976)*). Where the successor is a qualifying relative, it is worth noting that he/she will succeed to an assured tenancy, not a protected tenancy, and therefore will not be able to register for a fair rent.

Where more than one member of the family is eligible to succeed and a dispute arises, the issue will need to be decided by the courts and the RA 1977 does not indicate the grounds upon which the court should reach a decision, but in deciding relative merits, a claimant's age is relevant (*Williams v. Williams (1970)*).

Under the HA 1988, assured tenants are only allowed one succession. This is to a spouse or someone living with the tenant as husband or wife who will have the automatic right to succeed to an assured tenancy if the tenant dies, unless the tenant has succeeded to the tenancy. No one else in the family has an automatic right of succession. People living together might want to ask for joint tenancy to avoid possible arguments about succession rights later (DoE 1992a).

2.5.11 RESTRICTED CONTRACTS

Under the Rent Acts, tenants living with resident landlords had only limited protection in the form of a restricted contract (RA 1977, ss. 21 and 22). In *Gray v. Brown (1992)*, it was held that the terms of a tenancy must include clear words reserving the right of the landlord to live on the premises, and a term that the tenant would share the house with whomever the landlord might choose was not sufficient to deprive the tenants of protection. No restricted contract tenancies can be created after 15 January 1989 and these tenants enjoy no security of tenure. Court proceedings will always be necessary to remove such tenants, but the landlord only has to show that the contractual tenancy has been terminated.

2.5.12 ASSIGNMENT AND SUB-LETTING

A landlord may grant the tenant the right to assign the tenancy or sub-let to someone the tenant chooses. Usually, Rent Act and Housing Act tenancies prohibit the assignment of the whole of the property. If the tenant has paid a premium (that is, pecuniary consideration in addition to rent) for an assured tenancy under the Housing Act 1988, and there is nothing in the tenancy agreement which says or implies he/she may not assign or sub-let it, he/she has a right to assign the tenancy or sub-let to someone else. However, once the contractual tenancy has ended there is no right to assign or sub-let.

2.5.13 RENT CONTROL AND RENT RESTRICTION

Assured tenants and *assured shorthold* tenants pay market rents while *protected* tenants and *secure* tenants of housing associations can still have a 'fair rent' fixed by a Rent Officer or, on appeal, a Rent Assessment Committee. An application for a fair rent can be made by a protected tenant or their landlord, or jointly by the landlord and tenant. The application is made to a Rent Officer who will set a fair rent. The rent, once registered, applies for two years and no further application can be made until the end of the two-year period. It is normally the situation that the fair rent is lower than the market rent and it is not lawful for the landlord to charge more than the fair rent. If that is the case, the tenant can recover any rent paid over and above the fair rent that was charged. When assessing the property for a fair rent, the Rent Officer must consider all the circumstances except the personal circumstances of the landlord and tenant. In particular, he/she must take into account the state of repair of the house or flat, its character, locality and age and how much furniture is provided and what it is like; and any premium lawfully paid.

The Rent Officer must ignore any disrepair for which the tenant is responsible, any improvements that the tenant has made which he/she did not need to under the terms of the tenancy, and also he/she must assume that the demand for similar houses or flats available for letting in that particular area does not greatly exceed the supply, that is, the rent should not be forced up by the shortage (RA 1977, s.70). The landlord or tenant may appeal against the Rent Officer's decision and this appeal is heard by the local Rent Assessment Committee and their verdict is final. It is generally felt that it is unwise for a tenant to apply to the Rent Assessment Committee for a fair rent to be set aside as the Committees will, more often than not, increase the rent. Nationally, somewhere in the region of 80 per cent of appeals are overturned by the Rent Assessment Committee.

An assured shorthold tenant can apply to the Rent Assessment Committee for a market rent to be set. This is the legal maximum the landlord can charge. However, this only applies to the first period of the original agreement. For example, a tenant who takes a six-month *assured shorthold* can only have a Rent Assessment Committee decision on the rent for that period. If he/she enters into further agreement with the landlord, then the Rent Assessment Committee will not entertain a further application. In the case of an assured periodic tenancy the tenant can only apply to the Rent Assessment Committee on the anniversary of the tenancy. The assessment made by the Rent Assessment Committee is not the legal maximum rent the landlord can charge. If the landlord and tenant want to come to some other agreement about rent they may do so. However, in the event of a dispute the tenant does not have to pay the increase requested by the landlord as this will not be considered to be a binding agreement.

One of the difficulties experienced by *assured periodic* and *assured shorthold* tenants is the level of housing benefit paid for the new market rents. These are higher than the fair rent registered by the Rent Officer. If the local authority considers the rent to be excessive, housing benefit will be limited. In these circumstances, it is in the interest of the tenant to apply to the Rent Assessment Committee, since the local authority will usually pay benefit to the level of the assessed rent.

2.5.14 UNLAWFUL EVICTION AND HARASSMENT

Section 1 of the PfEA 1977 provides 'residential occupiers' with a degree of protection from unlawful eviction and harassment. Two separate offences are created by this provision, that is, attempting to evict without getting a court order; and harassing a residential occupier.

Section 1(3) of the PfEA 1977 as amended by the HA 1988 provides that:

> If any person with intent to cause the resident occupier of any premises
>
> (a) to give up occupation of their premises or any part thereof; or
> (b) to refrain from exercising any right or pursuing any remedy in respect of the premises or part thereof;
>
> does acts likely to interfere with the peace or comfort of the residential occupier or members of his household, or persistently withdraws or withholds services reasonably required for the occupation of the premises as a residence, he shall be guilty of an offence.

Section 3 of the PfEA 1977 excludes certain classes of tenancies and licences, including those sharing with resident landlords or members of their families and holiday or hostel lets. However, the Criminal Law Act 1977 (CLA 1977) still affords some protection since anyone who, without lawful authority, uses or threatens to use violence (against the person or against the property) to secure entry against the will of the lawful occupier will be liable to prosecution.

The offence of harassment can be committed by any person and not simply by the landlord, and can extend to harassment of any member of the household. The HA 1988 has made it easier to establish an offence as it is now only necessary to prove that the landlord knows, or has reasonable cause to believe, that the conduct is likely to cause the occupier to cease occupation. Previously, it had been necessary to show specific intent. It must be shown that the act is likely to interfere with the peace and comfort of the residential occupier. Penalties for the offence are a fine or imprisonment, or both.

Failure by a landlord to pay gas or electricity bills which resulted in disconnection on one occasion, for example, may not be sufficient to establish the offence (*R v. Abrol (1972)*). In this and other circumstances, a tenant's remedy may lie in a civil claim for an injunction for damages in the county court. Harassment and illegal eviction may, *inter alia*, give rise to a civil claim for assault and trespass, or breach of the tenant's covenant for quiet enjoyment. Damages can also be sought under s.27 of the HA 1988. The sum involved can be substantial. The amount is calculated by subtracting the value of the premises if the tenant had remained in occupation from the value of the premises with vacant possession.

Some local authorities employ a harassment officer. Part of his/her job is to investigate allegations of harassment and to prosecute if that is deemed appropriate. It is usually the case that the local authority brings criminal proceedings and the tenant would pursue damages through a civil prosecution.

2.6.1 REPAIRS AND IMPROVEMENTS

Many tenants are neither aware of their landlord's obligations to carry out repairs to their property, nor how to ensure that such repairs are carried out. In England, in 1986, people aged sixty or over occupied 61.9 per cent of properties lacking basic amenities, 39.3 per cent of unfit properties and 35 per cent of properties in poor repair (DoE 1988).

If there is a written tenancy agreement, it may contain express terms setting out the landlord's duty to repair. Whilst in the private sector the use of standard precedents usually restricts a landlord's liability to the statutory provisions, public sector tenancies may impose far wider obligations.

The main statutory provision is to be found at s.11 of the Landlord and Tenant Act 1985 (LTA 1985). A landlord is obliged to keep the structure, exterior, services and installations in repair and working order. This covers walls, roofs, windows, woodwork, plaster and installations for the supply of water, gas, electricity, sanitation, heating and hot water. The standard of repair must have regard to the age, character and prospective life of the dwelling and locality in which it is situated. The landlord must be given notice of the disrepair and a reasonable time to carry out the repairs.

The requirement for notice is not necessary if personal injury or damage is caused to tenants, licensees, members of their households, or visitors, due to the failure to repair if the landlord is found to have been negligent (Defective Premises Act 1972, s.265 (DPA 1972)). The DPA 1972 also imposes liability on builders and others who carry out work on the property in a negligent manner.

A tenant bringing a claim under these provisions would normally proceed in the county court for an order that the landlord carry out the repair and pays him/her compensation. However, under Part III of the Environmental Protection Act 1990 (EPA 1990), should the state of the disrepair or lack of facilities cause a statutory nuisance prejudicial to health or safety, the environmental health department of the local authority, or ultimately the magistrates' court, can order the nuisance to be eradicated.

Tenants can instigate a private prosecution in the magistrates' court under the EPA 1990. This remedy may be particularly important in cases of disrepair not actionable under s.11 of the LTA 1985, for example, in relation to dampness caused by condensation. Proceedings are generally quicker than in the county court and compensation of up to £5,000 can be awarded. However, Legal Aid is not available.

Local authorities also have a duty to investigate any complaint that property is unfit for habitation, or in a state of substantial disrepair. Notice can be served under the HA 1985 to compel repairs to be carried out (s.189), or to order the closure or demolition of the property (HA 1985, s.265). A tenant or occupier displaced in this way is entitled to be rehoused. The courts have held that where a local authority is itself responsible for the disrepair, it cannot be forced to serve notice on itself under the Act (*R v. Cardiff City Council, ex parte Cross (1983)*).

Direct action is also available to tenants. In some circumstances, it is legally possible for tenants themselves to carry out repairs. Where landlords are in breach of their contractual obligations to repair, a right exists in common law to do what is necessary and recover the costs out of the rent (*Lee Parker v. Izzet (1971)*). The procedure the tenant must follow before exercising this right is somewhat complex (Luba 1991). In addition, it is of limited value to tenants unless they have sufficient funds to finance the works in default. Where a tenant is in receipt of housing benefit, the paying authority will need to be informed of the tenant's intention to use this procedure, otherwise payment of housing benefit may be withheld. In order that direct action may be taken, benefit should be paid in cash rather than by means of credit. The right to use rent for repairs may not always be available, however. It is uncertain at present whether the right can be excluded by an express term in the tenancy agreement. Secure tenants of local authorities have access to a statutory scheme for the use of rent to pay for repairs mentioned above at para. 2.3.11.

The equitable rule of 'set-off' provides a similar remedy. This allows the tenant to claim not only the cost of repairs, but also the cost of any damage that may have resulted from lack of repair, for example the replacement of furniture, or carpets. The set-off can be raised as a defence to any claim for rent by the landlord. It would need to be shown that it would be inequitable to allow the landlord to recover the amount claimed in view of the counter-claim made by the tenant. Recent levels of damages are such that a tenant should be able to establish a set off sufficient to amount to a complete defence to the landlord's claim. Having said this, even the most straight forward set-off raised in a defence may serve to delay the final hearing of proceedings for arrears or possession for considerable periods (Luba 1991).

2.6.2 DISABLED FACILITIES GRANTS

Disabled facilities grants are available for structural work to a building which is required to meet the needs of a disabled person who lives there. The housing authority must satisfy itself that the work is necessary and appropriate to the needs of the person and it must consult the social services authority on this question. The housing authority must satisfy itself that it is reasonable and practicable to carry out such works having regard to the age and condition of the dwelling or the building in which it is situated (Local Government and Housing Act 1989 (LGHA 1989) s.114(1)).

Mandatory grants are available, but the authority must approve an application. Grants are available if the work is needed for any one or more of the following: facilitating access for the disabled person to and from the building, to a room or rooms used as the principal family room, to a room which can be used for sleeping or to one which has a lavatory, bath, shower or wash hand basin; providing a room with lavatory, bath, shower or wash hand basin; any work which could make it possible for the person to make use of such facilities; facilitating the preparation and cooking of food by the disabled person; improving or installing an adequate and suitable heating system; making it easier for the person to use lighting, heating or other forms of power either by moving the control arrangement or providing additional means of control; and, in cases where the disabled person is caring for someone else, facilitating access around the dwelling in order to carry out this responsibility (s.114(3)). In addition, a disabled facilities grant may be provided if the work is needed to make the dwelling 'suitable for the accommodation, welfare or employment of the disabled occupant', even if it does not fall into any of the above categories (s.114(4)).

The disabled person must normally live in the dwelling but, provided the works are intended for his/her benefit, the individual concerned does not have to be the owner or tenant. All grants are means-tested, but there is no upper limit on the amount of capital or income to be taken into account.

2.7.1 BUYING THE FREEHOLD

Since the introduction of the Leasehold Reform Act 1967 (LRA 1967), a lessee of at least three years' standing may compel the lessor, or landlord, to sell the freehold, or extend the lease by fifty years, if the lease is of a house (not a flat) below a certain rateable value and the original lease was for at least twenty-one years. The LRHUDA 1993 amends this legislation, abolishing the rateable value limit and extending the low rent test. However, leaseholders who only qualify under the 1967 Act (as amended by the new legislation), that is, who currently fall outside the Act because of the existing rateable value limits and low rent test, will only have a right to purchase a freehold, not the alternative option of lease extension (Katz 1994).

2.8.1 OWNER OCCUPIERS AND LONG LEASEHOLDERS

Owner occupiers in leasehold property are faced with the difficulty that the lease is a wasting asset. Recent legislation has gone some way to address this problem. The LRHUDA 1993 allows leaseholders collectively to buy the freehold on their flats. To be eligible, they must have lived in the property for at least a year. At least two-thirds of all flats in the block must qualify and at least two-thirds of those lease-holders must agree to buy. Landlords will be paid all reasonable costs and compensation for loss of value on other properties as a result of being forced to sell. The price of the freehold will be based on independent valuations of the property's market price (*Adviser* 1993).

Individual tenants have a further right to purchase a ninety-year lease from the term date of their current lease at a peppercorn rent, subject to the payment of a premium. However, a tenant must have occupied the flat as his/her only or principal residence for the last three years or periods amounting to three years in the last ten years (Diamond and McGrath 1993).

The Landlord and Tenant Act 1987 (LTA 1987) gives tenants of privately owned blocks of flats the right of first refusal on the sale by their landlord of his/her interest in the property. On receipt of a notice from the landlord of his/her intention to sell and the proposed price, the tenant has two months in which to accept, reject or make a counter offer. An acceptance will be valid if it is agreed by a bare majority of tenants. A rejection allows a landlord a year in which to dispose of his/her interest, provided it is not for less than the offer made to the tenant.

2.8.2   SERVICE CHARGES

Leaseholders of flats and, in some instances, leaseholders of houses, may have to pay a service charge to the landlord for the provision of common services such as repairs, maintenance, insurance or management expenses of the property as a whole or on an estate. These are a frequent source of complaint since leaseholders may feel that they have little control over the level of the charges which are made and the work that is done. Sections 18–30 of the Landlord and Tenant Act 1985 (LTA 1985) (as amended by the Landlord and Tenant Act 1987 (LTA 1987)) provide some protection to those who have bought flats on a long lease, whether the landlord is a private landlord, a council, a Housing Action Trust, a New Town Development Corporation, the Development Board for Rural Wales or a housing association; and protection also for those who rent property from a private landlord or a housing association and pay variable service charges in addition to rent.

A leaseholder who pays variable service charges has the right to ask the landlord how the service charge is made up, inspect the accounts and receipts and take copies, challenge the reasonableness of the charge and be consulted on major works. These rights can be exercised individually, or collectively if a recognised tenants' association exists.

Failure on the part of a landlord to comply with the above provisions is a criminal offence. In addition, disputes may be taken to the county court, regardless of the amount involved, whether by way of resisting a claim for a service charge, seeking reimbursement, or for a declaration whether or not the charge is recoverable or the works are to a reasonable standard (Arden and Hunter 1992). As a result of the difficulties encountered by long leaseholders over the management of their properties, qualifying tenants under the LRHUDA 1993 now have a right to a management audit (s.78). The purpose of the audit is to establish whether or not management functions are being discharged and service charges are being applied in an efficient and effective manner. The auditor must have regard to any code of practice approved by the Secretary of State, and has wide powers to inspect a property and obtain information from the landlord, or any managing agent employed by the landlord (Diamond and McGrath 1993).

Restrictions on levying service charges where properties have been disposed of by public sector authorities are contained in s.45 of the

HA 1985. Public sector authorities include registered housing associations as well as local authorities and other public bodies. For this purpose, 'disposal' includes the conveyance of freehold. Thus, the restrictions would apply, for example, where services are provided to an estate of houses.

2.8.3 IMPROVEMENTS AND REPAIRS

If owners or lessees are responsible for their own repairs and improvements then grants may be available from the local authority. On 1 July 1990 a new grant system was introduced by the Local Government and Housing Act 1989 (LGHA 1989). The local housing authority is responsible for administering the grants, the principal types being renovation grants, common parts grants, HMO grants and disabled facilities grants.

Renovation grants are mandatory where a dwelling is unfit for human habitation. Grants are means-tested with no upper resource limits. There are also higher limits for people with disabilities. The amount of grant available will depend on the claimant's financial position. A property can be described as unfit if it is structurally unstable, in serious disrepair, has dampness which could harm health, has inadequate lighting, heating and ventilation, an inadequate system of drainage, inadequately located toilet or bath, no proper facilities for preparing or cooking food, or no properly piped supply of water. Where the property is not regarded as unfit for human habitation then a renovation grant is at the discretion of the local authority which may approve it in such circumstances as putting the dwelling in reasonable repair, providing a dwelling by conversionof a house, providing adequate thermal insulation and adequate facilities for space heating (LGHA 1989, s.115). The provision of discretionary grants has recently been severely curtailed by the cuts in local government finances.

Common parts grants to repair or improve the common parts of buildings that are divided into flats can be applied for, either by the landlord or owner of the building, or a number of the tenants or leaseholders acting together. On an application made by a landlord the grant will be mandatory if it is needed to comply with a notice served under s.198 or s.190 of the HA 1985. Other grants are discretionary in circumstances similar to those for the renovation grants above.

Disabled facilities grants are available for adaptations to a building to provide facilities in a property for the benefit of a disabled person. (See para. 2.8.1 above.) Applications are assessed in conjunction with the social services authority and may not be approved unless the authority is satisfied that the works are necessary and appropriate to meet the needs of the disabled occupants and that it is reasonable and practicable to carry out the works having regard to the age and condition of the building (LGHA 1989, s.114(1)). It is not necessary to be registered as disabled. According to DoE Circular 10/90, para. 36, 'The assessment of whether the works are "necessary and appropriate" must involve consideration of whether the proposed adaptation or improvement is needed in order to enable the disabled occupant to remain in his [*sic*] own home, retaining or regaining as great a degree of independence as can reasonably be achieved.'

Landlords of houses in multiple occupation (HMOs), where the occupiers do not have their own self-contained accommodation, can apply for grants to repair and improve the property. As with common parts grants, the approval is mandatory where the application is by the landlord and the work is necessary to comply with a notice under s.189 or s.190 of the 1985 Act and discretionary in the same circumstances as for renovation grants.

In addition, discretionary grants are available for assistance with minor works for the provision or improvement of thermal insulation, the carrying out of works or repairs to a dwelling in a clearance area, repairs, improvements or adaptations to a property where the occupier of the property is sixty years of age or more, or adaptations to enable a person aged sixty or more to come and live in a carer's property. The maximum amount of assistance is limited to £1,000 per application with a limit of £3,000 in three years for one dwelling. Grants are only available to those in receipt of income support, housing benefit, council tax benefit or family credit.

A local authority may carry out a group repair scheme externally to a number of houses at the same time. The consent of the owners is necessary, and contributions may have to be made towards the costs of the works. The local authority also has power to declare renewal areas lasting for ten years, in which they may take action for improvements.

2.8.4 MORTGAGE DEFAULT

In 1991, record numbers of mortgage defaulters were evicted or were threatened with eviction. As a result the Social Security (Mortgage Interest Payments) Act 1992 (SS(MIP)A 1992) introduced a direct payments scheme for those on income support who qualified for assistance with some or all of the interest accruing under their mortgage. Under this scheme, the Benefits Agency makes payments of income support directly to the lenders. In some areas these rules have led to a more lenient attitude by the courts to those facing possession proceedings. However, if the property market improves and properties are more easily sold, this situation may change.

2.8.5 The courts have a number of statutory powers to deny possession to the lender. Under s.36 of the Administration of Justice Act 1970 (AJA 1970), a court may adjourn proceedings or stay or suspend for such period or periods as the court thinks reasonable. Some courts adopt a standard one- or two-year period over which the arrears must be repaid. However, in *First Middlesbrough Trading & Mortgage Company v. Cunningham (1974)*, it was held that the whole period of the mortgage could be the reasonable period. Where a mortgage is a 'regulated agreement' within the Consumer Credit Act 1974 (CCA 1974), then the court has wider power to reschedule the rate of payment of 'any sum' owed under regulated agreement and to vary the agreement in consequence of such an order.

2.8.6 DISPOSING OF OWNER OCCUPIED PROPERTY

Owner occupiers may decide, for a variety of reasons, that they are no longer able, or no longer wish to remain in their own home. The disposal of a substantial asset such as a house or flat can affect benefit entitlements and the amount to be paid for residential accommodation (see Chapter 4 at para. 4.6.1). Elderly persons may be caught in a dilemma whether or not to dispose of property. The house they live in may be too large for their needs, but they may hesitate to dispose of it for fear of depriving the family members of a valuable asset. They may, however, need to convert a capital asset into realisable income.

What choices are available? Capital may be realised by the sale of the property, and the purchase of something smaller or more suitable. This trade-down may result in considerable outlay in legal and related fees. Alternatively, a home income plan, sometimes called a mortgage annuity scheme, normally involves receiving a monthly income for life whilst retaining ownership of the home. Normally, an interest-only loan is raised on a proportion of the value of the property up to a maximum of £30,000. This is used to purchase an annuity income which is paid each month for life. The interest payable on the loan has to be deducted from the annuity and, because of this, many people are disappointed to find that the extra income is not as much as they hoped it would be, although the loan interest does attract tax relief. Problems can arise if someone with a home income plan wishes to move.

Home reversion schemes involve older home owners selling their homes to the reversion company in return for a lump sum, or in some cases an annuity income. The occupant remains in the house rent free or for a nominal monthly sum, on a lifetime tenancy. An administrative fee for arranging the sale is normally paid. However, in some cases the cash sum from the sale can be 35 per cent or less of the house value and will rarely be more the 60 per cent, even for people over eighty. Some building societies offer interest-only loans where the interest is rolled up, that is, repayment does not become due until the property is sold, so that neither the capital, nor the interest, is repaid during the elderly person's lifetime. However, deferred interest mounts up quickly and, at times of falling property values, the danger of the loan starting to catch up with the property value is considerable. In the past, many people have lost very substantial amounts of money through investment bond income schemes which should no longer be on the market (Age Concern 1991). Any elderly people wishing to consider a particular scheme should be strongly advised to seek independent financial and legal advice.

Many people with a house too large for their needs may choose to let part of it. It has been noted already that a tenant with a resident landlord will have no security of tenure under the HA 1988, although possession proceedings would have to be brought should the tenant not leave on being served with the requisite notice. One of the most commonly used options, however, is for elderly people to live with their families. At first sight, this may appear the most convenient and attractive arrangement. When the elderly person continues to live in his/her home, legal problems are unlikely to arise, except possibly where family members make a contribution towards the capital. Difficulties can arise, however, where elderly people give up their own property and move to live with relatives or friends. Sharing a house may prove difficult, and the parties may have fundamental disagreements. At worst, this can lead to costly and distressing litigation. Unless an elderly person becomes a joint owner, he/she may have no security of tenure and, ultimately, may have to move into residential accommodation. Again, expert advice should be sought so as to avoid complications arising later (see Chapter 7 at para. 7.18.2).

2.9.1 SHELTERED ACCOMMODATION

Sheltered housing units provide special facilities for elderly or disabled people which may include the service of a resident warden. In some areas, other support services are provided such as care officers, special home helps or a meal service. Research sponsored by the House Builders Federation in 1983 concluded that, had sheltered housing been available, about 12 per cent of elderly owner occupiers would choose to buy such accommodation (Baker and Parry 1983). According to a study by the National Institute of Social Work, up to approximately one-third of residents currently in residential homes could be successfully re-accommodated in specially adapted sheltered housing (Leigh 1987). However, completions of specialised dwellings for the elderly in England fell by a third between 1981 and 1990. Over this period, dwellings built by the private sector increased substantially, but were offset by a 63 per cent decrease in the number built by local authorities in new towns. In 1990, three-quarters of all specialised dwellings built for the elderly were for sheltered housing (CSO 1992).

The sheltered housing market is assuming many of the characteristics of a mixed economy. Conferences on housing for the elderly are frequently sponsored by private developers. The number of elderly persons accommodated in sheltered housing remains well below the estimated need. Many of the elderly from ethnic minorities, for example, apparently receive poor and inappropriate services. At least two housing associations, ASRA and CARIB, have been established to provide for the respective needs of elderly people from Asian and West Indian backgrounds (Smith 1988).

As indicated in para. 2.3.2, those living in sheltered accommodation provided by housing authorities will be secure tenants. Those living in sheltered accommodation provided by housing associations before 15 January 1989 will be secure, although after that date they will be assured tenants.

Sheltered housing in the voluntary or private sectors, entered into before 15 January 1989, is covered by the RA 1977, although it will fall outside the full protection of the Act if a substantial part of the rent is payable for 'attendance' (RA 1977, s.7). Attendance is not defined in the Act, but has been interpreted by the court to mean provision for the tenant of personal services which benefit his/her enjoyment of the premises (*Palser v. Grinling (1948)*). The emphasis has been on services being personal rather than communal, and would not include, for example, the cleaning of parts of the premises which are used in common. Section 7 will apply when the provision of personal services, which might include the services of a warden, constitutes a substantial proportion of the total rent. From decided cases, it would appear that this is legally satisfied if the cost of the attendance amounts to 14 per cent of the rent (Mitchell 1987). Since the attendance element is calculated from the commencement of the tenancy, Rent Act protection may be available for many whose dependence upon personal services is initially small. Should the cost of providing personal services subsequently rise substantially, the court might decide that the tenancy should then be brought within the statutory exception (*Seabrook v. Mervyn (1947)*).

For those entering sheltered accommodation in the voluntary or private sectors after 15 January 1989, whilst there is no similar exception under the HA 1988, the substantial attendance test will determine whether there is in fact a licence or a tenancy.

2.10.1   MOBILE HOMES

An increasing number of people, either by choice or through necessity, now live in mobile homes. The Mobile Homes Act 1983 applies to privately owned licensed sites and to local authority owned sites, but not to local authority sites for travellers. The site owner must give each owner a written statement setting out the terms of the agreement between them. Express terms, for example, as to pitch fees, can be referred to the court or to an arbitrator within six months of the date on which the site owner gave the resident his/her written statement. If there is only limited planning permission for the site, the owner must inform the resident in the written statement.

The resident has a right to keep his/her mobile home on site indefinitely unless either he/she, or the site owner, brings the agreement to an end. The site owner can bring an agreement to an end only after applying to the court or to an arbitrator. A resident has a right to sell his/her mobile home on site, and transfer the agreement to the purchaser. If the resident's spouse is also living in the mobile home at the time of the resident's death, he/she inherits the agreement and the deceased resident's rights. Where there is no such spouse, any member of the resident's family who was also living in the mobile home on his/her death, can inherit the agreement and the deceased resident's rights.

3   Care in the community

Lynda Bransbury

3.1.1 The majority of elderly people who need some form of support, even those who are severely disabled, continue to live in the community. Those over eighty-five are most likely to have serious disabilities and to be in receipt of services provided either through the NHS or their local social services authority (Audit Commission 1992). In recent years, much more emphasis has been placed on the importance of developing and expanding 'community care' services. There has, however, never been any consistency in what is meant by either 'community care' or 'community care services'. The White Paper *Caring for People* states that 'enabling people to live as independently as possible in the community is at the heart of community care' (DH 1989d). At the same time, the majority of the reforms proposed in that White Paper and subsequently enacted have been about the funding and organisation of residential services. Many of the services defined as 'community care services' in s.46 of the National Health Service and Community Care Act 1990 (NHSCCA 1990) relate to the provision of residential care (see Chapter 4).

Be that as it may, one of the cornerstones of the government's community care commitments is to achieve a shift of resources away from institutional care and to foster more services for people living at home. In practice, the distribution of transferred social security monies and other conditions of grant imposed on social services authorities seem to have consolidated existing patterns of expenditure on institutional, particularly nursing home, care, at least in the short run.

The high profile around 'care in the community' has undoubtedly reduced the Cinderella image of community care services within social services. However, the question remains whether the funding being provided will be adequate to transform the quality and range of provision in practice. It is not just that there is a serious dispute between the local authority associations and government over the adequacy of the overall funding (HC 1993), but there also seem to be implicit assumptions built into the funding formulae that 'care in the community' is a cheaper service to provide than a bed in an institution. This does not augur well for future developments, given the considerable costs of developing the complex packages of care which are needed if very disabled people are to be able to maintain a reasonable quality of life in the community.

3.1.2 A high percentage of elderly people are disabled or suffering from chronic illnesses. A person may need support from a social services authority as a result of mental illness, and not because they are elderly. The legislation relating to community care services has traditionally distinguished between those elderly people who also meet one of the statutory definitions of disability and those who do not. Greater duties have been imposed on social services authorities to assist and meet the needs of the former. The effect of the NHSCCA 1990, together with the Department of Health's *Policy Guidance*, has broken down some but not all of these distinctions. This chapter therefore starts by looking at a social services authority's powers and duties towards elderly people, whether or not they have disabilities. It then goes on to examine the legislation which applies to elderly people whose disability or ill health comes within the terms of s.29 of the National Assistance Act 1948 (NAA 1948). The provisions relating to disability cover a very wide range of physical and mental conditions which affect daily living.

3.2.1   ASSESSMENT DUTIES

Section 47(1) of the NHSCCA 1990 places a duty on social services authorities to carry out an assessment of a person's needs for 'community care' services, but only

> where it appears to a local authority that any person for whom they may provide or arrange for the provision of community care services may be in need of any such services.

Section 46 of the Act defines 'community care services' as those services provided under Part III of the NAA 1948; s.45 of the Health Services and Public Health Act 1968 (HSPHA 1968); s.21 of, and Sched. 8 to, the National Health Service Act 1977 (NHSA 1977) and s.117 of the Mental Health Act 1983 (MHA 1983). This covers the range of non-residential welfare services which a social services authority has the powers to provide to elderly people. See Chapter 5 at 5.6.24 for information on after-care provided under s.117 of the MHA 1983. Department of Health *Policy Guidance* requires that 'the aim of the assessment should be to ensure that all needs for care services are considered' (DH 1990). This *Policy Guidance* was issued under s.7A of the Local Authority Social Services Act 1970 (LASSA 1970) and therefore, while not as binding as a Direction, local authorities are required to follow it.

3.2.2 Section 47 does not provide an elderly person with the right to an assessment on request. Once someone requests an assessment, the authority must exercise its judgement based on the facts as to whether an assessment is necessary. An assessment can only be refused if the authority believes the person does not need any 'community care services' or if it believes it has no obligation towards the person. For example, this could apply to persons not 'ordinarily resident' in its area (see para. 3.8.2). The extent to which the duty to assess extends to carers is somewhat unclear (see para. 3.15.1).

3.2.3 The duty imposed on social services authorities by s.47 is to undertake assessments of need, but there is no requirement in the section to meet those needs, or to provide the individual with services. The provisions of s.47, in creating the framework for assessing need, must therefore be read together with legislation and directions which do impose a legal obligation on authorities to provide a 'community care service' once the need for it has been agreed. In this respect, s.47(2)(a) is very precise about the relationship between the 1990 Act and the Chronically Sick and Disabled Persons Act 1970 (CSDPA 1970). Anyone who is a disabled person within the meaning of s.29 of the NAA 1948, must be informed of their rights under s.4 of the Disabled Persons (Services, Consultation and Representation) Act 1986 (DP(SCR)A 1986), that is, to request an assessment of their need for any of the services provided under s.2 of the CSDPA 1970 (see para. 3.9.1 below).

3.2.4 The Secretary of State can issue directions under s.47(4) instructing social services authorities on the form and manner which assessments must take, but has not yet done so. At present, this is left to each authority and it is therefore unclear what procedures could or could not be held to constitute 'an assessment'. However, once an authority agrees to do an assessment, it must make a decision on what services, if any, are needed (s.47(1)(b)). It must also contact and collaborate with the district health authority (DHA) or the local housing authority if the person may need any of their services (s.47(3)).

3.2.5 Advice issued by the Social Services Inspectorate in the form of a letter issued from the Chief Inspector requires social services authorities to publish information about their assessment criteria and procedures. This should include criteria for identifying disabled people; deciding on the type and level of assessment; priority categories of need; when to involve other agencies and information on which staff are responsible for operating the criteria. It also states that all staff in contact with the public 'should be conversant with these arrangements' (SSI 1992).

3.2.6 The policy guidance issued by the Department of Health has consistently reiterated the government's intention that 'assessment should take account of the wishes of the individual and his/her carer' (DH 1989d). 'The individual service user ... should be involved throughout the assessment. ... They should feel that the process is aimed at meeting their wishes' (DH 1990).

3.2.7 Nothing in s.47 creates a specific duty to provide a written decision or explanation of the outcome following an assessment. It would, in practice, be extremely difficult for someone to exercise their statutory rights of complaint unless they were given both a decision and an explanation. This, therefore, creates an implicit duty on an authority to provide a reasoned explanation in writing. 'Service users and carers should be informed of the results of the assessment and/or any services to be provided. ... A written statement will normally be needed if a continuing service is to be provided. Written statements should always be supplied on request' (DH 1990). The Social Services Inspectorate advises authorities to give individual users a copy of their care plan which should 'spell out the extent to which their needs qualify for assistance' (SSI 1992).

3.3.1 WELFARE PROVISIONS AND THE ELDERLY

Section 45(1) of the HSPHA 1968 provides that:

> A local authority may, with the approval of the Secretary of State, and, to such extent as he may direct, make arrangements for promoting the welfare of old people.

This provision gave social services authorities new powers to provide or arrange services for elderly people who are not 'substantially' or 'permanently handicapped'. According to DHSS Circular 19/71 the aim should be 'so far as possible to prevent or postpone personal deterioration or breakdown'. Section 45 prevents authorities from paying any money directly to elderly people, except as remuneration for paid work undertaken in accordance with the above arrangements.

3.3.2 Local authorities only have the powers to make arrangements approved by the Secretary of State. DHSS Circular 19/71 sanctions arrangements for the following purposes: to provide meals and recreational facilities in the home or elsewhere; to provide information to elderly people about relevant services; to identify elderly people in need; to provide transport or help with travelling to and from local authority or similar services; to assist in finding suitable boarding out placements for elderly people; to provide visiting and advisory services and social work support; to provide practical assistance in the home, including adaptations and any other facility that would improve safety, comfort or convenience; to contribute towards the costs of wardens who provide welfare functions in sheltered housing and to provide warden services for people in private housing.

Since the Circular was published in 1971, the list of approved arrangements has not been expanded, although it was originally anticipated that it would be. The specific approval of the Secretary of State is required before an authority has the power to provide any other service not generally sanctioned by the provisions of this Circular.

No directions have been issued by the Secretary of State under s.45(1), which leaves the provision entirely at the discretion of each social services authority. The original reason given for not issuing directions which would have placed a duty on authorities to make these arrangements, was the absence of any practical experience in the field. Almost fourteen years later, this excuse seems to be wearing a bit thin. It cannot be argued that the NHSCCA 1990 makes directions unnecessary as the provisions of s.47 only impose a duty to assess, but do not extend authorities' duties to provide services to elderly people where need is assessed.

3.3.3 In making arrangements under s.45, the authority can employ, as its agent, a voluntary organisation or other person whose activities include the provision of services to elderly people. Section 45(3) requires the authority to satisfy itself that the organisation or person is capable of promoting the welfare of elderly people. Section 45 defines a voluntary organisation as a body carrying out its activities otherwise than for profit. This criterion may be satisfied if making a profit was subsidiary to the organisation's main objectives (*National Deposit Friendly Society (Trustees) v. Skegness Urban District Council (1959)*; see also *Victory (Ex Services) Association v. Paddington Borough Council (1960)*). An amendment to s.45 introduced by the NHSCCA 1990, allows organisations or individuals who provide services professionally or 'by way of trade' to be employed as the authority's agent (see paras. 3.16.1 to 3.16.4 on the problems which arise in relation to regulating private agencies providing domiciliary services).

3.4.1 BOARDING OUT SCHEMES FOR THE ELDERLY

Since 1972, social services authorities have had the power under s.45 of the HSPHA 1968 to help elderly people find suitable households in which they can board. There is no commonly accepted definition of what does or does not constitute a boarding out scheme. The term 'boarding out' has not been defined in either the 1968 Act nor Circular 19/71. In practice, no single or standard model of provision exists, and a variety of arrangements with differing origins, aims and practices have been developed in different areas. For example, some schemes are used for short term and respite arrangements; others provide more permanent homes for elderly people. The variety of purposes is reflected in the range of names used for different schemes. Two types of schemes stand at either end of the spectrum. At one end, elderly people go to stay in the home of the carer and the expectation is that they will be treated as a member of the family. These schemes are often known as elderly fostering or 'home from home'. At the other end, they are accommodated in lodgings or some similar establishment where board and lodging is provided on a commercial basis. These placements are sometimes referred to as 'supported lodgings'; a resident housekeeper or owner will usually provide some emotional or practical support.

3.4.2 Boarding out arrangements in one form or another were initially developed for people with learning disabilities rather than for elderly people. However, schemes catering for the elderly have become more common over the past ten years. The diversity of arrangements raises some complex legal issues which have not really been addressed. The most important ones concern the legal powers on which the authority is relying to provide assistance or fund provision and how this, in turn, affects the legal relationships between carer, elderly person and the authority. It is therefore important, but not always easy, to distinguish between when an authority is assisting an individual to find a suitable household (relying on its powers under HSPHA 1968) or when it is acting in pursuance of its duties under ss.21–6 of the NAA 1948 (see Chapter 4 at 4.5.1 to 4.5.6).

3.4.3 The status of elderly people as boarders under housing legislation is unaffected by which statute is relied on and depends on the kind of licence or tenancy agreement they are offered by their landlord. If the accommodation is provided under the NAA 1948, the primary relationship is between the authority and the elderly person, the carer acting on behalf of the authority. Most social service departments issue some kind of written 'contract' to residents when arranging residential placements. In practice, whether or not there is a written agreement between the authority and the resident, the carer has granted a licence by allowing the resident into the accommodation. On the other hand, if the authority has only assisted the person, using its powers under HSPHA 1968, and is not funding any part of the placement, then a contractual relationship exists between the elderly person and the person or organisation providing the placement. In this case, their housing status depends on whether they are offered a licence agreement or some form of tenancy. For example, most housing associations now offer assured tenancies to all their tenants, even those in shared accommodation. An assured tenancy gives them the right to exclusive occupation of one part of the premises for a fixed period at a fixed rent (see Chapter 2 at para. 2.5.5).

3.4.4 Where the authority is providing the service directly – such as where the carers are employees of the authority – it is unlikely that it can rely on its powers under the HSPHA 1968. While 'household' like 'boarding' is not defined in the Act or the DHSS Circular 19/71, an authority would be pressed to show that direct provision constituted assistance in finding a suitable household. Before April 1992, any funding provided by a social services authority towards the costs of lodgings, or a similar establishment (whether run by an individual or a commercial organisation), would not have been possible under the HSPHA 1968. Before that date, authorities could only employ voluntary organisations as their agents. Direct provision or use of a private provider arranged before 1992 would therefore

have fallen to be provided under NAA 1948 and the legal relationships between the elderly person, the carer and the authority are
fairly straightforward. These are dealt with in Chapter 4. In brief,
social services authorities would be responsible for the quality and
financing of the placement and the resident would be required to pay
a contribution to the authority towards the costs.

3.4.5 In all other cases, if some funding or other practical or financial
support is being provided by the authority to a carer who is not an
employee of the authority, it is very unclear whether the HSPHA
1968 or the NAA 1948 applies. The authority could be employing
the carer as its agent under s.45 of the 1968 Act or be funding
the provision under s.26 of the 1948 Act. If the former, then the
contractual responsibilities between the three parties are extremely
unclear. If the provider is acting as the agent of the authority in
providing accommodation, then it seems most probable that the
primary relationship exists between the authority and the resident,
even if, in practice, the resident is paying rent direct to the provider.
On the other hand, if the authority only contracts with the carer to
provide care or support, there could be a separate contract between
the resident and the provider for the accommodation. The question
of the authority's duty of care towards the resident and responsibility
for the quality of provision will depend primarily on its level of
involvement and the terms of any agency agreement (see para. 3.4.7).

3.4.6 If no money has been paid by the authority to the person
or organisation providing care, this arrangement should not fall
within the terms of the NAA 1948. The authority has simply acted as
an intermediary, putting the elderly person in contact with the household. In these cases, there is also a clear contractual relationship
between the resident and the provider creating either a licence or a
tenancy. The extent of an authority's duty of care towards a resident
is likely to depend on their level of involvement in arranging the
placement. For example, if all they have done is to make available
a list of all the establishments in the area and made it clear to the
person that they have no knowledge of the quality of the care, it
would be difficult for a subsequent negligence action to succeed
against them.

Where no money passes between the authority and the provider,
it could also be argued that it has no duty of care towards residents.
The authority might argue that it has simply assisted the elderly
person with advice, information or practical help in finding some-

where to live. On the other hand, even though there is no financial arrangement with the providers, some social services authorities actively recruit carers, provide training and only suggest placements which have been vetted. Others play an active part in deciding which household would be suitable for each individual. In these cases, a court might be more likely to hold that a duty of care existed between the authority and the resident.

3.4.7 The nature and extent of any legal liability would appear to depend upon whether the provider was regarded in law as acting as an agent for the authority. An agency can arise without formal agreement. For example, if someone gives the impression that another has authority to act on his/her behalf he/she may later be unable to deny the existence of an agency. The person on whose behalf the agent acts (known as the principal), can be held liable for the actions of an agent, as long as those actions are within the limits set by the agency. Equally, both agent and principal may be liable depending on the circumstances. For example, regardless of the contractual or agency arrangements, under the Occupiers Liability Act 1957 (OLA 1957) s.1(1) the occupier of any premises owes a separate duty of care for the safety of anyone who enters and remains there, even as a visitor.

No cases concerning the possible existence of an agency in relation to elderly placements have been reported. In *S v. Walsall Metropolitan Borough Council (1985)*, a case involving a child in local authority care placed with foster parents, the Court of Appeal held the authority not liable for the negligent acts of the foster parents in relation to the child.

This case may be persuasive authority for the view that no action in negligence against an authority would succeed in respect of harm sustained by an elderly person while boarding. However, it is difficult to judge how applicable the findings in this case would be to elderly boarding schemes. The child was placed with the foster parents under the provisions of the Boarding out of Children Regulations 1955. It was held that these provisions were entirely inconsistent with the notion that the foster parents were agents of the authority in carrying out their duties. The authority had a duty to provide accommodation for the child, which was satisfied by the boarding out arrangement. However, it was held that the foster parents were not fulfilling a duty to provide accommodation, but only providing a means whereby the authority could carry out its statutory duties towards the child. Clearly, if boarding out is being arranged under the HSPHA 1968 then, unlike the above case, no statutory duty arises, but the carer may be employed as the authority's agent under s.45.

Where the carer is employed as the authority's agent, s.45 of the HSPHA 1968 gives the authority powers to provide the carer with practical and financial support. This could include extending the authority's public liability insurance policy to cover claims for negligence by elderly residents or their relatives. If this were done, it would protect both the carer and the authority. However, some social services authorities take the view, particularly where there is no financial contract with the provider, that the authority does not have an insurable interest in the schemes. Authorities should, in any case, when seeking to recruit providers of boarding out schemes, advise them of the risks of negligence actions and the benefits of additional insurance cover.

3.4.8 Much of the funding for boarding out schemes has come from social security benefits, including housing benefit (HB). Changes to both social security and registration criteria on 1 April 1993 have affected the benefits payable and are described in more detail in Chapter 4. Before April 1993, there were two routes to benefit entitlement. First, residents in schemes run by independent providers registered under the Registered Homes Act 1984 (RHA 1984) before 1 April 1993, or which met the 'care' criteria, could claim the higher rate of income support (IS) towards the costs. In 1992–3, this was up to £185 per week. Second, residents whose placements offered a lower level of care were entitled to HB towards the rent and claimed IS and attendance allowance (AA) or disability living allowance (DLA) on the same terms as anyone else living independently in the community.

The April 1993 reforms have abolished the first route, although anyone resident in a scheme on 31 March 1993 has 'preserved rights' which means they remain entitled to the higher rate of IS. They lose preserved rights if they live away from a registered home for more than thirteen weeks or after fifty-two weeks in hospital. Benefits for new residents depend on whether the scheme is registered under the RHA 1984 or provided under Part III of the NAA 1948. If either of these applies, no HB is payable and IS is also affected. Benefit entitlement for residents in an unregistered establishment has not changed, but if their placement is being funded under Part III of the NAA 1948, again no HB is payable and attendance allowance (AA) or the care component of DLA stops after four weeks.

3.5.1 MEALS AND RECREATION PROVIDED BY DISTRICT COUNCILS

Schedule 9 of the Health and Social Services and Social Security Adjudication Act 1983 (HSSSSAA 1983) gives county district councils (that is, local authorities which are not social services authorities) the powers to provide meals and recreation to elderly people, either in their own homes or elsewhere. There is no definition of 'recreation' in the Act, but para. 10 of the Ministry of Health Circular 12/62 advised that recreation did not exclude the provision of 'work centres' or 'occupation centres' where elderly people earned small sums from the work they did, as long as this was ancillary to the prime purpose of the activity, namely to keep them fit and active by giving them an incentive to attend.

3.5.2 District councils can either provide these services themselves or employ a voluntary organisation which provides either meals or recreation for elderly people to act as their agent. Only voluntary organisations whose activities are not for profit can act as the authority's agent. Where a voluntary organisation is so employed, the district council can assist them in several ways to provide the service. These are: to contribute directly to the organisation's funds; to allow premises owned by the council to be used by the organisation on agreed terms, including services provided by council staff in connection with the premises and making available furniture, equipment, vehicles and other things (by gift or loan) (HSSSSAA 1983, Sched. 9, para. 2).

3.5.3 Paragraph 3 of Sched. 9 of the Act gives the Secretary of State the power to bring forward regulations regarding the qualification of staff employed and to create powers of inspection for any services or functions provided by a district council or its agent under Sched. 9. To date, no regulations have been made.

3.5.4 The powers granted to district councils under the HSSSSAA 1983 overlap with those assigned to social services authorities under s.45 of the HSPHA 1968 (see para. 3.3.1). In addition, the 1983 Act empowers health authorities to make grants to assist district councils in performing these functions. The NHSCCA 1990 requires each county council social services department not only to consult with its health authority, but also with its local housing authority, when identifying housing needs, before drawing up its community care plan. Hopefully, this requirement may lead to better co-ordination and distribution of functions between districts and counties than has been the case up to now.

3.6.1 HOME HELP AND LAUNDRY FACILITIES

Paragraph 3(1) of Sched. 8 of the National Health Service Act 1977 (NHSA 1977) requires every social services authority to provide or to arrange for the provision of home help for a household where such help is needed because of the presence of an elderly person. However, the legislation gives social services considerable discretion to determine need and therefore when to provide the service in individual cases. An identical duty applies if the need arises because of the presence of someone with a physical or mental disability, or who is suffering from illness. This duty towards chronically sick and disabled people overlaps with that relating to practical assistance in the home under s.2 of the CSDPA 1970 (see para. 3.9.1).

3.6.2 Social services authorities must provide the service or 'arrange for the provision' of home help, but in either case, it has a duty under Sched. 8 para. 3(1) to ensure that the scale of provision is adequate for the needs of its area. Services provided under Sched. 8 are 'community care services' within the meaning of s.47 of the NHSCCA 1990 and the provisions of that section therefore apply.

3.6.3 In addition, the authority has the power to provide or arrange laundry facilities for any household which is receiving home help or could qualify for the service under Sched. 8. This provision overlaps with health authority powers to provide laundry and incontinence services. However, in both cases, neither authority has a duty to make provision, so the availability of such services depends entirely on where a person lives. Some limited help is available to IS claimants through the Social Fund. Community care grants (CCGs) can be claimed towards the costs of washing machines and tumble driers. There is also some help with replacement clothing and bedding, for example, if it wears out more quickly than normal due to regular washing because of illness or old age (see Chapter 1 at para. 1.39.1).

3.7.1 TRAVEL CONCESSIONS FOR THE ELDERLY

Under the Transport Act 1985 (TA 1985), a local authority or two authorities acting jointly, may set up a travel concession scheme for use on public passenger transport services. Under s.93(7) of the Act, travel concessions cover men aged sixty-five or over and women aged sixty or over. The linking of concessions to pensionable age may well be challengeable under sex discrimination legislation. In one case, *James v. Eastleigh (1990)*, the court held that the council had unlawfully discriminated against Mr Jones because he had to pay more to go swimming than a woman of comparable age. Concessions can also apply to a companion travelling with an eligible person whose disability prevents him/her from using public transport without assistance. The power to provide free or subsidised travel under s.29 of the NAA 1948 does not apply to elderly people because, as a group, they are included in the terms of the Transport Acts and are therefore ineligible under s.29 (see paras. 3.8.1 to 3.8.5 below).

3.7.2 Local authorities have complete discretion whether or not to provide a concessionary scheme and what concessions to make. Some offer free travel throughout the day or restricted to certain times of day; others provide a percentage reduction in fares. Local authorities also vary in how the concessions are provided, for example, they may issue travel passes, or vouchers, or tokens. The absence of a mandatory scheme nationwide has led to considerable variation in what is available. According to the Department of Transport Circular 2/78, 25 per cent of expenditure on concessionary travel was concentrated on 10 per cent of elderly people and another 10 per cent lived in areas where there were no concessions at all.

3.7.3 According to Department of Transport Explanatory Notes on the provisions of the TA 1985 (Ref. P5V359), the concessions can apply across all forms of public transport, including taxis, ferries and rail services, and any other service specially designed to meet the needs of elderly or disabled people. Section 97(2) of the TA 1985 added to authority powers by enabling them to oblige operators of eligible transport schemes to make travel concessions. Under the Travel Concession Schemes Regulations 1986, operators participating in such schemes must inform the local authority of any change in fares, either when it takes place or not more than seven days later.

3.8.1 ELDERLY PEOPLE WITH DISABILITIES

In addition to the legislation which relates to the welfare of elderly people in general, provision enacted since 1948 places duties on authorities or gives them powers to assist people who are disabled or suffering from serious ill health. Anyone to whom s.29 of the NAA 1948 applies comes within the terms of the legislation affecting disabled people, regardless of their age.

3.8.2 Section 29(1) of the NAA 1948 provides that:

> A local authority may with the approval of the Secretary of State, and to such extent as he may direct in relation to persons ordinarily resident in the area of the local authority, shall make arrangements for promoting the welfare of persons to whom this section applies, that is to say, persons aged eighteen or over who are blind, deaf or dumb, or who suffer from mental disorder of any description and other persons aged eighteen or over who are substantially and permanently handicapped by illness, injury or congenital disorder or such other disability as may be prescribed by the Minister.

A social services authority only has the power to make arrangements for individuals 'ordinarily resident' in the area or if the authority in which the individual resides has agreed to the arrangement. 'Ordinarily resident' is not defined in the legislation, but it had become such a contentious issue by 1993 that the Department of Health was moved to issue a circular on the subject. DH Circular LAC (93)7 advises that it is the responsibility of each authority to make a decision and that the term should be given 'its ordinary and normal meaning'. The Circular also makes it clear that the provision of services for individuals should not be delayed because of uncertainty about which authority is responsible.

Each case should be considered looking at the length of time spent in the area, the continuity of residence and the person's intention. The little case law that has been reported does not relate to elderly people. However, in *Shah v. London Borough of Barnet (1983)*, Lord Denning suggested that ordinary residence was something that we adopt voluntarily and for settled purposes whether for a short or long duration (see also Chapter 5 at para. 5.2.1). The majority of elderly disabled people seeking help from their social services authority will have been resident in the area for some time, but there are some for whom residence will be an issue. One of the more common scenarios is where an elderly person has gone to stay with a relative and subsequently needs help because of the onset of serious disability. In such cases, particularly if their need for services arises shortly after their arrival, the authority may argue that the elderly person is ordinarily resident where they came from. The authority could also assume that the person had only come to stay in the area to take advantage of its better facilities. Where someone moves from one local authority area to another, the local authorities are expected to sort out the matter and decide between them where ordinary residence lies. The Secretary of State is responsible, under s.32(3) of the NAA 1948, as a last resort, for resolving disputes between authorities. The position may be even more complicated if the elderly person has come from another country and is now unfit or unwilling to return.

3.8.3 DHSS Circular 13/74 extended the definition of 'substantially and permanently handicapped' to cover people who are partially sighted or hard of hearing. The effect of the MHA 1983 similarly brought people suffering from 'mental disorder' within the ambit of s.29. The scope of s.29 is now quite broadly drawn but, according to para. 16 of DHSS Circular 45/71, does not extend to individuals whose condition is moderate, minor or likely to be temporary.

3.8.4 Social services authorities can provide a range of services to anyone to whom s.29(1) applies. They can provide holiday homes; free or subsidised travel for those who do not qualify for other travel concessions (see para. 3.7.1); and assist individuals to find accommodation, if this is needed to promote their welfare. Section 29 also gives them similar powers to make arrangements and provide services similar to those relating to elderly people under s.45 of the HSPHA 1968. (see paras. 3.3.1 to 3.3.3 above)

Although much of the provision under s.29 is largely discretionary, the CSDPA 1970 and the DP(SCR)A 1986 extend the duties placed on authorities towards people to whom s.29(1) applies (see paras. 3.9.1 to 3.10.2 below).

In addition, social services authorities are now required to provide certain services to everyone to whom s.29(1) applies as the result of the Secretary of State's approvals and directions under s.29(1) of the NAA 1948, published as Appendix 2 of DH Circular LAC (93)10. These are a social work service and advice and support to people in their own homes. They must also provide, in accordance with para. 3(1) of Sched. 8 of the NHSA 1977, facilities, in centres or elsewhere, for social rehabilitation and adjustment to disability, including help to overcome mobility or communication problems and social, occupational, cultural and recreational activities, including payments for work undertaken as part of these activities. Services provided under s.29 are 'community care services' within the meaning of s.47 of the NHSCCA 1990 and the assessment procedures must be followed (see para. 3.2.1 above).

3.8.5 Authorities must also compile and maintain a register of everyone ordinarily resident in the area to whom s.29(1) applies. The form and content of the register is left to authority discretion although authorities are advised in DH Circular LAC (93)10 to include individuals who 'at some future date may be in need of services' as well as those currently getting services. It is also suggested that it would be helpful to have different sections for each category of person registered. This Circular also stresses that whether or not an individual is registered is irrelevant in determining whether they are eligible for assistance under s.29. For example, some people specifically ask not to be recorded on any registers and assistance should not be withheld for this reason.

3.9.1 EXTENDED DUTIES TO ASSESS AND MEET NEED

The duties and powers to make arrangements under s.29 of the NAA 1948 were extended by the CSDPA 1970. The provisions of the 1970 Act must therefore be read in conjunction with s.29.

Section 1 of the 1970 Act requires local authorities: to inform themselves of the number of people in their area to whom s.29(1) applies and the extent of their need for services; to publish information about the services available; and to inform any user of such services about any other services which may be relevant to the user's needs. These requirements are separate from those relating to registers under s.29 (see para. 3.8.5) and are intended to improve the availability of accurate information from which to plan services.

3.9.2 Section 2(1) of the CSDPA 1970 places a statutory obligation on social services authorities to assess individual need and provide one or more of a range of specified services to meet that need. It also requires an authority to make arrangements which are necessary to meet an individual's needs for all or any of the following:

(a) the provision of practical assistance in the home;
(b) the provision ... of or assistance to that person in obtaining a wireless, television, library or similar recreational facilities;
(c) the provision ... of lectures, games, outings or other recreational facilities outside the home or assistance ... in taking advantage of educational facilities available to him [*sic*];
(d) the provision ... of facilities for, or assistance in, travelling to and from his home for the purposes of participating in any services provided under ... s.29, or with the approval of the

authority, in any services . . . which are similar;

(e) the provision of assistance . . . in arranging for the carrying out of any works of adaptation in his home or the provision of any additional facilities designed to secure his greater safety, comfort or convenience;

(f) facilitating the taking of holidays . . . whether at holiday homes or otherwise and whether provided under arrangements made by the authority or otherwise;

(g) the provision of meals . . . whether in his home or elsewhere;

(h) the provision . . . of or assistance . . . in obtaining a telephone and any special equipment necessary to enable him to use a telephone.

3.9.3 The range of services specified under s.2 are similar to those which can be provided to elderly people under s.45 of the HSPHA 1968, but unlike the 1968 Act, s.2 imposes a duty on an authority to act once it is satisfied that 'it is necessary in order to meet the needs of that person'. So, for example, the authority, having assessed the need for a home help, will have a duty to supply one to an elderly person to whom s.29 of the NAA 1948 applies. In the case of practical assistance in the home (CSDPA 1970 s.2(1)(a)) and meals (s.2(1)(g)), the authority must provide the service. For the other provision, the authority can decide whether to provide the service or simply assist the individual to obtain it. For example, some authorities tend to provide a fixed annual sum towards the costs of telephone rental. In all cases, the authority must satisfy itself that the level of assistance offered is adequate to meet the assessed need of the particular individual.

3.9.4 Once the individual's need for welfare services specified in s.2 of the CSDPA 1970 has been established, the authority must make necessary arrangements to meet it (DH 1990). The decision on what to provide cannot be fettered by the availability of finance (SSI 1992). On the other hand, the authority is expected to keep total expenditure on such services within the council's budgetary requirements for the year. The emphasis in s.2 on the authority's overriding duties towards individuals who are in need creates an inevitable tension with the requirement not to overspend and to have a proper and reasonable basis for setting priorities between those to whom s.2 might apply.

Authorities are only able to mediate between these conflicts, because s.2 leaves it to them to define when a particular service is needed. Most authorities have done this by developing criteria for defining 'need' and what services are available to meet these needs.

For example, authorities increasingly restrict assistance with telephone to people who live alone and have conditions where they may need to summon emergency help. Most of the case law relating to the 1970 Act relates to the extent to which such set criteria and blanket procedures conflict with an authority's duty to assess and meet the needs of a particular individual.

3.9.5 Once the authority identifies the need for one of the services under s.2, it must meet the need within a reasonable period. So it would not be unlawful *per se* to have a waiting list. The test would be whether this led to unreasonable or excessive delays in each individual case (Ombudsman investigations, Complaints Nos. 89/C/ 114, 91/C/0729 and 91/C/2038). An authority should, in each individual case, satisfy itself that a service user does not have a continuing need for that or an alternative service, before deciding to withdraw or reduce provision. Social services authorities which take blanket decisions to change their criteria of need or level of assistance will be vulnerable to legal challenges unless they have reassessed each current service user and satisfied themselves that the new policy would not be a breach of their duties towards that person under s.2.

3.9.6 It has also been held to be unlawful for an authority to decide not to provide assistance under one or other of the categories listed in s.2. The London Borough of Greenwich was held to have acted unlawfully in deciding to withdraw all assistance towards holidays, the argument being that each authority is required to be able to meet any of the items listed in s.2(1)(a)–(h) in each individual case.

3.9.7 When requested to do so by a disabled person or the person who cares for them, an authority must, under s.4 of the DP(SCR)A 1986, decide whether the person's needs require the provision of any service in accordance with s.2 of the CSDPA 1970.

The provisions of s.47 of the NHSCCA 1990 are also complementary to the CSDPA 1970 and the DP(SCR)A 1986. Anyone to whom s.29 of the NAA 1948 applies should be assessed as though they had made a request under s.4 of the DP(SCR)A 1986. The results of any assessment under the 1990 Act are then subject to the terms of s.2. So, if the assessment determines that a particular service is necessary to meet the person's needs, the authority must provide it if it is one of the services listed in s.2.

3.10.1 ADDITIONAL RIGHTS FOR PEOPLE WITH DISABILITIES

The DP(SCR)A 1986 was a private member's bill which had tacit government support and therefore got on to the statute book. The number of sections which still have not been implemented almost ten years later is a testament to the government's real commitment towards these issues.

The aim of the Act was to strengthen disabled people's right to have a say in the provision of services and to clarify the social services authority's obligations to assess their needs. The most significant provisions in this respect are to be found in ss.1, 2 and 3 of the DP(SCR)A 1986. After much prevarication, the Minister for Health finally announced, in a parliamentary answer in the House of Commons on 22 March 1991, that these sections would not be implemented.

3.10.2 Section 4 of the Act gives disabled people the right to seek assessment for services which the authority has a duty to provide under s.2 of the CSDPA 1970 (see paras. 3.9.1 to 3.9.7 above). Section 8 of the 1986 Act also requires that a carer's ability to provide support is taken into account in the assessment. The other sections of the DP(SCR)A 1986 which have been implemented relate to disabled students or are largely procedural.

3.11.1 EQUIPMENT AND APPLIANCES

Social services authorities have a duty to provide 'practical assistance' in the home under s.2 of the CSDPA 1970 (see paras. 3.9.1 to 3.9.7 above). One way to meet this responsibility is through the provision of equipment, such as handrails, bath seats or the installation of lifting equipment such as stairlifts or monkey poles. Some people will need equipment which cannot be installed without structural alterations or they may need to have major adaptations to their home such as ramps or doors widened. In these cases, both housing and social services authorities have some responsibilities (see paras. 3.12.1 to 3.12.4 below).

Many elderly people are very dissatisfied with the limited range of equipment which their authority offers and which is often unsuitable for their needs. The growth of regional centres which display a range of equipment designed to help with disabled living has made it easier for people to find out what would be best for them. In addition, users' rights to complain and get what they really need have been strengthened by the NHSCCA 1990. First, s.47 of the 1990 Act requires that the assessment is 'needs led' and not restricted to those items of equipment which the authority normally provides. Secondly, anyone who is dissatisfied with the assessment or with the equipment when it arrives has a right to make a formal complaint (see paras. 3.17.1 to 3.17.2 below).

3.11.2 The NHS also has some responsibilities for providing equipment and appliances, where such items are needed to meet 'health' rather than 'social' care needs. The White Paper *Caring for People* (DH 1989d) conceded that the distinction between the two can be blurred and recommended that 'health and local authorities will have to decide locally about how they share . . . responsibilities . . . for different services' (para. 6.6). In practice, this has resulted in much debate locally about, for example, when a bath is needed for social rather than health reasons. An added pressure in establishing boundaries is that equipment from the health service must be provided free of charge, whereas social services can choose whether to make a charge. The extent to which health and social services authorities have drawn up jointly-agreed procedures for clarifying who does what vary enormously in different parts of the country. In some areas, very little progress has been made; in others joint activity is very well developed, for example, there are some joint equipment stores.

Health authorities, including NHS Trusts, have responsibility for supplying such nursing equipment as incontinence pads, commodes and special beds. Some appliances are also available on prescription from general practitioners (GPs) or hospital. GPs can only prescribe items on the approved drugs list, which includes catheters, trusses and support hosiery. Hospital doctors can prescribe a wider range including surgical footwear, hearing aids and low vision aids. Wheelchairs (including a limited range of powered wheelchairs) are also provided and maintained by the Health Service. According to DHSS Circular LASSL 20/73 (June 1974), NHS and social services authorities have joint responsibilities for the supply and maintenance of environmental control systems, such as POSSUM which control electrical equipment for people with very limited movement.

3.12.1 ADAPTATIONS AND EXTENSIONS

Adaptations involve structural work being done to the home. This may be in order to install equipment or to meet the needs of a disabled person in some other way, for example, widening doors or installing a downstairs bathroom. Housing authorities and social services authorities have some joint responsibilities for these kind of alterations and are required to collaborate.

3.12.2 Whether the elderly person approaches the social services authority or the housing authority first, each is required to involve the other in the assessment of need. If a social services authority is undertaking an assessment under s.47 of the NHSCCA 1990, it must ask the local housing authority to assist in the assessment if it seems the person may need 'services which fall within the functions of a local housing authority (within the meaning of the Housing Act 1985) (and NHSCCA 1990, s.47(3)). The housing authority must consult with the social services department when making decisions on disabled facilities grants.

3.12.3 Grants towards structural work are available from local housing authorities under the Local Government and Housing Act 1989 (LGHA 1989). A disabled, elderly person to whom s.29 of the NAA 1948 applies (see paras. 3.8.1 to 3.8.5 above) may be eligible for both a renovation grant and a disabled facilities grant. (Information on who can apply for a renovation grant is to be found in Chapter 2 at para. 2.8.3.) Owner occupiers and tenants who are responsible for the repairs to their home can apply for a disabled facilities grant. The applicant must show that they are living in or intend to move into the dwelling and that it will be their main home. In the case of owner occupiers, this must be for at least twelve months. Eligibility depends on the applicant showing that the work is necessary and appropriate to meet the needs of a disabled person who lives there. Section 114(1) of the LGHA 1989 requires the housing authority to consult with the local social services authority before making a decision on this question.

Disabled facilities grants are mandatory for the items listed in Chapter 2; these include anything which 'facilitates access' either into the building or around the home. Discretionary grants are also available. Even where the grant is mandatory, the amount awarded will depend on the applicant's income and capital. Housing authorities are required to undertake a financial assessment of means which is very similar to that for income support (IS) (see Chapter 1 at para. 1.31.1). This can often result in applicants getting a grant which only covers part of the costs of the work. Many applicants cannot then afford to go ahead with the work.

3.12.4 Social services authorities have a duty under s.2(e) of the CSDPA 1970 to provide assistance 'in arranging for the carrying out of works of adaptation ... or additional facilities'. An authority could argue that it has fulfilled this duty by helping the person apply for a disabled facilities grant from the housing authority and by informing that authority that the work is necessary and appropriate. However, if an applicant fails to qualify for a disabled facilities grant or the grant is not enough to meet the costs of the alterations, the social services authority has an underlying responsibility. If a council is satisfied that the works are needed,

> they should ensure that the need is met within a reasonable time. Fulfilment of the duty to assist is not dependent on the availability of grant aid; where grant aid is not available, the responsibility of the Social Services authority remains and they should examine alternative means of provision with the applicant.
>
> (Ombudsman's investigation Complaint No. 91/C/0729)

Some authorities are seeking to avoid this responsibility by applying the same assessment of means as that used by the housing authority. This results in the amount of financial help available from social services being no higher than that from the grant. There appears to have been no case law on this practice to date, but it is arguable that an authority which refused assistance on these grounds would be in breach of its obligations under s.2.

3.13.1 MOBILITY NEEDS

The orange badge scheme introduced under s.21 of the CSDPA 1970 requires authorities to issue badges which provide some parking concessions when displayed in a vehicle used by disabled people with severe mobility difficulties. The Disabled Persons (Badges for Motor Vehicles) Regulations 1982 govern the issue of orange badges, specifying who is eligible, and the other conditions for use. The scheme only covers five categories of people, namely: recipients of either a mobility supplement paid with a war pension or the higher rate mobility component of the DLA; people who use a government-supplied vehicle or receive a grant towards the costs of using their own vehicle; someone who is registered blind; someone with a permanent and substantial disability which makes them unable to walk or causes very considerable difficulty in walking; or someone who drives regularly and has a severe disability in both arms which leaves them unable to turn the steering wheel by hand even if fitted with a turning knob. Parking concessions apply when the badge is correctly displayed in the vehicle and a person who comes into one of the above categories is either the driver or a passenger at the time (Department of Transport Circular No. 3/91). The scheme applies throughout England and Wales, although there are some local variations in addition to the national scheme. Orange badge holders travelling abroad may also be able to take advantage of concessions offered by the host country. Details of such concessions are available from the Department of Transport.

3.13.2 Authorities may charge a small fee for issuing the badge. Under the Disabled Persons (Badges for Motor Vehicles) Regulations, 1982, the maximum sum is currently £2. Authorities have only four grounds for refusing to issue a badge. These are if the applicant fails to pay the fee; where there is evidence that there was misuse of a previous badge (serious enough to have led to a conviction or which could have justified a conviction) on at least three occasions; the applicant does not provide enough information to show they meet one of the definitions of disability; or the authority does not believe the person is who he [*sic*] claims to be or believes the applicant would let someone else use the badge. Applicants have no rights of appeal against most decisions regarding orange badges. However, if a badge has been withdrawn or refused on grounds of misuse, they can then appeal to the Secretary of State. Wrongful use of a badge is an offence, giving rise on conviction to a maximum fine of £200.

3.13.3 Although stricter criteria of eligibility were introduced with the 1982 Regulations, there has been a substantial increase in the number of badges issued.

3.13.4 Exemption from Vehicle Excise Duty (road tax) is currently available for three categories of disabled people: anyone who has a government-supplied vehicle; a vehicle used solely by or for a recipient of the higher rate mobility component of the DLA or the war pension mobility supplement; and vehicles where a passenger receives AA. This last category was due to be abolished in 1993. The legislation has been held up for technical reasons. When the change occurs existing beneficiaries will be protected and continue to get exemptions under the old rules. Claimants of any of the qualifying benefits have to apply to the Department of Social Security for an exemption certificate before they can apply to the Vehicle Licensing Centre for an exemption. However, the final decision rests with the Vehicle Licensing Centre. There are no rights of appeal against decisions.

3.14.1 CHARGING FOR SOCIAL SERVICES

The statutes described in this chapter, under which social services authorities provide non-residential services, also empower them to charge for those services, if they wish to do so. Authorities cannot charge for assessments or for giving information and advice. In addition, authorities are required to charge for accommodation provided under Part III of the NAA 1948 (see Chapter 4 at para. 4.6.1).

3.14.2 While charges for non-residential services are at the discretion of each authority, the Department of Health has now made it known in its latest guidance (LAC (94)1) that the annual revenue support grant paid to local authorities is calculated on the assumption that they do make charges. It is assumed that nationally 9 per cent of the costs of domiciliary care for the elderly comes from charges. This provides a considerable financial incentive to increase or introduce charges. In practice, the financial pressures on authorities led more authorities in the 1990s to introduce charges or increase existing ones. Charges have generally risen at a level well above inflation. More than two-thirds of all local authorities in England and Wales were charging for respite care, home care, day centre attendance and meals on wheels by 1991.

3.14.3 Any charge for a non-residential service must be 'reasonable' (within the meaning of s.17 of the HSSSSAA 1983). The Department of Health, after more than two years of prevarication, finally decided not to issue detailed guidance for local authorities on charging policies. The rationale appears to have been that as s.17 places the responsibility with each authority, it would be inappropriate for that discretion to be fettered by DH guidance. Instead, in January 1994, an 'advice note' from the Social Services Inspectorate (SSI) was circulated by the Department of Health (SSI 1994). This advice has no formal weight, as it is not guidance, but is helpful in outlining the Department's views on some of the more problematic aspects of s.17.

There appear to be two separate tests of reasonableness within s.17. First, subsection (1) permits them to recover 'such charge (if any) for it as they consider reasonable'. The SSI advice suggests that social services authorities should take account of how much it costs to provide the service and the income profiles of service users as a group in deciding what is a reasonable charge. Authorities cannot charge more for the service than it costs to provide overall, but they can charge different rates for the same level of service if this reflects what they are being charged by different providers. For example, they could charge £2 for attendance at the council's day centre and £3 for the day centre run by a local voluntary group, if the latter costs more, but 'the authority should be able to explain to the service users the reason for this' (para. 6 of the SSI advice).

3.14.4 The second test of reasonableness relates to individual service users. Where an individual who 'avails himself [*sic*] of a service' satisfies the authority that he cannot afford the charge, 'the local authority shall not require him to pay more for it than it appears to them that it is reasonably practicable for him to pay' (HSSSSAA 1983 s.17(3)). So even if the authority has a charge based on a means-test, or has set a very low charge for the service, taking account of the ability to pay of service users as a group, they must still be able to assess under s.17(3) whether that charge is 'reasonably practicable' for a particular individual and, if not, be prepared to waive or reduce it further. Recent Ombudsman's inquiries suggest social services authorities will be vulnerable to legal challenges unless they have adequate systems in place to assess the impact of any changes in charges on existing users. In Greenwich, the Inquiry was discontinued as the Ombudsman found that the authority had 'taken all reasonable steps ... to ensure that the individual clients mentioned in this complaint had their cases thoroughly re-examined' (See Complaint No. 91(A) 3782).

3.14.5 Some authorities have fixed income thresholds from which to determine whether to waive charges. The Ombudsman's investigation into complaints against Essex County Council was dissatisfied with the way such thresholds operated there. Clients who could show they had a £10 excess of expenses over income had their charges waived. The Ombudsman criticised this approach on the grounds that 'this threshold was quite arbitrary and the council have been unable to justify how the figure was arrived at'. The conclusions went on to make the point that the closer a client's income was to the threshold, the higher their chance of having the fees waived, 'it was therefore crucial that such a financial criterion be well thought out'. (para. 63 of the Report by the Local Government Ombudsman into Complaints No. 90/A/2675 and others against Essex County Council 10 October 1991).

3.14.6   The wording of s.17(3) of the HSSSSAA 1983 raises questions regarding what duty an authority might have to service users who do not seek a review of the charge under this provision. The SSI Advice quoted earlier deals only with the authority's duty once the user has asked for help, but in many cases it would be reasonable to assume that an authority had enough information to have known that a user had a very low income or was in financial difficulties. Could an authority be held to be in breach of s.17(3) if it did not take steps to act at this point rather than waiting for the individual to ask for a review? Case law to date does not shed much light on this question. These cases, by definition, deal with duties towards individuals who have sought reviews under s.17(3). However, the general tone of High Court judgments and Ombudsman Reports imposes a very rigorous approach on authorities to ensure users are able to afford the set charges. Authorities have been particularly scrutinised regarding the steps taken to identify the likely impact on an individual user of a particular change in charges. (See para. 3.14.4 re. London Borough of Greenwich.) Whether this could be taken as an expectation that authorities should take such action in respect of the generality of users or solely when an individual complains, is open to interpretation. However, the SSI Advice note suggests that as a matter of good practice, authorities are required to consult users when any change in charges is under consideration (para. 30). The power to charge only applies to the person who is receiving the service. 'Authorities should have regard only to that individual's means in assessing ability to pay' (para. 18 of SSI Advice). No other member of the service user's family or their carer can be asked to pay the charge, nor can their income or capital be taken into account.

3.14.7   The power to charge is wholly separate from the authority's duty to provide assistance or a service. Where an authority has such a duty, for example, under s.2 of the CSDPA 1970 (see paras. 3.9.1 to 3.9.7 above), it cannot refuse to provide or withdraw the service if the user is not prepared or fails to pay the assessed charge. The authority has, of course, the same rights as any other creditor to pursue the debt through the county court. In practice, few authorities have chosen to do so in the past.

3.15.1 CARERS

The White Paper *Caring for People* (DH 1989d) acknowledged that 'the reality is that most care is provided by family, friends and neighbours'. It is estimated that around six million people provide some kind of support to others who have care needs; around 1.5 million of them providing more than twenty hours per week. Over a quarter of these carers are themselves elderly and many reported that they themselves had long-standing illness or disability (Green 1988). The fact that carers got a mention in the White Paper shows how much more aware we are of the numbers providing this kind of 'informal care', as well as the financial and personal costs of caring, than in the mid-1980s when a Family Policy Studies Centre report aptly described them as 'the forgotten army'.

3.15.2 Greater awareness of the importance of informal carers has been reflected in legislative changes since the mid-1980s. Carers are now required to be more involved in the planning and assessment of services for the disabled person they care for. A carer can request an assessment of the person's needs under s.4 of the DP(SCR)A 1986. An authority must under s.8 of that Act take into account whether the carer is able to continue to provide a substantial level of care on a regular basis, when deciding what services are needed. Section 46 of the NHSCCA 1990 requires authorities to consult with 'voluntary organisations as appear . . . to represent the interest of persons who use or are likely to use any community care services.' Policy Guidance (DH 1990) at para. 2.7 specifies that this includes organisations representing carers.

3.15.3 While authorities have been required to involve carers in assessments of the person being cared for, a carer's own needs and rights to services (separate from those of the person they care for) have not been strengthened or clarified in the new legislation. Most importantly, carers' access to assessment for their own needs under s.47 of the NHSCCA 1990 is ambiguous unless they are themselves elderly, disabled or chronically sick. During the Parliamentary Debates on the Act, Ministers repeatedly refused to accept amendments that would have clarified carers' access to assessment and services in their own right. Ministers argued that it was unnecessary to write carers into the legislation because the guidance would make it clear that authorities should assess carers' own needs. It certainly is the case that the Department of Health's policy guidance states that 'carers who feel they need community care services in their own right can ask for a separate assessment. This could arise if the care plan of the person for home they care does not, in their view, adequately address the carer's own needs' (DH 1990). As this guidance is issued under s.7A of the Local Social Services Authority Act 1970 (LASSA 1970), it could be argued that it carries some legal standing, but it remains questionable whether the courts would accept that carers under pension age would have grounds or locus to bring a legal action against an authority which refused to assess their needs for services.

3.15.4 Informal carers' rights to claim invalid care allowance and extra premiums with means-tested benefits are dealt with in Chapter 1 at para. 1.30.1.

3.16.1 CONTRACTING AND THE INDEPENDENT SECTOR

One of the cornerstones of the government's community care reforms was to 'promote a mixed economy of care'. In para. 1.11 of *Caring for People*, the government 'endorsed Sir Roy Griffiths' recommendations that social services authorities should be "enabling" agencies. It will be their responsibility to make maximum possible use of private and voluntary providers, and so increase the available range of options and widen consumer choice' (DH 1989d).

In the event, the government stopped short of imposing a compulsory competitive tendering regime on social services. Instead, they have relied on various exhortations and financial incentives to encourage or coerce authorities to make more use of contracting and independent sector providers of non-residential services.

This emphasis on the contract culture has also encouraged some authorities to move away from providing grant aid to voluntary organisations and instead offer them contracts for services. It is at present unclear the extent to which the EC Directive 92/50/EEC, known as the 'Services Directive', which was adopted in June 1992, may affect how social services authorities can fund or contract with organisations to provide services.

3.16.2 The government's stated objectives link improvements in consumers' choices to the promotion of a flourishing independent sector and contracting. In practice, the evidence to date suggests that the one does not necessarily flow from the other. Common and Flynn's study of twelve social services departments found that in ten of these authorities contracting had done nothing to increase choice (Common and Flynn 1992).

3.16.3 There are now far more independent agencies providing domiciliary and day services than ten years ago but, unlike the residential market, the growth of such services has been very slow. No reliable figures exist to show either the growth or distribution of services provided through voluntary or private agencies. Many of the agencies that do exist do not employ the carers, but simply act as an introduction service putting the carer in touch with someone who needs domiciliary help. Most private domiciliary help is provided by individuals who are employed directly by the person they help. Twice as many retired people rely on this kind of service than on a home care worker provided through their authority (Leat 1993).

3.16.4 Unlike the residential and nursing home sectors, private and voluntary providers and agencies are not required to register and are unaccountable for their quality of service or the trustworthiness of the carers. No checks are required regarding the criminal records of employees or carers introduced to prospective employers by agencies. The Joint Advisory Group of Private Domiciliary Care Associations has produced their own guidelines for the registration of agencies and providers. Some authorities are developing voluntary registration criteria and procedures, but the Secretary of State for Health is on record as opposing the introduction of any statutory registration requirements.

Clearly, where authorities are contracting with individual agencies, they can specify standards which have to be met and the Policy Guidance requires them to develop service specifications and ensure that systems are in place to ensure quality standards are met. Where services are provided under contract from the authority, therefore, there ought to be some controls over standards and quality. In practice, it is always difficult to know what is going on when services are provided in the home of the person needing care, but there are no safeguards at all for elderly people purchasing such services directly, regarding the quality or the trustworthiness of the carer who will come to their home. The expansion of unregulated domiciliary services therefore remains a worrying development given that they are provided to some of the most vulnerable and isolated members of our communities in the privacy of their own homes.

3.17.1 COMPLAINTS

Social services authorities were required under the provision of the Local Authority Social Services (Complaints Procedure) Order 1990 to have complaints procedures and arrangements for their publicity in place by 1 April 1991. Details of the procedures to be adopted

were set out in the Secretary of State's Complaints Procedure
Directions 1990 appended to the 1990 Policy Guidance.

> The intention of the Act is to allow access to a statutory procedure
> to anyone who is likely to want to make representations, including
> complaints about the actions, decisions or apparent failings of
> an SSD; and to allow any other person to act on behalf of the
> individual concerned.
>
> (DH 1990)

An authority does not have to deal with a complaint from someone
for whom it has no power or duty to provide a 'community care' service
(see para. 3.2.1 above). 'Complaints of a general nature which are not
concerned with an individual case are also likely to fall outside the
statutory definition' (DH 1990).

3.17.2 Once an authority receives a complaint, it must seek to resolve
it informally. If the complainant is still dissatisfied, the authority must
give or send them an explanation of the complaints procedures and
invite the complainant to make written representation on the issue.
The authority must also offer to advise or assist the person on how to
use the procedures or where to get independent advice.

Once the authority receives a written complaint, the directions
set out a clear timetable and procedures that must be followed. First,
the authority must consider the written representation and 'formulate
a response' within twenty-eight days. If this is not possible, the
authority must explain within this period to the complainant why it
cannot do so and when they can expect a response, which must be
within three months of the written complaint (para. 6 of the Direction).

The authority must give the complainant their response in writing.
Where the complaint was made on behalf of someone else, they must
also be informed in writing. The complainant then has twenty-eight
days in which to notify the authority in writing that they are still
dissatisfied and want the matter referred to a review panel. The panel
must meet within twenty-eight days of receiving the notification and
consider any written or oral submissions (para. 7). The panel must
make recommendations and record them in writing within twenty-
four hours of the end of the meeting. Written copies are then to be
sent to the authority, the complainant and anyone else with sufficient
interest in the matter. The authority must consider what action
to take in the light of the panel's recommendations and must write to
all the relevant people within twenty-eight days of the date of
the panel's recommendations giving their decisions, the reasons for

those decisions and any action they have taken or propose to take. The next section describes the courses of action that remain open to a complainant who is still dissatisfied.

13.7.3 The Ombudsman's investigation into complaints regarding appeals against home care charges already cited at para. 3.14.5 above provided some useful principles for the conduct of appeals in general. These included: that the information available to those hearing the appeal should be accurate and sufficient to allow them to reach a proper decision; the decisions taken should be as consistent as possible; and that those appealing should be aware of any rights to challenge the outcome. 'Finally it should be possible to give clear reasons as to why an appeal has been lost in order that the appellant can judge whether or not to pursue the matter further' (para. 61).

3.18.1 COMPLAINTS TO THE LOCAL GOVERNMENT OMBUDSMAN

It is the responsibility of the Parliamentary Commissioner for Local Administration, known as the Local Government Ombudsman, to investigate complaints of maladministration against local authorities. The Commissioners are appointed by government, but the Office of the Commissioner is an independent body which therefore acts as a watchdog over how authorities carry out their functions. The Ombudsman will investigate complaints where there appears to have been an injustice caused by maladministration on the part of the council. Neither 'injustice' nor 'maladministration' are precisely defined. However, injustice would cover mental distress or outrage as well as material or other tangible loss or damage. The term 'maladministration' limits the scope of the Ombudsman's investigation into how an authority has conducted itself or undertaken its functions. The Ombudsman's findings will not deal with whether a particular decision was right or wrong, but will consider how it was reached and whether the process complied with any legislative requirements imposed on the authority. The kind of issues that may justify the intervention of the Ombudsman would be delays in reassessing a resident when his/her needs change, or the lack of a clear explanation about what he/she is being charged, or any change in the charges.

3.18.2 Individuals can now make complaints direct to the Ombudsman, whereas in the past complaints had to be made through one of their councillors. Where someone is dissatisfied with how an authority has acted or failed to act, they should try to sort the matter out directly with the authority before applying to the Ombudsman. The Ombudsman would not usually investigate the matter until the person had exhausted their rights of complaint (see paras. 3.17.1 to 3.17.2 above). This is because s.26(5) of the Local Government Act 1974 (LGA 1974) provides that:

> Before proceeding to investigate a complaint, [an ombudsman] shall satisfy himself that the complaint has been brought . . . to the notice of the authority . . . and that the authority has been afforded a reasonable opportunity to investigate, and to reply, to the complainant.

In a letter in the Legal Action Group Bulletin in November 1993, Gordon Adams, Secretary to the Commission gave examples of when a complaint which had not been through the statutory complaints procedure might be investigated:

> if the procedure is taking too long, or if the complainant was not directed to the statutory procedure, when it was clear for some time that he/she wished to make a formal complaint, the ombudsman may well feel that the council has had a reasonable opportunity and so proceed to consider the complaint.

3.19.1 LEGAL REMEDIES

There are courses of action available to someone who is dissatisfied with a decision that has been made by a social services authority or with the way the authority has acted. The first is to take their complaint through the complaints procedure described in para. 3.17.1 above. If they remain dissatisfied and believe that the authority has failed to comply with any of its statutory duties, they can ask the Secretary of State for Health to intervene. Section 7(D) of the LASSA 1970 (inserted by s.50 of the NHSCCA 1990) empowers the Secretary of State to issue an order declaring the authority to be in default, if he/she is satisfied that the authority has failed, without reasonable excuse, to comply with any of their duties which are social services functions. This new default power replaces that originally contained in s.36 of the NAA 1948 and can be used where someone is, for example, unreasonably refused an assessment or if the authority fails to provide the appropriate service to meet assessed need. Applying to the Secretary of State in this way ought to be a faster way to achieve some redress than by pursuing a judicial review.

However, past experience suggests that applications can take many months to process and have rarely resulted in an entirely successful outcome (Cook and Mitchell 1982).

3.19.2 Judicial review is available to someone who believes the authority's decisions, procedures or actions to be unlawful, blatantly unreasonable or irrational. An application must be made to the High Court for leave to appeal. The courts only grant leave if they accept the appellant has '*locus standi*', which usually means that the person can show they are directly affected by the authority's actions or represent a group of people who would be, and that there are good grounds for the action. If an authority is shown to be in breach of its statutory duties, or to have acted unreasonably, the court can quash a decision (*certiorari*) and order it to be redetermined applying the law correctly (*mandamus*). Sometimes, the applicant's circumstances require urgent action, for example, the authority is about to withdraw services. In these cases, the courts can grant 'interim relief'. The purpose of interim relief is to maintain the status quo until the case is resolved. An order might therefore require the authority to maintain or restore the service which is the subject of the dispute. In addition, with the increasing reliance on actual or implied contracts between the authority, the user and the provider, there may be more grounds for dissatisfied service users suing the authority for breach of contract for the supply of services.

3.19.3 The case law on an authority's duty of care towards a user who is being provided with services by a third party is patchy and somewhat contradictory. There may therefore be grounds for a claim for damages where a service user has suffered physical or mental harm as a direct consequence of an action or omission by the service provider. However, the courts seem to have taken the view that no claims for damages arise from an authority's failure to meet its duties under s.2. of the CSDPA 1970. In the case of *Wyatt v. Hillingdon London Borough Council (1978)*, the Court of Appeal held that the 1970 Act 'which is dealing with the distribution of benefits ... to the sick and disabled ... does not in its very nature give rise to an action by the disappointed sick person ... and an action in damages is not appropriate'. The decision appeared to hinge on the fact that the person has another remedy available to them, namely to ask the Secretary of State to exercise the default powers as described in para. 3.9.1 above.

4 Residential and nursing care

Lynda Bransbury

4.1.1 A steadily growing number of people over sixty-five now live in residential establishments. However, only a very small percentage of the elderly population are cared for, or will need to be cared for, in such institutional settings. Survey evidence suggests there are 3.5 places in residential homes, and just over 1 place in nursing homes, for every hundred people aged sixty-five or over in the UK. About 124,000 of the 317,000 or so residential care beds are in local authority homes; the rest are in the private and voluntary sectors (Midwinter 1992). It would seem that only around one in ten of the retired population is likely to enter residential care at some stage in their lives, although this increases to one in five for those aged eighty-five or over.

However, while few elderly people make use of residential care, the majority of social services expenditure on services for the elderly is still spent on residential care (Audit Commission 1992). The pressures to maintain this expenditure seem set to continue for the rest of the century. The main cause of growing demand is the increasing numbers of very elderly people and, while this has slowed down, it is still predicted that there will be over a million people over eighty-five by the end of the century. In addition, more elderly people live alone; the pool of informal carers is shrinking as more women under sixty go into employment and elderly people are now discharged earlier after both acute medical and surgical treatment in hospitals (Audit Commission 1992). These practical pressures to maintain expenditure on residential placements within tight and cash-limited budgets sit uneasily against the strong commitment in the community care reforms that greater reliance be placed on funding domiciliary services to keep people at home.

4.1.2 It is too early to predict how the legislative changes which came into force on 1 April 1993 and the phased transfer of resources from the social security budget to social services departments (SSDs) will affect both demand and funding for residential and nursing home beds. Many private homes were already experiencing considerable financial difficulties before April 1993. While the private sector initially expanded because of the availability of social security benefits (see para. 4.2.1 below), there was plenty of evidence by 1991 (HC 1991) that many of the smaller homes were in financial difficulties. Homes were closing or facing bankruptcy, in many cases because of the gap between running costs and benefit payments. In some parts of the country a sizeable percentage of private homes have been going out of business each year in the 1990s. There is an expectation that this trend will have been accelerated by the reforms and that we shall see the numbers of private residential and particularly nursing home beds halted or reversed. Some commentators were predicting a 30 per cent reduction in nursing home beds in the first two years after the April 1993 reforms. In addition, there have been pressures on local authorities which led to a reduction in their own homes in many parts of the country before April 1993. The financing of residential care through benefits and special transitional grant continues to provide social services authorities with considerable incentives to divest themselves of their own provision. However, it is too early to see how the trends and conflicting pressures will shake out in the medium term or what they will mean for the balance between expenditure on residential and community services by the end of the century.

4.2.1 Prior to April 1993, there were two possibilities available to someone who needed some financial assistance with the costs of going into a residential home. They could approach their local social services department and ask the authority to help them by using its powers to provide accommodation under the National Assistance Act 1948 (NAA 1948). The authority would then decide whether the person needed residential care and, if so, whether to place them in one of its own homes or one run by a private or voluntary body. Alternatively, those with capital below a certain amount (£8,000 in 1992–3) could make independent arrangements to enter a private or voluntary home and then claim income support (IS) (a means-tested social security benefit) towards the fees. IS was also available to fund private nursing home beds. These people had no contact with their local social services authority, either before or after admission.

4.2.2 Throughout the 1980s, considerable anxieties were expressed from all quarters about some of the results from using social security benefits to finance private residential and nursing home care, the most important consideration being the rapid growth of homes owned by private companies and the resultant rise in social security expenditure. In the early 1980s, the Department of Health and Social Security (DHSS) (as it then was) sought different ways to curb this expenditure. This culminated in April 1985 by the replacement of locally set weekly limits with national limits set by Parliament each year. This meant that there was a maximum weekly amount which a resident anywhere in Great Britain could claim towards their fees, which depended on the type of care they received. For example, in 1992–3, the maximum amount of IS for a bed in a residential home for the elderly was £175 per week.

4.2.3 Together with the concern about escalating public expenditure, there was, by the late 1980s, considerable evidence of hardship to individual residents and homes in financial difficulties because of the fixed national limits. By February 1990, there were virtually no homes in the south of England charging at or below the IS limits. After several other bodies, including the House of Commons Select Committee on Health and Social Security, had drawn attention to the problems with admission to and financing of homes, Sir Roy Griffiths was given the job of coming up with a coherent solution. Sir Roy's report was very critical of having two routes for public subsidies towards the costs of fees. He argued that the two sources of funding – through benefits and social services budgets – should be unified and 'allocated on the basis of a proper judgement of each individual's needs' (Griffiths 1988). The government accepted this principle in the framework for community care set out by the 1989 White Paper *Caring for People*: 'that the provision of care at public expense should be preceded by a proper assessment of the individual's needs' (DH 1989d). The emphasis in both the White Paper and subsequent guidance, in line with Griffiths, has been to ensure that alternatives which could help the individual remain in the community are looked at first.

4.2.4 Griffith's other recommendation, which was finally accepted by the government, was to make social services authorities responsible for assessment of need and the funding of residential and nursing home beds at public expense. Residents who entered residential or nursing home care on or after 1 April 1993, can no longer claim IS towards their fees. Anyone in need of financial assistance with their fees now has to be assessed by their local social services authority (see para. 4.4.1 below). Once the authority agrees that there is a need for residential or nursing care, it becomes responsible for making the placement, funding it and collecting a contribution from the resident.

4.3.1 RESIDENTS IN INDEPENDENT HOMES BEFORE 1 APRIL 1993

There were 281,000 people living in registered care homes and nursing homes in February 1993 and claiming IS towards their fees; 233,000 of them were sixty or over. These residents were unaffected by the new regime for funding residential care from April 1993. They retain 'preserved rights' to IS and continue to claim the higher rate of IS towards their fees on the same basis that they did before April 1993.[1] They keep these 'preserved rights' if they need to move from one home to another. Preserved rights can only be lost if the resident is away from an independent residential or nursing home for more than thirteen weeks or after fifty-two weeks in hospital.[2] For example, a resident who leaves care, say for a trial period at home, will automatically requalify for the higher rate of IS if they need to return to a residential setting within thirteen weeks. Equally, a resident moved in an emergency from an independent home into a local authority home will requalify for preserved rights if they are then found a place in another independent sector home within thirteen weeks.

4.3.2 Some residents in independent sector homes on 31 March 1993 who were not getting IS on that date may be able to qualify for 'preserved rights' in the future. Anyone who was either self-financing or having their fees paid by someone else in April 1993 can claim 'preserved rights' to IS at any time in the future if their income and capital are low enough to qualify. For example, an elderly woman has been living in a private home since 1992. She has been paying part of the fees out of her savings and her son has been paying the balance. He has now retired and can no longer afford to make a contribution and her savings have gone down to £7,000. She will be entitled to the higher rate of IS towards the fees if her income is below the prescribed amount.

4.3.3 'Preserved rights' at least gave residents some transitional protection and stability in the funding of their fees, but these residents' level of IS remains pegged to the old national limits for the higher rate of IS. They therefore have no guarantees that their income will be sufficient to meet their fees. They have no security of tenure and may have to move if the gap widens between their income and their fees. A 1991 survey suggested that the average gap between

IS and fees out of London was around £54 per week. Evidence collected early in 1993 showed not only that many residents continued to face a considerable shortfall between their benefit and the fees, but that this gap was growing in many cases (LGIU 1993) Many of these residents are only able to stay where they are because of 'topping up payments' from charities, family or friends.

4.3.4 Section 26A of the National Health Service and Community Care Act 1990 (NHSCCA 1990) prevents social services authorities from providing financial assistance towards the costs of accommodation for the majority of elderly people who were already resident in a registered home on 31 March 1993. In effect, residents with preserved rights (see paras. 4.3.2 to 4.3.4 above) are excluded from any financial help. There are two exceptions. First, a resident who was getting topping up payments before they reached pension age can continue to receive help.[3] Second, elderly residents who have been evicted or served with a notice to quit from a residential care home or not allowed to return to the home they were living in after a period of temporary absence can be helped. In these cases, the authority can only 'make residential accommodation arrangements . . . in a home which is not owned or managed by the person or organisation which owns or manages the resident's current home, unless the whole home has been or is about to be closed down' (DH Circular LAC 93(6), para. 23). This provision means that the authority can only step in once an eviction notice has been served. It also means that if the authority decides to provide financial help, they must move the resident to another home. The resident will keep their preserved rights and the authority will meet the balance of the charge for the new placement. The authority does not have the power to leave them where they are even if it is clearly in the best interests of the resident. They must move them even if the only suitable alternative is in a home with much higher fees. The rationale behind this provision was concern that private home owners would start issuing eviction notices as a way of triggering topping up payments for their residents.

4.3.5 Regulation 8 of the Residential Accommodation (Relevant Premises, Ordinary Residence and Exemptions) Regulations 1993 prevents authorities from providing any financial assistance to residents over pensionable age in nursing homes. This applies even if they have been or are facing eviction. Although social services authorities have the power to make nursing home placements for anyone who needs care from 1 April 1993, they cannot do so for anyone who was already resident in a nursing home on that date.

Authorities in collaboration with health authorities will, however, be able to help all nursing home residents who face eviction or home closure with advice and guidance to help them to find alternative accommodation using their preserved rights and any other resources available to them. Residents ... retain their right of access to NHS services, and where the private care arrangements cannot continue, the NHS has a responsibility to assess the health needs of the residents, and to offer appropriate services within the resources available.

(DH Circular LAC(93)6, para. 28)

The implication of this guidance is that the health authority, not the social services authority, has an underlying responsibility for these residents.

4.4.1 ADMISSION AND CHOICE

Where it appears to a social services authority that an elderly person may be in need of residential or any other community care service, it should carry out an assessment under s.47 of the NHSCCA 1990. The basic principles and legal framework for assessment and decisions are described in Chapter 3 at para. 3.2.1, and any assessment for residential or nursing home care should meet the requirements set out there.

4.4.2 Once the authority has undertaken an assessment under s.47 and agreed that a need for residential or nursing care exists, Directions[4] issued by the Secretary of State are intended to ensure that the potential resident has some choice about which home they go into. In theory, therefore, an elderly person should be able to specify where they want to live within the UK (para. 2 of the Directions). For example, they may want to go to 'The Hollies' because they already have friends living there or to move to Wigan as it is near where their daughter lives.

In practice, the Directions limit the choices which potential residents can make. The 'preferred accommodation' must be suitable and available. It is for the authority to decide whether it is suitable. If there is no room in the home of their choice at the time of the assessment, local authorities should consider making a temporary arrangement until a place becomes available (para. 7.8 of Circular (92)27). The greatest obstacle to real choice, however, is para. 3(b) of the Directions. This requires that the preferred accommodation 'would not require the authority to pay more than they would usually expect to pay having regard to his [*sic*] assessed needs'. Paragraph 3(b) does not apply if the resident can find a third party (other than their spouse) who will meet the difference between what the authority would expect to pay and the fees for the home. This means that if, say, 'The Hollies' costs £50 per week more than the authority 'usually pays', an elderly person can only choose to go there if they can find a friend, relative or charity who will contribute £50 per week towards their care.

4.4.3 Recent case law may have strengthened residents' and prospective residents' rights to have some say in where they go. In *R v. Avon County Council, ex parte Hazell (1993)*, the court quashed the social services committee decision which had refused to send Mr Hazell to the home of his choice. It would appear that Avon County Council's reasons for its decision were that there was a suitable alternative, and the fees for the home of choice were above the figure which it had recently set as the maximum they could pay in the light of their budgetary position. It was, however, honouring commitments to existing residents even if the fees were above this ceiling. This case relates to decisions taken by the local authority before the Directions on choice came into effect. However, in giving judgment, Henry J. referred to the Directions and applied the tests set out in para. 3. In finding in favour of the appellant, he considered whether the accommodation was too expensive and argued that it was not, since Avon County Council was already funding other residents in this accommodation. This may be an important finding for the future. The financial constraints on social services departments are likely to result in local authorities reducing the maximum weekly amounts they are prepared to pay for different kinds of care. This judgment suggests that an elderly person would have a case against an authority who refused to accommodate them in the home of their choice on the grounds that the fees were now considered too expensive, if any residents in that home were already being funded by that authority.

4.4.4 Dillon L.J. in a Court of Appeal judgment in relation to home closures in Devon and Durham[5] also found that where there is a proposal to close a home or simply to move one or more residents from one home to another, those residents should be consulted well in advance and have a reasonable time to put their objections to the council and the residents' objections should be considered by the council (*R v. Devon County Council, ex parte Baker and Johns,* and *R v. Durham County Council, ex parte Broxson and Curtis (1993)*).

4.5.1 THE DUTY TO PROVIDE RESIDENTIAL ACCOMMODATION

Once an elderly person has been assessed as in need of residential or nursing care, the authority has a duty to meet that need using its powers under Part III of the NAA 1948. The duty extends to those in urgent need of accommodation, even if they are not ordinarily resident in the area (NAA 1948, s.24) (see para. 4.5.3 below). Local authorities are prevented from meeting the accommodation needs of most elderly people already resident in registered homes on 1 April 1993 (see paras. 4.3.4 to 4.3.5 above).

The authority can either provide the accommodation directly using its powers under s.21 of the NAA 1948; it can place the person in accommodation owned or managed by another authority, or it can use its powers under s.26 of the 1948 Act to make arrangements with another person or organisation to provide the accommodation.

4.5.2 A social services authority has no duty to provide accommodation for someone who is a hospital in-patient, or where the health authority or hospital trust has been paying for their care, for example in a private nursing home. Very often hospitals discharge elderly people when they still need substantial nursing care. This can apply to long-stay patients or those who have been in hospital for a few days, for example, following surgery. The legislation is unclear as to who is responsible for these patients if they cannot go home and have to be admitted to a nursing home. Guidance (para. 3 of Annex to DH Circular LAC(92)24) clarifies that social services are responsible for any nursing home placement which results from a joint health authority/local authority assessment. However, this still leaves room for disputes, for example where GPs admit someone in an emergency or a hospital patient is discharged into a nursing home. There remains some ambiguity over who is responsible for meeting continuing care needs for hospital patients (see Chapter 5 at para. 5.6.4 and 5.6.24).

In order to create as smooth an interface as possible, it has been a pre-condition for receiving community care grant that each authority has an agreement with the relevant district health authorities for dealing with patients being discharged from hospital. The protocol between the health authority and social services is supposed to set out a strategy and arrangements for deciding who pays for nursing home beds and how hospital discharges are integrated with assessments. Some arrangements are working better than others depending on the underlying relationships between health and social services in different parts of the country. However, if admission has occurred without prior consultation with the local social services department, or in breach of jointly agreed guidelines, social services have no responsibility for the placement.

4.5.3 The authority has duties under s.29 towards anyone ordinarily resident in the area. Section 24(3) of the NAA 1948 differs from s.29 in empowering authorities to provide accommodation for persons with no settled residence or who are not ordinarily resident in the area, but are in urgent need of accommodation. Directions issued as Appendix 1 to DH Circular LAC(93)10 require social services authorities to provide accommodation under s.21(1) for people who have been suffering from 'mental disorder', or for the prevention of 'mental disorder' who are ordinarily resident, or are in the area but have no settled residence (Direction 2(3)) and those who are ordinarily resident in another area but following discharge from hospital become resident in the authority's area (Direction 2(4)). The basic definition and case law on 'ordinarily resident' is dealt with in Chapter 3 at para. 3.8.2. However, there are particular issues relating to elderly people in need of residential or nursing care or already living in independent homes in the area. Problems can arise with defining which authority is responsible for someone who has been in institutional care for a long time. Circular LAC(93)7 offers some guidance on some of the questions that need addressing. Paragraph 10 covers those who have entered a residential establishment of their own volition in an area other than the one in which they lived previously. The Circular advises that if these residents subsequently need social services, they 'will look to the authority where the accommodation is situated'. In the case of hospital patients, the Circular builds on the provision of s.24(6) of the NAA 1948. Paragraph 14 states that a patient 'shall be deemed to be ordinarily resident in the area in which he was ordinarily resident before he was admitted to hospital. If they were not ordinarily resident in any area prior to their admission, then the powers of s.24(3) are applicable.' The Circular goes on to recommend this as a reasonable approach to people being discharged from similar institutions such as prison or resettlement units. However, it points out that no case law exists and disputes should therefore be resolved in the light of specific circumstances.

Paragraph 3 of DH Circular LAC(93)7 looks at who is responsible for assessing the needs of someone who 'arrives from abroad including those who are returning to this country having given up their residence abroad'. It could be implied that this paragraph relates to someone who has just come from another country, but the wording is open to interpretation. Authorities are advised that such a person could come within the terms of s.24(3) but if they do not, 'then the local authority where he has his settled residence should carry out the assessment.'

4.5.4 While this has not yet been tested in the courts, it is the Department of Health's view that s.21, as amended by the NHSCCA 1990, requires 'authorities to make some direct provision for residential care under s.21 of the 1948 Act' (para. 3, LAC (91)12). This advice has not deterred a number of authorities who have, over the past five years, transferred all their own homes to independent trusts or private companies. The Court of Appeal has upheld the principle that no decision to close a residential home provided under s.21 can be taken prior to holding a consultation exercise with the residents. It was found that it would have been sufficient to consult the body of residents as a whole, but that such consultation should give the residents time to put their objections to the council (see para. 4.4.4 above).

4.5.5 Amendments to s.26 of the NAA 1948, in the NHSCCA 1990, permitted authorities for the first time to make arrangements with private individuals for the provision of accommodation. The ethos of the community care reforms and the new funding arrangements have encouraged social services authorities to make more use of independent sector providers. The expectation has been that authorities will buy more places in private homes, but they have also been encouraged to switch from grant aid for voluntary and charitable bodies to contracting on 'fee per client basis or through a service contract laying down a given level of provision'.[6] These pressures have meant that far more local authorities are contracting for accommodation under s.26 than ever before.

4.5.6 Where the authority contracts with an independent provider, the authority is responsible for specifying the level of services to be provided; meeting the full costs of that service; assessing the resident's ability to pay and collecting a contribution from them. There are also legal responsibilities between the resident and the authority. The authority agrees to meet the resident's needs for accommodation for as long as the need arises; the resident must pay the assessed charge for that accommodation. Some authorities now issue residents with written contracts which set out the terms and conditions on which accommodation is provided. It is questionable whether any binding contract or legal relationship exists between the provider and the resident, even if the resident is making direct payments to the provider (see para. 4.6.7 below). For example, if the provider wants the resident to leave, they must notify the authority. It is then the authority's responsibility to find alternative accommodation for the resident, if their need for residential or nursing care continues.

4.6.1 CHARGING FOR RESIDENTIAL CARE

Where a resident is placed in accommodation under s.21 or s.26 of the NAA 1948, s.22 of that Act requires the authority to charge the 'standard rate fixed for that accommodation' unless the residents can show that they are unable to pay at that rate. In these cases, social services authorities must under s.22(3) assess a resident's ability to pay and charge accordingly, apart from the exceptions given later in this section. Authorities have little discretion in how they assess charges and are required to follow regulations issued under s.22(3) and the guidance in the *Charging for Residential Accommodation Guide* (CRAG). CRAG is issued under s.7(1) of the Local Authority Social Services Act 1970 (LASSA 1970) and is therefore binding on social services authorities in how they exercise these functions. New regulations – the National Assistance (Assessment of Resources) Regulations (NAARR 1992) which came into force on 1 April 1993, bring financial assessments under s.22 of the NAA 1948 broadly into line with the assessment of means for Income Support (see Chapter 1 at para. 1.31.1). Residents in homes on 1 April 1993 who would have been worse off under the new regulations remain assessed under the old system.

4.6.2   The standard charge is the maximum amount which the authority can charge each week. The 1948 Act does not specify how it is calculated, but an amendment to s.22 made by s.44 of the NHSCCA 1990 requires it to represent the full cost to the authority of providing that accommodation. Advice issued by the local authority associations suggests that where the accommodation is provided under s.26 of the NAA 1948 in an independent home, the standard charge should be set at the fee which the authority is being charged by the home. Where the accommodation is provided in one of the authority's own homes, the authority can take into account administrative and other costs as well as the specific costs of running that home. The authority can choose whether to pool the charges for all its own homes, so that all residents pay the same wherever they live, or have a different charge for each home. However, whether or not they pool charges, authorities do not have the powers to set standard charges at a rate which would recover more revenue overall than the full costs of providing the service. Standard charges can vary enormously, not only between individual authorities, but between different homes in the same area.

4.6.3 In practice, most social services authorities undertake a financial assessment of all prospective residents. Where a resident refuses to disclose information about their capital or income, the authority can then charge them at the standard rate. The financial assessment is based on the income and capital of each resident, whether single or married (see para. 4.7.1 below). The financial assessment must leave each resident with an amount for personal expenses (see para. 4.8.1 below). Residents are then expected to pay any income (as assessed under the NAARR 1992) above the personal allowance towards the costs, up to the standard charge. For example, if the standard charge was, say, £300 per week, a resident with £100 weekly income would keep £12.65 (1993–4) and the rest would go towards the charge, whereas another resident with £350 would pay the full standard charge and keep £50. Residents whose capital is above £8,000 must pay the standard charge until their capital falls below this amount; they are then assessed on their income. The minimum weekly charge is the rate of retirement pension, after deducting the personal allowance. In 1993–4, this was £56.10 which would have meant the authority was paid £43.45 and the resident kept the personal allowance of £12.65.

4.6.4 Regulation 5 of the NAARR 1992 permits authorities to charge whatever 'they consider reasonable' for any 'less dependent residents'. These residents are defined under reg. 2 as anyone who lives in an unregistered independent home or in a local authority home where no board is provided. The purpose of this provision is for these residents to be charged at a rate that allows them to have or develop a more independent way of life. It is therefore intended that these residents should be left with sufficient income to participate in everyday social activities and to meet any other commitments such as food or fuel. Authorities are also encouraged to exercise this power in respect of those residents who may have, or be seeking, some paid employment, so that they can see financial gains from working after paying travel and other work-related expenses. It is therefore up to the authority to choose what kind of financial assessment to apply and whether to disregard some or all of the resident's resources.

4.6.5 Social services authorities have discretion regarding the charges for temporary residents for the first eight weeks. Temporary residents are those whose stay is expected to last for less than fifty-two weeks. Authorities can, under s.22(5A) of the NAA 1948 charge whatever amount 'appears to them reasonable for him [*sic*] to pay'. However, if they decide to undertake a financial assessment, they must follow the regulations and guidance as set out in para. 4.6.3. Some authorities have used this power under s.22(5A) to provide incentives to use respite care. Some have, for example, provided free respite care, while others levy a small flat rate charge from everyone who uses the service, regardless of their income. After eight weeks, the authority must charge the standard rate and undertake a financial assessment of ability to pay under the NAARR 1992. However, where temporary residents go in and out of care, for example as part of a respite scheme, the discretion on charges applies to each new stay.

When social services authorities undertake financial assessments for temporary residents under the NAARR 1992, they cannot take payment of disability living allowance (DLA) or attendance allowance (AA) into account when assessing the resident's ability to pay. They must also disregard the costs of certain home commitments when assessing resident's incomes (NAARR 1992, Sched. 3).

4.6.6 Residents must be informed in writing of the charge they have been assessed to pay and how it has been calculated. This information should be provided at least annually and following any change in the assessment. Similar information should be provided to prospective residents. The notification must include the name of the person dealing with the assessment and how to instigate a complaint through the authority's complaints procedure (para. 20, LAC Circular (92)19. A resident, or prospective resident, who remains dissatisfied with the charge they have been assessed to pay can make a formal complaint, as described in Chapter 3 at para. 3.17.1.

4.6.7 The resident is required to pay the assessed charge to the authority. Authorities should inform residents of the assessed weekly charge and any reasons why the charge might fluctuate. Paragraph 14 of Circular LAC 94(1) requires authorities to note that where they are contracting for the accommodation, they are not required to specify how much the resident is being charged in the contract. Residents in all sectors will normally pay their charges directly to the authority. However, if they live in an independent sector home, s.26(3A) of the NAA 1948 (inserted by s.42(4) of the NHSCCA 1990) permits the charges to be paid to the provider, but only if the resident, the authority and the provider all agree to this. This provision was introduced primarily to help housing associations whose conditions of grant require them to have some form of landlord relationship with residents (but see the comments at 4.5.5 regarding the dubious legality of the relationship created). In these cases, the provider is simply acting as the authority's agent. 'Authorities should note that they remain responsible for the full amount should the resident fail to pay the home as agreed. In such a case the authority will recover the charge from the resident in the normal way' (para. 1.024 of CRAG). This applies equally where a third party is paying part of the fees as described in paragraph 4.4.2 above. If they fail to make the agreed payments, the authority is responsible for the shortfall, but could sue the person for breach of contract.

4.6.8 The latest Social Services Inspectorate Advice on charging, issued in February 1994, sheds some helpful light on charging residents for 'extras'. Some proprietors have been asking residents to pay additional charges for certain services and activities. Paragraph 20 of the SSI advice note makes it clear that proprietors should not be charging extra for anything which is already specified in the contract, even if they are paying someone else to provide this particular activity. In this respect, it will be essential for residents to check that all the services specified in their care plan, or agreed by the authority as necessary to meet the assessed needs, have been included in the contract between the authority and the home. It is also worth noting the advice at paras. 4.8.3 and 4.8.4 below regarding the use that can be made of personal allowances for 'extras'.

4.7.1 COUPLES

If one partner in a couple has been assessed as needing residential care, only that partner's income and capital should be taken into account when assessing their liability for charges. The authority has no power under the NAA 1948 to assess them on their joint resources. Even where both partners are admitted to a residential or nursing care home, they should each be assessed separately (para. 4.003 of CRAG). However, spouses are liable under s.42 of the NAA 1948 to maintain each other. Therefore, when either partner in a married couple is being provided with care at public expense, an authority can choose to invoke this provision and seek some contribution from the other.

4.7.2 However, they cannot use the financial assessment criteria (set out in para. 4.6.3) as the basis for determining a liable relative payment.

The latest guidance in DH Circular LAC (94)1 stresses that social services authorities cannot demand details of the spouse's capital or income. Authorities are advised that in each case they should decide 'what would be "appropriate" for the spouse to pay by way of maintenance. This will involve discussion and negotiation with the spouse, and will be determined to a large extent by ... financial circumstances in relation to ... expenditure' (para. 11.005 of CRAG). In the Department's view, it would not be appropriate, for example, necessarily to expect spouses to reduce their resources to IS levels in order to pay maintenance. Spouses who are dissatisfied with the level of contribution they are being asked to pay have the same rights as the resident to make a formal complaint, as described in Chapter 3 at 3.17.1.

4.7.3 The authority can, under s.43(1) of the NAA 1948, make a complaint to the magistrates' court against a liable relative who fails to pay the contribution set by the authority. It is then for the court to decide, depending on all the circumstances and the means of the liable relative, what is an 'appropriate' amount of maintenance to pay. At this stage, the court can require the spouse to provide details of their income and capital before making an assessment.

4.7.4 One partner in many elderly couples, usually the man, often has a considerably higher income than the other. If that partner needs residential or nursing care, the financial assessment takes all their personal income into account. This may result in the resident having to pay all or most of their income (except the personal allowance) towards the costs of care. On the other hand, the income which the partner who remains at home has in her own right may be insufficient to cover overheads or maintain their previous standard of living. This situation can arise whether or not the couple are married. In such cases, authorities have been strongly urged (para. 4.003A of CRAG and paras. 6 and 7 of Circular LAC(94)1) to consider using their discretion to leave the resident with a higher personal allowance (see para. 4.8.2 below).

4.7.5 Where one partner in a couple enters a residential or nursing home permanently, each of them will be treated as a single person for the purpose of claiming benefits. Each can therefore claim IS in his/her own right and the benefit will be calculated according to each partner's personal income and capital. This will also be the case if both partners are in institutional care, but living in different homes. Where they live in the same home, they will be treated as a couple if they share the same room, but otherwise it will depend on their circumstances.

4.7.6 The rules on claiming IS when one partner in a couple goes into temporary care are complex. If the couple are already claiming IS, their benefit will be recalculated as follows while one of them is in a local authority home. The amount for the partner who goes into care will be the 'Part III rate', that is, £56.10 in 1993–4, and the amount for the partner at home will be calculated as though he/she were a single person. For example, a couple both aged seventy-two would have received £98 in IS in 1993–4; if one of them was temporarily in a home, they would have received £119.45. This would have been made up of £56.15 for that partner and a single personal allowance and single pensioner premium for the other of £63.30. The couple are still claiming IS as a couple, so IS will continue to be paid to one of them on behalf of them both and based on joint income and savings.

4.7.7 Where one partner goes temporarily into an independent home, the couple can claim IS calculated in the following way. Benefit for the partner who remains at home will be calculated as though they were single. The benefit for the other partner will also be calculated as though they were single, plus the £45 residential allowance (see para. 4.12.1 below). If we take the couple in the example in the last paragraph, their benefit during a temporary stay would consist of £63.30 for the partner who remains at home and £63.60 plus £45 for the other, making a total of £171.60 per week. The couple would have their benefit recalculated in this way, unless to do so would give them less than they normally receive. The additional benefit during temporary stays can mean that some couples who are not normally on IS can qualify for it while one of them is in residential care. This applies to couples who have savings below £8,000 and joint incomes too high to qualify when they both live at home. The couple in the above example would be in this position if their income were above £98 but below £171 per week.

4.8.1 PERSONAL ALLOWANCES

In assessing each resident's ability to pay, the authority is required under s.22(4) of the NAA 1948 to ensure that they retain an amount for personal expenses. The minimum personal allowance is laid down each year in the National Assistance (Sums for Personal Expenses) Regulations (£13.10 from April 1994). It is the same for each resident whether they are in a local authority home or a residential or nursing home in the independent sector. Different rates, however, apply to hospital patients.

'The personal allowance is intended to enable residents to have money to spend as they wish, for example, on stationery, personal toiletries . . . ' (para. 5.001 of CRAG) (see para. 4.6.1 above). Since April 1993, residents in local authority homes, as well as the independent sector, have been expected to buy their own clothing out of their personal allowance. The only exceptions being 'in cases of special need or emergency (for example, all clothes are lost in a fire) the local authority may supply replacement clothing' (para. 5.001 of CRAG).

4.8.2 Section 22(4) of the NAA 1948 gives authorities the power to leave residents with whatever level of personal allowance 'as in special circumstances the authority may consider appropriate'. Authorities can use this power to reduce as well as increase the allowance. However, the examples cited in para. 5.005 of CRAG are all ones where authorities are being encouraged to increase the amount. Two of these are of relevance where one partner in an elderly couple is in a home. The first applies to temporary stays, and social services authorities are told to consider the needs of a partner who remains at home when setting the personal allowance. The second example encourages authorities to treat couples more fairly if one partner has a much higher income than the other and that partner needs to go into care. Authorities are advised to look at whether it is appropriate to increase the resident's personal allowance so that some of that income can be passed to the partner who remains at home, who might otherwise be unable to meet their commitments. However, there is little point in authorities taking this action if the partner who remains at home claims means-tested benefits, because the extra income would simply reduce their benefit income.

Another example given in CRAG for increasing the personal allowance may also be useful for elderly people who wish to maintain a fairly independent way of life while in a home. The guidance recommends that authorities should consider leaving a resident with more personal allowance if the only reasons they fail to qualify as a 'less dependent resident' (see para. 4.6.4 above) is because they live in a registered home or a local authority home that provides board.

While the guidance leaves the decision to each authority, they would have to provide sound justification for refusing to vary allowances if elderly residents fall into any of the examples given in para. 5.005 of CRAG. At the same time, these examples are not prescriptive and there will be other circumstances when an authority should be prepared to vary the personal allowance. The clearest example might be where an elderly person needs extra money to travel to keep in touch with close friends or relatives who may not be able to travel themselves. For example, this might occur where their spouse is in hospital or nursing care in another part of the country.

4.8.3 Residents are often offered extra services unrelated to the provision of accommodation, such as hairdressing, chiropody, attending day centres or leisure activities. They may be offered these by the authority or, if they live in an independent home, by the proprietor. In either case, they may be asked to pay a charge for such services. In this respect, it is important to note the advice in para. 4.6.8 above. Paragraph 20 of the SSI advice note referred to in para. 4.6.8 also covers activities which the authority assesses a resident as needing which are not covered in the residential contract. Day centre attendance would clearly come into this category. In these cases, para. 20 is clear that it is for the authority (not the proprietor) to charge the resident, under its powers in respect of non-residential services under s.17 of the Health and Social Services and Social Security Adjudication Act 1983 (HSSSSAA 1983). (See Chapter 3 at para. 3.14.1.) However, in charging for such services, authorities are told to bear in mind how little income residents have available for their other outgoings after paying for their accommodation. The proprietor can only contract separately with the resident for services which he/she has not been assessed as needing by the social services authority.

4.8.4 Paragraph 13 of Circular LAC (94)1 makes it very clear that none of the resident's personal allowance should go towards accommodation costs. It cannot be used to pay for 'more expensive accommodation' as described under para. 4.4.2 above. Many proprietors of private homes would like to be able to ask residents to use their personal allowances to buy a better room than that being purchased under the contract. Circular LAC (94)1 is extremely useful in demonstrating that this is not possible under the legislation and that social services authorities are required to ensure that all residents retain their personal allowance after meeting their accommodation costs.

4.9.1 THE FORMER HOME OF THE RESIDENT

A resident who is an owner occupier before they move into a home may find that the value of their home is taken into account when assessing their capital under the NAARR 1992 (see para. 4.6.3). These regulations, with one or two exceptions, align the treatment of capital resources with those for IS. Authorities now have very little discretion in how they assess the former home. The value of the home should never be taken into account in the case of temporary residents, that is, anyone whose stay is expected to last for less than fifty-two weeks if they intend to return there (NAARR 1992, Sched. 4, para.1).

4.9.2 In the case of permanent residents, the former home can only be treated as a capital asset if the resident is the owner and would have a beneficial interest in the proceeds of its sale (see para. 4.9.3 below if the home is jointly owned). If the resident is sole owner, the former home will be treated as a capital asset from the date it becomes un-occupied, even if it is up for sale. Where someone else still lives in the home, it must be disregarded as a capital asset if any part of it is occupied by the resident's partner, a child under sixteen whom the resident is liable to maintain, or another relative who is aged sixty or over or is 'incapacitated' (Sched. 4, para. 2). In this context, 'relative' means a parent, son, daughter, grandparent, grandchild, aunt, uncle, nephew or niece; or any partner of theirs; or a step-parent, step-son or step-daughter; a parent-in-law, son-in-law or daughter-in-law.

The authority also has the discretion under para. 19 of Sched. 4 to disregard the home if it is occupied by 'a third party where the authority consider it would be reasonable' to do so. It is entirely at the discretion of the authority to decide when to apply this disregard. For example, it could apply where the partner in a gay or lesbian relationship who owned their home was admitted to residential care. Paragraph 7.007 of CRAG suggests that one example of when it would be reasonable to disregard the home is 'where it is the sole residence of someone who has given up their own home in order to care for the resident, or someone who is an elderly companion of the resident, particularly if they have given up their own home.' Social services authorities are advised to review such decisions if circumstances change, for example, if the carer moves out.

4.9.3 Where the resident jointly owns the home with others, the resident is treated under reg. 27 of the NAARR 1992 as having an equal share of the beneficial interest in the home. Paragraph 7.012 of CRAG suggests that in valuing the resident's interest in jointly owned property, the value will depend on the resident's ability to assign the interest to someone else or there being a market for it.

4.10.1 CHARGES ON PROPERTY

The financial assessment may have taken into account the value of property, savings and the resident's former home (see para. 4.6.3 above and para. 4.11.1 below). If this has happened, the authority must specify the value which has been placed on these items. The resident will usually then find that they are liable to pay the standard charge, that is, the full costs of the accommodation. In these cases, once need has been assessed, the authority must provide the accommodation, but if the resident is unable or refuses to pay the assessed charge, a debt will start to appear on the resident's account. The authority then has the same rights as any other debtor to pursue these debts through the county court. This could result in the court ordering the resident to sell the assets in order to pay the debt. However, in practice, authorities are usually reluctant to take such action. Where the resident owns or has a beneficial interest in land or buildings, an authority does not, in any case, need to take such steps. Section 22 of the HSSSSAA 1983 gives them the power to place a charge on the resident's interest in the land which would allow them to recover the amount due from the proceeds of any sale of the land. The charge is on the resident's interest, not on the land itself, so the charge has no effect on joint ownership or tenancies. Whatever the resident's liability, the charge cannot be for more than the value of the resident's share of any proceeds from the sale of the property.

The provisions of s.22 of the HSSSSAA 1983 ensure that the authority does not need to force a sale of jointly owned property on the death of the resident if the land was held upon trust for sale.

4.10.2 It is for the authority to decide when to enforce payment of the debt once a charge has been registered, but it will usually be after the death of the resident. However, it was clearly the government's intention that s.22, in giving additional security, allows authorities to defer payment longer than this if appropriate. An example given during the debate on the HSSSSAA 1983 was where the home has been taken into account as capital, even though a relative lives there (HL 1992). In this case, if the debt were enforced on the death of the resident, the relative might lose their home or suffer financial hardship. The authority could therefore decide to delay enforcement until after the relative dies. Interest on the amount charged shall not accrue until after the death of the resident (s.24 of the HSSSSAA 1983). As the Secretary of State has not exercised her powers to direct the rate of interest, it shall be whatever rate is considered reasonable by the authority.

4.10.3 In order to force a sale of the property, the authority would have to apply to the court for an order. The court would decide whether it was fair to redeem the debt in this way at that time. The court would take into account such factors as the size of the debt compared with the value of the asset, the existence of other creditors and who lived there. If the court agreed that the debt should be redeemed, it can make an order requiring the property to be sold and the arrears paid. An authority which pursues arrears following the death of a resident must seek to recover them from the estate of the resident who had died and not from the resources of any beneficiary.

4.11.1 NOTIONAL CAPITAL AND DEPRIVATION OF RESOURCES

In certain circumstances, the authority can treat the resident, or potential resident, as having capital assets or savings which they do not actually possess at the time. Regulation 25 of the NAARR 1992 gives the authority the discretion to take into account 'capital of which he has deprived himself for the purpose of decreasing the amount that he may be liable to pay'. Any compensation or other payment in respect of personal injury cannot be taken into account if it has been placed on trust for the benefit of the resident.

4.11.2   The onus is on the resident to prove that they no longer possess a particular asset or capital. For example, they may have had a large redundancy payment in the previous twelve months. If much or most of this sum is no longer available, the authority will want evidence of how it has been spent. This may include receipts for expenditure, proof of debts having been paid, etc. If the resident fails to provide such proof, they will be treated as still possessing the asset or the money.

4.11.3   Where residents can show that the asset is no longer available to them, the authority must then decide whether 'deprivation of resources' has occurred. The question of when the transfer occurred is irrelevant, unless the authority wishes to recover the charges under s.21 of the HSSSSAA 1983 (see para. 4.11.5 below). Paragraph 6.064 of CRAG suggests that it would be unreasonable to treat a disposal as deliberate deprivation if it occurred at a time when the person was fit and healthy, and could not have foreseen the need for residential care. So the emphasis, as in reg. 25, is on the resident's motives and these can be difficult to establish. Many elderly people choose to hand over possessions or savings to their children and grandchildren for different reasons. Some are anxious, particularly if adult children live with them, that ownership of the family home should be sorted out before their death.

In considering whether deprivation has occurred CRAG advises that 'Avoiding the charge need not be the resident's main motive but it must be a significant one.' It cites examples of where the money has been used to pay off a debt which may or may not be treated as deliberate deprivation of resources. Another example of disposals concerned a man who bought a car two weeks before his admission and gave it to his son on entering the home. In this case, CRAG warns authorities of the importance of taking all the circumstances into account. It suggests that if at the time of purchase, the man was not expecting to go into a home or thought he would be in a position to continue driving the car, it would not now be reasonable to treat it as deliberate deprivation. This might have occurred because his admission resulted from an emergency or his condition deteriorated very quickly after the purchase.

A resident who has used up their savings by buying personal possessions may find the current value of these new belongings being taken into account in the assessment, even though personal possessions are normally disregarded.

4.11.4 Where an authority decides that deliberate deprivation of resources has taken place, it must first assess the value of the asset that has been transferred or spent and it can then treat this as 'notional capital'. In most cases, this will result in the resident being liable to pay the full standard charge. The authority must then 'decide whether it is realistic to attempt to recover the assessed charge from the resident bearing in mind that they may not have the means to pay the debt which will be accruing'.

An extremely complex formula governs how the resident's assets will be valued in the future once they are treated as having notional capital. This is known as the diminishing notional capital rule. Regulation 26 of the NAARR requires that, each week, the notional capital shall be reduced by the difference between the assessed charge and what the resident would have paid if there had been no notional capital. For example, the resident has been assessed as liable for the standard charge, say £300, because of the notional capital; whereas they would have been liable for the minimum charge, £43.45 (1993–4) if the transferred asset had not been taken into account. The formula reduces their notional capital by £256.55 per week (£300 minus £43.45). They will go on being liable for the standard charge until the formula reduces their notional capital to below the capital limit.

4.11.5 If an authority considers the resident has deliberately disposed of assets in the six months before the date when they moved into the accommodation (para. 6.060 of CRAG), they can rely on s.21 of the HSSSSAA 1983 to recover the costs from a third party. Section 21 imposes a liability on any third party who can be shown to have received the transferred asset as a gift. This applies whatever asset has been transferred to them. For example, they may be living in the family home and had the ownership transferred into their name. The third party can be required to pay the difference between the charge which the resident is able to pay and that which they would have paid if the asset had still been in their name. This applies whether or not the person had known the resident's motive in making the transfer. They cannot, however, be asked to pay more than the value of the benefit which they gained from the transfer.

4.12.1 BENEFITS PAYABLE TO RESIDENTS IN HOMES

Entitlement to benefits for residents in independent homes changed fundamentally on 1 April 1993. Those resident in a home on that date will usually have preserved rights to IS and are still assessed under the old rules. (see para. 4.3.1 above.) Residents who enter a registered home on or after 1 April 1993 will be entitled to the same personal allowances and premiums for IS as if they were living in their own home (see Chapter 1 at para. 1.31.5). Partners in couples will usually be assessed as single people (see para. 4.7.1 above). In addition, each resident will also usually be entitled to a residential allowance, £45 in 1993–4. This allowance is not paid if the home is run by a social services department. It is a deliberate financial incentive to place residents in independent rather than local authority homes. The residential allowance is a flat rate payment, regardless of what kind of care is being received or whether the home is registered as a residential or nursing home. Residents are entitled to IS calculated in this way, whether they go into the home independently or are placed there by their local social services authority. In practice, few residents on IS will be able to go into a home independently as the fees will far exceed their entitlement to benefits. Residents placed in an independent home by their social services authority will only be entitled to keep the personal allowance and will have to pay the balance of their benefits to the authority (see para. 4.8.1 above). They will also be unable to claim the care component of DLA or AA after four weeks (see para. 4.12.3 below). Housing benefit (HB) cannot be paid towards the accommodation charges if the home is registered.

4.12.2 Residents in local authority homes which provide board are only entitled to the 'Part III' rate of IS which is linked to the rate of retirement pension. This was £56.10 in 1993–4, of which the resident was entitled to keep £12.65 and the balance goes to the authority towards the charges (see para. 4.6.1 above). Housing benefit (HB) is not available towards the costs of accommodation provided under s.21 of the NAA 1948. Residents in homes which do not provide board will usually be entitled to claim IS and HB as if they were living independently in the community.

4.12.3 Residents in one of the authority's own homes, whether or not board is provided, that is, in accommodation provided under s.21 of the NAA 1948, can claim DLA (care) or AA for the first twenty-eight days of any stay. Entitlement then ceases as they are considered to be in accommodation where their care needs are being met at public expense. Residents in independent homes can claim AA as long as their accommodation is not being funded under s.26 of the NAA 1948. The resident will cease to be entitled to AA twenty-eight days after any social services authority agrees to become responsible for the placement. Residents who are to be discharged can make claims for AA in advance, or reactivate their old claims so that benefit will start to be paid from their first day at home. Entitlement to other social security benefits, such as retirement pension and the mobility component of DLA, are unaffected by admission to residential or nursing care, unless the person is a hospital in-patient.

4.12.4 Entitlement to benefits in independent residential settings from 1 April 1993 depends entirely on whether the establishment is registered under the Registered Homes Act 1984 (RHA 1984) (see paras. 4.15.1 to 4.20.4 below). Residents in registered homes can claim benefits as set out above. Residents in unregistered settings claim IS, HB and AA, as though they were living independently in the community.

4.13.1 REGISTRATION CATEGORIES IN THE INDEPENDENT SECTOR

A range of establishments which offer residential accommodation and personal care or nursing care fall within the registration criteria of the RHA 1984. Since April 1993, this includes establishments which cater for only one person, and at the other end of the spectrum are large nursing homes with sophisticated medical equipment, catering for over 200 residents.

The primary test of whether an establishment needs to register is not what it calls itself, which can often include 'rest home', 'guest house' or 'hotel', but whether or not both board and personal or nursing services are provided.

A person who deceitfully describes or implies that the establishment is a residential care home, nursing home or mental nursing home within the meaning of the 1984 Act will be guilty of an offence under s.24 unless the home is properly registered.

4.13.2 Several different codes of practice for the registration of residential care homes and nursing homes have been published. Authorities have been advised by the Secretary of State to regard *Home Life: A Code of Practice for Residential Care* (CPA 1984) as having the same status as guidance issued under s.7 of the LASSA 1970. The Secretary of State for Health speaking in parliamentary debate in 1983 said 'There will thus be a legally binding obligation on homes to conduct their affairs in a way that complies with the code of practice.' The nursing home handbook, *Registration and Inspection of Nursing Homes*, is published by the National Association of Health Authorities (NAHA 1985).

Both codes are relied on heavily by the two registration authorities in making decisions under the RHA 1984. However, neither has the force of law. In Registered Homes Tribunal Decision No. 27, the Tribunal found that the NAHA model guidelines 'is to provide some guidance which, while not binding, should be given its appropriate weight'.

4.14.1 THE ROLE OF INSPECTION UNITS

Social services authorities have been required since April 1991 to have an Inspection Unit which is responsible for inspecting residential care homes in both the public and independent sectors. The units are also authorised to be responsible for registration of voluntary and private residential homes. The aim of setting up the Inspection Units was to 'put the inspection of residential care in the public, private and voluntary sectors onto a common footing'. In practice, the work of registration, particularly following the Registered Homes (Amendment) Act 1991 (RH(A)A 1991) (see para. 4.16.1 below), has meant that little Inspection Unit attention has been focused on local authority homes to date (SSI 1993).

The Inspection Units were also set up to be 'free standing' in order to have an independent regulatory role. This has meant the Units are not part of the social services department as such and are directly accountable to the Director. The Director of Social Services is responsible for their management and organisation and for safeguarding their independence.

4.14.2 There is an inevitable tension between the different roles which Inspection Units have been given. On the one hand, they have a 'policing' role being responsible for registration and whether standards are being met. On the other, they are expected to play a key part in developing services and engaging private and voluntary sectors in developing a local strategy on community and residential care (DHSS Circular No. LAC (88)15 para. 6). The tensions are acknowledged in more recent advice from the Social Services Inspectorate:

> what is essential is that the inspection unit should retain its ability to make disinterested and objective evaluations of services including particularly the identification of unacceptable standards ... where conflict may arise between the inspector role and the advisory and supportive role the inspector role must come first and it must be clear when an inspector is conducting a formal inspection and when he/she is providing support.

(SSI 1991)

4.14.3 The work of the Inspection Unit is supported by an advisory committee which serves 'as a forum for the exchange of views between the ... registration authority, its officers and service providers ... and service users' (Policy Guidance 1990, para. 5.20). Social services authorities are free to determine the membership of their committee, but are encouraged by the policy guidance to involve both users and carers. The guidance also stresses the need for effective collaboration between the registration authority and the health authority, especially as the latter remains responsible for registering nursing homes (see para. 4.16.1 below).

4.15.1 RESIDENTIAL CARE HOMES

Section 1 of the RHA 1984 provides a definition of which establishments are required to be registered as residential care homes. It is the person who is responsible for the home who is registered, not the establishment. 'Registration is the culmination of a process designed to ensure that ... the person/s whose name/s appear/s on the Registration Certificate ... has/have satisfied all those requirements ... as to the fitness of those persons named and as to the suitability and fitness of the premises' (Tribunal findings in Registered Homes Tribunal Decision No. 153).

4.15.2 Registration only applies to 'establishments', but it applies equally whether the board and personal care are being provided free of charge or for profit. With the growth of more informal care arrangements, such as boarding out schemes (see Chapter 3 at paras. 3.4.1 to 3.4.8), it can be very difficult to define when care is being provided in an establishment or not. For example, where an elderly person has gone to live with a relative to have more care and support, it would presumably not be reasonable to suggest that this was an 'establishment' within the meaning of the 1984 Act, but if they had gone to stay with someone they knew only casually before moving in, would this be liable for registration? There appears to be no case law to date on these kind of arrangements although it is likely that some cases are in the pipeline as a consequence of small homes becoming liable for registration.

4.15.3 Registration only applies if both board and personal care are provided. There is no definition of 'board' within the RHA 1984. The question of what does and does not constitute board is becoming increasingly important. More residential establishments are providing cafeteria-style pay-as-you-eat catering, with residents having the choice about whether to eat in or out. Some projects which are trying to encourage more independent living involve residents in the shopping and residents do the cooking, with some supervision. There is therefore a question about whether any of these arrangements are offering board and if they are not, there is no requirement to register, regardless of the level of personal care being provided.

References to the provision of food in the Residential Care Homes Regulations 1984 which govern the conduct and activities in registered homes are unhelpful in clarifying when the provision of food may or may not constitute 'board'. Regulation 10(1)(k) refers to the provision of facilities so that residents can prepare their own food and refreshments and reg. 10(1)(l) relates to the supply of properly prepared wholesome food. Since April 1993, the HB legislation has defined board as follows:

> 'board' refers to the availability to the claimant in the home in which his accommodation is provided of cooked or prepared food, where the food is made available to him in consequence solely of his paying the charge for the accommodation or any charge which he is required to pay as a result of occupying the accommodation or both of these charges and is made available for his consumption without any further charge to him.

In *Otter v. Norman (1988)*, the House of Lords held that the provision of a continental breakfast was more than *de minimus* and constituted 'board' for the purposes of s.7 of the Rent Act 1977 (RA 1977). This might or might not be taken as further evidence that food has to be prepared or placed before the person at a mealtime before it constitutes 'board'.

4.15.4 Section 20 of the RHA 1984 defines 'personal care' for the purpose of s.1 as 'care which includes assistance with bodily functions where such assistance is required'. Neither the 1984 Act nor the Residential Care Homes Regulations 1984 provide any further guidance on what other types of assistance may or may not come within the terms of s.1. However, case law on this question, arising from Registered Homes Tribunal Hearings, has addressed these issues, one of the more significant being *Harrison v. Cornwall County Council (1992)*. This related to a home where two of the residents required high levels of emotional support and regular attendance arising from epilepsy and learning disabilities. The case hinged on whether for the purpose of s.1 someone who needed constant and regular 'attention', but who was able to manage their own bodily functions, was or was not in need of personal care. The Court of Appeal upheld the original Tribunal decision and found that the wording of s.20 allowed for the construction that a person who did not need assistance with bodily functions may yet be in need of personal care. Dillon L.J. in his judgment went on:

> assistance with bodily functions must be available if required, but it is not essential in order that there be 'personal care' that such assistance should in fact be required or given. Accordingly I agree with the view of the tribunal that the definition does not purport to be exhaustive and embraces care in many forms, emotional or psychiatric as well as physical.

4.15.5 The main grounds for cancelling registration are: if the annual fee is not paid; on any grounds that would have justified refusing registration in the first place (see para. 4.20.1 below) or if anyone, including the registered person, is convicted of an offence in respect of that home under the 1984 Act or regulations; if the registered person is convicted of an offence in respect of any other residential care home or that any other condition in force under the Act has not been complied with (s.10 of 1984 Act). The registered person should be given notice and the reasons for the proposal to cancel registration (see para. 4.20.1 below) and then has fourteen days in which to notify the authority that they wish to make representations. If the registered person wishes to do so, the authority cannot decide to cancel the registration until it has heard the representations. However, s.11 of the 1984 Act allows local authorities to apply immediately to a magistrate for an order cancelling the registration if it believes that the life, health or well-being of residents is at risk. The registered person has the right of appeal to a valuation tribunal if dissatisfied with any decision taken by the registration authority.

4.15.6 Any establishment which does provide board and personal care must be registered unless it is exempt from registration. It is an offence under s.2 of the 1984 Act to carry on a residential care home without being registered. A home which meets the definition in s.1 is not required to be registered if it is intended to be used solely as a nursing or mental nursing home, or is an NHS hospital or a hospital within the meaning of s.145(1) of the Mental Health Act 1983 (MHA 1983). A registered home which also provides some nursing care may be required to obtain dual registration (see para. 4.19.1 below).

4.16.1 HOMES FOR LESS THAN FOUR RESIDENTS

The RH(A)A 1991 amended the 1984 Act and removed the exemption from registration of homes which cater for fewer than four residents from 1 April 1993. However, it was Ministers' intention 'to apply a lighter touch to such homes' (DH Circular LAC (92)10, para. 3).[7] In particular, once a 'small home' is registered there is no continuing requirement to check routinely whether the standards set under reg. 10 of the Residential Care Homes Regulations 1984, or other requirements such as record keeping, are being met (Circular LAC (92)10, para. 3). Paragraph 9 states that 'authorities are neither required nor expected to inspect small homes, either on registration or regularly thereafter'. Sections 1(4) and (5) of the 1991 Act also gives the authority the power to waive or reduce the normal registration fee in the case of small homes.

Many people welcomed the introduction of the 1991 Act because of concerns that many unscrupulous proprietors were deliberately setting up small homes to avoid registration and keep standards low. In practice, the new provision is a mixed bag and cannot be considered in isolation from the impact of registration on residents' benefits. On the one hand, the expected gains from registration, in terms of inspection and accountability, are unlikely to materialise because of the 'lighter touch' approach. At the same time, registration wipes out any entitlement to HB and residents must then seek financial help from their social services authority. This will then mean that they lose entitlement to AA and most of their other income will be taken by social services as a contribution to their care (see para. 4.6.1 above). In effect, residents in registered placements lose any real independence of income. Many of those who have offered adult placements or 'home from home' schemes are being deterred from continuing because of the uncertainties of contracting with social services and the loss of any direct financial relationship between them and the person they care for.

An establishment which meets the definition in s.1 of the RHA 1984 does not have to register if it provides personal care and board for fewer than four people, all of whom are running the home, their employees or relatives.

4.17.1 NURSING HOMES

The Secretary of State for Health has delegated the registration functions for nursing homes under the RHA 1984 to district health authorities (DHAs).[8] DHAs do not have the power to delegate this function to anyone else. The Act defines which premises fall within the definition of a 'nursing home'. Two of these categories are relevant to the scope of this book. These are: 'premises used or intended to be used for . . . the provision of nursing for, persons suffering any sickness, injury or infirmity' (s.21(a)) and 'premises . . . used or intended to be used for the provision of all or any of the following . . . surgical procedures under anaesthesia . . .; endoscopy; haemodialysis or peritoneal dialysis; treatment by specially controlled techniques' (s.21(c)). Premises which fall within the definition of s.21(c) would be required to be registered even if patients did not stay overnight.

Some establishments which meet the definitions in s.21 are not required to be registered. These include hospitals or similar establishments run by a health authority or other public body, premises used wholly or partly for consultations by a medical practitioner, a chiropodist or dentist, except those using certain specially controlled techniques such as cosmetic surgery. The exemption also applies if the premises were used wholly or mainly as a private dwelling.

4.17.2 There is no definition of what constitutes 'the provision of nursing' in the Act. However, a definition is to be found in Annex 3 to *Managing Care* [9] This definition is intended to help inspection units define when establishments fall to be registered under s.1 of the 1984

Act and when they might not. Annex 3 states 'a nursing home provides the kind of care which requires the skills of a qualified nurse or the supervision of a qualified nurse'. It then offers a list which is 'neither prescriptive nor comprehensive' of a range of procedures, such as dressing wounds, feeding, management of complex or aggressive states. It suggests that if one or more of these is needed by a patient periodically in a twenty-four-hour period, or a resident needs constant nursing care, this could be considered to be 'nursing care'.

The National Association of Health Authorities Handbook (*Registration and Inspection of Nursing Homes* (1985)) provides advice and model guidelines to DHAs on their registration responsibilities. It argues that 'distinction between a resident and a patient may in the end be a subjective decision'. It goes on to suggest that the decision on whether an establishment ought to be registered as a nursing home should be settled on the basis of advice from the designated senior nurse in the registering DHA. Clearly, whether or not the decision is subjective, it must be seen to be reasonable and accord with the relevant legislation and case law.

4.17.3 Directions issued by the Secretary of State for Health in September 1984 require DHAs to inspect any premises in their district if they have reason to believe they should be registered (DH Circular HC(84)21 Annex C). The Circular to which the directions are annexed encourages DHAs to investigate even where the grounds for concern arise from hearsay. These requirements apply equally to mental nursing homes (see para. 4.18.1 below). Once granted, registration may at any time be cancelled on the same grounds (as are set out in para. 4.15.5 above) for residential care homes and the registered person has the same rights to notification and appeal.

4.17.4 Where some residents of a registered nursing home are receiving only board and personal care, the home may also be subject to dual registration (see para. 4.19.1 below).

4.18.1   MENTAL NURSING HOMES

A mental nursing home is defined in s.22(1) of the RHA 1984 as

> any premises used, or intended to be used, for the reception of, and the provision of nursing or other medical treatment . . . for one or more mentally disordered patients, whether exclusively or in common with other patients.

This definition does not cover establishments which provide day care only. Guidance on the facilities to be provided in mental nursing homes is contained in para. 50 of DHSS Circular HC(81)8. A mental nursing home can admit patients detained under the MHA 1983 if its application for registration specified that it intended to offer this service. If this applies, the nursing home has virtually the same powers and duties under the 1983 Act as a psychiatric hospital. (see Chapter 5 at para. 5.6.7 to 5.6.12).

4.18.2 Almost all the requirements regarding registration and decisions on registration that apply to nursing homes (see para. 4.17.1 above) apply equally to mental nursing homes. In addition, s.35 of the RHA 1984 provides specific powers to enter and inspect premises used, or thought to be used, as a mental nursing home. Where a mental nursing home is caring for detained patients under the MHA 1983, s.36 of the RHA 1984 provides for the temporary continuation of registration for two months following the death of the registered person or cancellation of registration by the registration authority.

4.19.1 DUAL REGISTRATION

Unlike its predecessor, the Residential Homes Act 1980, the RHA 1984 does not preclude one establishment being registered both as a residential care home and as a nursing home. The criteria for registration for the two categories are not distinct. If the home is providing both board and personal care to any resident, it would be an offence if it were not registered under s.1; if the same home is also providing nursing care either to the same residents or to others, it would be an offence if it were not also registered under s.21 of the RHA 1984. As numerous Tribunal decisions testify, the boundaries between 'personal care' and 'the provision of nursing' can often be blurred. The original purpose of dual registration was partly to overcome these difficulties and partly to give more residents the chance of staying in the same home as their needs increased. The effect of the RH(A)A 1991 has meant that nursing homes which provide just board and personal care for fewer than four residents have had to register under s.1 of the RHA 1984 since April 1993.

4.19.2 Dual registration applies to the whole establishment, although the manager can choose to provide the separate forms of care in different parts of the building. It also allows one resident to receive a wide spectrum of care services, from help with getting dressed to medication for terminal illness. Dual registration does mean that the establishment comes under the jurisdiction of two registration authorities – the local authority and the health authority. It is for authorities locally to come to some arrangements for dealing with dual registration. The need for co-operation and the desirability of joint inspections has been emphasised in Department of Health Guidance LAC(84)15. It would, for example, be perfectly feasible for the two authorities to set up an arrangement that allowed the home to be inspected and registered for both nursing and residential care under a single procedure.

4.20.1 REFUSAL ON REGISTRATION AND APPEALS

The registration authority may, under s.9(1) of the RHA 1984, refuse to register applicants in respect of residential care homes. They can do so if they consider that the applicants, or any other person concerned with carrying on the home, are not fit persons; the premises are not fit to be used; or the way in which the applicants intend to carry out the home is such as not to provide services or facilities reasonably required. However, the only grounds for refusing to register a 'small home' is if they are satisfied that the applicant, or any other person who will be concerned with carrying on the home, is not a fit person (s.9(2)). Section 25 provides the same grounds for refusing registration in respect of nursing homes. In addition, registration can be refused if the home, or other premises used in connection with it, are used, or proposed to be used, in any way improper or undesirable for such a home; it will not be under the charge of a registered medical practitioner or qualified nurse; or the required number of nurses are not on duty at such times as specified.

4.20.2 Circular LAC(91)4 issued as guidance under s.7(1) of the LASSA 1970 set out new arrangements giving registration authorities the right to ask for a check of criminal records as part of the registration procedures. By the date of the Circular, many authorities, including all those in Wales, had set up agreed procedures with local police forces to check the criminal record of any applicant for registration. In exceptional circumstances, checks can also be asked for on any person already in post or already registered. Where the applicant has a police record, they are not automatically treated as unfit to run the home. The authority must make a balanced judgement on their suitability taking account only of those offences which are relevant to the job or situation in question.

4.20.3 The authority must, under s.12 of the RHA 1984, give the applicant a written notice if they intend to refuse an application for registration as a residential care home, or attach any conditions to registration not already agreed between the applicant and the authority. The authority must also serve notice of its intentions to cancel registration, as described in para. 4.14.5 above. Any notice issued under s.12 must include the reasons for what it is proposing to do. The applicant then has fourteen days from the date of service of the notice to notify the authority that they wish to make representations. It is for the applicant to decide whether to make representation orally or in writing. These representations are not an appeal against the authority's decision as the final decision should not be taken until after representations have been made. Virtually identical procedures and rights apply, under ss.31–3, to decisions of the district health authority (DHA) in respect of registration for nursing homes and mental nursing homes.

4.20.4 Once either registration authority makes a final decision, there is a right of appeal under s.15 (registered care home) or under s.34 (nursing home or mental nursing home) to a registered homes tribunal. An appeal must be lodged within twenty-eight days of service of the notice of the authority's decision. The appellant may appear before the tribunal themselves or be represented. Legal Aid is not available for representation before a tribunal, although advice may be obtained before the hearing under the Green Form scheme. The decision of the tribunal, with reasons, will be sent to each of the parties, usually about four weeks after the hearing (para. 4.23 of *Registered Homes Tribunals Procedures* Department of Health 1989).

4.21.1 COMPULSORY ADMISSION TO RESIDENTIAL CARE

Section 47 of the NAA 1948 permits an elderly person to be compulsorily removed from where they are living to more suitable accommodation. This section only applies if the person is

(a) suffering from grave chronic disease or, being aged, infirm or physically incapacitated, are living in insanitary conditions, and
(b) they are unable to devote to themselves, and are not receiving from other persons, proper care and attention.

Section 47(1)(a) and (b)

The wording of s.47(1) is very narrowly drawn. It applies only to someone in need of care and attention who is also living in insanitary conditions. So authorities may be unable to use this power in respect of many people who are at risk because their living conditions are adequate. The person does not have to be suffering from mental ill health or disablement to fall within the scope of s.47. Social services authorities have other powers under the MHA 1983 in these cases (see para. 4.22.1 below). There is concern that some authorities are invoking s.47 to deal with verminous and insanitary living conditions when they could rely on less draconian powers under the Public Health Act 1961 (PHA 1961) and the Environmental Protection Act 1990 (EPA 1990). A Law Commission Consultative Paper has pointed out that under s.36 of the PHA 1961 an authority can require someone to move out of their home until it can be safely re-occupied and must provide the person with alternative accommodation free of charge (LC 1993c).

4.21.2 Metropolitan authorities, district councils and London boroughs have the power under s.47(2) to apply to the magistrates' court for an order to remove the person to a 'suitable hospital or other place' (subsection (3)). The authority cannot apply to the court until it has a written certificate from a medical officer employed by the DHA that, after 'thorough inquiry and consideration', removal is necessary in the interests of the person or to prevent injury or serious nuisance to others. In many areas, the District Community Physicians have been designated by the authority as the proper officer to undertake this work, but the appointment and authorisation of both medical and social work personnel to exercise any of the functions under s.47 is a matter for local co-operation between health authorities and local authorities.

4.21.3 An order under s.47 relates solely to the person's removal and detention elsewhere. It does not give authority for the person to be treated without their consent. An order, except under the emergency procedures described in para. 4.21.4 below, cannot be granted unless the person to whom it applies or 'some person in charge of him' has been given at least seven clear days' notice of the time and place at which the order is to be made (s.47(7)). The person managing the premises where the detained person will go also has to appear in court, or have been given a similar amount of notice of the time and place. An order will last for a maximum period of three months and the court has the powers to extend it for further periods of up to three months (s.47(4)). Once 'six clear weeks' has passed from the making of the order, the detained person, or someone acting on their behalf, can apply to the court for the order to be revoked (s.47(6)). The authority is responsible for meeting the costs of the accommodation and the detained person will be required to make a contribution towards the costs under the provisions of Part III of the 1948 Act, as described in para. 4.6 above.

4.21.4 The National Assistance (Amendment) Act 1951 (NA(A)A 1951) amended s.47 of the NAA 1948 and permits an order to be made without the required notice being given under s.47(7). Both the relevant medical officer and 'another registered medical practitioner' must certify that it 'is necessary in the interest of that person to remove him without delay' (s.1 of the NA(A)A 1951) before the court can make an *ex parte* order. There must also be evidence before the court that the person managing the premises is prepared to accommodate them. But unlike the full procedures, that person does not have to appear or be given seven days' notice. An order under s.1 of the NA(A)A 1951 can only be made for a maximum of three weeks. No application can be made to revoke the order. There remains concern that this procedure is not subject to effective judicial control. An *ex parte* application can be decided by a single magistrate and the person being removed does not have the opportunity to make their case. While s.1 of the NA(A)A 1951 was clearly intended as an emergency procedure, one study published in 1980 suggested that it was being used in 94 per cent of all removals (Norman 1980).

4.22.1 REMOVAL TO A PLACE OF SAFETY

Section 135 of the MHA 1983 applies to someone who is believed to be

suffering from mental disorder –

(a) has been, or is being, ill treated, neglected or kept otherwise than under proper control in any place within the jurisdiction of the justice, or
(b) being unable to care for himself, is living alone in any such places.

s.135(1)

Section 135 empowers a magistrate to issue a warrant authorising a policeman to enter the premises specified on the warrant with a view to removing the person to a place of safety. Force can be used, where necessary, to gain entry. The application for the warrant under s.135(1) is made by an approved social worker (ASW) who must provide information laid on oath that the person meets the above definition. The warrant does not have to name the person, but must give the address of the premises.

Section 135(1) is unclear about who makes the decision on whether the person should be removed. Section 135(4) requires the constable to be accompanied by a registered medical practitioner and an ASW, a person who is authorised to take or retake patients under the MHA 1983. It would therefore appear that these two professionals are responsible for deciding whether removal is appropriate and the policeman's role is to gain entry and effect the removal.

4.22.2 A s.135(1) warrant can apply to anyone who meets the definition given in para. 4.22.1 above. A warrant under s.135(2) is in respect of someone who is already liable to be detained under mental health legislation. A warrant issued under s.135 (2) must name the patient. A constable, an ASW, a member of staff from the hospital or any person authorised by the hospital management, has the power to remove the person named on the warrant to 'any place, or to take into custody or to retake a patient'. There is no requirement for the constable to be accompanied by either an ASW or a doctor.

4.22.3 Section 136 gives the police the power to deal with people who are in public places and who appear 'to be suffering from mental disorder and to be in immediate need of care or control'. The person can be removed to 'a place of safety'. The provisions of s.136 do not empower emergency admissions; its purpose is to allow the person to be assessed by a doctor and an ASW so that arrangements can be made for treatment or care, where necessary. This power is available to the police, whether or not the person is thought to have committed an offence. The Act does not define what constitutes a place of safety and it may well be a police station rather than a hospital, as hospitals are not required to accept someone who has been picked up by the police under s.136. Paragraph 10.5 of the latest Code of Practice states that 'preferred places of safety is a matter for local agreement'. It goes on to stress that whether the person is taken to a hospital or a police station, immediate contact should be made with both the local social services authority and relevant medical staff (DH/WO 1993).

4.22.4 Removal and detention authorised by any warrant issued under s.135 and s.136 must not exceed seventy-two hours. In the case of detention under s.136, the power to detain lapses as soon as the person has been seen by both a doctor and a social worker and they have decided that no further arrangements are needed for care or treatment. It is generally agreed that actions taken under s.135 or s.136 are subject to the Police and Criminal Evidence Act 1984 (PACE 1984). Paragraph 10.9 of the latest Code of Practice on the MHA 1983 makes this clear in respect of s.136 procedures and states that although the MHA 1983 'uses the term "remove", it is deemed to be an "arrest" for the purposes of the PACE 1984'.

4.23.1 GUARDIANSHIP AND MENTAL HEALTH

A patient may be received into guardianship under s.7 of the MHA 1983 if they are 'suffering from mental disorder, being mental illness, severe mental impairment, psychopathic disorder or mental impairment and mental disorder is of a nature or degree which warrants his reception into guardianship'. There is no requirement that the condition should be treatable as there is for admission to hospital under s.3 of the MHA 1983. The purpose of guardianship under s.7 of the MHA 1983 is to enable patients to receive community care where it cannot be provided without the use of compulsory powers. It provides an 'authoritative framework for working with a patient with a minimum of constraint to achieve as independent as life as possible within the community' (para. 13.1 of the Code of Practice). This form of guardianship is very different from that under s.37 of the 1983 Act which applies to mentally disordered offenders.

4.23.2 The application can be made by either the person's nearest relative or an ASW. The nearest relative can veto an application made by an ASW. Only the county court can overturn the relative's right of veto. The applicant must have seen the person within the previous fourteen days. The application for guardianship goes to the local social services authority which, in most cases, will then become the person's guardian. The Code of Practice requires decisions on guardianship to be taken following 'multi-disciplinary case discussion' (para. 13.3). However, it goes on to concede that if guardianship is being considered as an alternative to hospital admission, there may not be time to arrange such a meeting. A person may be kept under guardianship for up to six months from the date on which the application was accepted; the application can then be renewed for a further six months and after that at yearly intervals (s.20(2) of the MHA 1983). The person has the right to apply to a mental health review tribunal if they are dissatisfied with the decision.

4.23.3 Section 8 of the MHA 1983 sets out the three powers which the guardian has. These are: to require the person to live in a specified place; to require the person to attend a specified place for treatment, education, training or occupation; and to require authorised people to have the right of access to the person where they are living. These powers are quite tightly drawn. For example, the guardian can require the person to live in a particular place, but does not have powers to detain them there. If the person leaves without permission, they can be returned there if they are found within twenty-eight days. Equally, while the guardian can require the person to attend for treatment, treatment cannot be administered without the patient's consent.

4.23.4 It had been hoped that the guardianship powers would be a useful alternative to detention where someone could not be persuaded to accept support, medical treatment or practical help voluntarily. Guardianship was seen as a means of keeping individuals in the community. Paragraph 13.9 of the Code of Practice reinforces this by emphasising that guardians should not require 'patients' to live in a hospital, except in very exceptional circumstances, and even then it should be for as short a time as possible. In fact, very little use has been made of these powers; while practice varies between authorities, the use of guardianship has declined steadily since it was introduced.

4.24.1 PROTECTION OF PROPERTY WHILE IN RESIDENTIAL CARE

Section 47 of the NAA 1948 places a duty on the social services authority to protect the 'moveable property' and possessions of any-one who is a hospital in-patient; provided with accommodation under Part III of the 1948 Act (see paras. 4.5.1 above) or under s.47(3) of that Act (see para. 4.21.1 above). The duty only arises if the authority believes that there is a danger of loss or damage to the person's belongings and that no other suitable arrangements have been made. Where this applies s.47(1) requires the authority to take 'reasonable steps to prevent or mitigate the loss or damage'. The protection provided will depend on the circumstances. It could involve securing the premises, taking an inventory, arranging for fuel and water supplies to be turned off. It is argued that pets would constitute part of the resident's moveable property and that the authority would therefore have a duty to ensure that they were well cared for. The authority can, at all reasonable times, enter the person's former home in order to carry out these duties. It can also seek reimbursement from the person of any expenses involved in undertaking its duties.

4.25.1 COMPLAINTS PROCEDURES

Any user or potential user of a social service has a right of complaint against any decision made by that authority. The details of how the complaints procedure operate are set out in Chapter 3 at para. 3.17.1. Local authorities are under a duty to have complaints procedures that 'are understood by staff, users and elected members'. Every resident should have received information, in a form they could understand, about their rights to make a complaint; how to do it, and the name of someone to contact if they want to make a complaint. In practice, elderly people living in homes are least likely to exercise their rights to complain:

> Too often we hear from people who say they do not dare to make a complaint, even though they know what they are supposed to do in theory. People must be encouraged to believe that it is alright to say how they feel, and staff need help in learning how to deal with comments and complaints. Otherwise the whole exercise will be meaningless.

(Meredith 1993)

4.25.2 Residents who live in independent sector homes may have particular difficulties making complaints. The best way to deal with small things which are unsatisfactory, or not to their liking, is to try to negotiate change directly with the person running the home. If this fails, or more serious issues arise, the person has the right to make a formal complaint to the authority which placed them there. Without independent advice and support, they may feel too vulnerable to complain. Residents, particularly if housebound, may also face considerable practical obstacles. There may have been little or no contact with the authority after they went to live in the home; they may have lost the information which explains who to contact. It may also be extremely difficult to write a letter or get it posted without having to reveal what its contents are about.

4.25.3 In practice, therefore, complaints procedures are not effective in ensuring that elderly residents are either happy or satisfied with the quality of their care and environment. Poor practices will continue to go unchecked in every sector without more rigorous and regular monitoring and inspection. In this respect, both the Inspection Units (see para. 4.14.1 above) and the officers placing the contracts have essential but distinct roles to play. In addition to its routine duties of inspection and monitoring standards, the Inspection Units deal with complaints about the conduct of homes, staffing levels and quality of staff. A complaint can be made by a concerned person and the Unit then has a duty to investigate. In addition, regardless of whether complaints have been made, the authority should ensure that proper procedures are in place to monitor whether the service specification for each resident is being properly met and how that resident feels about how they are being treated.

4.26.1 LEGAL REMEDIES

There are several courses of action available to someone who is dissatisfied with a decision that has been made by a social services authority, or with the way the authority has acted. In most cases, the legal remedies described in this section are only available to applicants who can show they had exercised their rights under the complaints procedures described in 3.19 and paras. 4.25.1 to 4.25.3 above and are still dissatisfied with the outcome or where the complaints procedure can be shown to be inappropriate (see Chapter 3 at para. 3.17.1). If the applicant believes that the authority has failed to comply with any of its statutory duties, he/she can ask the Secretary of State for Health to intervene. Section 7(D) of the LASSA 1970 (inserted by s.50 of the NHSCCA 1990), empowers the Secretary of State to issue an order declaring the authority to be in default, if he/she is satisfied that the authority has failed, without reasonable excuse, to comply with any of their duties which are social services functions. This new default power replaces that originally contained in s.36 of the NAA 1948 and can be used where someone is, for example, unreasonably refused an assessment or if the authority fails to provide the appropriate service to meet assessed need. Applying to the Secretary of State in this way ought to be a faster way to achieve some redress than by pursuing a judicial review. However, past experience suggests that applications can take many months to process and have rarely resulted in an entirely successful outcome (Cook and Mitchell 1982).

4.26.2 An applicant who believes an authority's decisions, procedures or actions to be unlawful, blatantly unreasonable or irrational, can seek judicial review (see Chapter 3 at para 3.19.1). The provisions of s.7(D) make it unclear when a dissatisfied user or potential user can seek judicial review in respect of a social services decision which may be unreasonable or erroneous in law. There is an argument that they are precluded from applying for judicial review because s.7(D) offers an alternative remedy. However, s.7(D) only applies to social services functions. In the Devon and Durham cases cited earlier in this chapter, Dillon L.J. addressed these questions and accepted that these complaints regarding insufficient consultation were for the courts' jurisdiction, in part because it was questionable whether 'consultation' was a social services function within the meaning of s.7. Dillon L.J. and Simon Brown L.J., in a separate judgment on the cases, acknowledge that this is a developing area of law. Simon Brown went on to outline his approach to the question as follows:

> which of two available remedies – or perhaps more accurately avenues of redress – is preferred will depend ultimately upon which is more convenient, expeditious and effective. Where Ministers have default powers, application to them will generally be the better remedy . . . unlike the court, moreover, he can direct a solution rather than merely leave the authority to redetermine the question. Where on the other hand, as here, what is required is the authoritative resolution of a legal issue . . . I would regard judicial review as the more convenient alternative remedy.

4.26.3 As suggested in Chapter 3 at para. 3.18.1, the increasing reliance on actual or implied contracts between the authority, the user and the provider, may provide more grounds for dissatisfied service users suing the authority for breach of contract for the supply of services. However, the legal and contractual relationships between user, provider and the authority are, as yet, largely untested where the authority is contracting with an independent provider for the provision of accommodation, care or both. Earlier case law, cited in Chapter 3, suggests that there may be grounds for a claim for damages where a service user has suffered physical or mental harm as a direct consequence of an action or omission by the service provider. The case law on an authority's duty of care towards a user who is provided with services by a third party is patchy and somewhat contradictory.

4.27.1 *Local government Ombudsman* Judicial review is available to someone who believes the authority's decisions, procedures or actions to be unlawful, blatantly unreasonable or irrational. An application must be made to the High Court for leave to appeal. The courts only grant leave if they accept the appellant has '*locus standi*', which usually means that the person can show they are directly affected by the authority's actions or represent a group of people who would be, and that there are good grounds for the action. If an authority is shown to be in breach of its statutory duties, or to have acted unreasonably, the court can quash a decision (*certiorari*) and order it to be redetermined applying the law correctly (*mandamus*). Sometimes, the applicant's circumstances require urgent action; for example, if the authority is about to withdraw services. In these cases, the courts can grant 'interim relief'. The purpose of interim relief is to maintain the status quo until the case is resolved. An order might therefore require the authority to maintain or restore the service which is the subject of dispute.

NOTES

1 Regulation 3 of the Social Security (Amendments consequential upon the introduction of Community Care) Regulations (1992) SI No. 3147.
2 Regulation 19(1ZF) of the IS General Regulations, as inserted by Regulation 3 of the Social Security (Amendments consequential upon the introduction of Community Care) Regulations (1992) SI No. 3147.
3 Regulations 6 and 7 of the Residential Accommodation (Relevant Premises, Ordinary Residence and Exemptions) Regulations (1993) SI No. 477.
4 NAA 1948 (Choice of Accommodation) Directions (1992) issued with DH Circular No. LAC (92)27.
5 *R v. Devon County Council, ex parte Baker and Johns* and *R v. Durham County Council, ex parte Broxson and Curtis*, 1993.
6 *Purchase of Service*, Department Health Social Services Inspectorate Practice Guidance 1991.
7 RHA 1984 – Small Residential Care Homes. Department of Health Circular No. LAC (92)10 dated September 1992.
8 NHS Functions Directions to Authorities and Regulations 3, 5 and 7 of the Administration Arrangements Regulations SI No. 1991/554.
9 Welsh Office (1991) Managing Care: Guidance on assessment and the provision of Social and Comunity Care, April 1991.

5 Health care

Gwyneth Roberts

5.1.1 HEALTH AND THE ELDERLY

Most people over sixty-five lead active, energetic and independent lives in the community. However, the likelihood of suffering from an acute or chronic condition increases with age. Over four million people over sixty-five suffer from some degree of physical, mental or sensory disability, ranging from very slight to severe, with women, in particular, being more prone to chronic illness in old age (OPCS 1990). As a result, elderly people, in general, make greater use of health care provision than other age groups (OPCS 1988).

However, self-referral may be misleading as an indicator of need, since old age is often seen as synonymous with ill health, decline, dependency and frailty (Caldock and Wenger 1993; Victor 1991). It may not be surprising, therefore, that many older people refuse, for as long as possible, to be labelled as sick (Tinker 1992). They may also believe that medical conditions occurring in old age are less likely to respond to care and treatment (Wenger 1988). As a result, a condition may be well advanced before being assessed as 'serious' (ADS 1993), and a doctor is consulted (Johnson 1972). Information, advice and support, as well as access to preventive, curative and rehabilitative services, are important in overcoming such problems. Older people should be encouraged to seek help at an early stage, and, if necessary, helped to do so.

It is equally important, however, that care and treatment are not imposed. A dilemma can sometimes arise between the right of the individual to control over his/her body, and to take risks, and society's concern to protect those deemed unable to protect themselves. The difficulty is to avoid intrusive paternalism, with a possible loss of dignity and choice, without allowing individuals to suffer neglect, discomfort, or pain. The issue is of particular significance as the numbers suffering from mental infirmity increase (HAS 1982; ADS

1993). There are no easy answers in this complex area, but that is no excuse for riding rough-shod over the rights of vulnerable people. The general legal principle, to which there are few exceptions, is that medical care and treatment can be given only with the consent of the patient (McIntosh 1990; Law Commission 1993b).

5.2.1 ENTITLEMENT TO HEALTH CARE

Most people over retirement age, regardless of nationality or origin, are automatically entitled to health care in the NHS. Problems can sometimes arise, however, for individuals who have been in this country for only a short period of time. Under the National Health Service (Charges to Overseas Visitors) Regulations 1989, (and the National Health Service (Charges to Overseas Visitors) Amendment Regulations 1991) those who are classified as 'overseas visitors' are liable to pay for most hospital care. Nevertheless, treatment at an accident and emergency, or casualty, department is exempt (reg. 3(a)), although the exemption ceases to apply if a patient is formally admitted as an in-patient or registered at an out-patient clinic. The diagnosis and treatment of certain notifiable diseases, and treatment given at special clinics for sexually transmitted diseases are also exempt (reg. 3(c)). In relation to HIV/AIDS, however, only a diagnostic test, and any associated counselling, are exempt (reg. 3(d)). Psychiatric treatment for detained patients, and patients received into guardianship, under the Mental Health Act 1983 (MHA 1983) is also exempt (reg. 3(e)) (see Chapter 4 at paras. 4.23.1 to 4.23.4), as is treatment given as a condition in a probation order made under s.3(1) of the Powers of the Criminal Courts Act 1973 (PCCA 1973) (reg. 3(f)). Services such as domiciliary nursing and ambulance transport are also exempt.

In general, a person is classified as an 'overseas visitor' if he/she is not 'ordinarily resident' in the UK (reg. 1(2)). The residence test depends upon whether a person is living here 'lawfully and voluntarily and for settled purposes as part of the regular order of his/her life for the time being'. There must be a recognisable purpose for being in the country, plus a sufficient degree of continuity for such residence to be described as 'settled' (*Akbarali v. Brent London Borough Council (1982)*; *R v. Barnet London Borough Council, ex parte Shah (1983)*). The Department of Health (DH) advises health authorities and NHS Trusts to treat those who intend remaining in the UK for less than six months as overseas visitors. Establishing a person's residence should be a question of fact in each case, however, using the judicial test set out above. A stay of less than six months might be sufficient, in some circumstances, to qualify a person as 'ordinarily resident' here.

The relevant regulations also contain a list of those with complete or partial exemption from the rules. For example, a person who has lived in the UK for at least twelve months is entitled to free hospital treatment (even if he/she was absent from the UK for up to three months during that time) as is any person who has come to this country to take up residence permanently (including former residents returning after an absence abroad). Immigrants who have come here with the hope of settling permanently are also exempt, except where their application has been refused. If an appeal is successful, however, any charges which have already been levied must be repaid. War disablement pensioners and war widows receiving UK pensions are also exempt, as are those receiving any other benefit under a personal injuries scheme. Refugees are also exempt, as are those who have applied for refuge or asylum. A person detained under the Prison Act 1952 (PA 1952), or Immigration Act 1971 (IA 1971), is also exempt. Pensioners from an EU country are also exempt, unless they came to this country expressly to receive medical treatment. If so, they must obtain prior authorisation for the treatment they receive.

Overseas visitors with only partial exemption include UK state pensioners living abroad, who had previously lived in the UK for a continuous period of at least ten years, or who have ten years continuous service for the Crown. The nationals of other EU countries are also partially exempt, as are the nationals, or residents, of a country with which the UK has a reciprocal arrangement. In general, this category of overseas visitor is exempt only in relation to treatment 'the need for which arose during the visit'.

If an overseas visitor is exempt, the exemption he/she enjoys extends also to members of his/her family. A person's family, for this purpose, are his/her spouse, any children below the age of sixteen, and children between the ages of sixteen and nineteen in full-time education at a school or college of further education, but not including university, or other forms of higher education. In relation to visitors from another EU country, however, the definition of 'family' may be wider, depending on the social security rules of the country from which they come.

The main category of overseas visitor with no exemption at all from paying for most hospital treatment are short-term visitors from a country such as India, Pakistan or the United States, with which the UK has no reciprocal agreement in this respect. Since the test is residence, and not nationality, some British nationals may find themselves subject to charges for the treatment they receive. Individuals in need of hospital treatment, who are uncertain about their residential status in the UK, would be well advised to check carefully whether or not they are classed as 'overseas visitors' under these regulations, and if so, whether they are exempt.

5.2.2 The Health Service Commissioner (see Chapter 6 at para. 6.4.23) reported recently on two cases in which charges were levied on patients on the grounds that they were not eligible for hospital care under the NHS. In the first case, the patient had returned to the UK after an absence of several years, and sought treatment for a condition which had been diagnosed and treated while he was living overseas. He agreed to pay a deposit to cover the cost of follow-up treatment, thinking it would be repaid when he produced evidence showing that he intended to reside permanently in the UK. The hospital refunded part of the deposit, but kept most of it to cover treatment which the patient received before evidence had been produced. The administrative staff at the hospital regarded him as a private patient until he acquired NHS status, although he was initially interviewed under procedures for dealing with overseas visitors. The Ombudsman was satisfied that the patient had returned to the UK to take up permanent residence, and that he should have been immediately and wholly exempt. Hospital staff had failed, at the initial interview, to establish his intentions, and had not followed DH guidance precisely. The authority apologised for the hardship caused, and agreed to take steps which would ensure that, in future, proper procedures were followed. The deposit had also been refunded in full.

In the second case a South American woman, who could speak no English, was on a six-month visit to her daughter. She was admitted to hospital in an emergency, and treated for a condition suspected of being infectious. During her mother's stay in hospital, the daughter was led to believe that treatment would be free under the NHS. On the day on which she was discharged, the daughter had been told that she might, after all, have to pay for her mother's treatment and care. The district health authority (DHA) then sent her a bill, and subsequently began legal proceedings to recover the debt. The Ombudsman's investigation revealed a series of procedural errors. The officer responsible for establishing liability to pay had not been told of the patient's admission until the day on which she was discharged, because nursing staff did not know that he should have been given the relevant information. The nurses were under the impression that the medical records staff would identify such patients from the routine daily returns. The consultant in charge of the woman's treatment had not been approached. In fact, the complainant had received a substantial bill for her mother's treatment. The Ombudsman also criticised the subsequent handling of the case. The DHA treasurer believed, on the basis of inaccurate information, that he had a statutory duty to collect the charge. Procedural failures threw doubt on whether the DHA could be satisfied that liability had been established. It agreed to improve its procedures, and waived the charges already levied for the woman's treatment. Had proper procedures been followed, the patient would almost certainly have been wholly exempt, since her treatment was for a possible communicable disease (Health Service Commissioner 1990).

5.2.3 ENTITLEMENT IN THE INDEPENDENT SECTOR

Health care is also available in the independent sector, but here a person's entitlement is determined by the terms of the agreement under which treatment is to be provided. Provision in this sector of medicine has grown considerably since the late 1970s. The number of patients treated at independent hospitals grew between 1981 and 1986 by almost a half to over 400,000, and day cases doubled to a 1,000,000. By the end of the 1980s, 17 per cent of all elective surgery carried out in England, including 28 per cent of hip replacements, and 19 per cent of all coronary artery by-pass grafts, were in this sector (DH 1989a).

Speed and convenience are two of the reasons why individuals may opt for private care. Treatment is often more easily obtained, making this sector of medicine more attractive to those who are in need of acute care and treatment. Taking out private insurance has also become more common. By 1989, 5.34 million people, or 9 per cent of the UK population, had some form of insurance. The nature and extent of treatment which is covered by an insurance policy depends on its terms and conditions. Private health insurance is generally restricted to acute medical or surgical conditions, whereas long-term care for chronic complaints, such as those afflicting many elderly people, are not likely to be included. In any case, some medical insurance schemes do not accept individuals aged sixty, or sixty-five and over, as first-time contributors. Without insurance cover, the cost of private care falls on the individual and could prove prohibitive. Those who are already covered by insurance may also find that, when they reach retirement age, their premiums go up substantially. Current government policy, however, is to encourage older people to take out medical insurance by making tax relief available for those aged sixty or over. Tax relief is also available where premiums are paid by another person, such as a son or daughter, on behalf of a person aged sixty or over.

5.3.1　THE NHS AND THE INDEPENDENT SECTOR

There has always been an interrelationship between the NHS and the independent sector, as, for example, in the provision of pay beds at NHS hospitals. In addition, the independent sector makes provision, such as hospices, and nursing and convalescent homes, in areas where NHS coverage has traditionally been more limited. About 70 per cent of hospice beds and about 78,000 nursing homes beds are in this sector of medicine (DH 1989a).

The boundary between the NHS and independent sector is likely to become increasingly blurred in future, following the introduction of an internal NHS market under the provisions of the National Health Service and Community Care Act 1990 (NHSCCA 1990). As a result, a considerable proportion of services to patients in the NHS is now determined by so-called 'contracts' made between the commissioners of health care and the providers of services. The main commissioners are the district health authorities (DHAs) which are responsible for purchasing a range of services to meet the health care needs of the resident population of their areas. The other main commissioners are general practitioner fundholders (GPFHs) who are able to purchase certain kinds of hospital care for patients on their list (DH 1989a). The main providers of health care, on the other hand, are the Directly Managed Units (DMUs), that is, hospitals and community health services directly managed by DHAs, and the NHS Trusts. However, NHS commissioners are also able to contract with the independent sector, and are encouraged to do so where that would lead to better value for money, and more efficient care (DH 1989a). Contracts between NHS commissioners and providers in the independent sector are likely to become more common in certain areas of health care, such as long-term nursing provision (Laing 1993), which are of particular significance in the care of older people.

5.4.1　ACCESS TO HEALTH CARE

Since most elderly people live at home, their primary need is for health care in the community. Increasingly, even chronic conditions such as diabetes and stroke, can be effectively supported in the community rather than in hospital (Tomlinson 1992). There has been increasing emphasis recently on the importance of enabling elderly people to remain independent, healthy and in their own homes for as long as possible, with more stress being placed on care in the community as a means of preventing or deferring long-term care in residential homes or hospitals (DHSS 1981; DH 1989d). There are problems, however, in establishing and maintaining community care (Silvey 1991). As a result, some elderly people enter care who, with better help and support, might have remained at home (Henwood 1992). Primary health care has a particular role to play in this respect, in assessing need, and in providing skilled help with the problems and disabilities which may develop with age (DH 1989d; DH 1991a).

5.4.2 PRIMARY HEALTH CARE

Primary health care in the NHS consists of two separate services which together provide patients with a range of services. They are the family health services (FHS), organised and administered by Family Health Services Authorities (FHSAs); and community health services (CHS), organised and provided by DHAs, and by NHS Trusts (see para. 5.3.1 above).

Access to the NHS usually takes place through self-referral to a family practitioner working for the FHS, that is, to a general practitioner (GP), a dentist, or an optician. The other health professionals in the FHS are community pharmacists. Although their main function is to dispense and supply patients with drugs and appliances, usually as prescribed by GPs and dentists, they also offer advice to members of the public on request, especially to individuals who are uncertain whether or not to consult a GP about a particular problem.

Family practitioners are independent contractors working for the NHS on the basis of service agreements entered into with the FHSA, and not with their patients. The main terms of these service contracts are agreed nationally and are set out in the relevant regulations. Additional terms of service relating, for example, to the location and times of surgeries, are negotiated between individual family practitioners and the local FHSA.

5.4.3 OBTAINING CARE

It may be too readily assumed that elderly people, as a group, have little difficulty in gaining access to family practitioner services (FPS). Some elderly people, however, face particular problems in obtaining the care which they need. Difficulties can arise in a number of ways: from lack of information and advice, or because the availability of FPS in the NHS can vary from place to place. For instance, access to GP care may be more difficult in inner city areas, where there is often a shortage of doctors, and those working in such areas tend to be older, and in single-handed practices. They may also employ fewer practice staff (Acheson 1981; DHSS 1987; Tomlinson 1992). However, the elderly inhabitants of the inner cities are likely to have more complex health problems, as a result, for example, of poor housing, homelessness, drug dependency and chronic mental or physical illness (ACHEW 1989; Scheuer *et al.* 1991; Bloomsbury CHC 1991). There is growing concern that individuals of this kind may be seen as expensive, time-consuming and/or troublesome. As a result, they are more likely to be rejected by the family practitioners they approach (see para. 5.5.3 below). In other parts of the country, problems arise not so much from a general shortage of family practitioners, as from the fact that many of them offer private care only. In some areas, this is particularly true in relation to dental and optical services.

5.4.4   Lack of information can also be a problem, especially for some groups of elderly people, such as those who are members of ethnic minorities or who came here originally as refugees. They may have language and communication problems (Ham 1992), or suffer from cultural isolation, or separation from their wider families (Norman 1985; Schweitzer 1991). They often fail to access mainstream services, remaining a stark example of unmet need (ACHEW 1989; Bloomsbury CHC 1982; Scheuer *et al.* 1991; Bloomsbury CHC 1991).

5.4.5   PROVIDING INFORMATION

One of the responsibilities of FHSAs is to provide the public with information about FPS in their area. The Patient's Charter also stresses the importance of ensuring that information about FPS is made available to patients, and that practitioners comply with their contractual obligations to provide practice leaflets and other information (DH 1991b) (see para. 5.5.1 below). One of the ways in which FHSAs must carry out their duty to provide information is by compiling and maintaining directories of GPs, dentists and opticians practising in their area. The directory relating to GPs, for example, must contain specific personal and professional information about every GPs on the FHSA's practice list. Individual GPs may also ask for additional information to be included, such as what languages they speak (other than English), and their particular clinical interests. The directories must be available at FHSA offices, and at other locations such as hospitals, main post offices, public libraries, Community Health Council offices, and Citizen's Advice Bureaux.

5.5.1 GENERAL MEDICAL SERVICES

The general medical services (GMS) provided in the community by GPs are an important aspect of the FHS. In many instances, GPs are an individual's first point of contact with the NHS. GPs also treat the vast majority of problems brought to them without referring the patient elsewhere.

In theory, the relationship of doctor and patient is the result of the exercise of choice by both parties. In an attempt to increase patient choice, the government has introduced measures aimed at providing individuals with more information about individual GPs. As a result, every GP must produce a practice leaflet and make it available to the FHSA, to every patient on his/her list, and to any other person who, in the GP's opinion, might reasonably require it. Where a GP is in partnership, one practice leaflet relating to the partnership as a whole is sufficient.

A practice leaflet must include certain information, such as the full name, sex, and medical qualifications of the doctor, and the date and place of his/her initial registration as a medical practitioner. It must also provide information about the way a practice is run, for example, whether the GP works single-handed, or in partnership, or part-time, or on a job-sharing basis, or in a group practice. It should also list any other staff who work in the practice, and their roles. The times at which the GP is available for consultation must be given, with arrangements for off-duty cover. There should also be information about how to arrange an urgent and non-urgent domiciliary visit. If an appointments system is in force, the leaflet should state how patients can obtain urgent and non-urgent appointments, as well as repeat prescriptions. In a dispensing practice, information about the arrangements for dispensing medicines and appliances should also be included. If clinics are held, their purpose, frequency, and duration should be mentioned, as well as details about any other services which the GP offers, such as minor surgery. A practice leaflet should also state whether there is suitable access to the practice premises for disabled patients, and if not, why they are unsuitable for certain kinds of disability. Any arrangements for receiving comments about the way services are provided must also be included. The geographical area covered by the practice must also be described with either a sketch, diagram or plan of the area (National Health Service (General Medical Services) Regulations 1992, reg. 47; Sched. 12).

GPs must also prepare annual reports for the FHSA on the range of services they offer and the workload undertaken by them during the year. In this way, the government hopes to encourage GPs to focus more clearly on the provision of high-quality patient-orientated services, and the need to plan and set objectives for their development and improvement (DHSS 1987).

5.5.2 REGISTERING WITH A GP

General practitioners are responsible for providing a comprehensive and continuous system of care for their patients. Because of the nature and extent of their responsibility, registration is normally a pre-requisite of the doctor–patient relationship. Registering with a doctor may be of particular importance for elderly people. It has been suggested that non-registration should be treated as a possible pointer to other unmet social need (see para. 5.4.3 above).

To register with a GP, a person may approach any doctor who is in practice locally. If a person is incapable of making the approach personally – because, perhaps, of physical or mental infirmity – the request can be made by a relative or carer. If the GP agrees to accept him/her, the patient's medical card, or if it is unavailable for some reason, an application form, must be sent to the FHSA, so that the patient's name is added to the doctor's practice list. The FHSA then issues the patient with a new medical card (reg. 20; Sched. 2, para. 6). The Merrison Committee recognised that for some people the right to choose a doctor was theoretical only, yet its existence was felt to be highly valued (RCNHS 1979).

5.5.3 ALLOCATION

For various reasons discussed above (see para. 5.4.3), some elderly people face particular difficulties in registering with a GP. Since everyone resident in the UK is legally entitled to be registered with a doctor, though not to be on a particular doctor's list, an individual who is having difficulty finding a GP to accept him/her should be encouraged to contact their local FHSA. The FHSA will try to find a GP willing to accept him/her as a patient. Failing that, an individual can make a written request for allocation by the FHSA.

In deciding to allocate a patient to a doctor, the FHSA must take certain factors into account, such as the distance between the person's residence and the practice premises of doctors in the area; whether, during the previous six months, a GP in the same locality has asked for the applicant to be removed from his/her list; and any other relevant circumstances. An allocation cannot be made without the Secretary of State's consent if a GP's list is at, or above, the maximum permitted by the regulations. If the Secretary of State's refuses to give his/her consent, the FHSA must ask if the person wishes to be re-allocated to another GP. If so, the FHSA must do so as soon as possible, seeking the Secretary of State's consent, where necessary.

A GP can appeal to the FHSA within seven days of having a person allocated to his/her list, in which case, the FHSA must review its decision. If, on review, the FHSA confirms its original decision, it must notify the GP within seven days. If, however, the FHSA revises its decision, it must, in addition, notify the patient, and the GP to whom the patient has been re-allocated. Until then, the GP to whom the patient was originally allocated remains responsible for his/her treatment and care (reg. 21).

GPs can ask to be exempt from having patients allocated to them. In reaching its decision, the FHSA must have regard for the doctor's age, state of health, and the number of patients already on his/her list. (reg. 21)

5.5.4 TEMPORARY RESIDENCE

An elderly person who intends living in an area for up to three months, perhaps during a short-term stay at a residential home, can apply to a GP for acceptance as a temporary resident without having his/her name removed from the list where he/she is already registered. If, however, he/she stays in the area for longer than three months, this temporary arrangement can be brought to an end. The FHSA for the area where the individual was previously living can remove his/her name from the GP's list. If practicable, the patient should be told that this has happened, and of his/her right to apply to be put on the list of a doctor in the area where he/she is now living, including that of the GP who has been treating him/her as a temporary resident (reg. 26). If the GP agrees, the patient is then to be treated as his/her patient. If a temporary resident has difficulty in finding a GP to accept him/her, he/she can ask to be allocated to a GP in the usual way (reg. 21) (see para. 5.5.3 above).

5.5.5 IMMEDIATELY NECESSARY TREATMENT

In exceptional circumstances, GPs can be responsible for individuals who are not on their practice list. GPs who are available must treat any person who needs 'immediately necessary' treatment as the result of an accident or emergency occurring within their practice area, provided the patient's own GP is not able to attend. A doctor who is elderly, or infirm, or exempt from having persons allocated to his/her list (see para. 5.5.3 above) may be relieved of this responsibility during weekdays, from 7 p.m. until 8 a.m., and at weekends, from 1 p.m. on Saturdays until 8 a.m. on the following Monday.

GPs must also give 'immediately necessary' treatment for up to fourteen days to a person they have refused to accept as their patient who is without a doctor, unless, during that time, the person is accepted by, or allocated to, another GP (Sched. 2, para. 4).

5.5.6 PROVIDING SERVICES

GPs are personally responsible for the care of their patients on a twenty-four-hour basis. They can divest themselves of this responsibility only as long as they take reasonable steps to ensure continuity of treatment by another doctor acting as their deputy. Local FHSAs must be told about any standing deputising arrangements (unless the deputising doctor is the GP's assistant, or has his/her name on the FHSA's medical list), and of any intention to enter into arrangements with a commercial service (Sched. 2, paras. 20–1). An FHSA must consent to arrangements of this kind and must ensure that they are adequate. It may also impose any condition it considers reasonable or expedient (para. 22). Before imposing a condition or refusing consent, however, an FHSA must consult the Local Medical Committee (which represents medical practitioners in the locality). Deputising arrangements must be reviewed from time to time, and the FHSA may withdraw consent, or alter any conditions which had previously been imposed. There is a right of appeal to the Secretary of State against an FHSA's refusal to agree to the use of a commercial deputising service, or the imposition of conditions (para. 22).

A GP is responsible for the acts and omissions of a deputy, except if the deputy's name is also on the FHSA's medical list, in which case the deputy is personally responsible for any acts or omissions (Sched. 2, para. 20). In such circumstances, any complaint must be brought against the deputy, and not the patient's GP (see Chapter 6 at para. 6.3.6).

A GP may delegate treatment to another person, such as a nurse, only where it is clinically reasonable to do so, and the GP is satisfied that the person to whom the task is delegated is competent to carry it out (Sched. 2, para. 19(2)(b)). Some of the tasks, such as screening, which GPs must now carry out under the 1990 contract, may be delegated to another member of the GP's practice team (DH 1989e).

5.5.7 TREATING PATIENTS

A GP's foremost obligation is to treat patients at his/her practice premises. The place and times of consultation must be approved by the FHSA or, on appeal, by the Secretary of State. Unless prevented by an emergency, or unless adequate cover has been arranged, GPs must be available to attend and treat patients during surgery hours. They are normally expected to be available for consultations, health promotion clinics and home visits, for not less than twenty-six hours on five days a week, (or, with the permission of the FHSA, on four days a week) for at least forty-two weeks a year, at times which are convenient for their patients. Slightly different rules apply to GPs who job-share (Sched. 2, para. 29).

Where an appointments system is in operation, a GP is not obliged to treat a patient who attends without an appointment, unless delay would jeopardise the patient's health, and provided he/she is offered another appointment within a reasonable time. A GP must take reasonable steps, however, to ensure that a consultation is not deferred without his/her knowledge (Sched. 2, para. 17).

Appointments systems can be particularly problematic for elderly patients without access to a telephone. Although the number of households with a telephone in which one or both members are aged sixty or over had increased to 91 per cent by 1990, it is only 78 per cent in the case of one-adult households aged sixty or over (OPCS 1990). Some practices operate both an appointments system and 'open' surgeries at which patients simply turn up and wait to be seen. The importance for many elderly patients of contact with their GP may be seen from the fact that nearly 22 per cent of all those over sixty-five interviewed as part of the General Household Survey in 1983 had seen a doctor at the surgery during the previous month (CSO 1986), and over 90 per cent of people aged seventy-five years or over consult their GP at least once a year (OPCS 1986). This may underestimate need, however, since evidence also indicates that elderly people are often discouraged from visiting the surgery because of problems with transport, because surgeries are arranged on an appointments system, or because they are not always sure of being seen by their 'own doctor' but by another GP in the practice. Although most of those interviewed in this particular study realised that they could make an appointment to be seen by their own doctor, they were easily deflected by receptionists who seemed to be putting them off by offering consultation at a different time, or with a different doctor from the one they had anticipated they would see (Wenger 1988). Some practices attempt to overcome some of these problems by providing 'off-peak' surgery hours specifically for elderly patients.

A receptionist at the GP's surgery is usually a patient's first point of contact with his/her doctor. The Merrison Committee received complaints from patients and from a number of Community Health Councils (CHCs), that some receptionists were over-protective of the GP for whom they worked and apparently made it difficult for patients to see the doctor. The Committee recognised the demanding nature of the work and recommended that they should receive more training (RCNHS 1979).

5.5.8 A GP'S DUTY TO PATIENTS

A GP's main responsibility to patients is set out in Sched. 2, para. 12(1) of the terms of service. Patients must be provided with 'all necessary and appropriate personal medical services of the type usually provided by general medical practitioners'. In doing so, a GP is not expected to exercise a higher degree of skill, knowledge and care than GPs as a class may be reasonably expected to exercise (para. 3), a standard which is similar to that operating under the rules of negligence at common law.

In addition, however, the current regulations set out a number of specific services which GPs are expected to provide, particularly in relation to health promotion, health education and disease prevention. GPs are specifically required to give appropriate advice to patients on their general health, on diet, exercise, smoking habits, consumption of alcohol, and on the misuse of drugs or solvents. Patients must be offered a consultation, and, where appropriate, physical examination, to identify or reduce the risk of disease or injury, as well as vaccinations and immunisations. GPs must also arrange for patients to be referred to other NHS services (see para. 5.5.21 below) and advised how to obtain help from a social services authority (Sched. 2 para. 12).

5.5.9 NEWLY REGISTERED PATIENTS

In most circumstances, GPs must offer a consultation for all newly registered or allocated patients. The purpose is to take a medical history of the patient and his/her family, and to investigate his/her current state of health. Certain social factors should also be investigated, such as his/her housing and family circumstances, and lifestyle (including diet, exercise, smoking habits, consumption of alcohol, and misuse of drugs or solvents) which might affect his/her health. The patient must be offered a physical examination, including measuring height, weight and blood pressure, as well as a urine test. The results of the examination should be recorded in the patient's medical notes. The GP must also assess the patient's need for medical care, and offer to discuss his/her conclusions with the patient, unless doing so would result in serious harm to the patient's physical or mental health (Sched. 2, para. 14).

5.5.10 PATIENTS NOT SEEN WITHIN THREE YEARS

A GP must offer to see any patient, aged between sixteen and seventy-five, who has not consulted him/her, nor attended a clinic, during the previous three years, unless he/she has already been offered a consultation during the previous twelve months. The purpose of the consultation is to assess the patient's need for personal medical services (Sched. 2, para. 15). It should follow similar lines to that offered to newly registered, or allocated, patients (see para. 5.5.9 above).

5.5.11 PATIENTS AGED SEVENTY-FIVE AND OVER

Patients aged seventy-five years of age or over must be offered an annual consultation, and domiciliary visit, to assess whether they need personal medical services. If the offer is accepted, the GP must, during the consultation, assess and record any matters which appear to be affecting the patient's general health, including, where appropriate, his/her sensory functions, mobility, mental and physical condition, including continence, social environment, and use of medicines. If a GP makes a domiciliary visit, he/she should record any of his/her observations which are relevant to the patient's general health, such as whether carers and relatives are available (DH 1989e). The GP must also offer to discuss with the patient what conclusion he/she has reached about the general health of the patient, if it is unlikely to cause serious damage to his/her physical or mental health (Sched. 2, para. 16).

5.5.12 Doubt has been expressed about the value of routine health checks for every elderly person, and the benefits which are likely to result from using scarce resources in this way (Tulloch and Moore 1979; Williamson 1987). It has been estimated, for example, that a practice of 2,000 patients is likely to contain at least 150 patients over the age of seventy-five (Richards 1993). Assuming that a domiciliary assessment would take at least an hour, 150 hours of the GP's time would be required to complete the screening, case analysis and management of all such patients (Richards 1993). Nevertheless, since some elderly people may be reluctant to approach their GP with complaints which they regard as either too trivial for the doctor's attention, or as an inevitable part of growing old, screening of this kind may reveal a considerable amount of unmet physical, psychological and social need among elderly people (Bergman 1973; Taylor and Buckley 1987). Whether such need can, in fact, be met without a substantial increase of resources is another matter (Victor 1991). In practice, the screening of elderly patients in this way may be delegated to other members of the primary health care team (see paras. 5.5.15 and 5.5.24 below).

5.5.13 OTHER SERVICES

GPs may also offer additional services, such as minor surgery, to patients who are registered with the practice. The kinds of surgery which can be performed include injections for varicose veins and haemorrhoids, the aspiration of joints and cysts, and the removal of abscesses, cysts, thrombosed piles, warts, and foreign bodies. Before a GP may carry out minor surgery, however, he/she must satisfy the FHSA that he/she has the medical experience, training and facilities which are needed (regs. 32–3).

Having minor surgery performed by a GP at the practice where they are registered, is likely to be more convenient, and quicker, for an elderly person than having to attend hospital.

5.5.14 PRACTICE PREMISES

Responsibility for providing proper and sufficient practice premises 'having regard to the circumstances of [their] practice' rests primarily with GPs as independent contractors (Sched. 2, para. 27). Some GPs, particularly in rural areas, also hold branch surgeries. If the main, or the branch, surgery needs improving, grants are available for the purpose. Nevertheless, the standard of practice premises varies

(Tomlinson 1992), and the government has expressed concern that, in some areas, a substantial proportion are below minimum standards. Some of the elderly people interviewed in one study mentioned that one of the constraints preventing them from visiting their GP was that they found the waiting room at the doctor's practice premises depressing (Wenger 1988). A major objective has been to improve premises, particularly in deprived areas, by increasing the assistance available to GPs (DHSS 1987). GPs must also allow a member or officer of the local FHSA or Local Medical Committee, or both, to visit their practice premises on request.

5.5.15 Over 6,000 GPs practice from health centres. These are often purpose-built and, as a result, are more likely to be suitable for providing a range of services, some of which may be provided for the patient by other primary health care professionals who either visit or work at the health centre. One development, for which there is government support, is the establishment of primary health care teams consisting of doctors, health visitors, nurses, and sometimes other professionals such as social workers, physiotherapists and chiropodists, and possibly practice managers (DHSS 1987). Not all primary health care teams are based at health centres, but it is suggested that where they work from such premises the quality and accessibility of primary care is improved (RCHS 1979).

5.5.16 For the elderly, there are advantages and disadvantages in registering with a GP who works at a health centre. One advantage is the likelihood of closer co-operation between doctors, community nurses, and the other professionals providing health care in the community. Better preventative, and all-round care, is also more likely. Premises are often purpose-built and may have easier access for those with limited mobility, as well as being better equipped and more welcoming for patients. A disadvantage is that when a practice moves to a health centre, a local surgery may close and patients may have further to travel. As a result, it may be more difficult for older patients to get to see their GP.

5.5.17 HOME VISITS

Patients wishing to consult their GP are normally expected to attend his/her practice premises during surgery hours. A GP is, however, required to attend the patient elsewhere within his/her practice area, or at the address where the patient was living when accepted by the doctor, or at any other place at which the GP has agreed to visit, if the patient's condition requires it (Sched. 2, para. 13). Where, however, a patient moves to live outside his/her GP's practice area, he/she must be told that the GP is no longer obliged to visit and treat him/her. The patient should also be advised to obtain the GP's agreement to visit him/her at the new address, if and when his/her condition requires it, or seek acceptance by another GP. He/she must also be told that if the advice has not been acted on within thirty days, his/her name will be removed from the GP's list (reg. 23(2)–(3)).

The number of consultations held at a patient's home increases with age, so that more than half the contacts with patients over seventy-five years of age take place in their home (RCGP 1986), a likely reflection of the increased frailty and more restricted mobility of those in this age group. Some GPs visit older patients regularly, or arrange for a health visitor or district nurse to call (see para. 5.5.24 below). There seems to be no particular consistency, from practice to practice, in either the frequency or pattern of such visits (Wenger 1988). Regular contact with a GP or other health service professional, although helpful, does not necessarily result in the elderly person revealing all his/her symptoms. Deferential attitudes towards doctors and other professionals, and a reluctance to complain, are characteristic of many in this age group.

5.5.18 PRESCRIBING

Another responsibility placed on GPs is to issue prescriptions, which are then dispensed by community pharmacists. They must, however, supply any appliances or drugs which are needed for the patient's immediate treatment (National Health Service (Pharmaceutical Services) Regulations 1992, reg. 19) In certain circumstances, GPs may also be permitted to dispense directly to their patients, that is, where patients would otherwise suffer serious difficulty in obtaining drugs, medicine and appliances from a pharmacist because of distance, or inadequate communication, or because they live in a rural area which is more than a mile from a pharmacy (National Health Service (Pharmaceutical Services) Regulations 1992, reg. 20).

Since 1986, GPs may not prescribe a scheduled drug, that is, any of the drugs listed in Sched. 10 of the National Health Service (General Medical Services) Regulations 1992. A further restriction is placed on GPs by s.18 of the NHSCCA 1990. Under this provision, FHSAs must give each practice in its area an annual notice, in writing, specifying the practice's indicative budget for the year. GPs are expected to 'seek to secure' that, except with FHSA's consent, or for good cause, their prescribing costs do not exceed this amount. Initially, allocations reflected a practice's existing spending patterns, but there is a gradual shift towards a weighted capitation formula, which takes account of certain social and epidemiological factors, as well as other special factors, such as the need of certain patients for unusually expensive drugs. The object is to 'bring downward pressure on those practices which are above average [in cost]' (DH 1989c), reflecting the government's wish to control the high cost of prescribing in the NHS. According to the DH, patients will always get the medicines they need. Nevertheless, FHSAs can impose sanctions on practices which overspend their budget. The introduction of indicative budgets is, therefore, expected to have greater impact than the limited prescribing list introduced in 1986 (Hughes and McGuire 1992). Moreover, GPFHs must restrict their prescribing costs to the budget set for them by the FHSA.

GPs can continue to prescribe privately any items they choose. Although GPs may not charge for issuing a private prescription, the full cost of purchasing the drug will be borne by the patient.

An aspect of prescribing practice which causes continuing concern is repeat prescriptions issued without the patient being re-examined by the doctor. Individual GPs vary in the extent to which they allow the practice to continue without a further consultation. A high incidence was reported by those interviewed by Wenger in her sample of elderly people (Wenger 1988). In several instances, patients had not been seen for over a year, but continued to take drugs on a repeat prescription. In one case, possibly extreme, the practice had continued unchecked for five years. Unpleasant side-effects were often reported and endured by elderly patients who perceived their doctor as unsympathetic and authoritarian, and were, therefore, reluctant to ask whether the prescription should be repeated.

5.5.19 DISPENSING DRUGS, MEDICINES, AND APPLIANCES

Normally, dispensing services, provided by a community pharmacist, should be available for not less than thirty hours a week over five days, although an FHSA may approve shorter hours if satisfied that the service which is being provided is still likely to be adequate. (National Health Service (Pharmaceutical Services) Regulations 1992, Sched. 2 para. 4) Most FHSAs also organise a rota so that dispensing is carried out outside normal opening hours, for example, in the evenings to coincide with local surgery times, as well as on Sundays and during bank holidays. In an emergency, a pharmacist may issue drugs (except those on a special list) without a prescription. The GP who has requested the pharmacist to do so must provide a prescription within seventy-two hours (para. 3(9)).

Prescription charges are waived for those of retirement age or over, that is, sixty-five for men and sixty for women. A particular difficulty for elderly patients lies in the way medicines and drugs are labelled, for example, 'as directed' or 'as needed'. Lack of information, or a breakdown in communication between doctor and patient via pharmacists, seem common (Wenger 1988) with too much responsibility being placed upon patients.

The Nuffield Report in 1986 recommended that community pharmacists should be encouraged to become more active in the continuing education of other community health workers, such as those responsible for residential homes for the handicapped and the elderly (Nuffield Foundation 1986). The supervision of the supply and safe-keeping of medicines in residential homes is seen by government as particularly important. Under current regulations, pharmacists who regularly provide drugs to residents of a home registered under the Registered Homes Act 1984 (RHA 1984) (as amended) (see Chapter 4 at para. 4.13.1) may offer advice on the safe-keeping and correct administration of such drugs, as well as keeping records of visits to the home.

Another supplemental service which a community pharmacist may offer is to keep records of drugs supplied to a person who is exempt from paying the statutory charges (see para. 5.5.20 below); or who, in the opinion of the pharmacist, is likely to have difficulty in understanding the nature and dosage of a drug, and the times when it should be taken, and it is likely that the same drug, or one similar to it, will be prescribed in future (reg. 16).

Pharmacists also give advice on minor ailments to individuals calling at their shop. The Merrison Committee wished to encourage this within limits and suggested that setting up pharmacies at health centres would be a step in the right direction (RCNHS 1979).

5.5.20 CHARGES

There are no charges for GP care and treatment in the NHS. The only occasion when a GP may charge an NHS patient a reasonable fee for treatment is when a person claiming to be on the GP's list fails to produce his/her medical card when requested, and there is reasonable doubts about his/her claim. An application for a refund may be made to the FHSA within fourteen days (or longer period, not exceeding a month, which the FHSA considers reasonable in the circumstances). If the FHSA is satisfied that the person was, in fact, on the doctor's list when treatment was given, the amount charged must be deducted from the doctor's remuneration and reimbursed to the patient (National Health Service (General Medical Services) Regulations 1992, Sched. 2, paras. 4(3), 38(f), 39).

Some of the services provided by GPs fall outside the NHS scheme and, for these, a charge may be made. Such services include a medical examination given on the request of an insurance company, or issuing an international certificate of vaccinations. In general, however, elderly people in this country are relieved of financial anxiety when consulting their GP.

5.5.21 REFERRAL

GPs must refer patients, when necessary, to other parts of the NHS, such as specialist and hospital services as well as advising patients how to avail themselves of services provided by a local social services authority. Knowledge about the community care arrangements in their area is particularly important in ensuring that elderly patients get the care and support they need. The General Medical Services Committee advocates the use of a simple standardised referral form to provide authorities with relevant factual information about the patient's health, where necessary. GPs should ensure that patients have given informed consent to information being provided for this purpose.

Failure, or refusal, to refer a patient could form the basis of a complaint to the FHSA (see Chapter 6 at paras. 6.3.3 to 6.3.11). The complainant would need to establish that referral was necessary in the particular circumstances of the case. A more likely action is for the patient to change doctors and then request a referral.

There might be grounds also for an action in negligence at common law, as the result of a doctor's failure to refer a patient (see Chapter 6 at para. 6.5.1). In such case, action is available whether the patient was being treated privately or on the NHS. The plaintiff would need to show that the doctor's failure to act was unreasonable and that he/she suffered loss as a consequence.

5.5.22 CHANGING DOCTORS

One of the aims of recent changes in GP contract was to make it easier for patients to change from one GP's list to another. The government hoped that simplifying the system would, when coupled with more comprehensive and accessible information, make people more discriminating in their choice of practice and doctor. This would lead to greater competition, which would encourage doctors to improve the quality of their services (DHSS 1987). In reality, patients often have little choice, particularly if they live in a rural area, or an inner city.

Under the current rules, a person can simply apply, in the usual way (see para. 5.5.2 above) for acceptance by another GP. If a person has difficulty finding a GP to accept him/her, he/she may apply to be allocated to another GP's list (reg. 22).

5.5.23 REMOVAL FROM A GP'S LIST

A GP may apply to have a patient removed from his/her list without giving any reason (Sched. 2, para. 9(1)). Removal takes effect from the date on which the patient is accepted by another GP (see para. 5.5.2 above), or allocated to another doctor's list (see para. 5.5.3 above), or on the eighth day after the application was made, whichever is sooner. There is one proviso, however, in that if a patient is being treated on the date on which removal would normally take effect, the FHSA must be informed, and removal will take effect either on the eighth day after the FHSA is notified that the person no longer needs treatment, or on the date which the person is accepted by, or allocated to, another doctor, whichever is sooner (para. 9(2)). If a patient moves outside the area, or his/her whereabouts are no longer known to the FHSA, his/her name can be removed from the list of the GP with whom he/she is registered at the end of six months, unless the FHSA is satisfied that the GP remains responsible for the patient's general medical care, including visiting and treating him/her when necessary (reg. 23).

For certain patients, removal from a GP's list can present considerable difficulties, for example, those who live in a rural area where there are few or no other practices within a reasonable distance. Since elderly people, on the whole, tend to be uncomplaining patients, they may, perhaps, be the least likely to find themselves removed from a GP's list. Nevertheless, some 'difficult' individuals, possibly suffering from some form of mental disorder or mental infirmity, may find themselves removed from a GP's list. The allocation system can be important in ensuring that such patients are not left without a doctor.

5.5.24 THE COMMUNITY NURSING SERVICES

Community nursing services (particularly district nurses and health visitors) make an important contribution to the care of elderly people.

Although employed by a DHA or NHS Trust, community nurses are often attached to a health centre, or to one or more general practices, sometimes as members of a primary health care team. Better team-work at primary health care level is seen as important in raising the standard of the services available to elderly patients in the community. The Cumberlege Report (DHSS 1986) proposed that community nursing services should be planned, organised and delivered on a neighbourhood basis. While recognising the advantages of this proposal in providing an effective service, the government did not believe that there was one way only of organising nursing services. The decision should rest with the relevant DHA or NHS Trust (DHSS 1987).

District nurses are qualified Registered General Nurses (RGNs) who have undertaken additional training to enable them to provide skilled nursing care in the community, including residential homes (DHSS 1977). They should also give general advice to elderly patients on how to care for themselves and offer particular help over such problems as incontinence (DHSS 1981). They may act as leaders of a district team which can include State Enrolled Nurses (SENs) and auxiliaries who carry out certain tasks such as bathing and dressing frail ambulant patients (DHSS 1977; DHSS 1981). District nurses often assess and, if necessary, re-assess the needs of patients and their families, as well as monitoring the quality of care (DHSS 1977). Community Psychiatric Nurses (CPNs) are becoming increasingly important members of primary health care teams. They have a relatively long tradition of caring for older people with mental health problems (Adams 1989). CPNs are also involved in assessing patients with dementia, and in providing them, and their carers, with support and intervention (Matthew 1990).

Health visitors are primarily concerned with promoting better health and preventing illness and disability by giving advice, education and support. Their training should enable them to understand relationships within the family and the effects upon these of normal human processes, such as ageing.

5.5.25 District nurses and health visitors may themselves initiate visits, or may be asked to see a patient by a hospital doctor, a social worker, or a relative, or by the patient him/herself. Often, however, it is a patient's GP who will refer an elderly person to them. Community nurses often pick up problems which then need to be referred to a GP, or to a social services department, or to a voluntary organisation. Because of the increasing number of elderly people in the community, with more of them frail or infirm, the community nursing services may be over-burdened and unable to visit patients as often as they might wish. Wenger found that visits from district nurses were, however, more likely to be regular than those from any other health professional. Their support of elderly people and the carers of those who are very dependent was much appreciated (Wenger 1988). The majority of those who receive care from the community nursing services will have a named nurse or health visitor allocated to them. Under the *Patient's Charter*, however, this is expected to apply in all cases.

The profile of the community nursing work-force, particularly that of district nurses, is likely to change considerably in the future. Newly qualified nurses who have followed a Project 2000 training programme may work in either hospital or community settings without further specialised district nurse training. This is likely to result in a smaller number of specially trained district nurses providing supervision for less experienced or qualified colleagues.

5.5.26   GENERAL DENTAL SERVICES

General dental services are another aspect of the FHS with significant bearing on the health of elderly people. Access to NHS dental care has become increasingly difficult of recent years, particularly in some areas (ACHEW 1992). An elderly person may not always know what treatment, if any, is available, or may have difficulty in finding a local dentist to accept him/her for NHS treatment. If so, the FHSA should be asked for information and advice. To ensure that the public is properly informed about NHS dental care, FHSAs must ensure that up-to-date copies of certain documents, including the local directory of dentists (see para. 5.4.5 above) are available at their offices, and other convenient places in the area. However, FHSAs have no powers to allocate a patient to a dentist's list (see para. 5.5.3 above).

5.5.27   OBTAINING DENTAL CARE

To obtain general dental care under the NHS, a person must register with a dentist. In theory, the relationship of dentist and patient should be the result of the exercise of choice by both parties. In an attempt to increase patient choice, the government has introduced measures aimed at providing individuals with more information about individual dentists. As a result, every dentist must produce a patient information leaflet and make it available to the FHSA and to any person who may reasonably require one. Where a dentist is in partnership, one leaflet relating to the partnership as a whole is sufficient.

The leaflet must contain specific information including the full name, sex, and dental qualifications of the dentist, and the date and place of his/her initial registration as a dental practitioner. It must also contain information about any other dentists working in the practice; whether a dental hygienist is employed; and whether orthodontic treatment is available. It must also list the days and times when the dentist is available to treat patients, whether the surgery is accessible without using stairs, and whether the premises are accessible to a person in a wheelchair. The dentist may also include information about any languages he/she speaks, other than English (National Health Service (General Dental Services) Regulations 1992, Sched. 5).

5.5.28 REGISTERING WITH A DENTIST

The procedure for registering with a dentist is similar to that for registering with a GP, in that individuals may approach any dentist practising in their local area, and ask to be accepted as the dentist's patient. Where a person is incapable of applying in person, the application may be made on his/her behalf by a relative or carer. Dentists are free to accept or refuse patients without giving any reason (reg. 18(1b)).

5.5.29 PROVIDING SERVICES

Dentists are normally expected to provide treatment personally, except where they are temporarily prevented from doing so by illness, or other reasonable cause, in which case, care and treatment can be provided by a deputy or assistant (Sched. 1, para. 35(1)). Where two or more dentists are in partnership, or the dentist employs an assistant, treatment may be given by a partner or assistant as long as reasonable steps are taken to ensure continuity of care for the patient (para. 35(2)). Where a dentist intends being absent from his/her practice premises for more than twenty-eight consecutive days, he/she must notify the FHSA and provide the name and address of the dentist responsible for providing care during his/her absence (para. 35(9)).

5.5.30 Getting to the surgery can be a problem for some elderly people and they may need help with transport. Their GP, a community nurse, a health visitor or a community dentist may be able to offer advice and assistance. A dentist is entitled to levy a charge if an appointment is cancelled at very short notice. The amount charged will vary from dentist to dentist, as will the definition of 'short notice'. A dentist must visit and treat a patient at the place in which he/she normally resides, or is temporarily residing, if it is not more than 5 miles from his/her surgery and the patient's condition requires it (Sched. 1, para. 24). Dentists are not otherwise obliged to make domiciliary visits. A person who has a disability which causes him/her difficulty in receiving dental care can contact a dentist with special interest in the field. The British Society of Dentistry for the Handicapped will put a disabled person in touch with a dentist in their local area. Community dentists, that is, dentists employed by a DHA, also treat disabled people who cannot attend for treatment at a surgery. Community dentists may also make annual visits to residential establishments in order to give residents a dental examination.

5.5.31 CONTINUING CARE AGREEMENTS

The 1990 contract has placed greater emphasis on preventive care. As a result, most general dental treatment is now provided on the basis of a continuing care arrangement, which normally lasts for two years in the first instance, but may be renewed for periods of two years at a time. Under a continuing care agreement, a dentist must carry out any treatment necessary for maintaining a patient's oral health. The patient must be given a treatment plan, showing what care and treatment (if any) is needed to secure and maintain his/her oral health. It should include the estimated cost of treatment under the NHS, and the cost of any care which is to being done privately (Sched. 1, para. 4(1)(b)). Certain kinds of treatment will not normally be available on the NHS and can only be done privately, such as putting white fillings into back teeth.

A patient may ask the dentist to provide him/her with a new treatment plan at any time. A treatment plan must also be provided whenever it is proposed to mix NHS and private treatment during the same course of treatment, and if certain kinds of treatment are needed, including three or more fillings, extracting more than two teeth, or extracting a tooth which, in the dentist's opinion, is likely to present special difficulty.

5.5.32 EMERGENCY CARE

Dentists must provide patients with care in an emergency, that is, when a patient suffers severe pain as a result of his/her oral condition, or his/her oral health is likely to deteriorate significantly if no treatment is given (Sched. 1, para. 6(2)). They must make reasonable arrangements to ensure that patients receive prompt care and treatment, as soon as appropriate, either personally or from another dentist (para. 6(1)). Emergency cover does not, however, include repairing or replacing dentures (para. 6(2)). Patients should be told how to obtain emergency treatment, for instance, what number to ring for out-of hours service. FHSAs must also ensure that emergency cover is provided in their area.

5.5.33 PAYING FOR TREATMENT

Most dental treatment under a continuing care agreement is subject to charges. However, treatment to stop bleeding must be given free of charge. A dentist must also repair or replace a restoration, that is, any filling, inlay, pinlay or crown, which fails within twelve months of being provided, either by him/her, or another dentist acting on his/her behalf, or a dentist from whom a continuing care arrangement was transferred (Sched. 1, para. 4(1)(f); paras. 7(1) and (2)). The obligation to repair, or replace, does not arise, however, where the patient has received private treatment from the dentist during the previous twelve months, or where another dentist has provided him/her with occasional (but not temporary) treatment (see para. 5.5.38 below). Nor does the obligation arise where, at the time, the dentist advised the patient (and indicated on the treatment plan and on the patient's record) that the treatment was only intended to be temporary, or that in his/her opinion, a different form of treatment would have been more appropriate for securing the patient's oral health, but the patient insisted on the restoration which was provided. The duty does not arise either if, in the dentist's opinion, the condition of the tooth is such that it cannot be repaired or replaced so that different treatment is required, or that the need for the repair or replacement arose because of trauma (para. 7(3)).

Charges for dentures and bridges should include minor adjustments which may be needed after being fitted. Major alterations, made more than a few months after the fitting, must be paid for by the patient. When dentures become broken, the patient is liable to pay for their replacement. If, however, the dentures were themselves faulty, the patient should take them back to the dentist who should send them to a denture repair laboratory. There is no charge for this service, except where the dentures were fitted privately. Where repairs are not carried out properly, a patient may have grounds for making a complaint to the FHSA (see Chapter 6 at paras. 6.3.13). No charge may be made for a call-out to the surgery in an emergency, although the dentist may charge for any treatment given as a result, except when the patient is entitled to free treatment. A home visit is also free, as is calling out a second dentist or doctor to the surgery to give an anaesthetic when a dentist is providing emergency treatment.

5.5.34 A dentist may ask for charges to be paid wholly, or partly, in advance, and may refuse to treat a patient until payment is made. NHS dental treatment is free for certain groups only, such as those on income support (IS) or family credit (FC), or whose partner receives either benefit, as well as those on a low income, that is, capital and income which is below IS level. Where an elderly patient's income, or that of his/her partner, is such that the patient does not qualify for free care, it may be low enough for him/her to be eligible for help with part of the cost of treatment. After making an assessment, the DSS issues eligible claimants with a certificate which is valid for six months. This can be used to get free or cheaper dental treatment. Where a person is not eligible in this way, about 80 per cent of the cost of NHS treatment must be paid. The maximum charge is now £250 for a course of treatment. If the dentist prescribes a drug which is not on the approved dental list, the patient will have to be given a private prescription and must then pay the full cost of the drugs. Alternatively, the patient could visit his/her GP to get the prescription.

Anxiety about the cost of treatment may deter some elderly people from seeking dental care. An analysis of national statistics suggests that people over sixty-five, who are not exempt, are half as likely to have costly treatment as those who are. However, non-exempt patients are four times as likely to receive emergency treatment, suggesting that elderly people who fall into this group put off visiting a dentist for as long as possible (Birch 1988). It is particularly important, therefore, that those who are eligible for free or cheaper treatment should receive it.

5.5.35 If a patient needs various kinds of more expensive treatment, the dentist must obtain the permission of the Dental Practice Board (DPB) before the work may be carried out under the NHS. The DPB may refuse to authorise complex treatment if is not thought to be needed, or if a cheaper form of treatment would be as satisfactory. If the DPB refuses to approve a proposed course of treatment the patient may have cheaper treatment done on the NHS, or he/she may appeal against the decision within four weeks. In that case, a hearing before two independent dentists will be held. The alternative is to pay for the work to be done privately. Where the DPB gives approval for more expensive treatment to be done, any additional cost is added to the normal cost of the treatment.

5.5.36 REFERRAL

If a patient needs care and treatment which the dentist cannot provide because he/she lacks the necessary facilities, experience or expertise, he/she must refer the patient, with his/her agreement, to another dentist, to a hospital, or another NHS service (Sched. 1, para. 12(1)). No charges are made for dental care received as an in-patient. For most other in-patients, however, only emergency treatment is free, except for long-stay patients who are entitled to free care when necessary, including dentures. Where a person receives out-patient dental treatment, however, he/she will have to pay for dentures, crowns and appliances in the same way as in general dental practice.

5.5.37 TERMINATING A CONTINUING CARE AGREEMENT

If a dentist wishes to discontinue a continuing care arrangement, he/she must give the patient notice in writing not later than three months before the date on which the agreement is due to lapse, or such shorter period as is reasonable in the circumstances. The dentist must also try to complete any care and treatment which he/she had agreed to provide for the patient and which is outstanding, and any further treatment that is necessary to secure and maintain his/her oral health (Sched. 1, para. 10).

A continuing care arrangement also comes to an end if the patient enters into an arrangement with another dentist; or agrees with the dentist, or any other dentist, that the care and treatment should, in future, be provided privately (Sched. 1, para. 8(2)(b)). A patient may ask for a summary of the care and treatment he/she received when he/she is transferring to another dentist. The summary, for which the patient may be charged, should be provided within twenty-eight days (para. 15).

5.5.38 OCCASIONAL TREATMENT

A dentist may also provide occasional treatment for a patient in certain circumstances, such as on referral from a dentist who does not have the necessary facilities, experience or expertise to provide the treatment which the patient needs. If occasional treatment is being given, the range of treatment is more restricted than under a continuing care arrangement.

5.5.39   CHANGING DENTISTS

A patient may change dentists at any time. If he/she wishes to change during a course of treatment, he/she may have to pay the first dentist for the full course. When this happens, he/she should contact the FHSA to see whether a refund is possible. It is always sensible to find a second dentist in advance who is prepared to complete a course of treatment already started by another dentist.

5.5.40   OPTICIANS

The general ophthalmic services (GOS) are another aspect of the FHS which are important in providing proper care for older people. Since eyesight is likely to deteriorate with age, elderly people need regular attention and care from an optician. There may also be specific problems which can lead to loss or impairment of vision. Poor vision can have an adverse effect on mobility, with greater dependency and social isolation. As people grow older, they should have regular sight tests so that suitable glasses can be prescribed and any incipient problems are diagnosed as quickly as possible. It is also important that they see an optician or their GP as soon as possible after noticing any particular difficulty or discomfort. The GOS's primary function is to provide sight-tests, and prescriptions for spectacles, where necessary. Lists of those who work for the NHS locally must be compiled and held by the local FHSA and should also be available elsewhere in the community. Where a problem needs further or different care or treatment, an individual should be referred to the hospital eye service, for example, or to a social services department.

5.5.41   Sight tests can only be carried out by a registered ophthalmic medical practitioner or a registered ophthalmic optician (optometrist). Annual sight tests are no longer available free of charge except for certain groups. Elderly people, as a group, have no exemption, although some opticians offer tests at a reduced cost for elderly people. Some elderly people, however, are exempt from paying for the test, either because they (or their partner) is on IS or FC, or they need complex lenses, or they are registered blind or partially sighted, or they have been diagnosed as suffering from diabetes or glaucoma, or they are either the parent, brother, sister or child of a person who has been diagnosed with glaucoma, or they are patients at a hospital eye clinic. Those on a low income may also be able to get help with the cost of the test. Those who are eligible for a voucher should tick the entitlement box when signing a sight test form. If the sight test indicates that new spectacles are needed, the optician must issue both a voucher and a prescription. Prescriptions may be made up by an unregistered supplier, except if a person is registered blind or partially sighted.

5.5.42 Spectacles are no longer available under the NHS. Elderly people who are prescribed new spectacles or lenses must pay for them unless they, or their partner, are eligible for help because they are receiving IS or FC, or on grounds of low income. In such cases, vouchers are automatically issued which can be used to obtain spectacles, or contact lenses, in the private market, either free of charge or at a lower cost. Those entitled to free or cheaper glasses on the grounds of low income should apply to the DHSS on form AG2. After the claim has been assessed, the DSS will send the claimant a certificate entitling him/her to free or cheaper treatment. Vouchers are valid for a single transaction only, and must be used within six months of the date of issue. Vouchers can also be used to purchase contact lenses. Those who need complex/powerful lenses, but are not automatically entitled to an NHS voucher, are entitled to a voucher which helps with part of the cost, as are those on a low income which is above the limit for free treatment. War pensioners who require sight tests, or glasses, as a result of a condition for which they receive a war pension, may be able to claim back some or all of the cost from the Department of Social Security (DSS).

5.5.43 Elderly people who need special glasses may be referred to the hospital eye service. If a prescription is issued by a hospital consultant, the same rules on eligibility for free or cheaper glasses or contact lenses apply. If a person requires frequent changes of spectacles or contact lenses on clinical grounds, only the first pair must be paid for. If, however, a person is entitled under the voucher scheme, he/she will also be entitled to help with the cost of the first prescription. Special vouchers can be issued for items not covered by the standard voucher scheme, such as particularly expensive glasses or contact lenses.

5.5.44 In some areas, it may be difficult for an elderly person to locate an optician whose practice he/she can reach conveniently.

Opticians are not obliged to make home visits, but may be prepared to visit where there are good reasons why a person cannot make the journey to their practice premises. Opticians can charge for a home visit. In some areas of the country, however, there are free visiting schemes in which opticians may participate on a voluntary basis. Alternatively, an elderly person can ask their GP, a district nurse (DN) or a health visitor (HV) whether transport can be arranged, or ask to be referred for to hospital eye service which may arrange for the patient to be visited at home.

5.5.45 CHIROPODISTS

Problems connected with mobility are particularly significant in old age. Services offered by chiropodists help elderly people to keep active and independent. Unlike most other NHS services, chiropody is available only to certain priority groups, including women over sixty and men over sixty-five. Chiropodists work mainly at clinics run by the local DHA, although about a quarter of their contacts with patients take place at the person's home, with a further one-eighth at the chiropodist's surgery. The principal drawback in obtaining chiropodist care in the NHS is the length of waiting lists in some areas. As a result, many elderly people may have no alternative but to opt for private care.

5.6.1 SECONDARY HEALTH CARE SERVICES

As individuals grow older, they are more likely to need hospital care. According to the General Household Survey for 1988, over 20 per cent of men and 16 per cent of women over seventy-five reported that they had been in hospital during the previous year, compared to about 9 per cent of the population as a whole (OPCS 1988). Most elderly people become hospital patients by referral from their GP to a hospital consultant's out-patient clinic. Non-fund-holding GPs may only refer their patients to those hospitals with which the local DHA has a contract for the services which are needed. GPFHs, however, may contract directly, up to a financial limit, from a variety of possible providers, such as directly managed hospitals, NHS Trust hospitals or hospitals in the independent sector, for certain kinds of hospital care. These are elective in-patient treatments, such as hip replacements and cataract operations, and day care treatment, but not emergency or medical admissions; out-patient services such as physiotherapy, and including continuing out-patient treatment and out-patient attendances following in-patient and day care surgery; and diagnostic tests and investigations, such as X-rays, radiological tests and blood tests, including those ordered by a hospital consultant. Once a patient has been referred, decisions over treatment are for the hospital consultant who may take clinical responsibility for the patient (DH 1989b).

Since April 1992, DHAs should ensure, in accordance with the *Patient's Charter*, that all NHS service providers make available for patients, detailed information about their services, including quality standards and maximum waiting times. This applies, also, when DHAs and GPFHs are contracting for services. They must satisfy themselves, through their monitoring procedures, that the information is available, and easily accessible, to patients.

5.6.2 GETTING TO HOSPITAL

For a variety of reasons, such as limited mobility, difficulties in relation to transport, or the cost of getting there, elderly people may find it difficult to make their own way to and from hospital, either to see a consultant or to be admitted as an in-patient. In such circumstances, the patient's GP or the hospital where they are going, should be asked whether transport can be arranged, either by ambulance or by hospital car. For those using public transport, or other means of getting to hospital, financial help may be available if they (or their partner) are receiving IS or FC, or if they receive a war or Ministry of Defence disablement pension and are being treated for that disability in an NHS hospital. Help with hospital travel costs for NHS treatment may also be available on grounds of low income. If the hospital confirms that the patient needs someone to accompany him/her on the journey, that person is also eligible for help with travel costs. A claim for travel expenses can be made on arrival at the hospital. Evidence, such as an order book, must be produced to show that the person is eligible for financial help. Proof of entitlement as a result of low income can be obtained by sending form AG1 to the Agencies Benefits Unit (ABU) in Newcastle-upon-Tyne for an assessment to be made. The ABU will send back a certificate stating whether full or partial entitlement may be claimed. The certificate is valid for six months. If travel costs have already been paid by an individual falling into either of the above groups, a refund may be claimed within a month of the payment being made. Those unable to travel to hospital, because they lack sufficient funds, should ask the local DSS office for a Crisis Loan from the Social Fund.

A person who is visiting a patient in hospital may be able to obtain help with fares from the Social Fund if the patient is a war or Ministry of Defence disablement pensioner being treated for that disability, or is a close relative receiving IS support.

5.6.3 THE CONSULTATION

NHS patients have no right to insist on being seen by a particular consultant, not even the consultant to whom they have been referred by their GP. It is the consultant who decides whether or not to examine the patient, and whether to delegate the task to another doctor in his/her team. However, the consultant carries the ultimate responsibility, for example whether or not to treat the patient, and if so in what way.

5.6.4 REFERRAL

A consultant may refer a patient for out-patient treatment, such as physiotherapy. Under the *Patient's Charter*, patients should be given a specific appointment, and be seen within thirty minutes of the appointment time. If a patient requires X-rays, a blood test and other procedures prior to the appointment, these should be carried out prior to the out-patient consultation (DH 1991b). Similar arrangements for transport to and from a clinic can be made, and for the payment of fares (see para. 5.6.2 above).

In some areas, patients may be referred by a consultant (and sometimes by a GP) to a geriatric day hospital for nursing care or re-habilitation.

Many older people, however, need continuing care in a geriatric or psycho-geriatric hospital or unit. The number of such beds has gone down considerably of recent years, despite the fact DHAs are required to ensure that 'their plans allow for the provision of continuous residential health care for those highly dependent people who need it' (DH 1989d). In a recent survey of Community Health Councils, 77 per cent of respondents stated that, between 1987 and 1990, the provision of continuing care beds in their area had been reduced. The beds which had disappeared had not, however, been off-set by other NHS facilities. As a result, some elderly people, their relatives and carers faced a situation in which there was no NHS provision for non-acute nursing needs (ACHEW 1990b). In evidence to a House of Commons Select Committee, the Alzheimer's Disease Society stated that relatives and older people were not necessarily aware of their right to insist on staying in hospital, or continue to receive an NHS funded bed, but were often being vigorously encouraged to seek a placement in an independent nursing home. According, however, to DH Circular (HC(89)5): 'no NHS patients should be placed in private nursing or residential care homes against their wishes where it would mean that they or any relative would become personally responsible for paying for the care they received' (DH 1989f). In its report, the Select Committee stressed the importance of providing more NHS convalescence care to ease the pressure on hospitals to clear beds, while providing users and carers with more time to consider the available options and to create more imaginative and flexible care packages (HC 1993). In general, however, it does not appear that DHAs are purchasing beds in the independent sector to replace the continuing care beds which are no longer available at NHS hospitals. As a result, only 28 per cent of carers in a recent survey by the Alzheimer's Disease Society reported that they had access to an NHS continuing care bed, whereas 15 per cent of carers reported that there was no long-term care available locally (ADS 1993).

This lack of long-term NHS care has recently been highlighted by the Health Service Commissioner in a special report to the Secretary of State for Health. The Ombudsman upheld a complaint that failure to make long-term care available within the NHS for a patient suffering from brain damage was unreasonable and constituted a failure in the services which should be provided (HSC 1994).

5.6.5 ADMISSION TO HOSPITAL

Admission to hospital normally takes place as a result of a consultant's decision to admit. In certain circumstances, however, a patient may be admitted to hospital without following this normal route.

In an emergency – where, for example, an elderly person has a heart attack while out shopping, or is involved in a road accident – he/she may be taken straight to a hospital out-patient accident, emergency or casualty department, and, if necessary, be admitted from there, for in-patient treatment. Not all hospitals have such departments, however, and even where they do, they may be open only at certain times, and, possibly, not at all at the weekend. If a situation is not urgent, the patient's GP should be contacted. If, however, the GP decides that the patient should be admitted to hospital, he/she has authority to do so if a bed is available locally. If necessary, the GP will contact the ambulance service. Where it is not possible to contact the GP, or if he/she refuses to visit, but it is felt that immediate treatment is needed, an elderly person may be taken direct to an accident or casualty department for attention and possible admission to hospital. Only in a serious emergency should a 999 call be made to the ambulance services. In any case, the ambulance services are likely to try to contact the person's GP first, and usually will only come directly to the patient's house if they fail to contact the person's GP. Where an emergency ambulance is called, it should, in accordance with National Charter Standards set out in the *Patient's Charter*, arrive within fourteen minutes in an urban area, nineteen minutes in a rural area, and twenty-one minutes in a sparsely populated area, and a patient should be seen immediately at an accident and emergency department and have their need for treatment assessed by a trained health care professional (DH 1991b).

Under s.158 of the Road Traffic Act 1988 (RTA 1988), NHS hospitals and GPs are allowed to charge a fee for emergency treatment following a road traffic accident. A charge of this kind, levied against the user of any vehicle involved in the accident, is usually paid by the insurance company. The maximum charges to be levied for treatment and care in such circumstances have been increased by the provisions of the Road Traffic Accidents (Payments for Treatment) Order 1993.

5.6.6   WAITING LISTS

Under the *Patient's Charter*, patients should be guaranteed admission for treatment by a specific date, which should be not later than two years from the date when they were placed on a waiting list (DH 1991b). No patient should have to wait over eighteen months for a replacement hip or knee operation or for a cataract operation. All patients on a day-case waiting list, on or after 1 April 1992, should receive a letter from the hospital (usually in the consultant's name) informing them of the guaranteed date by which they will be admitted for their particular treatment. There should also be guaranteed admission within a month, for urgent in-patient or day-case treatment. In exceptional circumstances, this waiting time may have to be exceeded, for example where, in the judgement of the GP and patient, it would be best to wait rather longer than the guaranteed period to secure the specialised services of a particular doctor, or where highly specialised treatments, such as organ transplants, are needed, and the availability of treatment does not rest simply on the efficient planning of resources. Where a patient asks for the operation to be deferred, and it is not possible to offer another date within the guarantee period, providers should offer the patient personalised arrangements for treatment as soon as possible after that time. If the patient is medically unfit at the time when the treatment is to be given, every effort should be made to secure treatment as soon as the patient is fit.

If an operation is cancelled twice in succession, on the day on which a patient was due to be admitted to hospital, he/she should be admitted within a month of the date of the second cancellation. If, while a patient is in hospital, an operation is cancelled twice in succession, the patient should be re-admitted within a month of the date of the second cancelled operation. This National Charter Standard is aimed specifically at reducing distressing circumstances caused by organisational problems.

5.6.7 ADMISSION TO HOSPITAL UNDER THE MENTAL HEALTH ACT 1983

Apart from an emergency when it may not be possible to obtain a person's consent, a patient's agreement is normally required before a patient can be admitted to hospital and be given treatment. The other main exceptions to this rule arise under s.47 of the National Assistance Act 1948 (NAA 1948) (see Chapter 4 at paras. 4.21.1 to 4.21.2) and in relation to the compulsory admission to hospital of mentally disordered patients as defined under s.1 of the MHA 1983.

In practice, most mentally disordered patients enter hospital informally. Indeed, s.131 of the MHA 1983 states that nothing in the Act should be construed as preventing a person needing treatment for mental disorder from being admitted in that way. Mental disorder is defined by s.1(2) as 'mental illness, arrested or incomplete development of mind, psychopathic disorder and any other disorder or disability of mind'. There are four specific categories: mental illness, severe mental impairment, mental impairment and psychopathic disorder, each of which is further defined by the Act.

5.6.8 An application for compulsory admission to hospital under the MHA 1983 can be made only by an approved social worker, as defined in s.114 of the Act, or by the patient's 'nearest relative', as defined in s.26 of the Act. Before making an application, the approved social worker (ASW) must interview the patient in a suitable manner, to satisfy him/herself that detention in a hospital or mental nursing home is, in all the circumstances of the case, the most appropriate way of providing the care and medical treatment which the patient needs (s.13). In all cases, whether an application is made by an ASW, or by the patient's nearest relative, it must comply with either s.2, (admission for assessment); s.3, (admission for treatment); or s.4, (admission for assessment in an emergency) and with the other statutory provisions in the 1983 Act which relate to medical recommendations and other related matters. If the application is for admission for treatment under s.3 of the Act, the patient's nearest relative may object. It is possible, however, for any other relative, or any person with whom the patient is residing, or any approved social worker, to apply to the county court for the functions of the patient's nearest relative to be transferred to the applicant, or to any other proper person who is willing to act.

5.6.9 A person who appears to be mentally disordered can also be detained in hospital under other sections of the Act. Under s.136, a police constable is authorised to remove to a place of safety any person found in a public place, who appears to be mentally disordered and in immediate need of care and control, if it is thought to be necessary in his/her own interests or for the protection of other people. The purpose of detention, which may last no longer than seventy-two hours, is for the individual to be assessed by a doctor, and interviewed by an ASW, so that arrangements can be made, if necessary, for his/her treatment or care. A place of safety under the Act includes (apart from a hospital), local authority social services accommodation, a police station, a mental nursing home, a residential home for mentally disordered persons or any other suitable place the occupier of which is prepared temporarily to receive the person. According to the revised *Code of Practice* on the Mental Health Act, it is always good practice, where a hospital is being used as a place of safety, for the patient not to be formally admitted, although he/she may have to be cared for on a ward. Where such policy is adopted, it is essential for the person to be examined by a doctor in the same way as if he/she had been formally admitted (DH/WO 1993).

The use of s.136 should also be locally monitored to establish how and in what circumstances it is being used, particularly in relation to certain categories of people, such as those from particular ethnic or cultural groups; and in order that consideration can be given to making changes in the mental health service which have the result of reducing the use of the section (DH/WO 1993).

Where a person has been removed to a place of safety under s.136, he/she is entitled, under s.56 of the Police and Criminal Evidence Act 1984 (PACE 1984), to have a person of his/her choice informed about his/her removal and his/her whereabouts. Where a police station is being used as a place of safety, he/she also has a right of access, under s.58 of PACE 1984 to legal advice. In other circumstances, access to legal advice should be facilitated when it is requested.

5.6.10 Section 135 also includes a 'place of safety' provision. Under this section, a magistrate may issue a warrant authorising a police constable to enter premises, if necessary by force, and without the consent of the occupant, to remove a person thought to be mentally disordered, with a view to making an application for admission to hospital, or for making other arrangements for his/her treatment or care. Detention under s.135 cannot exceed seventy-two hours.

Before issuing the warrant, the magistrate must have information on oath from an ASW, that there is reasonable cause to suspect that a person believed to be mentally disordered has been, or is being, ill-treated, neglected or kept otherwise than under proper control; or being unable to care for him/herself, is living alone. An ASW and a doctor must accompany the constable when executing the warrant.

5.6.11 A criminal court can order a person, brought before it in relation to an alleged offence, to be admitted to hospital in the circumstances, and on the conditions set out in ss.35–40 of the MHA 1983.

5.6.12 Concern has been expressed by the Mental Health Act Commission (MHAC), in its Biennial Reports, about the professional, ethical and practical dilemmas often facing staff in dealing with two patient groups in particular, that is, long stay informal patients who lack mental capacity; and patients who are subjected to *de facto* detention in a locked ward or room. Many of these patients are elderly. The MHAC has become increasingly aware of the lack of clearly defined rights and safeguards in relation to such patients. In one hospital, for example, visiting Commissioners found twelve locked wards, although only a few of the patients in them were formally detained under the Act. These problems are intensified when hospitals close and many of the patients move into the private and voluntary sectors. About a half of all mentally infirm patients, not living at home, are being looked after in the independent sector. Professionals and staff do not necessarily recognise the extent to which some of these patients are deprived of their liberty. Situations, such as these, highlight the need for a proper legal framework in which decisions relating to mentally incapacitated adults can be made (Law Commission 1991, 1993b, 1993c) (see Chapter 7 at 7.21.1).

However, growing concern about the current situation is reflected in the increasing number of requests for advice about *de facto* detention. The Commission encourages hospital managers (HMs) to introduce written policies clarifying the status and rights of any informal patient who is subject to *de facto* detention, and to introduce requirements for their implementation to be monitored (MHAC 1987, 1989, 1991). As far as good practice is concerned, the revised Code of Practice suggests that 'the safety of informal patients who would be at risk of harm if they were allowed to wander out of a ward or nursing home at will, can usually be secured by means of adequate staff and good surveillance.' Combination locks and double-handled doors to prevent frail elderly people from wandering out should be used as little as possible, and only in units where there is a regular and significant risk of patients wandering off accidentally and as, a result, being at risk of harm. Every patient should have an individual care plan which states explicitly why and when he/she will be prevented from leaving the ward. It points to the need for clear policies on the use of locks and other devices, and that a mechanism should be in place for reviewing decisions on these. Where a patient may leave the ward accidentally, he/she may legitimately be deterred by such devices. If, however, patients persistently and purposely attempt to leave, whether or not they understand the risk involved, consideration must be given to assessing whether they would more appropriately be detained formally under the Act, rather than remaining as informal patients. No patient should be deprived of appropriate daytime clothing during the day with the intention of restricting their freedom of movement, nor of other aids necessary for their daily living (DH/WO 1993).

5.6.13 CONSENT TO TREATMENT

The general rule is that however elderly, frail, or infirm a person may be, he/she must freely consent to being medically treated, otherwise a tortious and actionable wrong is committed against him/her (see Chapter 6 at paras. 6.5.1 and 6.5.4). A patient normally gives his/ her consent expressly by signing a consent form. The consent form usually describes the operation it is intended to perform, but may also contain the additional phrase 'and proceed'. This phrase permits the surgeon to carry out any further surgery deemed immediately necessary.

Consent need not always be given expressly, however, since, in some circumstances, it may be implied from a person's conduct. For example, if a person with backache attends a physiotherapy department, agreement to receive treatment which is reasonable for that condition may be assumed from the individual's conduct, unless the contrary is clearly expressed or implied by the patient.

A question arises, however, whether consent is real unless it is given on the basis of full knowledge of the possible consequences. In *Sidaway v. Board of Governors of the Bethlem Royal Hospital and the Maudsley Hospital (1985)*, the House of Lords held that English law does not recognise the doctrine of 'informed consent', namely, that a patient has a right to be informed of all the possible risks involved in the proposed treatment. The doctor is required to act only in accordance with the practice accepted as proper at the time by a reasonable body of medical opinion.

5.6.14 TREATMENT WITHOUT CONSENT

At common law, treatment can only be given without a person's consent in cases of urgent necessity, for instance, operating to save a person's life, or to prevent an individual acting in ways dangerous to him/herself, or others. Even so, treatment must only be such as is reasonable and sufficient in the circumstances of the particular case. According to McCullough J. in *R v. Hallstrom, ex parte W (1986)*: 'It goes without saying that, unless clear statutory authority to the contrary exists, no one is . . . to undergo medical treatment or even to submit himself to a medical examination without his consent.' According to the Hallstrom judgment, this general rule applies (apart from the statutory exceptions set out below) to mentally disordered patients as well, as confirmed by the recent decision in *Re C (1993)*. The facts of the case were that C, a mentally disordered patient, suffered from a life-threatening condition. Plans for invasive surgery were made, but C refused to give his consent. C applied to the court for an injunction to restrain the authorities from taking action. The question which arose was whether the presumption of competence had been rebutted in this case. It was held that any patient who understands the nature, purpose and effects of any proposed medical treatment, is capable of refusing the treatment, even if his general capacity is impaired by chronic mental illness. Mr Justice Thorpe analysed C's decision-making process into three stages: first, comprehension and retaining information about the treatment; second, believing it; and, third, weighing the information, balancing risks and needs, in order to arrive at a choice. When that test was applied, the presumption that C had the right of self-determination had not, in this case, been displaced. He understood the nature, purpose and effects of the treatment and had arrived at a clear choice.

5.6.15 This general presumption that adults have full legal capacity, is, however, open to rebuttal (*per* Lord Donaldson M.R. in *Re T (Adult: Refusal of Treatment) (1993)*). Where an elderly person is mentally incapacitated to the extent that he/she cannot give his/her consent, the légal position is more complex. A particular problem arises, in this context, in relation to patients who are suffering from dementia. In its Second Biennial Report, the MHAC discusses the difficulty of using the MHA 1983 to detain and treat elderly patients suffering in this way. The Commission noted the delicate balance which needs to be maintained in such circumstances. Staff might be understandably reluctant to employ formal detention under the Act, even with respect to a difficult elderly patient. On the other hand, where a patient was not detained and not subject to the provisions of Part IV of the MHA 1983, staff might hesitate to provide positive treatment.

The Law Commission has recently pointed to the

> fundamental tension in this area between the need to allow professionals scope to do their best for their patients, and the need to protect those who cannot protect themselves from treatment, however well-intentioned, which they may not want or need. The law must attempt to find a balance between these considerations.
>
> (Law Commission 1993b)

In *Re F (Mental Patient: Sterilisation) (1990)*, the House of Lords held that although no person or court can give consent on behalf of an incapacitated person, the court may grant a declaration authorising treatment to be given because of necessity if such treatment would, also, be in the patient's best interests. According to Lord Goff,

> not only (1) must there be a necessity to act when it is not practicable to communicate with the assisted person, but also (2) the action taken must be such as a reasonable person would in all the circumstances take, acting in the best interests of the assisted person.

In the words of Lord Brandon, the treatment

> will be in the best interests of such patients if, but only if, it is carried out in order either to save their lives or to ensure improvement or prevent deterioration in their physical or mental health.

In deciding a patient's 'best interests', according to Lord Goff, the decision, may, in practice, involve others besides the doctor. 'It must surely be good practice to consult relatives and others who are concerned with the care of the patient. Sometimes, of course, consultation with a specialist will be required; and in others, especially where the decision involves more than a purely medical opinion an interdisciplinary team will in practice participate in the decision' (*per* Lord Goff).

The decision in *Re F* has been criticised on several grounds (Law Commission 1991). In Consultation Paper 129, the Law Commission proposes a statutory formulation of the test of capacity to consent, and of the basis for making a treatment decision once it is established that the person is incapable of making his/her own decision. The role of a judicial forum in resolving specific questions is also discussed (Law Commission 1993b).

5.6.16 There are specific statutory rules, however, in relation to detained mental patients who refuse treatment for their mental disorder. The legal position in such cases is covered by Part IV of the MHA 1983 (other than where the detention is for a short period of time only). Under the statutory provisions, it is not necessary to obtain a patient's consent for treatment for mental disorder which is given by the responsible medical officer (that is, by the doctor in charge of the patient's treatment), except for certain categories of treatment which are set out in the Act. In consequence, psychosurgery, and the surgical implantation of hormones, can be only carried out on a detained patient (and, in these exceptional circumstances, on an informal patient) with his/her express consent, and with the agreement of an independent doctor specifically appointed for the purpose, who, in accordance with s.57 of the Act, has also consulted two other persons concerned with the patient's treatment. Where electro-convulsive therapy (ECT) treatment is proposed, or where a course of medication has continued for three months during a period of detention, treatment can be given or continued only with the detained patient's express consent, and the issue of a certificate given by the responsible medical officer, or an independent doctor specifically appointed for the purpose, which confirms that the patient's consent is real and valid. In this case, however, if the patient refuses his/her consent, or is incapable of giving it, an independent doctor appointed specifically for the purpose may, after consulting, in accordance with s.58, and with two other persons concerned with the patient's treatment, certify that the treatment should be given, in that it is likely to alleviate or prevent his/her condition from deteriorating. The procedures under s.57 and s.58 apply to treatment given either on a single occasion, or in accordance with a plan of treatment. Because of the danger of consent to treatment being without limit of time, s.61 provides a procedure for reporting, and reviewing, treatment given under s.57 and s.58, and for the cancellation of any certificates granted under those sections.

5.6.17 Sections 57 and 58 do not apply to urgent treatment given under s.62 of the Act, that is, to treatment which is immediately necessary to save a patient's life. Urgent treatment includes treatment which is immediately necessary to prevent serious deterioration to the patient's condition, or which is immediately necessary to alleviate serious suffering; or which is immediately necessary, but is the minimum interference necessary to prevent the patient from behaving violently or being a danger to him/herself or others. If the proposed treatment would also be irreversible or hazardous, however, the patient's consent and/or a second opinion which accorded with s.57 or s.58, would have to be obtained, however urgent the circumstances.

5.6.18 WITHDRAWING CONSENT

Under general rules of law, a patient may withdraw consent to treatment at any time, except where the doctrine of necessity applies (see para. 5.6.14 above). This includes mentally disordered patients who are in hospital informally. Where a mentally disordered patient, detained under the MHA 1983, has given consent to treatment under s.57 or s.58, he/she may withdraw that consent at any time before the treatment, or plan of treatment, is completed (unless it is treatment which is urgently needed to save his/her life). If it is proposed to continue treating the patient after consent has been withdrawn, the statutory procedures in ss.57 and 58 must be invoked, except where the responsible medical officer considers that discontinuing treatment would cause serious suffering to the patient.

5.6.19 ADVANCE DIRECTIVES

Advance directives are a means whereby individuals can, when rational and lucid, anticipate an event, such as serious illness, which might cause them to become incapable of giving or refusing consent to treatment at some future date. An example of an advance directive is a 'living will', that is, a document which enables a person to declare that he/she does not wish to be kept alive by medical technology, such as a life support machine, if his/her condition has deteriorated to the point that it is no longer reversible.

It was held in *Re C (1993)* (see para. 5.6.14 above) that the High Court has jurisdiction to grant an injunction in relation to any future medical treatment, such as a patient becoming incapacitated at some future date.

In Consultation Paper 129, the Law Commission has set out its preliminary proposals for anticipated decision-making. It considers the relevance of decisions made before the onset of incapacity, and whether the law should grant treatment providers an explicit but limited authority to take certain decisions after appropriate consultation. The Commission proposes that a person should be able to execute an enduring power of attorney (EPA), giving another person the authority to give or refuse consent on his/her behalf to some or all medical treatment. A judicial tribunal should, also, be able to appoint a 'treatment proxy' where necessary to act on behalf of the incapacitated person (Law Commission 1993b).

5.6.20 WITHDRAWAL OF MEDICAL TREATMENT

It has been held in the case of *Airedale NHS Trust v. Bland (1993)* that the withdrawal of artificial feeding did not constitute a criminal act. It was further held, in this case, that a doctor is not under a duty to maintain a patient's life where the continuance of intrusive life support is not in the patient's best interests. However, doctors who are faced with a situation in which a patient is in a persistent vegetative state (PVS) must seek a declaration from the court in every case.

Although the principle of the sanctity of human life forbids positive measures being taken to cut short the life of a terminally ill patient, this does not prevent the discontinuance of treatment which merely keeps the patient alive. Where a patient is in a PVS, and will inevitably die without such life-prolonging treatment, the test to be applied, in the absence of clear instructions from the patient when he/she was of sound mind, is the duty of doctors to apply treatment which, in their informed opinion, is in the best interests of an unconscious patient. Although the ultimate power and duty to review situations of this kind rests with the court, it will be reluctant to place a doctor in the position of having to carry out treatment which he/she considers contrary to the best interest of the patient (*Airedale NHS Trust v. Bland (1993)*).

5.6.21 LEAVING HOSPITAL

In general, patients may leave hospital at any time even during a period of treatment, although such action could be unwise, and could result in a deterioration in the patient's physical and/or mental health, for which the hospital staff could not be held responsible. Normally, patients should wait to be discharged by the consultant in charge of their case. In the case of an elderly patient, arrangements for domiciliary care may also be needed (see para. 5.6.24 below).

In certain circumstances, however, a patient can be prevented from leaving hospital. There are common law powers which can be used if a patient is a danger to him/herself or other persons. Under s.47 of the Health Services and Public Health Act 1968 (HSPHA 1968), patients suffering from one of the notifiable infectious diseases, such as tuberculosis or infectious jaundice, can also be prevented from leaving hospital; as can persons admitted to hospital under s.47 of the NAA 1948, (see Chapter 4 at paras. 4.21.1 to 4.21.4) and patients detained under the MHA 1983. Statutory powers can also be used to prevent any patient from leaving hospital if it is thought that an application for admission as a detained patient under the MHA 1983 ought to be made (see para. 5.6.22 below).

5.6.22   DETAINING INFORMAL PATIENTS UNDER THE MENTAL HEALTH ACT 1983

Under s.5(2) of the MHA 1983, the doctor in charge of a patient's treatment, or the doctor nominated to act in his/her absence, can report to the hospital managers (HMs) that, in his/her opinion, an application for the patient's compulsory detention in hospital ought to be made under the Act. The delivery of the report to the managers of the hospital authorises the patient's detention in hospital for a period of up to seventy-two hours, during which time an application for admission for assessment, or admission for treatment, can be made. This section could be used if, for example, it was felt that an elderly patient, who had perhaps entered a general hospital for the treatment of a physical ailment, was suffering from a mental disorder which justified detaining him/her for assessment or treatment in a psychiatric hospital or ward, and the patient was unwilling to be admitted informally. For this purpose, the HMs are either the DHA, or special health authority (SHA), or the directors of the NHS Trust responsible for managing the hospital in which the patient is detained; or in relation to a special hospital, the Secretary of State; or, in relation to a mental nursing home, the person or persons registered in respect of the home under the RHA 1984.

A patient who is in hospital informally, but receiving treatment for mental disorder, can be compulsorily detained if the conditions set out in s.5(4) of the MHA 1983 exist. Section 5 enables a patient to be detained for up to six hours by a first level nurse qualified in mental nursing, if he/she considers the patient to be mentally disordered to such a degree that it is necessary for the patient's health or safety or the protection of others for him/her to be restrained from leaving, and it is not practicable to secure the immediate attendance of the doctor in charge of the patient's treatment. A written record of the circumstances of the case must be made in the prescribed form, and delivered to the HMs. The nurse's authority to detain lapses at the end of six hours, or when a doctor with authority to make a report to the managers under s.5(2), arrives on the ward, whichever is sooner.

5.6.23 THE END OF DETENTION

There are a number of ways in which the right to detain a patient admitted to hospital under the MHA 1983 can be brought to an end. In the first place, a patient can be detained only for the period specified in the section under which an application for detention was made, unless a subsequent application under a different section of the Act, or an application to extend the period of detention has been made under the Act. Second, the responsible medical officer or the HMs or his/her nearest relative, may bring detention to an end in accordance with s.23 of the Act. Discharge by the nearest relative may be prevented, however, by procedures set out in s.25(1). Third, a patient may apply, and in some circumstances, must be referred, to a Mental Health Review Tribunal (MHRT) which has power to release the patient. A nearest relative, whose right to discharge the patient has been prevented, may also apply to the MHRT in accordance with s.66 of the Act. Under s.17 and s.18, a patient who remains absent from hospital, with or without leave, is discharged automatically after absence for a specified period of time. In an NHS Trust, only the non-executive directors may carry out this function which they must carry out in person.

5.6.24 AFTER-CARE

For many elderly patients, their families and carers, leaving hospital can present considerable problems in relation to continuity of care and adequacy of support in the community. Under the provisions of s.3(1) of the National Health Service Act 1977 (NHSA 1977), a duty is placed on the Secretary of State for Health to provide facilities for 'the after-care of persons who have suffered from illness as he considers are appropriate as part of the health service'. However, difficulties can arise over the extent of the responsibility of NHS authorities, on the one hand, and the responsibility of social services authorities, on the other.

Department of Health Circular HC(89)5 and WO Circular WHC(90)1 are the most recent guidance for hospitals to the procedures to be followed when a patient leaves hospital. The Circulars set out a number of basic ground rules, such as the importance of ensuring that hospital wards and departments have up-to-date discharge procedures, that these have been issued to all concerned, that their effectiveness is monitored, and that they are amended, where necessary. The aim should be to encourage and restore independence wherever possible, and, in other cases, to facilitate the smooth transfer of the patient to alternative care in the community, where that has been agreed.

Patients should only be discharged on the authority of the doctor responsible for their treatment and care. Where authority is delegated, its extent should be clearly understood by all concerned. Patients should not be discharged until the doctors are agreed, and management is satisfied, that everything reasonably practicable has been done to organise the care which the patient needs in the community. The patient, and, if appropriate, his/her family and/or carer(s), should be involved in planning his/her discharge. To ensure that arrangements are complete, responsibility for checking that action has been taken should be given to one member of staff. If arrangements are changed, the importance of ensuring that support, already planned for the patient's return to the community, will still be available.

The DH/WH issue a booklet to help health authorities review their procedures. This stresses that special care is needed in planning the discharge of certain groups of patients, including those who live alone, those who are frail, and elderly patients who live with an elderly carer. For this purpose, people living in sheltered housing, and other warden-assisted accommodation, should be treated as living alone, since wardens, normally, only assist in emergencies. Other groups who need special care are patients who are seriously ill, and may be returning for further treatment at a later date; patients who are terminally ill; patients with continuing disability (including those discharged from long-stay hospitals to return to the community, and those with sensory impairment); psychiatric patients; patients who have been in hospital for an extended stay; patients in need of special assistance, for example, those who are incontinent, or need community nursing, paramedical or rehabilitation services; patients with communication difficulties; and people who are homeless or live in hostel accommodation (DH 1989f).

In a recent report, however, the House of Commons Select Committee on Health refers to evidence that arrangements for hospital discharge were placing undue pressure on patients and their relatives and carers, effectively depriving them of a real choice about the type of care they received after discharge, although Circulars HC(89)5 and WC(90)1 stressed the importance of fully consulting users, relatives and carers before discharge. The Circulars also stress the importance of liaison with social services and housing departments about alternative arrangements if it appears likely that the patient will not be able to return to his/her current place of residence. Such arrangements must be made in good time and be acceptable to the patient and, where appropriate, the patient's relatives or carers. They should be fully aware of their nature, purpose and likely consequences.

5.6.25 In relation to social services authorities, the duty to provide after-care services arises under s.21(1)(b) and para. 2(1) of Sched. 8 of the NHSA 1977. According to s.21:

> A local social services authority may, with the Secretary of State's approval, and to such extent as he may direct shall, make arrangements for ... the after care of person who have been [suffering from illness].

DHSS Circular (83)10 contains Ministerial directions only in relation to services for those who are, or have been, suffering from mental disorder. Paragraph 4 of the Circular directs authorities to provide centres (including Training Centres and Day Centres) or other facilities (including domiciliary facilities), whether in premises managed by the local authority or otherwise, for training or occupation of persons who are, or have been, suffering from mental disorder. Since services provided under s.21 are defined as 'community care services' under s.46(3) of the National Health Service and Community Care Act 1990 (NHSCCA 1990), social services authorities have a duty to carry out an assessment of a mentally disordered person's needs for such services, but only in accordance with s.47(1) of the Act (see Chapter 3 at paras. 3.2.1 to 3.2.6).

Social services authorities also have a joint duty to provide after-care for mentally disordered patients under s.117 of the MHA 1983, that is, for patients who are leaving hospital after being detained under s.3, or s.37, of the Act (or having been transferred to hospital from prison under ss.47 and 48). Under s.117, the duty to provide after-care is placed on the DHA and the local social services authority jointly, and in conjunction with voluntary organisations. The two authorities must provide after-care services for a person to whom the section applies, until they are satisfied that he/she in no longer in need of them. In making these provisions, DHAs, NHS Trusts and social services authorities are asked to ensure that their staff are aware of the care programme approach as laid down in Circular HC(90)23/LASS(90)11 and the principles set out in the Welsh Office mental illness strategy (DH/WO 1993).

The revised Code of Practice sets out a procedure to be followed after the decision is taken to discharge a patient. Discussions should be held on a multi-professional basis to ensure that a care plan is set up to manage the patient's continuing health and social care needs. Those who should be involved in the discussions include the patient's responsible medical officer, a nurse involved in the patient's care, a social worker specialising in mental health work; the patient's GP, a community psychiatric nurse, a representative of a relevant voluntary organisation (where appropriate and available); the patient if he/she so wishes, and/or a relative, or other nominated representative. The issues to be considered include the patient's wishes and needs; the views of any relevant relative, friend or support of the patient; the possible involvement of other agencies; proper assessment; the appointment of a key worker; and the identification of any unmet need. The care plan should also take into account the patient's social and cultural background. There should be an agreed time-scale for implementing the plan, and for keeping it under regular review (DH/WO 1993).

6 Complaints and redress of grievances in health care

Gwyneth Roberts

6.1.1 HEALTH CARE PROBLEMS

The issues relating to health care which most often give rise to complaints by patients can be categorised in three main ways. First, there may be complaints over the way in which services are organised and delivered, and/or the standard of care provided; second, there may be complaints over gaps, deficiencies, and delays in the provision of services, often arising from lack of resources; and, third, there may be complaints which allege actual harm or injury to a particular individual, which may amount to the torts of negligence or trespass to the person. These different types of complaints give rise to different procedures which are examined below.

6.2.1 ACCESS TO MEDICAL RECORDS

Access to medical records can be particularly important for patients wishing to make a complaint, or to bring a legal action against a health professional or a health authority. There are various statutory provisions under which a person may apply for access to information. Under the Data Protection Act 1984 (DPA 1984), 'data subjects' have a right to check the accuracy of personal records held about them on computer. Under s.29(1) of the Act, however, the Secretary of State may exempt certain data. Medical data, for example, is exempt if, in the opinion of the doctor, access to it could cause serious harm to the patient's physical or mental health, or could lead to the patient identifying another person (other than the health professional involved in his/her care), who had not consented to his/her identity being disclosed. Whether a patient would suffer from 'serious harm' as a result of being given access to records is for the doctor to decide.

6.2.2 The Access to Health Records Act 1990 (AHRA 1990) extends the provisions of the DPA 1984 to health records made manually after 1 November 1991, that is, to records made in connection with the care of an identifiable individual by, or on behalf of, a health professional. A 'health record' means any information (including expressions of opinion) about an individual's physical or mental health. For this purpose, a 'health professional' includes, not only doctors, dentists, opticians and chemists, but nurses, health visitors (HVs), chiropodists and physiotherapists, and other professionals (s.2), and 'care' includes any examination, investigation, diagnosis and treatment of an individual (s.11). Application for access can be made in writing by the patient, by a person acting with the patient's written authority, or by a person appointed by a court to manage the affairs of an incapable patient, or by the personal representative of a patient who has since died, or by a person who may have a claim arising out of the patient's death (s.3). Application is made to the 'holder' of the data, which may be the patient's GP, a family health services authority (FHSA), a district health authority (DHA), or NHS Trust, or any health professional by whom, or on whose behalf, the record is held (s.1(2)). Similar exemptions apply under the 1990 Act to those set out in the DPA 1984. An applicant may ask for incorrect, misleading, or incomplete records to be amended. If the holder refuses access, or refuses to amend an alleged inaccuracy, the applicant may complain to the DHA or NHS Trust or FHSA. If the applicant remains dissatisfied, he/she may apply to the court for an order to compel the record holder to comply with the statutory provisions.

Where information in a health record would otherwise be unintelligible (because, for example, of the use of technical medical language) an explanation must be provided (s.3(1)(a)–(f)). It is not clear, however, on whom the duty to explain is placed.

6.3.1 COMPLAINTS ABOUT THE ORGANISATION AND STANDARD OF SERVICES

The first category of complaints are those concerned with the way in which a service is organised, and/or the standard of care provided. Complaints of this kind may be dealt with according to any one of a number of procedures. Complaints against family practitioners, and complaints about hospital care and treatment, are dealt with differently. This can create particular problems for those who are uncertain which procedure to use, or whose complaint relates to several parts of the NHS. For example, a complaint may relate to the organisation and standard of care in services received both in hospital and from a GP (ACHEW 1990a). The reason for this diversity of procedures lies in the history of health care rather than in any rational development of an appropriate and suitable complaints system (Stacey 1974).

In June 1993, the government announced the setting up of an independent review of all complaints procedures in the NHS. Its report, and recommendations for change, are expected early in 1994.

6.3.2 COMMUNITY HEALTH COUNCILS

Patients can seek the help and advice of their local community health council (CHC) when bringing a complaint. In some areas, members and/or officers of the local CHC will also assist in presenting a complaint to the appropriate body. The Secretary of State does not regard that as a formal role for CHCs, but is prepared to allow it to happen on an informal basis. If an individual changes his/her mind and decides not to proceed with an alleged grievance, the CHC might, however, use the case as an example of poor standards of service. It could then make its views known to the relevant body since one of the main responsibilities of a CHC is to keep the health services in its locality under review, and make recommendations for its improvement. Under the Community Health Councils Regulations 1985, CHCs have a statutory right to be consulted by the local DHA and FHSA whenever these bodies propose 'any substantial development of health services in the Council's district or ... any substantial variation in the provision of such services', although, in exceptional circumstances, DHAs and FHSAs may take a decision without consultation in the interests of the service. In such cases, a CHC must be immediately notified and given reasons for the lack of consultation. A CHC can also require a DHA or FHSA to provide it with such information as it reasonably requires about the way in which services are being planned and operated. A CHC has right of access for the purpose of inspecting premises controlled by a DHA, FHSA or NHS Trust. Given that it has such powers and duties, and given that it has representatives from the local community serving on it, contacting a local CHC can be of advantage to a patient with a possible grievance.

6.3.3 COMPLAINTS AGAINST FAMILY PRACTITIONERS

The current system for complaining about family practitioner services has been criticised in that it works unevenly from one part of the country to another; is complex and long-drawn out; does not deal adequately with some of the problems which most worry patients; is weighted in a number of ways against the complainant; is not widely known or understood and does not, therefore, provide adequate consumer safeguards. A particular cause for misunderstanding is that the system which originated with the health insurance scheme of 1911 is designed not so much as machinery for the redress of grievances by patients, but as a means of ensuring that family practitioners comply with their terms of service. In essence, the system is concerned with enabling FHSAs to sanction any practitioner who is in breach of his/her contractual obligations.

6.3.4 PROCESSING COMPLAINTS

All complaints received within the statutory time limit must be screened to check whether they allege that the practitioner has breached his/her terms of service. Many of the complaints brought against family practitioners fall outside the terms of service, such as allegations of discourtesy, brusqueness or rudeness. In such cases, the FHSA may attempt to resolve the matter through correspondence, or offer the complainant access to an informal conciliation process. The aim of conciliation is to ensure that the complaint is fully aired to the satisfaction of both parties, and to attempt to re-establish good relations between the parties. A complainant may also be offered informal conciliation in relation to an allegedly minor breach of service. If the complainant agrees, he/she must be advised at the outset that participation in the informal procedure does not affect his/her right to opt for a formal investigation at any stage in the procedure. Where, however, a complaint involves a potentially serious breach of service it should be referred for formal investigation, from the start.

Since most complaints against family practitioners are brought against GPs, what is mainly discussed below is the way in which the procedures work in relation to them. Parallel procedures exist, however, for bringing complaints against the other family practitioners (that is, against dentists, opticians and pharmacists) who also have contracts with the FHSA. These procedures are discussed in more detail in para. 6.3.13 below. In all cases a complaint will be treated as valid if it is made, initially, to a regional health authority (RHA) (or to the Welsh Office (WO), in Wales), or to a DHA, rather than direct to the FHSA.

6.3.5 COMPLAINTS AGAINST GPS

A complaint against a GP can be made by a patient, by anyone acting with the patient's consent, or by anyone acting on behalf of a patient who, because of old age, sickness or some other infirmity, is incapable of bringing the complaint him/herself (National Health Service (Service Committees and Tribunal) Regulations 1992, reg. 6). A complaint may also be brought in relation to a person who has since died.

Normally, a complaint must be made in writing, except where the FHSA is satisfied that the complainant is illiterate because of a physical disability, or some other reason (such as a language problem). Oral complaints must be tape-recorded and transcribed by the FHSA (reg. 5(5)).

Complaints against GPs must be made within thirteen weeks of the event giving rise to it. Complaints falling outside this limit may be allowed only on the grounds of illness, or some other reasonable cause, and only with the consent of the doctor concerned, or the Secretary of State. If a late complaint is not allowed, there is a right of appeal to the Secretary of State (Sched. 3; Sched. 4, para. 1) Where a complaint is not sufficiently detailed, the complainant must be asked to provide the FHSA with the necessary details, within twenty-one days.

6.3.6 PRE-HEARING PROCEDURES

If there seem to be grounds for holding a formal hearing, the FHSA must send a copy of the complainant's statement to the chairman of the Medical Services Committee (MSC). Having considered it, the chairman must decide whether, in his/her opinion, there are reasonable grounds for believing that the GP has failed to comply with one or more of the terms of service. If the chairman decides that the complainant's statement does not disclose a breach of service, the FHSA must inform the complainant, and invite him/her to submit a further statement, within fourteen days. If no further statement is received or if, after giving the matter further consideration, the chairman is of the opinion that no hearing is necessary, he/she must bring the matter to the MSC, which may either dismiss or uphold the chairman's decision. If the MSC upholds the chairman's decision, it may report to the FHSA without holding a hearing.

If, however, the chairman considers there are reasonable grounds for believing that one, or more, of the terms of service has been breached, he/she must identify each term, and inform the FHSA. The GP must be told, and asked for his/her comments within four weeks. Where comments are received, they must be sent to the complainant, who has fourteen days in which to make any observations. If the chairman, after considering any further comments, or observations, decides that a hearing is unnecessary, that decision, too, must be brought before the MSC, which may either dismiss or uphold the chairman's decision. If it upholds the chairman's decision, the MSC may report to the FHSA without holding a hearing.

If no comments are received, or if the chairman considers, on the basis of any he/she receives, that there is a material difference between the parties over the facts of the case, or that a hearing is necessary for some other reason, the FHSA must arrange a hearing, inform the parties, and send them copies of all the relevant correspondence, comments or observations which are to be produced as evidence at the hearing. If the complaint concerns a GP's deputy who is also on the FHSA's medical list, the complaint is deemed to have been made against both doctors. If, in the chairman's opinion, the evidence shows no personal failure by the patient's GP to comply with his/her terms of service, the MSC may limit its investigation to the complaint made against the deputy.

6.3.7 NOTICE OF HEARING

Both the patient and the doctor (or doctors) (see para. 6.3.6 above) must be given at least twenty-one days notice of the date, time, and place of the hearing. They must also be given the names of members of the MSC, so that they can identify any person with an interest in the case. The secretary of the Local Medical Committee (LMC) (which represents doctors in the area) must also be given notice of the hearing (Sched. 4, para. 4(2)). Within fourteen days of being notified, the parties must provide copies of the documentary evidence they are proposing to produce at the hearing, including the names of any witnesses. They must also be given copies of evidence submitted by the other party. They must also let the FHSA know in writing whether or not they intend to be present at the hearing, and must be told the possible consequences of not being present (see para. 6.3.8 below). Where the MSC is satisfied that the complainant has failed to comply with this request, or is refusing to attend without reasonable cause, it may consider the complaint, and report to the FHSA without holding a hearing (Sched. 4, para. 4(3)). In that case, however, it may not make a recommendation to the FHSA which would adversely affect the GP against whom the complaint was brought unless he/she has previously given his/her consent to this action being taken. The chairman may postpone a hearing on the application of either party, if it is not reasonably practicable for them, or any witness, to attend on the day of the hearing, or for any other reason (Sched. 4, para. 4).

6.3.8 THE HEARING

Hearings are held in private, although a member or officer of the LMC may attend as an observer. The MSC consists of a lay chairman, three lay members of the FHSA, and three doctors. No one who is in practice, or who has ever been in practice, as a doctor, dentist, optician or chemist, may sit as a lay member. This applies, also, to nurses, midwives and Health Visitors, and any person who is, or has ever been, an officer or employee of an FHSA, an RHA, a DHA or a CHC (Sched. 2, para. 11). The quorum at a hearing is five, that is, the chairman, two lay members and two doctors. This must be maintained during the whole of the hearing, with a balance between the lay and the professional members. No more than two officers of the FHSA may attend.

Before starting the proceedings, the chairman must ask each member if he/she has any direct or indirect interest in the matter to be discussed. If any member declares an interest, he/she may not take part in the proceedings, although a deputy may act in his/her place (Sched. 4, para. 6(3)). The White Paper *Promoting Better Health* referred to fair treatment as essential if complaints were to be properly resolved (DHSS 1987). If the respondent GP is a member of the FHSA, the complaint must be transferred to another FHSA for investigation.

Both sides may be assisted, or represented, by another person such as a friend, or member or officer of a CHC or LMC. Both parties may give and call evidence and put questions to the other party, and to any witness, either directly or, if the committee directs, through the chairman. A representative may, also, address the committee, and put questions to witnesses. Barristers and solicitors may not act as representatives, but may attend only as advisers.

If, during the hearing, an issue arises which relates to an event or matter, which, in the chairman's opinion, was not sufficiently disclosed to the GP prior to the hearing, he/she may direct it to be excluded. If no direction is given, the hearing must be adjourned, unless the GP and chairman agree that the hearing should proceed. Before being invited to give his/her consent, a GP who has no representative present, must have the opportunity to consult the representative of the LMC.

If either party fails to appear, the hearing may be adjourned if the committee is satisfied that absence is due to illness, or some other reasonable cause. Before doing so, it must invite the observation of the party who is present.

6.3.9 THE DECISION

At the end of the hearing, the MSC must decide whether or not a breach in the terms of service has occurred. A majority decision is possible if the committee is not unanimous. In the event of a tie, the chairman has a casting vote (reg. 8(1)). A report containing the committee's findings and recommendations must then be prepared for submission to the next meeting of the FHSA. The complainant may withdraw his/her complaint, in writing, with the committee's agreement, at any time before the report's submission.

The FHSA may either accept the findings and recommendations of the MSC, or may reach its own conclusions on the facts. The FHSA may then decide either (a) to dismiss the complaint; or (b) withhold an amount not exceeding £500 from the GP's remuneration; or (c) recommend to the Secretary of State that an amount exceeding £500 should be withheld from the GP's remuneration. It may also determine that (a) any expenses incurred by the patient as a result of his/her breach should be deducted from the doctor's remuneration; (b) the GP be warned to comply more closely with his/her terms of service in future; (c) a limit is placed on the number of patients the GP may have on his/her list; or (d) to refer the GP to an NHS Tribunal with a recommendation that the continued inclusion of the GP on the medical list would be prejudicial to the efficiency of the service.

A copy of the FHSA's decision, and the MSC's report, must be sent to both parties. They may also request that copies be sent to a member of the House of Commons, or the House of Lords. They must also be told of their right of appeal to the Secretary of State. The Secretary of State must also be sent copies.

6.3.10 APPEALS

The parties may appeal to the Secretary of State within one month of the decision, and report, being sent to them. An appeal must be accompanied by a statement of the facts, and of the arguments which form the basis of the appeal. On appeal by the patient, the Secretary of State may dismiss it without holding a hearing, on the grounds that the patient had no reasonable grounds for the appeal, or that it is otherwise vexatious or frivolous. On appeal by the GP, however, an oral hearing must be held, unless the appellant does not require it. The appeal is in the form of a hearing before three officers of the DH or WO. In this case, barristers or solicitors can represent the parties, as can officers or members of any organisation of which the appellant is a member, or a member of his/her family, or a friend. The tribunal reports its decision to the Secretary of State who then informs the parties in writing.

6.3.11 Complaints to FHSAs often allege failure to make a home visit when requested, and the condition of the patient requires it; or refusal to refer a patient's case to a consultant when the patient's medical condition required it. The MSC cannot review a reasonable exercise of clinical judgement by a doctor, but can be asked to adjudicate on whether or not the practitioner took all reasonable steps in the exercise of that judgement, for example, whether or not the diagnosis was made without proper and necessary examination of the patient. One complaint, upheld by an MSC, concerned a GP who twice visited a patient and, on the second occasion, diagnosed gastro-enteritis and gave appropriate treatment. Two days later, the patient's condition worsened and his wife asked for a further visit which was refused. She was told, however, to contact the GP again if the patient's condition continued to give cause for concern. Later the same day, another request was made, and the GP arranged for a deputy to call on his behalf. The patient died from a burst appendix shortly after the deputy arrived. The MSC recognised the difficulties of making an early diagnosis of the patient's condition and that the GP sincerely believed in the correctness of the diagnosis which had been made. Nevertheless, it held that a visit ought to have been made, although it also recognised that the GP had been influenced by a history of unnecessary requests for visits made by the patient over the years. The committee also accepted that the GP had in the past given satisfactory service to both the patient and his wife (*Family Practitioner Services* 1985).

Another complaint, made on behalf of an 86-year-old patient, alleged failure to visit and treat a patient whose condition required it. A telephone call had been made at 11.45 a.m. on a Monday as a result of which medicine was made available and collected for the patient, but the doctor did not call. A further call was made at 6.45 a.m. the following day, followed by another at 7.30 a.m. At 10.30 a.m. on the same day, the doctor's wife was told that a doctor from another practice had attended and treated the patient. The MSC considered that the GP, following the telephone calls and with knowledge of the patient's previous medical history of a heart complaint, should have made a visit. He was, therefore, in breach of his terms of service which obligated him to render to his patient all necessary and appropriate medical services, and to visit if the patient's condition required it (*Family Practitioner Services 1982*).

6.3.12 PATIENTS' COMMITTEES

A relatively recent development in the field of primary health care is the setting up of patients' committees in some practices and health centres to act as a forum for expressing patients' opinions about the organisation and running of the practice or health centre, and as a means of communicating to the doctors working there, the problems raised by patients in the context of service delivery. A National Association for Patient Participation was formed in 1978 to support the work of individual Patient Participation Groups (PPGs), to share information and experience between groups, and to spread the idea and practice of patient participation generally. The establishment of a group depends largely on the interest and encouragement of the doctors within the practice or health centre. There are over 300 PPGs throughout the country. In general, there are three main ways in which they tend to function. Groups try to improve, and publicise within the practice, the facilities which are provided for patients, and try to act as a forum where the views of both doctors and patients can be heard, and where constructive efforts can be made to improve the practice. They also try to further health education in the practice, as well as setting up self-help schemes. PPGs also engage in fund-raising activities to purchase equipment for the practice to which they are attached.

6.3.13 COMPLAINTS AGAINST DENTISTS, OPTICIANS AND PHARMACISTS

FHSAs also deal with complaints against dentists, opticians and pharmacists. Complaints against dentists must be made to the Dental Service Committee within thirteen weeks of the patient becoming aware of grounds for the complaint, or six months of the completion of treatment, whichever is sooner. The Dental Service Committee consists of a chairman, who must be a lay person, and six other members, three of whom must be lay members appointed by the FHSA, and three of whom must be dentists appointed by the Local

Representative Committee of dentists. Some FHSAs, also, choose to have a Denture Conciliation Committee whose function is to listen to complaints about dentures.

A complaint against an optician must be brought within thirteen weeks of the event giving rise to the complaint. Complaints are heard by the Ophthalmic Service Committee consisting of a chairman, who must be a lay person, and seven other members, three of whom must be lay members appointed by the FHSA, two of whom must be ophthalmic medical practitioners, appointed by the LMC, and two of whom must be ophthalmic opticians, appointed by the Local Optical Committee.

A complaint against a pharmaceutical chemist must also be brought within thirteen weeks of the event giving rise to it. Complaints are heard by the Pharmaceutical Service Committee consisting of a chairman, who must be a lay person, and six other members, three of whom must be lay members, appointed by the FHSA, and three of whom must be community pharmacists, appointed by the Local Pharmaceutical Committee.

In all these cases, the procedure is similar to that described above in relation to GPs.

6.3.14 NHS Tribunals are bodies, separate from FHSAs and MSCs, set up to consider recommendations, usually from FHSAs, that a family practitioner's continued inclusion on the medical, dental, ophthalmic list or pharmaceutical list would be prejudicial to the efficiency of the service in question. An NHS Tribunal consists of a chairman who must be a practising barrister or solicitor of at least ten years' standing, and two members appointed by the Secretary of State, one of whom must be a lay person, and the other a professional person. A decision in favour of the practitioner is final, but if the Tribunal decides against the practitioner, he/she has a right of appeal to the Secretary of State.

6.3.15 COMPLAINTS ABOUT HOSPITAL SERVICES

Until recently, no statutory procedure existed in relation to complaints about the organisation and standard of services in hospitals. The Hospital Complaints Procedure Act 1985 (HCPA 1985), required the Secretary of State to direct health authorities on the complaints procedure to be set up in hospitals in their area for which they were responsible. Following the circulation of a consultation document, the Secretary of State issued directions on the arrangements to be made for dealing with complaints made by, or on behalf of those who are, or have been, hospital patients. The directions were extended to include NHS Trusts by DH Circular EL[91]107 and WO Circular DGM(91)138.

6.3.16 In accordance with the directions, every DHA and NHS Trust must designate an officer at each hospital, or group of hospitals, for which they are responsible, to receive and be accountable for all formal complaints made by or on behalf of a patient. In a DHA, the unit general manager (UGM), and in an NHS Trust, the chief executive, is regarded as the appropriate person. Where a patient is dead, or unable to act, the complaint may be made by a close relative, friend or suitable representative person or body. Where the complaint is made on behalf of a person who is capable of complaining, the designated officer must satisfy him/herself that the complaint is made with his/her knowledge and consent.

6.3.17   MAKING A FORMAL COMPLAINT

A formal complaint must be made, or recorded, in writing. According to Circular HC(88)37 and Circular WHC(88)36, issued at the same time as the directions, where a complainant cannot put the complaint in writing, the designated officer should ensure that a record is made, and must ask the complainant to sign it. Refusal to sign the record should not, however, delay the investigation. The complaint ought normally to be made within three months of the event giving rise to it, although the designated officer should, if satisfied there was good cause for the delay, have discretion to allow a longer period.

6.3.18   INVESTIGATING A COMPLAINT

Arrangements for dealing with formal complaints must allow complainants an opportunity to bring any relevant information or comments which they wish to make to the attention of the designated officer, who should ensure that he/she has a full picture of the incidents on which the complaint is based. This may involve holding a preliminary interview with the complainant to clarify the issues or obtain further information. It may be possible to resolve matters satisfactorily at this stage, but care should be taken not to prejudice the outcome of any further investigation.

Members of staff involved in the complaint should also be given an opportunity to bring relevant information and comments to the attention of the designated officer. However, care must be taken not to introduce delay by allowing staff excessive periods for comment. The aim should be to process complaints as speedily and thoroughly as possible at every stage.

After carrying out the investigation, the designated officer must prepare a report, which must be sent to the complainant, any person involved in the complaint, and any other person, as required by the DHA or NHS Trust (such as the manager of another department or service). If a complaint is upheld, the letter should give reasons for any failure in the service, and state what steps have been, or will be, taken to prevent a recurrence. Where appropriate, it should contain an apology. If the complainant remains dissatisfied, he/she should be advised take the complaint to the Health Service Commissioner (HSC) (see para. 6.3.24 below), unless the complaint clearly falls outside the HSC's jurisdiction, or the complainant is proposing further action through the courts.

6.3.19 INFORMAL COMPLAINTS

Arrangements must also exist for staff at a hospital to seek to deal with complaints informally. A complainant may also ask for the designated officer's assistance in dealing with a complaint which is likely to be dealt with informally. Informal complaints need not be in writing, but the Circulars mention the importance of making a note in cases where the complaint is not readily settled, and where a dispute as to the precise nature of the complaint might arise, particularly where a formal investigation is likely. If an informal complaint is not dealt with to the satisfaction of the patient, staff should advise the complainant to make a formal complaint to the designated officer at the hospital.

6.3.20 Designated officers are not responsible for investigating complaints which fall into the following categories: (a) those concerning the exercise of clinical judgement by a hospital doctor or dentist which cannot be resolved by discussion with the consultant concerned; (b) those relating to serious untoward incidents involving harm to a patient; (c) those relating to the conduct of medical or hospital staff and requiring the holding of disciplinary proceedings; (d) those giving reasonable grounds for police investigations as to whether a criminal offence has been committed. The designated officer's duty in such circumstances is to bring the matter to the attention of the DHA or NHS Trust so that appropriate action is taken.

6.3.21   Health authorities and NHS Trusts are required to take all necessary steps to improve public perception of the complaints system. They should publicise arrangements for dealing with complaints and, as far as possible, ensure that patients, visitors, local CHCs and members of staff are fully informed. The Circulars refer to various ways in which arrangements can be publicised, including information in admission booklets, leaflets, notices placed in DHA or NHS Trust premises, particularly reception areas. Consideration should be given to providing information in ethnic and minority languages. Awareness of complaints procedures should also form part of staff training and development.

6.3.22   DHAs and Trusts are required to make arrangements for reports to be prepared every three months to make it possible to monitor progress, to consider trends, and to take remedial action where necessary.

6.3.23   COMPLAINTS ABOUT SERVICES PURCHASED FROM NON-NHS PROVIDERS

Where DHAs (and GP fund holders (GPFHs)) (see Chapter 5 at para. 5.3.1) purchase hospital services from providers in the independent sector, they must stipulate in their contracts that complaints about those services will be dealt with according to procedures similar to those set out in the directions made under the HCPA 1985. Contracts with independent provider units should ensure that each provider designates an officer to act on behalf of the chief executive, or general manager, to receive and investigate complaints. However, any formal response should come from the chief executive or general manager. The complaint should be dealt with in accordance with written procedures, reflecting the principles of the NHS complaints procedures, and agreed with the purchasing authority. Information about these, including how, and to whom, to complain should be disseminated within the provider unit through advice to patients and by displaying notices. The unit's management should monitor the arrangements and keep the relevant purchasing authorities informed about progress in dealing with complaints. When a service is purchased by a DHA, the provider unit should ensure that the complainant knows to which purchasing authority to turn if they remain dissatisfied with the outcome of a complaint. The DHA should be notified of every such incident.

6.3.24 REFERRAL TO THE HEALTH SERVICE COMMISSIONER

An elderly patient, or if he/she is incapable of doing so, a member of his/her family, or if he/she has died, his/her personal representative, or some other individual or body, such as a DHA, CHC, or Citizen's Advice Bureau (CAB), may take a complaint to the Health Service Commissioner (or Ombudsman) whose function is to investigate allegations of injustice or hardship suffered either as a result of the failure of a relevant body (which includes RHAs, DHAs, NHS Trusts, and FHSAs) to provide a service which it is under a duty to provide, or as the result of a failure in the way in which a service was made available. The HSC can also investigate allegations of maladministration resulting from any other action taken on behalf of an authority. There is no statutory definition of 'maladministration' but it is said to include 'bias, neglect, inattention, delay, incompetence, ineptitude, arbitrariness and the like' (HC 1966). Maladministration, therefore, covers a wide range of possible action or inaction, such as giving wrong information, failing to follow agreed policy, or procedures, unjustified delay in responding to a complaint, or an unsatisfactory investigation of the original complaint.

A complaint must normally be made in writing not later than one a year from when the matter came to the notice of the complainant, although the HSC has powers to extend the time limit if that is considered reasonable. The HSC must be satisfied that the relevant body has been given notice of the complaint and had reasonable opportunity to investigate it and to give a reply.

The HSC must also be satisfied that the original complaint was brought to the attention of the body against whom it is brought, and that it was given a reasonable opportunity to investigate the matter and give a reply. The HSC may interview any person with information about the matter complained about, and may also examine all relevant documents.

Certain matters are excluded from the HSC's remit. The HSC cannot usually investigate matters which would come within the jurisdiction of the courts or a tribunal, unless it is considered unreasonable to expect the complainant to make use of such procedures. Nor can the HSC investigate matters which concern the action or omission of a family practitioner in providing a service, although the administrative failures of an FHSA, alleging, for example, poor communication, or delay in dealing with a complaint, could be examined by the HSC. Also excluded from the HSC's jurisdiction are matters concerned solely with clinical judgement relating to diagnoses and treatment, an omission which led to much public and official disquiet and eventually resulted in the introduction of the procedure referred to at para. 6.3.28 below. The HSC cannot deal with matters concerning personnel matters, an authority's commercial or contractual dealings, or serious incidents or major breakdown in services, which are matters to be dealt with by means of a public inquiry set up by the Secretary of State.

The HSC can interview any person if it is thought he/she could provide information on the matter complained about, and can also examine any relevant documents. On completing an investigation the HSC submits a report of the finding to the patient, who remains anonymous, and to the relevant body, but cannot ensure that any changes are made as a result of the investigation. The HSC's powers are limited to investigating and, if necessary, to publicising the complaint and the findings, and trying to persuade the relevant body to act on the suggestions and recommendations made by him in his report. If the HSC decides not to conduct an investigation, a statement, with the reasons, must be sent to the complainant, to the relevant body and to any Member of Parliament who may have assisted in making the complaint.

6.3.25 The following are examples of cases involving elderly patients where a complaint was upheld by the HSC. In the first, an elderly woman was referred to an ophthalmic consultant by her GP. After nearly twelve months without any acknowledgment from the hospital, and since telephone calls elicited no further information, her daughter became so concerned about her deteriorating condition that she took her mother to the accident and emergency department at the hospital. Enquiries by the HSC revealed that the referral had not been processed in the normal way, which was why the patient had not received a letter of acknowledgement after being referred by her GP, nor told how long she might have to wait for an appointment. However, even if the referral had been processed correctly, the category of urgency to which she was accorded, would have meant a wait of some sixteen months. The DHA had taken steps to bring this excessive waiting period down, and was continuing to make efforts to make further improvements.

At the accident and emergency department, the woman had waited for six and a half hours, in uncomfortable surroundings, before being seen by a doctor. Her anxiety had been increased by the fact that she had not brought essential medication with her. The HSC found that the department operated a triage system for allocating priority to patients who were waiting to be seen, and she had been placed in the least urgent category which inevitably meant some delay. Nevertheless, the length of time she had to wait had been excessive. It seems that the staff had forgotten, or overlooked, how long she had been waiting. Since the complaint was made, the DHA had introduced changes aimed at alleviating problems of this kind particularly for elderly patients, and had agreed to continue to monitor their effectiveness (HSC 1992).

6.3.26 Another case revealed serious faults in the observation and supervision of patients, the absence of an effective monitoring of standards, and poor staff discipline at a hospital. An elderly man had been admitted for treatment of a severe heart condition at a hospital which was due to close. He died within a few days of being admitted. The case tragically highlighted the cumulative effects of fundamental failure in basic nursing care and professional standards. The curtains had been drawn around his bed, and no one was able to account for the last half hour or so of his life before he was discovered collapsed on the floor. His son was dissatisfied with the explanation given to him about his father's death. The HSC's investigations revealed that several trained nurses had overlooked basic nursing procedures, and that shortcomings in the handover from one shift to another were largely to blame for what had happened on the evening in question. Those coming on duty had not been told about the patient, and the nurse who was taking charge had not made a tour of the ward immediately after the ward report. These matters illustrated far more profoundly than any training manual why basic nursing procedures were required, and why they needed to be respected and vigorously applied. Evidence showed that these were not isolated incidents but had been prevalent for some time because of a general laxity in standards. How was it that such a deterioration had not been apparent to senior nursing staff? In the opinion of the HSC, there was lack of effective monitoring and a degree of fatalism in the face of the hospital's closure. The DHA's documentation was also woefully inadequate. The HSC severely criticised ward staff and senior management. The DHA had drawn up new care and management procedures for the equivalent ward at another hospital and, equally important, had agreed to ensure that arrangements for managerial and professional oversight of standards operated effectively (HSC 1990).

6.3.27 Discharge arrangements are another area where the HSC has expressed concern (see Chapter 5 at para. 5.6.24). Elderly women living alone seem particularly vulnerable. In one case, a woman aged eighty-five had been admitted to hospital following a fall at home. About six weeks later, she visited her home with an occupational therapist and community liaison nurse (CLN) for a discharge assessment. Her daughter, who was the woman's main carer, was herself convalescing after an operation. She asked the CLN to delay her mother's discharge until she was well enough to look after her, and believed that the CLN had agreed to find a bed in a rehabilitation ward. A week or so later, the daughter was telephoned by the hospital and told that her mother was on her way home. Her mother was re-admitted to hospital the following day with a broken femur after several falls at home. She died two weeks later. Her daughter complained that her mother had been discharged despite the CLN's agreement to find her a bed, and that hospital staff had not made adequate discharge arrangements, or informed her of the discharge until her mother was already on the way home by ambulance. The CLN denied that he had promised to find a rehabilitation bed, and there seemed to have been a genuine misunderstanding about the arrangements. The misunderstanding would not have happened if he had written to the daughter confirming the outcome of their discussion. The DHA had taken steps to ensure that a plan of action arising from a home visit was recorded in future, and confirmed with the patient or carer. However, the ward staff had also erred in not following their normal practice of identifying the appropriate relatives and liaising with them about discharging the patient. The HSC upheld this part of the complaint and criticised all the senior ward staff for not identifying one person as responsible for liaison with the relatives. Senior management had not ensured that all ward sisters, at the very least, were aware of the policy, nor had they monitored its application. New procedures for discharging patients had subsequently been introduced (HSC 1990).

6.3.28 COMPLAINTS ABOUT CLINICAL DECISIONS

There is a non-statutory procedure, set out in Circulars HC(88)37 and WHC(88)36, for investigating complaints made by, or on behalf of, a patient about the clinical judgement of medical members of staff. If the patient has since died, or has limited competence to deal with the complaint because of physical or mental disability, the complaint may be made by a relative, or carer or other suitable person or body. At the first stage, responsibility for investigating the complaint is placed on the consultant him/herself, who should try to resolve the complaint within a few days, preferably by offering to see the complainant in order to discuss matters and attempt to resolve the patient's anxieties. He/she should also involve any other member of the medical staff who has been concerned with the care of the patient. It may also be helpful, at this stage, to discuss matters with the patient's GP. Should there be delay, the consultant should contact the complainant, and give an explanation. A brief, strictly factual, record of the discussion should be placed in the patient's hospital notes. If the consultant feels there is a significant risk of legal action being taken, he/she should bring it to the attention of the district general manager (DGM) or Chief Executive. Where there are non-clinical aspects to a complaint, the consultant should inform the DGM or Chief Executive so that they can be dealt with by an appropriate member of staff.

Normally, it is the DGM or Chief Executive who sends the complainant a written reply on behalf of the authority or Trust, having agreed any reference to clinical matters with the consultant. On occasion, however, the consultant may wish to write directly to the complainant, referring to clinical aspects of the complaint.

If the patient is dissatisfied with the outcome, at this stage, he/she may renew the complaint either to the DHA, or NHS Trust, to one of its managers, or the consultant. If the complaint has not yet been put in writing, the patient should be asked to do so before it is considered further. The consultant should then inform the regional medical officer (RMO) in England, or the Medical Officer (Complaints) (MO(C)) in Wales, informing the DGM or Chief Executive at the same time. The complaint is then discussed by the RMO, or MO(C), and the consultant, who may feel, as a result, that a further talk with the complainant might resolve matters. If it fails to do so, or if the consultant feels that no purpose would be served by such a meeting, the RMO, or MO(C), should discuss with him/her whether it might be valuable to offer the complainant an independent professional review.

At the third stage, an independent professional review is set up involving two consultants working in the same specialty, one of whom is from another health region. This procedure is not followed, however, if the complaint is likely to be subject to more formal action by the DHA, or NHS Trust, or if the patient is likely to initiate action via the courts. The independent professional review involves discussing matters with the medical staff concerned with the patient's care and treatment, as well as with the patient. The meeting with the patient is by way of a medical consultation where clinical aspects of the problem are fully discussed. The consultant should not be present, but should be available if required. The complainant may be accompanied, if he/she so wishes, by a relative or personal friend. He/she might also wish to ask his/her GP to be present. If the independent consultants feel that the medical staff have exercised their clinical judgement responsibly, they should try to resolve the complainant's anxieties. They may, on the other hand, feel that discussions with the medical staff would avoid similar problems arising in the future. If so, they should inform the complainant and provide him/her with an appropriate explanation of how it is hoped to overcome any problems which have been identified. They should also report their findings to the RMO, or MO(C). At any stage in the investigation, the independent consultants may decide that, because of exceptional circumstances, the complaint would be best pursued by some other means. If so, they should inform the RMO or MO(C).

When the review is completed, the District General Manager (DGM), or Chief Executive, must write formally to the complainant on behalf of the DHA or NHS Trust, sending a copy to the consultant. Where appropriate he/she must explain what action has been taken as a result of the complaint, although in relation to clinical matters he/she will follow the advice of the RMO, or MO(C). The patient obtains no further remedy or recompense under the procedure.

6.3.29   PUBLIC INQUIRIES

Under s.22 of the National Health Service Act 1977 (NHSA 1977), the Secretary of State may hold a public inquiry in connection with a matter of particular public concern. Several public enquiries were held in the late 1960s as the result of public concern about incidents of mismanagement and cruelty at a long-stay hospital. These inquiries led to the establishment of the Hospital Advisory Service, (now the Health Advisory Service (HAS)). The functions of HAS, which is an independent body, include the scrutiny, maintenance and improvement of overall standards in areas of the NHS where patients may be particularly vulnerable. Included in its current remit are geriatric and psychiatric services both in hospital and in the community. After a visit by a team from HAS, a report is prepared and sent to the Secretary of State and the health authority or NHS Trust concerned, and to local CHCs. Health authorities and NHS Trusts are expected to implement HAS recommendations and to monitor their implementation. The reports are now available to members of the public.

6.3.30 MENTALLY DISORDERED PATIENTS

The Mental Health Act Commission (MHAC) was set up to protect the interests of patients detained under the Mental Health Act 1983 (MHA 1983). The Commission is also responsible, under s.120(1)(b) of the Act, for investigating two categories of complaints. First, a patient may complain, either at the time of detention or later, about any matter which occurred while he/she is, or was, detained under the Act in a hospital or mental nursing home, and which he/she considers has not been satisfactorily dealt with by the managers of the hospital or mental nursing home. Secondly, the MHAC may receive complaints from any person in relation to the exercise of powers or the discharge of duties, conferred by the Act in respect of detained patients.

Most complaints arise in the course of hospital visits, either when the Commissioners interview the patient, or during discussions with staff. Often, problems result from lack of communication between the patients and those caring for them. The majority of complaints are resolved during the visit, at either ward or departmental level, or at the formal 'feedback' session at the end of the visit. Where the patient wishes to remain anonymous, the Commissioners may raise a complaint as a general issue at the 'feedback' session at the end of a visit. Where it is not possible to do so, and, at the same time, defend the patient's anonymity, the Commissioners will record the complaint, and raise it later should an appropriate opportunity arise. Complaints are only pursued without consent of the patient in exceptional circumstances, for example, where work practices affect patients as well as staff.

Where a more serious complaint is involved, Commissioners check what has already been done by the managers (see paras. 6.3.15 to 6.3.23 above). Where a patient has difficulty in making a complaint, the Commissioners discuss the procedure with him/her and assist, where necessary. For example, a letter of complaint may be written by a visiting Commissioner. Patients sometimes telephone the Commission for information and advice which may result in a complaint being lodged. Complaints are also received in writing, and may vary from a brief request for advice or information to very detailed accounts. A vetting procedure has been introduced, aimed at deciding whether a complaint falls within the Commission's jurisdiction, and whether or not a special visit is needed. Visits are made where a complaint appears to be serious, or the complainant seems particularly disadvantaged, or it is felt that a letter may have concerned a more serious issue than is immediately apparent from its contents.

Complainants are informed about the outcome of their complaint, either by the hospital or the Commission. If the Commission, or the complainant, remain dissatisfied, further action is taken, including visiting the patient, discussing the matter with the hospital, referring the complaint to another agency, or the Commission's appropriate regional group, or, occasionally, the Central Policy Committee (MHAC 1987, 1989).

The Commission has established a formal policy to deal with complaints, and to enable it to act in a consistent manner (MHAC 1993). A major feature is the inclusion of time limits, intended to ensure that complaints, received in writing, are acknowledged within two working days of being received; that a more detailed response is provided within three weeks of its receipt, or that an appropriate holding letter is sent; and that the investigation of most complaints is concluded within fourteen weeks, unless to do so would mean sacrificing the quality of the investigation. A major aim is investigating complaints promptly, effectively and fairly, within a reasonable time-scale. The policy also emphasises the need to keep complainants informed of the progress and outcome of the investigation, a matter over which the Commission had been criticised in the past. However, since Commissioners work only part-time, and are not specifically trained to investigate complaints, apart from the limited training initiatives of the Commission itself, the Commission regards dealing with complaints to the standards which it has set itself as presenting the Commission with a major challenge (MHAC 1991).

One of the major gaps in the Commission's powers is that it cannot protect the interests of informal patients, who are the majority of those who are in hospital, or mental nursing home, at any time. Under s.121(4) of the MHA 1983, the Secretary of State has power to direct the Commission to keep the care and treatment of informal patients under review, but there have been no directions of this kind to date. The Commission had asked the government to extend its remit to cover three particular aspects of the care of informal patients. These were (i) the use of restraints, such as medication, or denial of clothing, which prevented informal patients from leaving hospital or any part of a hospital, other than restraints arising under s.5 of the Act (see Chapter 5 at para. 5.6.22); (ii) intentional deprivation of the company of other patients, or of amenities normally enjoyed by the patient; and (iii) any form of medical treatment which includes the imposition of a stimulus with the intention that the patient should find it unpleasant or uncomfortable, apart from treatment for a physical illness or disability (MHAC 1987).

In its first Biennial Report, the Commission expressed increasing concern about the situation of two categories of informal patients in particular, that is, long-stay patients who lack mental capacity, and patients who, for various reasons, are subject to *de facto* detention in a locked ward or room (MHAC 1985).

6.3.31 The absence of a single complaints procedure for complaining about the organisation and standard of care in hospitals is clearly unsatisfactory. The Ministerial directions issued under the HCPA 1985 hardly go far enough to make the process of complaining less daunting for patients wishing to register their dissatisfaction with the services they receive. There is, apparently, great variability in the implementation of the Act, with few DHAs taking seriously their responsibility to advertise and produce publicity material about the complaints procedure (ACHEW 1990a). The position of those who are vulnerable, such as the elderly in long-term care, whose dependence upon staff may make them less likely to criticise standards of care, gives rise to particular concern. The public inquiries referred to above show how easily mistreatment of patients can remain hidden within the institution. It is important, therefore, that staff should feel able to bring complaints on behalf of patients. A useful model procedure for staff complaints and for managers in handling them is to be found in the publication *Protecting Patients*, available from the National Association of Health Authorities and Trusts.

Another matter of considerable concern as, increasingly, vulnerable people move out of long-term care in hospital into the community, is the absence of a proper complaints system in this part of the NHS. Complaints about community health services do not come within the procedures set down by the directions made under the HCPA 1985 and Circular HC 88(37) and Circular WHC(88)37. However, the DH recommends that these procedures should also be used with respect to community health services.

6.3.32 PROFESSIONAL MISCONDUCT

An allegation of professional misconduct, concerning either NHS or private practice, should be directed to the Council or Board which is concerned with maintaining standards of care in that particular profession.

Complaints about the professional misconduct of a doctor must be referred to the General Medical Council (GMC) which has jurisdiction, under s.36, and ss.38–45 of, and Schedule 4 to, the Medical

Act 1983 (MA 1983), over questions of serious misconduct which might bring the medical profession into disrepute, and over matters relating to criminal conviction. 'Serious professional misconduct' is not defined in the Act, but has been judicially described as 'serious misconduct judged according to the rules, written or unwritten, governing the profession'. The formal rules which currently govern the GMC's procedures are set out in regulations issued in 1988, and described in *Professional Conduct and Discipline: Fitness to Practice* (GMC 1993).

Complaints are initially screened by a medical member of the GMC who will decide if the case falls within the Council's jurisdiction, and should be referred for consideration by the Preliminary Proceedings Committee (PPC). A complaint cannot be rejected at this stage without the agreement of a lay member of the Council, specifically appointed to advise the medical screener. The PPC, which sits in private, determines, on the basis of written evidence and submissions, whether the case should be more fully investigated by the Professional Conduct Committee (PCC). The PPC can also refer the case to the Health Committee (HC) to determine whether a doctors's fitness to practice is seriously impaired by a physical or mental condition. If the PPC decides not to refer the case to the PCC, it may decide that no further action is necessary, or may send the doctor a warning letter, or letter of advice (where, for example, the doctor had a first conviction for driving under the influence of alcohol, or where his/her professional conduct had, apparently fallen below the proper standard, but was not so serious as to warrant a public inquiry). If the PPC refers the case to the PCC, or to the HC, it may also order the doctor's suspension, or that his/her registration should be conditional, for up to two months, until the matter can be considered by the PCC or HC. The doctor must be given the opportunity to appear, and be heard, as to whether such an order should be made.

If the PCC finds a case proved, it may decide to close the case; or it may postpone its decision until further evidence is provided; or it may place conditions, for up to three years, on a doctor's registration, in order to protect the public, or the doctor's own interests; or it may suspend a doctor for up to twelve months; or remove his/her name, immediately, from the register of those allowed to practice. The kinds of conditions which may be imposed are that a doctor must not practice in a certain area of medicine, or that he/she must take specific steps to remedy an evident deficiency of knowledge, clinical skills, professional attitudes, management or communication. Where a direction by the PCC affects a doctor's registration, he/she has a right of appeal, within twenty-eight days, to the Judicial Committee of the Privy Council. The direction does not come into effect until the twenty-eight days have expired, or, where an appeal is lodged during that time, until it has been heard, which could be as long as twelve months. However, the PCC may, if it considers it necessary in the interests of the public, or the doctor, make an interim order, which suspends the doctor immediately. This suspends registration during the twenty-eight-day period, or, where an appeal is lodged, until it has been heard. A right of appeal against such an order lies to the High Court.

A direction removing a doctor's name from the list of practitioners, is effective until the doctor makes a successful application for it to be restored, except where an appeal against the direction is successful. An application cannot be made until at least ten months after the date on which the order was made. Where an application is unsuccessful, a further period of at least ten months must elapse before a further application may be made. Each application is determined on its merits, having regard, among other things, to the nature and gravity of the original offence, the length of time since removal, and the conduct of the applicant in the interim.

6.3.33   Under s.35 of the MA 1983, the GMC is also responsible for maintaining and improving standards of professional practice by advising doctors on what behaviour is acceptable, and on matters of medical ethics. General advice on these matters is formulated by a Committee on Standards of Professional Conduct and Medical Ethics, and is usually disseminated in the Council's Annual Reports, as well as in *Professional Conduct and Discipline: Fitness to Practice* (GMC 1993).

According to the GMC's *Annual Report* for 1992, the number of complaints went up between September 1991 and August 1992 by almost 20 per cent. Of the 1,320 complaints received during that period, however, 14 per cent were redirected elsewhere, and in 44 per cent of cases, no disciplinary action was taken. By the time the *Annual Report* was published in July 1993, 25 per cent were still under consideration, and others had been dealt with informally. Only thirty-five cases (2.7 per cent) were referred to the PCC, with a further twenty-four being referred to the HC. With the addition of cases carried over from the previous year, the PCC considered forty-three cases in all. Four doctors were struck off the list, thirteen were suspended, six had conditions placed on their registration, nine were admonished and the rest were cleared. Nearly 600 complaints concerned poor medical treatment while others concerned the behaviour of doctors, including breach of professional confidence, rudeness, violence and exercising undue influence over patients. The GMC has proposed that a new disciplinary category should be introduced to deal with matters such as rudeness or consistently poor performance. Such a change would require legislative changes which were not likely to come into force until at least 1995. The Council's President and Chair of the PCC said that the Council was 'surprised and disappointed' at this delay in finding Parliamentary time for the introduction of such procedures.

A complaint about the professional misconduct of a dentist should be directed to the General Dental Council, about an optician to the General Optical Council, and about a community pharmacist to the British Pharmaceutical Council, all which have disciplinary powers, including removal from the list of those registered to practice.

6.3.34 COMPLAINTS AGAINST OTHER HEALTH SERVICE PROVIDERS

In relation to services provided by chiropodists, complaints often arise because of the delay which occurs between an assessment of need and the availability of treatment. Referring the problem to the DGM or Chief Executive may help to secure care more quickly, but other action, such as alleging a breach of statutory duty, is not likely to succeed (see para. 6.4.2 below). Complaints concerning the standard of services given by a chiropodist should be directed to the DGM or NHS Trust, in the first place. Where maladministration is being alleged, a complaint can also be made to the HSC.

The body regulating the professional conduct of chiropodists is the Chiropodists Board of the Council for Professions Supplementary to Medicine, to which any complaint concerning professional misconduct should be directed. The Disciplinary Committee of the Board has power, in serious cases, to remove a person from the list of those registered to practice. Only state registered chiropodists may work within the NHS.

6.3.35 COMMUNITY NURSES

Complaints about the provision of services by district nurses and HVs lie initially to the DGM or NHS Trust. There is also right of access, where appropriate, to the HSC. The UKCC for Nursing, Midwifery and Health Visiting handles serious complaints of a professional nature. The UKCC can remove a practitioner found guilty of a serious breach of conduct from the register of those permitted to practice.

6.4.1 COMPLAINTS ABOUT GAPS, DEFICIENCIES AND DELAYS

A major cause of complaint in the NHS is that gaps, deficiencies, and delays in the provision of service, have a detrimental effect upon patients in need of care and treatment. There is often a shortage of geriatric beds in local hospitals, for example (see Chapter 5 at para. 5.6.4), or long waiting lists for operations such as hip replacements. In such circumstances, what action can an individual take in order to try to obtain the services which are needed? Three kinds of legal action may be available, although on existing evidence, success is often uncertain or unlikely. The legal possibilities are: to sue for breach of statutory duty; to apply to the courts for judicial review of an administrative decision; and to request the Minister concerned to exercise his/her default powers.

6.4.2 BREACH OF A STATUTORY DUTY

The NHS is available to its users as a result of duties placed upon the Secretary of State by ss.1 and 3 of the NHSA 1977. Section 1 of the Act places a duty upon the Minister to promote a comprehensive health service designed to secure improvement in the physical and mental health of the people of England and Wales, and in the prevention, diagnosis and treatment of illness. The Minister also has a duty under s.3 of the NHSA 1977 to provide accommodation, facilities and services for the prevention of illness and for the care and after-care of people suffering from illness, to such extent as he considers appropriate and necessary.

6.4.3 One possible course of action is to sue for alleged breach of one or more of these statutory duties. The primary task of the person bringing the action is to show that the duty relates to him/her, either as an individual, or as the member of a specific group, and is not owed to the public in general. Success, therefore, depends upon the court's interpretation of the presumed intention of Parliament when enacting the legislation. Judicial attitudes in this context can be illustrated by the (unreported) decision of the Court of Appeal in *R v. Secretary of State for Social Services and Others, ex parte Hincks (1981)*. Four individuals, including three elderly persons, who had been on a waiting list for orthopaedic surgery for up to three years, brought an action against the Secretary of State, the regional health authority and the local health authority, alleging breach of statutory duty because plans to build an extension to a particular hospital had been abandoned as the result of financial cutbacks. The applicants also sought a declaration that the respondents were in breach of the duty set out in s.1 of the Act to continue to promote a comprehensive service designed to secure improvements in health and the prevention of illness, and were also in breach of their duty under s.3 to provide accommodation, facilities and services in order to fulfil those purposes. The plaintiffs also sought damages for the pain and suffering which they had suffered as a result of the time spent in waiting for treatment, and an order to compel performance of these statutory duties (see para. 6.4.4 below).

The applicants' attempt failed since they were unable to establish a right of action for breach of statutory duty. The Court of Appeal held that the terms of s.3(1)(a), which specifically relates to the provision of hospital services, required the Secretary of State to provide accommodation, facilities and services only 'to such extent as he considered necessary to meet all reasonable requirements'. The duty was not absolute and Lord Denning suggested that for an action to succeed, the way in which the Minister had exercised the discretion given to him had to be so unreasonable that no reasonable Secretary of State would have acted, or not acted, in that particular way. According to Lord Bridge, current government policies in the economic and financial fields were to be regarded as proper limitations on a Minister's statutory duties to provide services. It would seem that the question of how much is to be made available by way of resources, and of how these resources are then to be allocated to particular services, is regarded as a matter of political decision-making lying outside the jurisdiction of the courts (Braham 1985). Action for breach of statutory duty is, therefore, of limited value and unlikely to be of much use to elderly people unable to secure the services they need because of financial stringency unless it could be shown, perhaps, that the Minister's decision was so unreasonable as to be *ultra vires* and possibly open to judicial review. Subsequent attempts at using actions for breaches of statutory duty have been no more successful in their outcome than they were in the Hincks case.

However, s.117 of the MHA 1983 is an exception in that it creates a specific duty to provide after-care services for certain categories of mentally disordered patients (see para. 6.4.4 below). It has also been argued (Gordon 1993) that an implied duty to provide community care services, such as after-care under s.21 of and Sched. 8 to the NHSA 1977, arises whenever any category of mentally disordered patient has been assessed as needing such services (see Chapter 3 at para. 3.2.1 and Chapter 5 at para. 5.6.25).

6.4.4 JUDICIAL REVIEW

Another possible course of action available to an aggrieved patient would be to invoke the supervisory jurisdiction of the High Court by making use of a procedure known as judicial review. This is the means by which the High Court exercises control over the wrongful administrative acts or omissions of public authorities and officials by the use of the prerogative orders of mandamus, certiorari and prohibition. The procedure for applying for judicial review is now governed by Order 53 of the Rules of the Supreme Court, and by s.31 of the Supreme Court Act 1981 (SCA 1981).

6.4.5 Applicants for one or more of these prerogative orders – to quash, restrain, or to require the performance of a public duty – must first obtain the leave of the court which will only be granted if the court considers the applicant has shown a 'sufficient interest in the matter to which the application applies'. An order may be refused if the court considers that a suitable alternative remedy is available to the applicant, such as a statutory right of appeal to the Minister, appeal to some other court, or the use of default powers (see para. 6.4.6 below). If these hurdles can be overcome, however, judicial review is one of the main methods by which the decision of a public body, such as a health authority, can be controlled by the courts, particularly where it can be argued that there is a specific duty to provide certain services. In *R v. Ealing District Health Authority, ex parte Fox (1992)*, an application for the judicial review of a decision by a health authority not to provide after-care services to a mentally disordered patient succeeded since the applicant fell within the scope of s.117 (see Chapter 5 at 5.6.24).

6.4.6 DEFAULT POWERS

Another possible course of action is to ask the Secretary of State to exercise the default powers set out in s.85 of the NHSA 1977. Under that section, the Secretary of State can declare a regional health authority (RHA), or DHA, or an FHSA or a Special Health Authority (SHA), or NHS Trust, plus a number of other bodies, to be in default for failing to discharge any duty placed upon them by the Act. (This power parallels default procedures available under local government legislation.) If the Minister exercises his/her power, members of the authority are dismissed, and others are appointed in their place. It is rare, however, for Ministers to exercise such powers, and the procedure is, therefore, of limited value in itself. The threat of drawing the attention of a Minister to a particular problem by asking him/her to exercise his/her default powers has, however, been used by a number of groups seeking to obtain services for disabled people (Cook and Mitchell 1982). If the Secretary of State refuses to exercise his/her default powers, is it possible to take legal action in the courts? The position is not clear since judicial opinion seems divided on this point. It has been suggested that legal action can be brought if a public body had apparently acted *ultra vires*, that is, beyond the powers granted to it by statute, or where the decision affects an individual who is a member of the class of individuals to whom the statutory duty is owed (Hoggett 1990).

6.5.1 ACTIONS IN NEGLIGENCE OR TRESPASS TO THE PERSON

The third category of complaint which may arise in relation to health care concerns harm or injury suffered by an individual which, it is alleged, amounts to the tort (or civil wrong), either of negligence or of trespass to the person. A patient may seek financial compensation for an injury suffered as the consequence of the act or omission of someone involved in his/her care. Such actions are available to patients in either the public or the private sector of medicine. For NHS patients, the various complaints procedures described above are, generally, no bar to taking action in the courts as well. The possibility of using the judicial process will, however, normally prevent a complaint being made to the HSC (see para. 6.3.24 above). For private patients, an action in tort, or possibly an action for breach of an express or implied term in the contractual agreement entered into for the provision of care and treatment, may be their single form of redress. Actions for breaches of statutory duty, or for judicial review, and requests to the Minister to exercise statutory default powers are not available. Nor is the complaints machinery of the NHS open to them.

Under s.139 of the Mental Health Act 1983 (MHA 1983), mentally disordered patients detained under the MHA 1983 cannot bring a legal action in relation to acts committed under the provisions of the Act without first obtaining the leave of the High Court, and no liability will arise unless the act complained of was done in bad faith or without reasonable care.

6.5.2 NEGLIGENCE

The three essentials of the tort of negligence are that the defendant owes a legal duty of care to the plaintiff; that there was a breach of that duty; and that, as a consequence, harm was suffered by the plaintiff. The standard of care expected of a defendant is that of a reasonable person, so that, for example, a doctor must conform to the standard which can reasonably be expected of a person fulfilling a doctor's role or function. If there is a standard practice in a particular field, deviation from it could be regarded as evidence of negligence. Action which did not observe accepted practice might, however, be held to be warranted because of the special circumstances of the case. It is for the plaintiff to show first, what would have been normal or usual practice; second, that the defendant did not follow such practice; and third, that the alternative course which was, in fact, followed was one which no professional person of that status or experience, displaying reasonable skill and ability, would have taken in acting with reasonable care. In *Bolam v. Friern HMC (1957)* it was said that a doctor must 'exercise such care as accords with the standards of reasonably competent medical men at the time', and that the test 'is the standard of the ordinary skilled man exercising and professing to have that special skill'. This could be subject, however, to the exercise of a higher duty if the practitioner had knowledge of special risks. According to Lord Scarman in *Maynard v. West Midlands RHA (1985)*: 'a doctor who professes to exercise a special skill must exercise the ordinary skill of his speciality'. The defendant is not expected to avoid all possible risks, nor will he/she be negligent because of an error of judgement where all reasonable care was taken, nor because of some mischance.

In some circumstances, the rule *res ipsa loquitur* – the thing speaks for itself – may apply. In such cases, if injury can be shown by the plaintiff, negligence will be presumed, and it will be for the defendant to rebut the presumption. If the defendant succeeds, the burden of proof then shifts back to the plaintiff to show that the injury was caused by the defendant's negligence. Although *res ipsa loquitur* has been successfully pleaded in a number of cases of alleged medical negligence, it has been suggested that judges are generally resistant to its application in this field (Samuels 1983).

There may be a particular duty of care towards patients who present special risks, such as elderly persons who are mentally confused. In such cases, suitable precautions should be taken if there is a danger that they may injure themselves or other persons. Their mental state might be such that constant supervision is necessary to ensure that they come to no harm.

6.5.3 VICARIOUS LIABILITY

Where it is alleged that a tort has been committed by an employee, it may be possible to bring the action against the employer as well as, or as an alternative to, suing the employee. This is not possible where the person concerned is an independent contractor, such as a family practitioner, or a doctor in private practice. In those cases, action can only be brought against the person who is alleged to have committed the tort. The rules relating to vicarious liability are not discussed in detail here but the rationale is that an employer, such as a DHA or NHS Trust, should be made liable for any wrong suffered as the result of the actions of those who are its employees and acting within the scope of their employment, because this gives economic advantage to the individual claiming damages. In *Cassidy v. Ministry of Health (1951)*, the plaintiff lost the use of his left hand and suffered severe pain as a result of negligent post-operative treatment. The Court of Appeal held the hospital liable because the negligent act was carried out by those employed by the hospital authority. Similarly, in *Roe v. Ministry of Health (1954)* it was held that, had negligence been proved, the defendants would have been vicariously liable for the actions of an anaesthetist who at the time of the alleged tort was working part-time for the NHS, although the rest of the time was spent in private practice.

6.5.4 TRESPASS TO THE PERSON

Another possible form of legal action is to sue in the tort of trespass to the person, either for assault or battery. Such action is possible where it is alleged that medical treatment has been given without the consent of the patient, (see Chapter 5 at paras. 5.6.13 to 5.6.18) or where a patient is wrongfully restrained, or detained against his/her will and prevented from leaving the premises. The most difficult cases are, again, likely to arise where a patient is mentally disordered or mentally confused. The statutory position in relation to consent to treatment by detained mentally disordered patients is discussed elsewhere (Chapter 5 at paras. 5.6.16 to 5.6.17). Important proposals for changes to the law in relation to adults with mental incapacity are contained in the Law Commission's Consultation Paper No. 129 (Law Commission 1993b) (see Chapter 5 at para. 5.6.15)

6.5.5 SUMMARY

The purpose of this chapter has been to indicate the main processes and procedures for making complaints and seeking redress in the field of health care. These tend to be slow and bureaucratic to use, complicated, and often weighted against the complainant. For example, delays of well over a year are not uncommon before FHSA Service Committee decisions are ratified (ACHEW 1991). The Council on Tribunals has called for the introduction of independent adjudicating authorities to replace the current system of service committees, for the appointment of legally qualified and independent chairmen, and for proper training for those involved in the process of hearing complaints (Council on Tribunals 1990). The existing situation may present particular problems for elderly people since, as a group, they may not find complaining easy, especially against those in positions of authority or power over them. Yet many elderly people may be particularly vulnerable when they enter the health care system, whether in the public or independent sector, because of their social, psychological and physical status. They need, not only information about their rights, but advice and support in bringing complaints and in seeking redress for their grievances.

Over fourteen years ago, the Merrison Committee argued for a 'simple, well-understood mechanism through which people who use the NHS can suggest how it [could] be improved and complain when things go wrong' (RCNHS 1979). Since then, some changes have been made, but far more comprehensive and radical reform is needed, particularly as a result of the setting up of the internal market in the NHS which has led to far more complex patterns of health care delivery.

7 Personal and family matters

Aled Griffiths

7.1.1 MARRIAGE BREAKDOWN

Britain has the second highest rate of marriage breakdown in Europe (Rae 1994). This increase in the divorce rate affects all age groups. Over a third of all marriages in 1991 were remarriages where either or both members of the couple had been divorced. The remarriage rate for divorced women and widows is much lower than their male counterparts (CSO 1994). Those who experience marriage breakdown in old age face particular problems. Some of the issues relevant to their position are discussed below.

7.2.1 DIVORCE

The only ground upon which divorce can be granted is that a marriage has broken down irretrievably. Irretrievable breakdown must be evidenced, however, by the existence of one or more of the following facts: that the respondent has committed adultery and that the petitioner finds it intolerable to live with the respondent; that the respondent has behaved in such a way that the petitioner cannot reasonably be expected to live with him/her; that the respondent has deserted the petitioner for a continuous period of at least two years immediately preceding the presentation of the petition; that the parties have lived apart for a continuous period of two years immediately preceding the presentation of the petition and that the respondent consents to the granting of the decree; that the parties have lived apart for a continuous period of at least five years immediately preceding the presentation of the petition.

In calculating whether or not the parties have lived apart for the requisite length of time, any cohabitation for a period, or periods, not exceeding six months in total is ignored. A similar six-month rule applies where the parties continue to live together after the discovery of an act of adultery, or after the occurrence of the incident, giving rise to a petition based upon the respondent's behaviour. Cohabitation for more than six months is a bar to presenting a petition based upon adultery, but no specific statutory restriction exists in relation to a petition based upon the respondent's behaviour.

Divorce petitions founded upon five years' separation can be refused where it is shown that the dissolution of the marriage would cause grave financial or other hardship to the respondent (see para. 7.2.4).

7.2.2 The vast majority of divorce petitions are now undefended. Nevertheless, the need for the petitioner to show irretrievable breakdown of the marriage has resulted in considerable litigation over the years. Some of the reported cases have particular relevance for those who are elderly. For instance, what amounts to unreasonable behaviour, or what must a spouse reasonably be expected to endure where a husband or wife's difficult behaviour arises from deteriorating health? First, it appears that what amounts to unreasonableness is subjective. In *Birch v. Birch (1992)*, the wife filed a petition for divorce after twenty-seven years of marriage, on the grounds of her husband's unreasonble behaviour. In essence, she complained of his dogmatism, dictatorial, didactic and chauvinistic attitude. The Court of Appeal decided that such behaviour towards a sensitive wife amounted to unreasonable behaviour with which she could not be expected to live. Second, it appears that a spouse is expected to put up with passive behaviour. In *Thurlow v. Thurlow (1976)*, the wife's mental deterioration arising from epilepsy led her to being progressively unable to perform domestic tasks. She 'threw items', caused damage to household equipment, and wandered in the street causing distress and worry to her husband. She also became incontinent and had to be admitted to hospital when her husband could no longer cope. The evidence indicated that her condition was unlikely to improve. The husband's petition, alleging it was not reasonable to expect him to continue to live with her, was successful. The judge acknowledged the existence of a marital duty to accept and share the burdens of a spouse's illness, but the length of the wife's illness had to be taken into consideration, as well as the ability of the petitioner to bear the stress which it had imposed upon him. It was implied, however, that relying on this ground might not be possible where the respondent's behaviour was merely passive. Should a person be permanently comatose, the only available remedy might be a decree based upon evidence of five years' separation.

Another relevant issue in this context is the mental element necessary in order to establish desertion. Even where *de facto* separation exists, there can be no desertion unless one spouse intended to remain permanently separated from the other. Where, for example, separation had resulted from the poor health of one of the spouses, that, in itself, would not constitute desertion unless coupled with evidence that the respondent wished to have nothing more to do with the petitioner (*Smith v. Smith (1973)*). A person suffering from mental illness might be incapable of forming the necessary intention to desert. If, however, it could be shown that the respondent had formed an intention to desert prior to becoming mentally ill, the petition might succeed even though the respondent had become ill before the beginning of the two-year period of separation necessary to establish desertion. Section 2(4) of the Matrimonial Causes Act 1973 (MCA 1973) provides that:

> ... the Court may treat a period of desertion as having continued at a time when the deserting party was incapable of continuing the necessary intention if the evidence before the court is such that, had that party not been so incapable, the Court would have inferred that his desertion continued at that time.

Where one spouse behaves so unreasonably that he/she effectively drives the other from the matrimonial home, there may be grounds for bringing a petition against that person for 'constructive' desertion. In effect, the spouse remaining in the home is deemed to be in desertion because of his/her behaviour.

7.2.3 In order to establish grounds for divorce on the basis of having lived apart, the parties may be treated as living separately even though they live in the same house. The courts have distinguished between living in the same accommodation and living in the same household. In *Fuller v. Fuller (1973)*, the wife had left her husband for another man. Some time later she took the husband in as a lodger, because he was suffering from a serious heart condition and was too ill to live by himself. It was held that the couple were to be treated as if they were living apart. It is not clear whether this distinction would be applied by the court in circumstances where the couple were living within the same residential establishment. It might be necessary to show more than that the couple were no longer sharing the same bedroom.

7.2.4 Where a petition is based on the fact of five years separation (see 7.2.1 above), the defence of 'grave financial hardship' may be available to the respondent. It could be used, for example, where a marriage had been in existence for many years, and the wife, being the respondent, would lose the benefit of her husband's occupational pension were a divorce to be granted. The defence can, however, be met by the petitioner making alternative financial arrangements which satisfy the court, such as providing a compensatory insurance policy (*Le Marchant v. Le Marchant (1977)*). A spouse's entitlement to social security benefit might be sufficient to overcome the statutory defence (*Reiterbund v. Reiterbund (1975)*). Where 'other hardship' is alleged, that, too, must be 'grave' (*Parker v. Parker (1972)*). In practice, the courts have been reluctant to accept this defence. For instance, evidence that a 62-year-old widow with a weekly income of £60 would lose the possibility of a widow's pension of £15 per week if her husband died was held not to constitute grave hardship (*Jackson v. Jackson (1993)*). Thus, the courts have refused to grant a decree only in exceptional circumstances.

When it was first proposed that divorce should be allowed on the basis of five years' separation, it was labelled a 'Casanova's Charter' by critics who believed it might be used by some husbands to divorce a wife who was becoming less physically attractive in their eyes. In fact, more women than men have used this ground of recent years, as the basis for divorce.

7.2.5 Undefended petitions are now dealt with under a special procedure, first introduced in 1973, which allows evidence to be presented in written form. Much of the trauma associated with court proceedings is removed since neither party need be present in court. If the divorce court registrar is not satisfied that the petitioner has proved his/her case, further evidence can be submitted, also in writing.

7.2.6 Once a decree absolute has been awarded by the court, it is not possible to set it aside. In *Callaghan v. Hanson-Fox (Andrew) (1991)*, the petitioner unsuccessfully sought to set aside the decree absolute on the ground that it had been obtained through fraudulent statements in the petition. After twenty-two years of marriage, the petitioner's wife had filed for divorce to which he had consented. The wife died intestate shortly after the divorce was made absolute and the court refused to render the divorce ineffective.

7.2.7 In 1993, the government published a Consultative Paper entitled *Looking to the Future: Mediation and the Grounds for Divorce* (Lord Chancellor's Department 1994). The main proposal is the introduction of 'no fault' divorce, coupled to a twelve-month period for reflection and consideration. The aim is to promote mediation. As the summary of the report states, 'mediation does not sit easily with the current divorce process where, in 75 per cent of cases, adultery or behaviour is alleged. Mediation is said to encourage couples to resolve issues for themselves, reduce tension, and facilitate longer lasting agreements'. On the other hand, critics believe that mediation can disadvantage a weaker spouse and does not prevent the parties from subsequently employing lawyers to go over the ground again.

At present, the number of families being seen by any form of mediation service is relatively small, with the focus primarily on disputes concerning children (Rae 1994).

7.3.1 JUDICIAL SEPARATION

A spouse may decide to petition for judicial separation rather than divorce. This might be because of adherence to a particular religious faith, which prohibited or frowned upon divorce, or it might be based upon hope of eventual reconciliation. It may also be used as a remedy by those experiencing marital problems during the first year of marriage when divorce is not possible. The grounds for judicial separation are the same as those for divorce.

7.3.2 Where a decree of judicial separation is granted, the court's power to make various financial awards can be invoked. The decree terminates the duty to cohabit, and removes consent to sexual intercourse which is implied by the existence of marriage, so that a husband who had intercourse with his wife against her will might be guilty of rape. The standard of proof which a wife must establish in order to show that she had been raped by her husband is the same as in a criminal prosecution, that is, beyond reasonable doubt (*N v. N (1991)*). So long as the decree is in force, it cannot be alleged that either spouse has deserted the other. The existence of a decree of judicial separation also affects a spouse's right to inherit under the rules of intestacy (see para. 7.9.1), although he/she could apply for reasonable provision under the Inheritance (Provision for Family and Dependants) Act 1975 (I(PFD)A 1975) (see para. 7.13.1). An undefended petition for judicial separation is also dealt with under the 'special' procedure (see para. 7.2.5 above).

7.4.1 FINANCIAL MATTERS

Divorce and judicial separation often lead to disputes about money and property. On application, a divorce court can order lump sum payments to be made by one spouse to the other, as well as award maintenance payments to an ex-spouse or to support any dependent child. The Matrimonial and Family Proceedings Act 1984 (MFPA 1984) amended the provisions contained in the MCA 1973 which previously required the court to place the parties, as far as practicable, in the position they would have been in had no divorce taken place. The MCA 1973, as amended, sets out new guidelines for the court in making financial arrangements. The court's duty is to have regard to all the circumstances of the case, first consideration being given to the welfare of any child under eighteen. Particular regard must also be given to a number of other matters, including the income, earning capacity, property and other financial resources of either of the parties to the marriage, as well as any which they are likely to possess in the foreseeable future. Other matters which must be taken into account by the court include: (i) the age of each party and the duration of the marriage; (ii) any physical or mental disability of either of the parties; (iii) the contribution which each has made or is likely, in the foreseeable future, to make to the welfare of the family, including any contributions by looking after the home and caring for the family; (iv) the conduct of each of the parties, if that conduct is such that it would, in the opinion of the court, be inequitable to disregard it, and the value to each of the parties to the marriage of any benefit (for example, a pension) which the party will lose the chance of acquiring.

Another change introduced by the MPFA 1984 was that the court must consider whether it would be appropriate for the financial obligation of each party towards the other to be terminated as soon after the grant of the decree as the court considers just and reasonable. If it is thought an order for periodical maintenance payments would be appropriate, the court must then consider whether these should be sufficient only to enable the spouse receiving them to adjust, without due hardship, to the termination of his/her financial dependence on the other party.

Where a settlement is not limited by the 'clean break' principle, the courts can vary a maintenance arrangement at any time on the grounds that circumstances have changed. In *Re W (Dec'd) (1975)*, an ex-wife's claim was upheld twenty-nine years after the divorce. She had been granted a divorce on the basis of her husband's desertion in 1946, but following professional advice, did not claim maintenance because of her earnings. The husband resisted his ex-wife's later efforts to obtain maintenance and was thereby able to amass capital which should have gone towards his wife's maintenance. On his death, he left an estate worth £28,000. The wife, then aged seventy-five years, had very limited resources. It was held that, having regard to her age, it would be just for her to receive £11,000.

In deciding the quantum of the sum to be awarded, the courts have used as a guideline the so-called 'one-third rule', as set out in *Wachtel v. Wachtel (1973)*. It must be emphasised, however, that the rule has been used flexibly, and that its application will vary according to the circumstances. There will be some situations where more than one-third is appropriate. In other circumstances, where the marriage was brief, or the wife is qualified and able to earn a reasonable living, a lesser amount may be awarded.

The age of the parties could be a significant factor in deciding questions of maintenance, particularly where there is a considerable age gap between the husband and wife. In *Compton v. Compton (1985)*, the Court of Appeal was influenced by the fact that the wife was only forty years old and had good earning capacity, whereas the husband was over sixty years and had retired. In *S v. S (1977)*, it was held that where a marriage was short-lived, and particularly where the parties were not young, the primary consideration was the needs of the wife. Regard should be had to the effects of the marriage, mainly on the wife, but also on the husband. The resources and obligations of the parties should be ascertained and balanced against each other in relation to all the circumstances of the marriage.

7.4.2 Divorce can have important implications for social security and private pension rights. A woman under sixty must build up her own national insurance record, but on reaching pensionable age can rely, if that is to her advantage, upon contributions paid by her former husband during the marriage. If a woman remarries before reaching the age of sixty, she can no longer rely upon her ex-husband's contribution record. A woman divorced after the age of sixty, can rely, if necessary, on her ex-husband's record, in claiming a state pension. The DSS produces a leaflet (NP32A) outlining a person's entitlement to a pension after divorce. Special rules enable divorced women to claim short-term benefits such as sickness or unemployment benefit if they have not been in paid work, or have not paid full National Insurance contributions.

Private pension schemes rarely provide for an ex-spouse. In this respect, provision in Britain lags behind that of some countries, such as the Netherlands, where an ex-wife has a legal right to a proportion of her previous husband's occupational pension and to a proportion of the state widow's pension, depending on how many years they were married. In Britain, an ex-wife might be advised to consider making provision for herself from her own resources. There are several possibilities, but the simplest and cheapest way of securing a degree of protection is probably to take out a term life assurance policy on the life of her former husband. As mentioned above, a divorce court can always make financial orders to compensate for loss of state benefits. The value of occupational pension schemes are rarely taken into proper account by solicitors or judges, however, possibly because their potential value is not fully appreciated (*H v. H (Financial Provision Capital Assets) (1993)*). Should there be cause for concern, it might be appropriate to consult a pensions consultant or an actuary. The Law Society has drafted a model letter of instruction to an actuary for the purpose of valuing an occupational pension (*Family Law* 1993).

It also appears from a recent case that it is possible for a court, in limited circumstances, to vary a husband's pension fund in order to provide an annuity for a wife (*Brooks v. Brooks (1993)*). In this case, the couple were married in 1977 and the husband's company, a small family business, established a pension fund in 1980. The trustees of the fund were the husband and his sister, the company accountant. The trustees were enpowered to pay benefit at their discretion to various beneficiaries, including Mr Brooks' spouse, widow, or dependant. At the time of divorce proceedings, Mr Brooks was under pensionable age, and the judge decided that he could vary the pension fund to provide the wife with an annuity and pension. The case, however, may only have limited application (Chatterton 1993). Until this decision, it had always been thought that a pension fund could not be touched and divided on divorce. The company in question was very much a family company and, as the law stands, it is doubtful if the courts would vary large pension funds.

7.4.3 In May 1993, the Pensions Management Institute published a report based on the findings of a Working Group. It proposed, *inter alia*, that there should be a statutory presumption in favour of valuing pensions on divorce, and that pension splitting should be possible. It must be hoped that the government will ensure that such proposals become law so that inadequate divorce powers do not continue to lead to inadequate pensions for those who have taken care of the family (Masson 1993).

7.4.4 THE MATRIMONIAL HOME

One of the most important settlements on divorce relates to the matrimonial home, which may be sold (if owner occupied), or surrendered (if a tenancy), or one party may remain in it. Arrangements of this kind can result from an agreement between the parties, or can be ordered by the court, which has wide powers to apportion legal interests in the home as it sees fit. The court order might provide for sale of the property to be postponed, contingent upon some event, or it might transfer the property to either of the parties.

It is common practice for solicitors, prior to the actual divorce or judicial separation, to draw up 'Consent Orders' to deal with any interim arrangements which may be needed. In effect, these amount to legal contracts between the parties. It seems, moreover, that if one of the spouses should die, the right to enforce a Consent Order vests in the deceased person's estate. The leading case in this context involved an agreement that the husband should pay his wife a lump sum, and that she, in turn, would transfer her interest in the matrimonial home to him. The husband honoured his part of the agreement but died before his wife had completed hers. Although there was no apparent legal authority, the court declared that the husband's executors could enforce the agreement against the surviving spouse (*Warren-Gash and Another v. Lane (1984)*). No such discretion exists where the parties are unmarried. In those circumstances, the court can uphold existing legal interests only, but might be prepared to recognise an implied trust which would protect, as beneficiary, a non-owner who had contributed to the acquisition of a capital asset (*Cooke v. Head (1972)*).

7.5.1 COHABITATION

There is a distinct lack of any legislative framework to regulate the respective rights of cohabitees (Jackson 1990). People who live together should put their affairs in order since the property rights of cohabitees, as indicated below at para. 7.18.2, are tenuous and may lead to very complicated legal problems (Barlow 1993; Moroney 1993). Living together precedents have been drafted and an advice handbook is also available (Welstead 1990).

7.6.1 FINANCIAL PROVISIONS IN THE MAGISTRATES' COURT

Under the Domestic Proceedings and Magistrates' Court Act 1978 (DPMCA 1978), a magistrates' court (sitting as a domestic court) has jurisdiction to order financial provision to be paid by one party to the other while a marriage is in existence. The grounds are (i) that the respondent has failed to provide the applicant with reasonable maintenance; (ii) that the respondent has failed to provide, or make reasonable contribution towards reasonable maintenance for a child of the family; (iii) that the respondent has behaved in such a way that the applicant cannot reasonably be expected to live with the respondent; and (iv) that the respondent has deserted the applicant.

7.7.1 DOMESTIC VIOLENCE

Should one of the parties to a relationship be the victim of domestic violence, the law can provide a degree of protection through orders and injunctions. Where the parties are married to each other, application can be made either to a magistrates' court or to the county court, but where a couple is unmarried, only the county court has the necessary jurisdiction (DPMCA 1978; Domestic Violence and Matrimonial Proceedings Act 1976 (DVMPA 1976)).

To succeed in a magistrates' court, it is necessary to show physical violence was used or threatened against the applicant, and that the order is necessary for his/her physical protection. If so, a protection order may be granted. In the county court, it is necessary to show only that the individual suffered 'molestation', which can include 'pestering', 'harassment', or 'mental torment' (*Vaughan v. Vaughan (1973)*). In such cases, the county court may grant an injunction protecting the other party from molestation. Orders are available in both courts to exclude the offender from the matrimonial home, and to provide for the arrest and, where necessary, the detention of the violent partner. Difficulties, leading to acts of domestic violence, sometimes occur when elderly couples find themselves spending almost every hour in each other's company (Griffiths and Bhowmick 1978).

7.7.2 It should also be noted that violence, or threat of violence, is not essential to justify making an ouster order under s.1(3) of the Matrimonial Homes Act 1983. In the recent case of *B v. B (1993)*, the Court of Appeal held that a husband's jealous, argumentative, unyielding nature was sufficient to justify an order.

7.7.3 However, in some circumstances, protection from molestation may not be given by means of a non-molestation order. In *Wookey v. Wookey (1991)*, a wife aged seventy-two had obtained a non-molestation order from the county court restraining her husband, aged seventy, from assaulting, molesting, or otherwise interfering with her, and from entering the former matrimonial home. The husband was not capable of understanding what he was doing, and the Court of Appeal decided that an injunction of this kind should not be awarded in such circumstances, even though his wife had desired the extra security associated with a power of arrest. The court concluded that an order would have no deterrent effect and that, in any event, the Matrimonial Homes Act 1983 was the appropriate mechanism for dealing with the problems associated with the husband's behaviour.

7.8.1 GRANDPARENTS AND GRANDCHILDREN

Prior to the Children Act 1989 (CA 1989), grandparents had limited opportunities to protect the welfare of their grandchildren (Crook 1994; Samuels 1993b). Under the CA 1989, however, that situation has been replaced by a single, far more comprehensive code which enables grandparents to apply for rights in relation to their grandchildren in certain circumstances. Most court hearings which bear directly on the welfare of a child, or where the interests of a child may have to be taken into account, are now classed as 'family proceedings'. A court has power, in such proceedings, to make an order, either when an application is made to it, or of its own accord. In reaching its decision, the court will be bound by two golden rules: first, that the welfare of the child is the paramount consideration; and, second, that no order must be made unless to do so would be better for the child than no order at all. If an issue is contested, (or if a local authority is involved, for example, in care or supervision proceedings) the court must also have regard to a welfare checklist which refers, among other factors, to the wishes of the child.

Under the new provisions, grandparents may apply for a s.8 order, either in existing family proceedings, or by making a fresh application. Section 8 orders include a residence order, settling the arrangements to be made as to the person with whom the child is to live; a contact order, requiring the person with whom the child lives, or is to live, to allow the child to visit or stay with the person named in the order, or for that person and the child to have contact with each other in some other way; a prohibited steps order, which determines that the person with parental responsibilities may not take certain steps in relation to the child without the consent of the court; and a specific issue order which gives directions for determining a specific question in relation to any aspect of the exercise of parental responsibility in relation to a child.

As non-parents of the child, grandparents will usually need the court's consent to apply for some or all s.8 orders. However, a person who already has a residence order in his/her favour can apply without leave for a s.8 order. Any person with whom the child has lived for at least three years, or who has the consent of any person with parental responsibility for the child, can also apply, without leave, for a residence or contact order. The three-year residence period need not be continuous, but it must not have begun more than five years before the application is made, nor ended more than three months previously. If the child is in local authority care, the consent of the authority must be obtained. Where leave must be obtained, specific guidance for the court is set out in s.10(9) of the Act. It has, however, been said that the need to seek consent will 'scarcely be a hurdle at all to close relatives such as grandparents . . . who wish to care for or visit the child' (Law Commission 1988).

In many cases, what grandparents are seeking is a contact order. More rarely, perhaps, there will be grandparents who are seeking a residence order, either because they are already caring for the child, or wish to become his/her carer. Apart from determining with whom the child is to live, an additional advantage of a residence order is that it confers parental responsibility upon any person in whose favour it is made. A residence order does not, however, deprive parents of the parental responsibilities which are theirs by right. Indeed, certain powers are vested only in a child's parents, such as the power to consent to adoption.

A grandparent who applies for a residence order may have a hard task in certain circumstances. In *Re W (A Minor) (Residence Order) (1993)*, the Court of Appeal confirmed that in the event of competing residence order applications between a natural parent and other relatives, such as grandparents, 'there is a strong presumption, that other things being equal, it is in the interests of the child that it shall remain with the natural parents'. However, the welfare of the child can override these presumptions as happened in *Re U (A Minor) (1993)*. The odds on grandparents obtaining a residence order may be better as against non-relatives (Crook 1994).

Unless they have already been granted a residence order, grandparents will always need the court's consent to apply for a prohibited steps or a specific issue order. They may seek a prohibited steps order, for example, to prevent a child being removed from the country, or to prevent contact with a particular individual. Specific issue orders can relate to such matters as medical treatment and education, matters which normally fall within the natural domain of parents.

7.8.2 ADOPTION

Grandparents may themselves want to adopt a grandchild, or may fear that the granting of an adoption order will result in no contact with their grandchild. On making an adoption order, the court can impose 'such conditions as it thinks fit' (Adoption Act 1976 (AA 1976), s.12(6)). This power has been held to be wide enough to enable the court, in exceptional circumstances, to make a contact order in favour of any relative, if that is in the best interests of the child (*Re J (1973)*; *Re S (1975)*; *Re C (A Minor) (1988)*). Two recent cases give grandparents who want to preserve contact with a grandchild some hope.

In *Re D (A Minor) (Adoption Order: Validity) (1991)*, the Court of Appeal refused to make an order under s.12(6) of the AA 1976 to restrain a grandfather from having contact with a child who was about to be adopted. The child in question suffered from a severe mental disability, and had been placed with long-term foster parents who subsequently applied to adopt the child. The foster parents had wanted to exclude contact with the grandfather, but the Court of Appeal concluded that their legislative powers did not extend to prohibiting contact with third parties, even during the period of the child's minority. In this case, the subject of the adoption order had, in any event, almost attained the age of majority.

The case of *Re U (Application to Free for Adoption) (1993)* is even more encouraging. A child had been taken into care following a number of non-accidental injuries. The child was placed with short-term foster parents and the grandparents maintained regular contact and wanted to adopt. The Adoption Panel, however, decided that they were unsuitable and applied to the court for an order which would free the child for adoption. The application was dismissed and the judge made a residence order in favour of the grandparents. The Court of Appeal confirmed the decision, but varied the order by making a family assistance order requiring the council to make available one of its officers to advise and assist the grandparents for a period of six months, or until such time as the grandparents applied to adopt the child.

7.8.3 GRANDPARENTS AND LOCAL AUTHORITIES

Previous to the CA 1989, where a child was in the care of a social services authority, there was often considerable risk of contact being lost between the child and his/her grandparents. The local authority had considerable discretion whether or not to allow contact with the child, and, if so, to what extent. Under the 1989 Act, however, greater emphasis is placed on trying to ensure that parents as well as other members of a child's family, such as grandparents, have a continuing involvement with the child. A child is being 'looked after' by a local authority, either because he/she is a child in need, who in accordance with local authority's preventive and supportive functions, is being accommodated under a voluntary arrangement, or he/she is in care under a care order. In the first case, the local authority will not acquire parental responsibility for the child. In the second case, parental responsibility will be shared between the local authority and those already vested with parental responsibility for the child.

When it is looking after a child, an authority's main duty will be to safeguard and protect the child's welfare. But the Act also places a number of specific duties on the authority. For example, before making any decision in relation to the child, the authority must, as far as reasonably practicable, ascertain the wishes and feelings of the child, his/her parents, any other person with parental responsibility, and any other person whose wishes and feelings the authority considers relevant (s.22). It is hoped that grandparents will normally be treated as falling within this category. In addition, the child's family, including grandparents, should be involved in plans for the child. Under Sched. 2, para. 15, a local authority has a duty to promote contact between a child who is being looked after by the authority and his/her family.

A grandparent who is dissatisfied with contact arrangements may apply to the court for a s.8 contact order, but the conditions set out in para. 7.8.1 above will apply. Grandparents with parental responsibility over a child may remove a child who is simply being accommodated by a social services authority, at any time. Particular rules apply to children who are subject to care proceedings, or who are already in care. Reasonable contact should be allowed with a child's parents, a guardian, anyone with a residence order, or who has obtained a High Court order, such as wardship. The child, his/her parents, the local authority, or any of the above, can also apply to the court for a contact order under s.34 of the Act, either during care proceedings, or subsequently. Others can apply only with the leave of the court. If a child is in care under a care order, a grandparent, who has parental responsibility for a child, can apply to the court for a residence order. If the order is granted, the care order will come to an end.

7.9.1 WILLS AND INTESTACY

Some 550 women are widowed every day and some 120 husbands lose their wives (*Money Care* 1985). In addition to experiencing the trauma of bereavement, many of those who are widowed face financial uncertainty as a result of the spouse's death. A simple way of reducing stress for the surviving spouse is to execute a will. Where no will exists, the rules of intestacy will apply in distributing the deceased's estate. Many people mistakenly believe that, should they die intestate, everything will automatically go to their husband or wife. This is not necessarily so. If the estate is of sufficient value, other relatives may benefit, thus reducing the amount available for the surviving spouse. Another problem is that cohabitees have no automatic right to inherit under the rules of intestacy. The Law Commission (1990) has suggested that those who have been cohabiting for two years or more should be eligible to inherit under the intestacy rules, but to date the law remains unchanged. It is, therefore, usually vital to make specific provision for the other partner.

The only occasion upon which a widow or widower is guaranteed the whole of a deceased person's estate on an intestacy is where there are no children or other relatives, such as parents, brothers and sisters. For many people, it will be of little concern to learn that their children have an automatic right to share in their estate in certain circumstances. They might react differently, however, on learning that, where there are no surviving children, the deceased spouse's parents could possibly benefit. If there are no surviving parents, their share will be distributed to other specified relative(s) in the order set out in the statutory provisions (see para. 7.10.1 below).

However much or however little a person owns, there are good reasons for making a will. An added advantage is that one or more suitable person(s) can be chosen to act as executor(s)/trix, with the responsibility of proving the will and of carrying out its directions. On an intestacy, those appointed as administrators are invariably entitled to a share in the estate. Moreover, where a person dies intestate there can be unseemly family discord over what the deceased said or wanted. 'He wanted me to have the 'x', not you.' A will makes it clear exactly what the deceased's wishes were (Samuels 1993a). More importantly, there may be special reasons for making a will, such as the need to provide for the long-term needs of a child with learning disability (Ashton 1993b). Similarly, it may be necessary to provide for carers (Hailstone 1993). Also, the cost of administering an estate could be greater than the cost of proving a will. The powers granted to administrators are relatively limited, and sometimes inadequate, whereas executor(s)/trix can be given wide powers to insure, invest or otherwise manage the deceased person's assets.

7.9.2 MAKING A WILL

A valid will can be executed quite simply and easily. In general, it has to be made in writing, but otherwise need not be in any particular form, nor use any special terminology. A word of warning is needed, however. The wording of a will affects its legal meaning and it is always wise to seek professional advice if the drafter is uncertain of the effect of what is proposed. The Legal Advice and Assistance Scheme can be used to engage a solicitor to draft a will if the financial criteria are met. In any event, for a simple transaction such as this, the cost of professional services should be relatively low. The Law Society, in its pamphlet, *Making a Will Won't Kill You* (Law Society 1993), suggests that solicitors are always prepared to give estimates. If difficulties arise, it might be advisable to quote from this pamphlet.

Alternatively, standard form wills with instructions are available from newsagents and elsewhere. *Which*, the consumer magazine, also publish a guide and action pack. The disadvantage of these is that they may not provide the individual with the formula necessary to give effect to his/her wishes. Another danger, in drafting a will, is that the testator/trix may use ambiguous language (*Muir v. Lloyds Bank (1992)*). For example, if a testator states that: 'I give everything equally to my wife and three sons', it is not clear whether he means to give one half to his wife and for the other half to be shared amongst his three sons, or whether he means to give them all one quarter each. A similar problem arises where a will creates an unintended life interest with such words as 'I leave everything to my wife and after her death to my children.' According to the Law Reform Committee, this type of provision, which frequently occurs in home-made wills, has usually been interpreted as restricting the wife's inheritance to a life interest (Law Reform Committee 1973, 1980). In other words, the wife would not be entitled to the capital but only to interest arising from it. In many cases, this may not have been the testator's intention. A change in the law was enacted in s.22 of the Administration of Justice Act 1982 (AJA 1982). This provides that:

> Except where a contrary intention is shown it shall be presumed that if a testator devises or bequeaths property to his spouse in terms which in themselves would give an absolute interest to the spouse, but by the same instrument purports to give his issue an interest in the same property, the gift to the spouse is absolute notwithstanding the purported gift to the issue.

Under this provision, therefore, the wife would get everything. It should be noted, however, that the circumstances to which the section applies are limited and that it will help resolve only the second of the two situations referred to above (Mackay 1983).

7.9.3 There are few limitations on what may be disposed of by will. Testators should, however, give careful consideration to whether they wish to provide specific or general legacies. A specific legacy is the gift of a specific object, such as 'My Ford Escort car'. A general legacy is a gift to be provided from the testator's general estate. It is irrelevant whether its subject matter forms part of the testator's property at his death. Usually a general legacy is in the form of a gift of money. The problem with specific gifts is that they may no longer be available at the testator's death, with the result that the intended beneficiary will receive nothing. In the example given above, it might have been better for the will to have simply provided the gift of a car.

It is also possible for a will to contain a power of appointment to trustees to the effect that they distribute gifts as they see fit. In *Beatty (Dec'd), Hinves v. Brooke Re (1990)*, the testatrix requested the trustees to distribute the chattels among such persons as they think fit within two years of her death. The court held that the arrangement was valid.

If the words 'tax free' are added to specific gifts, this ensures that, subject to there being sufficient monies available, any liability for tax will come out of the estate and will not be deducted from the gift. Where appropriate, the will should also make clear whether or not property is being left free of any liability for mortgage repayments.

After making individual legacies, it is important for the testator to leave the residue of the estate to a particular person or body. If that is not done, a partial intestacy will arise and part of the deceased's estate will be governed by the rules of intestacy rather than by the terms of his/her will.

7.9.4 Once made, a will is valid unless and until revoked by the person making it, or altered by a codicil, or declared invalid by a court. The marriage of a testator/trix usually revokes a will previously made, except where it is clear from its terms that marriage to a particular individual was not intended to have that effect. The granting of a divorce will also, in most cases, revoke an existing will insofar as it applies to a former spouse (AJA 1982). An ex-spouse, disinherited by divorce, who has not remarried, can, however, apply for provision to be made for him/her under the I(PFD)A 1975 (see para. 7.13.3 below) although success is by no means certain.

7.9.5 MUTUAL WILLS

Mutual wills depend on an agreement that the wills were to be irrevocable after the death of the first to die. In the recent and important case of *Re Dale (Dec'd), Proctor v. Dale (1993)*, the husband and wife made identical wills in 1988 in favour of their two children, J and A, in equal shares. The husband died first leaving a net estate of £18,500. After his will had been proved, the wife made a new will which gave a legacy of £500 to J and the residue of the estate, £19,000, to A. J claimed that her parents had made a binding and irrevocable agreement and it was held that the wife's refusal to perform her part of the bargain constituted a fraud on the husband. The wife could not escape from her binding obligation.

7.9.6 CHOOSING EXECUTOR(S)/TRIX

Persons of eighteen years of age or over can be appointed executor(s)/trix of a will. It is possible, therefore, (and not uncommon) for a husband and wife to name each other as executrix and executor, either alone or in conjunction with others. If one of the executors/trix is a professional person, such as a solicitor, he/she must be authorised by the terms of the will to charge for any services undertaken as a result of this appointment. Otherwise only reasonable expenses can be recovered. The will does not become invalid if it provides for an executor/trix to receive a bequest. Those with an interest of this kind must not, however, act as witness, nor must their spouse.

Some bank managers encourage the practice of appointing a bank to act as executor. Banks have specialist departments dealing with this kind of work and are experienced in investment and trust management. All banks make additional charges for work to be carried out which vary in amount from one bank to another. Fees usually, however, represent an all inclusive figure which is expressed as a percentage of the gross value of the estate, in some cases as much as 6 per cent. Banks invariably appoint a solicitor to do some of the work. As a result, it may also be necessary to pay a solicitor's fee from the assets.

7.9.7 CAPACITY TO MAKE A WILL

In order for a will to be valid, the person executing it must be *compos mentis*, that is, mentally competent. The well-established test of mental capacity is that the testator/trix understands the nature of the act, the extent of his/her property, and any moral claims he/she ought to consider. In other words, an individual must know that he/she is making a will, the broad extent (though not the value) of his/her property as well as those individuals he/she ought to bear in mind (*Banks v. Goodfellow (1870)*). Although the general rule is that a person must be competent at the time of executing the will, it may be sufficient to show that mental capacity existed when the testator/trix was giving instructions. It will be valid if the testator/trix was lucid at the time, even if generally confused (*In the Estate of Bohrmann (1938)*). This rule can be of practical importance where a person is ailing (*Parker v. Felgate (1883)*).

In *Re Glynn (Dec'd) (1990)*, the deceased gave instructions to two independent persons to draw up his will. After giving instructions, but before executing the will, he suffered a massive stroke and became disorientated and unable to communicate. The two independent persons subsequently visited the testator in hospital and read the will to him. He nodded and made an X at the foot of the will. Held, upholding the will, that in executing it, the deceased was merely confirming former instructions. He was deemed to have understood that his instructions were reflected in the will even if he did not, in fact, remember the contents of the instructions in detail.

Being deluded does not automatically deprive a testator/trix of the necessary mental capacity. In the leading case of *Banks v. Goodfellow (1870)* the testator suffered from delusions of being persecuted by a particular individual (who, in fact, was dead), as well as by devils and spirits. The court held that since the delusions had no influence upon the will's contents, it could be treated as valid. Where only a part of a will is affected by a delusion, it might be possible to show that the remainder is valid.

Proving mental capacity can be difficult. Where problems could arise, it may be advisable to ensure the will is witnessed by a medically qualified person. It is common practice to include in a will a statement to the effect that the person making it fully understands its effect. That should also be done if a testator/trix has an obvious impediment, such as a visual handicap or if he/she is hard of hearing.

Fraud and/or undue influence can also affect validity. It has been said that in executing a will a testator/trix 'can be led but not driven' (*Hall v. Hall (1868)*). In other words, persuasion, appeals to the affection, or to the ties of kindred, or pity for future destitution, or the like, are all legitimate. On the other hand, pressure of a kind which overpowers the testator's judgement would invalidate the will. Talking incessantly to a feeble person might be sufficient to affect a will's validity (*Wingrove v. Wingrove (1885)*). It need not be shown that physical force was used. Litigation is not common since the burden of proof falls upon the person alleging fraud or undue influence. Where the person benefiting from the will or the gift stands in a special relationship to the donor, however, there is a presumption of undue influence. The burden of proving that the will was freely made then rests with the beneficiary. These special relationships, known as 'fiduciary relationships', include those of doctor and patient; solicitor and client; and priest and parishioner, and carer. The courts have stressed that the list of such relationships is never closed (*Allcard v. Skinner (1887)*). It is not established whether or not the staff of a residential home are regarded as having a fiduciary relationship towards those who are resident there.

A presumption of undue influence can also arise where no recognised category of special relationship exists but there are special social or domestic circumstances which could affect the will's validity. *Re Craig (Dec'd) (1970)* concerned the will of an 84-year-old man who had made substantial gifts to his secretary-companion. The gifts were set aside by the court, even though the medical evidence confirmed the testator was not lacking in mental capacity, but rather a 'very gentle, dependent and vulnerable old man'. In *Simpson v. Simpson (1992)*, the testator made a will leaving all his residuary estate to his third wife and other gifts to children. The testator became terminally ill and after a suicide attempt, his condition deteriorated markedly. In subsequent months the testator transferred a number of assets to his wife's name without consulting his solicitor, a long-standing friend. Held, that a presumption of undue influence arose as a result of the testator's increasing lack of capacity, his increasing dependence on his third wife, and the fact that the transfers were not in keeping with his normal pattern of behaviour.

7.9.8 DEPOSITING THE WILL

Once executed, a will should be deposited in a safe place and the executor(s)/trix told of its location. If it cannot be found on the death of testator/trix it may be presumed to have been destroyed with the intention of revoking it (*Eckersley v. Platt (1886)*). If it were to be found some time afterwards, complex problems could arise. Those who had already benefited from the estate, either on the basis of an earlier will, or according to the rules on intestacy, would be liable to return that which had been already received (*Ministry of Health v. Simpson (1951)*). This could cause financial difficulty if, for example, a gift had been disposed of by the beneficiary. Testators/trix would be well advised to deposit the will at a bank or with a solicitor. The safest procedure, however, is to deposit the will with the Principal Registry of the Family Division of the High Court. This should ensure that there are no problems since a search will be automatically carried out to see if a will had been placed there on the death of the testator/trix. A registration fee of £1 is charged for this service.

It is also useful to compile a list of personal documents for use by the executor(s)/trix. Age Concern has published a guide which sets out the information which should be included (Age Concern 1994). The list should be shown to the executor(s)/trix before being deposited in a safe place.

7.9.9 DISPOSAL OF ONE'S BODY

One reason for making a will is that the testator/trix wishes to arrange for the disposal of his/her body. A clause can be inserted in a will specifying whether the body is to be buried or cremated, although instructions of this kind do not normally have any legal force (Cremation Regulations 1965). It is possible, however, to bequeath part of one's body for medical research.

7.9.10 An alternative method of achieving that objective is set out in the Anatomy Act 1984 (AA 1984). This makes it possible for a person's body to be used for medical research on the basis of a request made orally, or in writing, during a person's last illness and in the presence of two or more witnesses (s.4). The phrase 'last illness' is not defined in the Act, and a dispute over its designation could arise in particular circumstances. The AA 1984 also permits a body to be used for anatomical research if there is no reason to believe that the deceased, his/her surviving spouse, or his/her relatives had expressed any objection to the body being used in this way. Individuals who do not wish their body to be used for anatomical research should object in writing, or orally before two witnesses (McFarlane 1984).

7.9.11 It is not uncommon for wills to include directions as to the conduct of the deceased's funeral. Individuals with particular wishes in this regard would be well advised, however, to make other arrangements to ensure they are known, since a will may not be made public until after the funeral has taken place. It would be better, therefore, to prepare a separate letter containing specific instructions. A number of organisations exist to help ensure a person's wishes are carried out.

Salford Age Concern's Funeral Manning Society, for example, enables individuals, on payment of a small fee, to register their instructions. When a person dies, his/her relatives can telephone the society and be given the relevant information. The society will also undertake to negotiate the price of a funeral with firms of undertakers and will give direct help in arranging it.

A number of commercial schemes have also been established to meet this need (Age Concern 1994). Age Concern in association with Chosen Heritage, for instance, provide a Funeral Plan.

7.10.1 INTESTACY

Where a person dies without having made a will, or where a will proves invalid, an intestacy arises. There were some 60,000 cases of intestacy in England and Wales in 1992.

Who inherits property on an intestacy, and in what proportions, is determined by the relevant statutory rules and regulations. The Family Provision (Intestate Succession) Order 1993 came into force in December 1993 and will apply to the estates of all persons dying intestate on or after that date.

When a married person dies without leaving a will, the surviving spouse is entitled to receive a fixed sum (the statutory legacy), provided the assets are sufficient. The statutory legacy will amount to

(a) £125,000 if the intestate is also survived by children, or
(b) £200,000 if there are no children, but the intestate is survived by certain close relatives. An explanatory table is provided in Appendix II.

7.11.1 DISTRIBUTING THE ESTATE

A will must normally be proved, that is, it must be produced by the executor(s)/trix before the Probate Registry with a statement setting out the value of the estate and including a promise to administer it. Once probate has been granted, twelve months is normally allowed for settlement of the estate. Fees must be paid to the Registry proportionate to the estate's value. A solicitor's services are not always necessary in this context since the Registry will assist those applying for probate. A solicitor's advice may be needed, however, in distributing an estate should a will's provisions prove complex.

Where a person dies intestate, letters of administration directing an administrator to settle the deceased's estate are normally required. The administrator will usually be the deceased's closest relative.

The fees which must be paid to obtain probate and letters of administration come from the estate itself.

7.11.2 STATUTORY NOMINATIONS AND SMALL ESTATES

Some statutes allow for disposal of certain assets by means of a written nomination operating at death. Examples of property which can be dealt with in this way include national savings certificates and funds in an industrial and provident society. The formal requirements for statutory nomination resemble, but are not identical, to those for making a will. The effect is essentially the same, since a nomination has no force until the nominator dies. If the nominee pre-deceases the nominator, the nomination fails.

Application to the Probate Registry is not necessary if the value of an estate is less than £5,000 (Administration of Estates (Small Payments) (Increase of Limit) Order 1984), or consists of property subject to statutory nomination. Some statutory nominations are being phased out, however, and in any case, it is usually better to dispose of all assets by means of a will, since a statutory nomination, once made, tends to get forgotten.

7.12.1 FUNERAL ARRANGEMENTS

For many people there is stigma in not being able to make financial provision for their own funeral. They may also become anxious about the financial burden which could fall upon relatives or friends in meeting the costs. This worry is often very real, since the amount needed to pay for a funeral can be considerable. The National Association of Funeral Directors, based in Solihull, West Midlands, has a code of practice for funeral directors which it encourages members to display. Members of the Association offer a basic funeral and will provide a written estimate of costs. Additional costs, such as flowers, crematorium and cemetery fees, doctors and clergy, often exceed the actual costs of the funeral, and the funeral director will also advise on these issues (Age Concern 1994).

The only social security grant now available to meet funeral expenses is payment from the Social Fund. To qualify, the claimant must be responsible for arranging the funeral, although that responsibility can be delegated to someone else (see Chapter 1 at para. 1.37.1).

7.12.2 BURIALS AND CREMATIONS

Everyone has a right to be buried in the churchyard of the parish in which they died, provided there is space available. If the deceased has paid for a plot in the churchyard, there will be a document referred to as a 'faculty', and the latter will need to be produced. However, it should be noted that the parochial council is entitled to have a policy of refusing to reserve grave spaces in a churchyard, but the court is not bound by such a policy and has a discretion to grant a faculty when appropriate. In *Re West Pennard Churchyard (1991)*, a petitioner sought to reserve a grave space for herself in the church-yard. The local church council opposed the petition as being against its normal policy on burial plots. Held, granting the petition, that the parochial church council had no power to refuse to bury her in the churchyard of the parish, that was her common law right. The council was entitled to decide where in the churchyard the burial was to take place; it was also entitled to have a policy to oppose the reservation of particular spaces, but the court was not bound by such a policy. On the facts of the case, the petition would be granted.

7.12.3 It should also be noted that a grant of faculty for the exhuma-tion of remains from a consecrated churchyard and their re-interment elsewhere will only be made in exceptional circumstances. In *Re St Peter's Churchyard, Oughtrington (1993)*, the petitioner sought permission to move his wife's body to the graveyard of a parish church where space had become available, and where both the petitioner and his wife had been active members for many years and where members of his wife's family were buried. The petition was unopposed. The burial had occurred some eight years previously and the coffin would have decayed considerably. The petition was refused.

In order to prevent any body being cremated where there is possi-ble doubt about the cause of death, there are very strict rules about certification which can increase the cost of cremation. The majority of cremations are run by local authorities, and some will charge higher rates to non-residents. Information and advice is to be found elsewhere (Age Concern 1994).

7.12.4 LOCAL AUTHORITIES AND HOSPITALS

District councils must arrange for the burial or cremation of any person who has died, or been found dead, in their area, if it appears that no other suitable arrangements can be made. The local authority may recover the costs of the funeral from the dead person's estate, or from any person liable to maintain the deceased immediately before his/her death. The authority must not arrange for a person to be cremated rather than buried where it has reason to believe that the deceased wished to be buried, even though cremation would be cheaper. Hospital authorities have a duty at common law to arrange for the burial or cremation of a deceased patient. This obligation is invariably carried out by the district council or London borough council of the area in which the hospital is located (Public Health (Control of Diseases) Act 1984 (PH(CD)A 1984), s.46).

7.12.5 Bereaved individuals may find it difficult to cope with funeral arrangements. Funeral directors are often a useful source of advice, assistance and support in such circumstances. Members of the National Association of Funeral Directors pledge adherence to a Code of Practice which, amongst other things, requires members to give written estimates, and to ensure that information about social security benefits is made available.

7.13.1 FAMILY PROVISION

Where the provisions of a will, or the rules of intestacy, or a combination of both, fail to make reasonable financial provision for a deceased person's dependants, they can make an application to the court under the I(PFD)A 1975. Those who can apply are: the wife or husband of the deceased; a former wife or husband who has not re-married; the deceased's child (or any person treated by the deceased as a child of the family); and any dependant who immediately before the deceased's death was being maintained, wholly or partly, by him/her (s.1(1)). The I(PFD)A 1975 states that a person is to be treated as 'being maintained' if the deceased 'otherwise than for full consideration, was making a substantial contribution in money or money's worth towards the reasonable needs of that person'. The effect of this provision is contrary to what many people expect. In order to succeed, an applicant must show that the balance of generosity was tipped in favour of the deceased. In other words, it has to be shown that the applicant was dependent on the deceased and not vice versa. In *Re Wilkinson (1977)*, the deceased had provided board and lodging for her sister who, in return, did some light housework, helped the deceased to dress, and acted as her companion. The sister's application under the Act succeeded since the judge took the view that she had been dependent on the deceased. The value of her services was outweighed by the value of the board and lodging which she had received.

Although the Act requires the deceased's contribution to be 'substantial', the payment, in 1975, of £5 per week to a pensioner who had no other means of support was sufficient to satisfy the test.

7.13.2 Somewhat ironically, therefore, the wording of the legislation seems to penalise carers who give more than they receive. In the leading case of *Bishop v. Plumley (1991)*, the Court of Appeal clarified the position and provided additional security for carers. Held, that in deciding the balance of dependency, the care and support provided by the carer should not be taken into account in deciding whether the person in question was being 'maintained' by the deceased.

7.13.3 PROVISION FOR SPOUSES

As might be expected, it is spouses who apply most frequently under the 1975 Act and provision for them is more generous than for other applicants. Very substantial sums have been awarded on occasion. In *Re Besterman (Dec'd) (1984)*, the husband had left the bulk of his £1 million estate to the University of Oxford. On making an application under the Act, his widow received an overall sum of £378,000. According to the court, a useful rule of thumb was to take, as the normal starting point, the one-third rule established in the divorce case of *Wachtel v. Wachtel (1973)*. In other words, the widow would normally be entitled to at least one-third of the capital assets of the estate.

In the later case of *Re Bunning (Dec'd) (1985)*, the court implied that a more generous test could be applied, taking into account the fact that it was no longer necessary to make provision for the deceased person. In other words, the court implied that more than the one-third rule in *Wachtel v. Wachtel (1973)* might be applied in some circumstances. In *Re Bunning (Dec'd) 1985*, the separation had been for the relatively short period of four years, whereas in *Re Rowlands (Dec'd) (1984)* the application succeeded even though the separation had lasted forty-three years. It seems clear that had the applicant, who was ninety years of age and living with a married daughter, been able to show unmet financial needs, she would probably have been awarded a more substantial amount than was, in fact, awarded. It was unlikely, for instance, that she would ever need to become resident at a private nursing home. Indeed, her future seemed secure.

In deciding whether or not to award reasonable financial provision, the courts will take into account the conduct of the parties. An applicant sometimes succeeds, however, even if he/she had acted badly towards the deceased. In *Re Snoek (Dec'd) (1982)*, the widow could offer no explanation for her anti-social conduct; it was 'just for experience'. The court decided, nevertheless, that this behaviour did not quite cancel out her earlier contribution to the marriage, in managing the home for her husband, and in bringing up their four children. It decided, in the circumstances, that she should be awarded the 'modest' sum of £4,000.

Had the deceased proceeded with the petition for divorce filed a few years before his death, the outcome might have been different. Although ex-spouses who have not re-married can apply under the Act, it seems, from the precedent established by the Court of Appeal in *Re Fullard (1981)* that they will succeed in limited circumstances only. The applicant and the deceased married in 1938 and were divorced in 1976. Both received legal advice. As a result, it was agreed that the wife should pay £4,500 for her husband's share in the matrimonial home, and that neither party should make maintenance payments to the other. The agreement was not embodied in a court order. The husband then took lodgings with an elderly lady who later inherited his entire estate. This consisted mainly of money which his ex-wife had paid him for his share in the matrimonial home. By the time of the application, Mrs Fullard was of retirement age, but still working in order to pay off the mortgage she had taken out in order to buy her husband's share of the home. Nevertheless, her application failed. From this case, it would seem that former spouses will succeed only if at least one of three possible situations exists: first, that there was no proper settlement of financial matters on divorce; second, that there has been a significant change of circumstances between the date of the divorce and the death; or, third, that a continuing financial obligation existed, or that actual provision was being made for the applicant, which terminated on death (Oughton 1984).

7.13.4 An example of the second of these situations arises where a substantial capital fund is unlocked by the death of the deceased. The late spouse might be very well insured, for example. In order to succeed, however, it would be necessary to show that the premiums had been paid before the divorce took place. The third situation will be more common, although it is unfortunate, perhaps, that the courts generally place such emphasis on the need to show the commitment to have been long-standing. Financial vulnerability can be greater, the shorter the length of the marriage. Given the introduction of the clean-break principle by the MFPA 1984, such commitments are likely to become less common. Section 8 of the 1984 Act allows the court, on application by either party, to bar the other party from making future application under the I(PFD)A 1975, s.81. Before the introduction of this provision such arrangements were possible only with the agreement of both parties. The inheritance provisions can now be avoided even if there is no agreement between the parties, provided the court approves the requisite order (s.15).

Following the decision in *Re Fullard*, it is now more difficult to obtain Legal Aid so as to make an application under the 1975 Act. The court also suggested that judges should abandon their previous practice of ordering that the costs of an unsuccessful spouse should be met from the deceased's estate, apart from exceptional cases. Applicants with weak claims should, therefore, be advised of the risks involved.

It is not, however, crucial for those who remain married to show that the relationship was long-standing. In *Re Clarke (Dec'd) (1991)*, P and the deceased had married in 1976 when they were seventy-one and seventy-six respectively. The deceased had two children by his former marriage and P had sold her house on marriage and placed the proceeds of sale into a building society. They lived off their pensions and kept their finance separate. The deceased's will provided little for P, with the bulk of his substantial estate going to the children and grand-children. Held that P was entitled to claim and that she should be rehoused, have a reasonably comfortable income, and that she should have something to fall back upon to deal with future contingencies.

A similar approach was adopted in *Moody v. Stevenson (1992)*. A married B and moved into her house, but some years later B moved into a nursing home where she subsequently died. Her will left every-thing, including the house, to her step-daughter who in time sought possession. The widower's claim under the Act succeeded. The court had to consider what provision the applicant might expect if there had been divorce rather than a death, and concluded that A was entitled to live in the house as long as he was willing and able to do so.

7.13.5 PROVISION FOR CHILDREN

Neither a child of the deceased person, nor a person treated as a child of the family during the course of a marriage, need be a minor in order to apply under the Act. An elderly or middle-aged person can do so even though he/she was not treated as 'a child of the family' before becoming an adult. In *Re Leach (Dec'd) (1985)*, a 55-year-old social worker was awarded £19,000 from her step-mother's estate, although she was thirty-two at the date of the deceased's marriage to her father. A similar decision was given in *Re Callaghan (Dec'd)*

(1984) where the court placed considerable weight upon the fact that the deceased had apparently adopted the role of grandfather in respect of the applicant's children. The applicant had also given the deceased much care and support.

The above cases can be contrasted to the recent case of *Harlow v. National Westminster Bank PLC and Others (1994)*. Again, this child was middle-aged, but in this case the applicant's mother and father had separated when he was two years old. His father had never provided for him, but left a valuable estate which was largely to be divided between various charities. His application was refused – the obligations referred to in s.3(1)(d) were held to refer to obligations the deceased had immediately before his death.

7.13.6 TIME LIMITS

An application under the I(PFD)A 1975 must be made not later than six months from the date of a Grant of Probate or, in the case of intestacy, not later than six months from the date upon which Letters of Administration were taken out. The court can use its discretion, however, to extend the time limit in accordance with established guidelines.

7.14.1 *DONATIO MORTIS CAUSA* – GIFTS IN CONTEMPLATION OF DEATH

An individual believing him/herself close to death, or contemplating a dangerous journey or activity, may wish to arrange beforehand for the transfer of property to be made to another person should death occur. In order to make a gift of this kind successfully, the following criteria must be satisfied: the gift must have been made in contemplation of death; the gift must have been delivered to the individual in question; the gift must have been conditional upon the death of the donor; and it must have been capable of passing as a *donatio mortis causa*.

Until the Court of Appeal decision in *Sen v. Headly (1991)*, it was generally believed that land could not be transferred this way. The deceased had been admitted to hospital suffering from cancer and he was aware of his condition. The deceased and the plaintiff had a close relationship over thirty years and in the course of visiting, some three days before he died, he gave the plaintiff a steel box which contained some deeds and added 'The house is yours Margaret. You have the keys. They are in your bag. The deeds are in the box.' The court held that land was capable of passing by way of *donatio mortis causa*, and that delivery of the deeds had secured an effective transfer. Indeed, the legal requirements have been relaxed further. In *Woodward v. Woodward (1992)*, a terminally ill father told his son to hang on to car keys, saying 'Keep the keys, I won't be driving it any more.' A dispute arose between the son and the widow and the court held that there had been an effective transfer. The fact that the registration documents and the spare keys had not been delivered was not important. The correct inference from the father's words was that he intended making a gift of the car to the son.

Should a dispute arise, the burden of proving the validity of the arrangement falls upon the person receiving the gift, but evidence from the donee alone could be sufficient to establish its effectiveness.

7.15.1 THE FORFEITURE ACT 1982

Anyone found guilty of causing another person's death is usually prevented from benefiting under the will, intestacy, statutory nomination, or *donatio mortis causa* of his/her victim. The Forfeiture Act 1982 (FA 1982) modifies this rule with respect to manslaughter if it can be shown that justice requires it. *Re K (Dec'd) (1985)* was the first case to come before the courts after the passing of the Act. A 62-year-old widow, who had pleaded guilty to her husband's manslaughter, was allowed to inherit a life interest, valued at £412,000, in her husband's estate and a half-share in the matrimonial home, valued at £85,000. The deceased had subjected the applicant to frequent and unprovoked violence. Following a quarrel, she shot him. In reaching its decision, the court seems to have taken into account the conduct of both the offender and the deceased. In *Re H (Dec'd) (1990)*, P, who was severely depressed and on anti-depressant drugs, killed his wife. The evidence showed that he bore no responsibility for his actions. It was held that the forfeiture rule did not apply, the test was whether there had been deliberate intentional and unlawful violence, or threats of violence. In this case, no such violence was present, so the Act did not apply.

The question whether or not the provisions of the FA 1982 could be applied to a person found guilty of a so-called 'mercy killing' has not yet come before the courts. A useful review of case law is to be found elsewhere (Cretney 1990).

7.16.1 LIFETIME GIFTS

The practice of making lifetime gifts is referred to here for two reasons. First, the courts are more ready to assume the existence of 'undue influence' where gifts are transferred during a person's lifetime than when they are made under a will. Indeed, two recent decisions of the Court of Appeal revealed the difficulties which can occur when an elderly person advances a capital sum to a younger relative in return for the right to spend the rest of his/her days in the relative's house. In *Cheese v. Thomas (1994)*, an 86-year-old widower contributed £43,000 towards the cost of purchasing a house, the total cost of which was £86,000. The defendant, a great-nephew, contributed the difference by means of a mortgage and the house was conveyed to the nephew. Some months later, the nephew defaulted on the mortgage and his uncle initiated legal action claiming that he should be regarded as a joint owner. The county court rejected the latter argument, but accepted an alternative argument that the transaction should be set aside on the basis of undue influence. The Court of Appeal confirmed the decision, emphasising that the relationship between the two parties was of a fiduciary character, and that in the cicumstances undue influence was to be presumed. It should be noted that the defendant was an innocent fiduciary who had not acted with impropriety. In *Baker v. Baker (1993)*, the facts were rather similar. The 75-year-old plaintiff, a secure tenant, agreed with the defendants, his son and daughter-in-law, to provide capital to purchase a house in which he could subsequently live rent free. The relationship broke down, but in this case there was no question of undue influence since the plaintiff, though elderly and frail, was mentally sound and articulate. The 75-year-old was therefore not entitled to have his capital returned. He was simply entitled to compensation because of his loss of expectation – a much smaller sum.

Where a fiduciary relationship exists or there are special circumstances, the gift may be set aside unless it can be shown that the donor received proper independent advice, which was given with knowledge of all the relevant circumstances. In *Inche Noriah v. Shaik Allie Bin Omar (1929)*, an elderly Malayan woman executed a deed of gift in favour of her nephew who had been responsible for managing her affairs for some time. Although she had the benefit of independent advice, the lawyer who gave it was unaware of all the facts of the case. The court held that the gift should be set aside on the grounds that the presumption of undue influence had not been rebutted.

The above decisions reveal the legal pitfalls associated with entering into informal arrangements of this kind. Moreover, even where there is no question of undue influence, the granting of interest-free loans can lead to tax traps. Put simply, such loans may be interest-free, but not tax-free (Liddington 1993).

A detailed discussion of tax law is beyond the scope of this book, but some of its features are discussed at paras. 7.16.2 to 7.16.3.

7.16.2 CAPITAL GAINS TAX

Where assets, such as property, or shares, or other valuables are sold or given away, the transferor may have to pay Capital Gains Tax (CGT) should the real or notional gain arising from the transaction be above the annual exemption rate. From April 1994, the exemption will be £5,800 per year. The gain is obviously notional where the asset is given away as a gift, but for tax purposes it is deemed to have been disposed of at market value.

It is not the value of the asset as such that is important, but the increase in its value between acquisition and disposal. Tax is usually paid on the difference between the price at acquiring it and value at disposal. Until April 1988, a flat rate of 30 per cent was levied on chargeable gains. From April 1988, however, the rate payable reflects the individual taxpayer's rate of income tax. The tax rate, therefore, rises to 40 per cent for higher rate taxpayers, but drops to 25 per cent for standard rate tax payers.

7.16.3 Certain assets, such as a person's main or only residence, and savings certificates are exempt from CGT. Until the 1988 Budget, there was also an exemption for one other residence occupied by the dependent relative. The Budget abolished tax relief on homes provided for a dependent relative and the change applies to all disposals after 6 April 1988. Arrangements made prior to that date, however, will continue to qualify for relief from CGT. To qualify, the property must be let rent-free and for no consideration, although the rules permit the dependent relative to be liable for the rates, and for the cost of repairs to the dwelling arising out of normal wear and tear. In this context, a 'dependent relative' means any relative of the taxpayer or his/her spouse who is incapacitated, by age or infirmity, from maintaining him/herself. It includes the taxpayer's mother, and mother-in-law if she is separated or widowed. For the exemptions to apply to a widower, he would need to be incapacitated. Only one dwelling can qualify for this exemption.

For the reasons given above, few family transactions are likely to give rise to CGT. Moreover, persons eligible should take maximum advantage of the rule that there can be no chargeable gain on any asset transferred from one spouse to the other, whether by gift or sale. Tax savings are possible (Ray 1993; Dunham 1994).

To be eligible for retirement relief and thereby achieve a permanent reduction or elimination of liability to CGT, the individual needs to be aged fifty-five or over. However, premature retirement is possible on the ground of ill health which partly depends on the function performed by the claimant. In a partnership, where the ill health of one brings the end of the partnership, only the partner who is disabled will benefit and not the healthy partner. Physical retirement from business is not always necessary, but in the case of sole traders it may be desirable to dispose of the whole business rather than attempt to dispose of part of it, as the latter may be difficult to establish to the satisfaction of the Revenue. Company directors who have ceased to work full-time may claim retirement relief provided the part-time working involves an average of ten hours or more a week since full-time work ceased (Gunn *et al.* 1992).

7.17.1 INHERITANCE TAX

Capital Transfer Tax (CTT) was introduced in 1975 to replace estate duty. Whereas estate duty was levied on the value of property upon the death of a person, CTT introduced a levy, subject to certain exemptions, on lifetime transfers of property. The Finance Act 1986 (FA 1986) changed the name of CTT to Inheritance Tax (IHT) and, in relation to transfers made on or after 18 March 1986, reverted to the principle of charging tax on lifetime gifts only when they had been made within seven years of the donor's death.

Transfers within the seven-year period are now subject to a tapering charge. The value of gifts transferred during the seven years before death will be added to the value of the deceased person's estate. Where the total value is above the tax-free limit, IHT is payable. The IHT tax-free limit is currently £150,000 (1993–4).

Exemptions and reliefs similar to those discussed in respect to CGT are also available, but the introduction of 100 per cent agriculture and business property relief from IHT in the Finance (No.2) Act 1992 (F(No.2)A 1992) was very good news for businessmen and farmers (Kirby and Liddington 1993). Technical procedures exist to deal with problems caused by ownership of a succession of businesses in order to ensure that no loss of relief occurs. In addition, gifts of up to £3,000 in any tax year are exempt, as are gifts made in contemplation of a marriage. For instance, a £5,000 exemption is allowed on gifts by one of the parents of a bride or groom, whereas grandparents can give £2,500 each, free of IHT.

The FA 1986 also introduced an important change to the law in respect to gifts with reservation which occur when the donor continues to enjoy some benefit from the gift. The most common example is where an individual transfers ownership of his/her house to another but continues to live there. Where such arrangements are made but the donor continues to benefit from the gift, then the whole value of it will be counted as part of his/her estate for the purpose of IHT. Where the donor no longer benefits from the gift, however, liability for tax depends upon whether the change in circumstances had occurred more than seven years before death. For example, where an elderly person who had previously transferred ownership of his/her home, later enters a residential home, there may be no liability for IHT. Where death occurs within the seven-year period, however, the amount payable will depend upon the number of years that have passed since entry into the residential home took place.

7.18.1 INTENTION TO CREATE LEGAL RELATIONS

There is a legal presumption that social and domestic arrangements do not create legal relations between the parties. The party wishing to establish the existence of a legal contract must present evidence to rebut the presumption. A factor which may weigh heavily with a court is whether or not the arrangements were spelled out in detail. In *Berryere v. Berryere (1972)* a grandmother attempted to recover from her daughter money she had spent on bringing up her grand-daughter. The grandmother had made it clear that she expected her daughter to share responsibility for the child. The daughter undertook to pay a regular sum each month for the child's maintenance. Only three payments were made, however, and nothing was then paid for some nine years. The court held that the presumption had not been rebutted in this instance and that the claim must fail. Legally binding contracts are possible between members of a family, neverthe-less, as in the case of *Hagger v. de Placido (1972)*. In that case, the court recognised the existence of a contract between a 29-year-old tetraplegic and his mother and brother who had undertaken to nurse him. Agreements by which grandparents care for their grandchildren might be treated in the same way but only where an intention to create legal relations was clearly established.

7.18.2 LIVING WITH RELATIVES

The courts have been more prepared to presume a contractual intention where the agreement between the parties relates to joint residency. An example would be an elderly person moving to live with a son or daughter and his/her family, or vice versa.

Difficult problems can arise in arrangements of this kind. In *Parker v. Clarke (1960)*, a young couple sold their house and moved to live with elderly relatives on the basis of a promise, made in writing, that they would be left a share in the property. A later claim that there had been no intention to create legal relations was rejected by the court. It was held that the younger couple would not have taken the important step of selling their own home on the basis of a social arrangement only. The couple were successful in obtaining damages for the loss of a share in the house.

The case of *Broughall v. Hunt (1983) (unreported)* illustrates some of the difficulties. This case involved a more common arrangement in that a 70-year-old woman moved to live with her daughter and son-in-law. Her bedroom was in a new extension to the house, which was not self-contained, and to which she contributed £1,000. Much of the building work was done by her other two sons-in-law. Some years later the relationship broke down and she left. The court decided that she had a contractual licence to occupy the premises for as long as she wished, and that the licence had been improperly terminated by her daughter and son-in-law. She was awarded £1,500 damages (although, given the legal costs, the net benefit to her must have been minimal). Her daughter and son-in-law fared much worse, however. They faced having to sell their home in order to meet the estimated legal costs of £10,000, a reflection of the very complicated legal problems involved. An excellent discussion of the issues and similar cases is to be found in a College of Law publication (1992), and elsewhere (Warburton 1993).

Another point worth noting here is that where capital has been transferred, the courts may impute a trust giving the beneficiary a right to a share in the value of the property, as well as a right of occupation until it is sold. Rights created in this way could have the effect of blocking a future sale. Where no capital changes hands, however, an elderly person moving to live with relatives may have only a licence to occupy. Those contemplating arrangements of this kind would be well-advised to draw up an agreement establishing that a licence to occupy only is being created. This would establish the limited nature of the transaction and set out the period of notice required to end it. If an elderly person had exclusive occupation of a separate part of the premises, however, then a tenancy might arise.

Where capital is transferred, it should be specified whether the sum in question is intended as a loan or as payment for a beneficial interest in the property. If a loan is intended, a charge under seal should be made on the legal estate, so as to give the person concerned protection similar to that of a mortgagee. If, on the other hand, a beneficial interest is intended then the best solution might be to use co-ownership as the basis of a trust for sale (Keeling 1992).

Individuals contemplating joint residence would be well advised to consult a solicitor. They may feel some reluctance in doing so, since setting out the terms of the agreement in a formal document might seem like a declaration of bad faith. Formalising arrangements helps to protect both parties, however, and can also help foster mutual undertanding, and allay suspicion about motives. Circumstances can change, often quickly and dramatically. Events such as divorce, redundancy, or death can render arrangements unworkable which were previously feasible.

7.19.1 IMMIGRATION

'Dependent relatives' can be admitted into the United Kingdom on the basis of rules established under the Immigration Act 1971 (IA 1971). The primary requirement is for applicants to show they are without other close relatives in their own country to whom they can turn in time of need. Entry to the United Kingdom is possible under these rules even though close relatives remain in the country of origin but they are unable or unwilling to assist the dependent relative. These rules apply to three categories of persons: (i) widowed mothers and widowers, and parents of a person resident in this country, who are travelling together, and one of whom is at least sixty-five; (ii) parents and grandparents in other circumstances who have not remarried and more distant relatives; and (iii) parents and grandparents who have remarried. These provisions have resulted in complex litigation. Useful advice in this context is available from the Joint Council for the Welfare of Immigrants.

7.20.1 ELDERLY ABUSE

Evidence suggests that some 'old elderly' people are vulnerable to physical and/or mental abuse from those who care for them. One estimate puts the number at risk as high as 500,000 (Eastman 1984), but such claims have not been validated. As indicated elsewhere, there has been no major study of the prevalence or incidence of abuse in Britain (Decalmer and Glendenning 1993). Although not denying that abuse exists, other commentators feel that the extent of the problem is as yet unknown. They are critical of those who, on somewhat thin evidence, advocate the introduction of protective measures which might encroach upon the freedom of many elderly people (Traynor and Haslip 1984). Be that as it may, it seems little use is made of legal and quasi-legal processes as a means of protection and redress, and possible explanations for the dearth of litigation are provided elsewhere (Griffiths, Roberts and Williams 1993).

7.20.2   One explanation relates to the way in which abuse is defined. A commonly quoted definition is that it involves 'the systematic maltreatment, physical, emotional or financial of an elderly person by a care-giving relative'. It may take the form of physical assault, threatening behaviour, neglect, abandonment, (for example, locking an elderly relative in a bedroom) or sexual assault (Eastman 1984). Elderly abuse is thus given a wide and imprecise definition.

7.20.3   Where abuse is alleged, two forms of legal intervention exist. These consist of civil actions in tort alleging some form of trespass to the person, or criminal proceedings for assault. Trespass to the person consists of battery, assault, or false imprisonment. An assault can arise whenever a person has reasonable cause to fear that direct harm is to be directed at him/her. The tort of battery, however, requires actual, direct, and intentional application of force to the person. The least touching of another person could constitute battery, although the everyday collisions of ordinary life are outside its scope. Battery can arise without real hostility in the perpetrator so long as the act is against the will of the plaintiff. An unwanted kiss, for example, or cutting hair without consent, or spitting at a person, could amount to battery.

False imprisonment is the infliction of physical restraint not expressly or impliedly authorised by law. The tort cannot arise where a person consents to restrictions being placed upon his/her person, but consent cannot be implied simply because no resistance is shown. A person can be falsely imprisoned without knowing it, for example, when asleep (*Meering v. Grahame White Aviation Co Ltd (1920)*). The tort does not arise, however, unless a person's freedom of movement and action has been restrained in every direction.

It is surprising, perhaps, that allegations of false imprisonment involving elderly people living in residential homes, or with relatives, are not more common, given recent scandals in some residential homes and other evidence of restrictions placed upon elderly people. Claims are made, for instance, that elderly people living with relatives are sometimes locked up, confined in small rooms, and kept isolated from other members of the family (Eastman 1984). Carers of elderly people, particularly when they are in positions of authority, may, unwittingly, even if not deliberately, be committing the tort of false imprisonment. For instance, it was alleged and acknowledged in Tribunal Case No. 131 (Registered Homes Tribunal) that elderly residents in one home had been confined to their bedrooms by the insertion of a nail into the door frame. One of the few cases involving an elderly person in an action for false imprisonment is reported here simply to illustrate some of the characteristics of the tort. A 72-year-old shopper was accused of shop-lifting on the mistaken suspicion that she had stolen a greetings card. Her handbag was removed from her 'for a few minutes'. Following a fifteen-minute wait in an open changing cubicle, she was taken to the local police station in a police van. She received £1,520 damages for false imprisonment, as well as substantial damages for trespass to goods because of the removal of her handbag (*White v. W P Brown (1983)*).

7.20.4 A characteristic of the three torts discussed above is that physical harm must have been directly threatened or inflicted upon the plaintiff. Where physical harm is caused indirectly, liability may arise under the so-called rule in *Wilkinson v. Downton (1897)*. The rule is sometimes referred to as the 'wrongful interference principle'. The tort is underdeveloped but has considerable potential in this context (Brazier 1992; Fricker 1992). For instance, if someone were to shout at an elderly person descending a difficult staircase, with the intention of giving him/her a shock, that person might be held liable for any physical injuries which resulted, even though no direct force had been applied. An action might succeed even where there was no intention of causing actual physical injury, since the intention to cause shock may be sufficient to establish 'wrongful interference'. It should be noted, however, that no parallel criminal proceedings exist in this case. Another possible course of action might be in the tort of negligence if it could be established that the person caring for the elderly person had a duty of care towards him/her. The elements of this tort are discussed in Chapter 6 at para. 6.5.2.

7.20.5 Some actions are both criminal and tortious and can give rise both to prosecution and a civil action for damages. In general, it does not matter which proceedings are brought first, although the usual practice is for civil proceedings to be stayed until criminal proceedings have been completed. Some statutes, however, provide that criminal proceedings brought under them are a bar to future civil action.

Section 45 of the Offences Against the Person Act 1861 (OATPA 1861) bars civil proceedings if, for example, summary criminal proceedings for common assault have been brought. The rule barring civil proceedings can be evaded, however, by the simple expedient of suing first and making a criminal complaint later.

The OATPA 1861 sets out a number of criminal assaults ranging in seriousness from common assault to assault with the intention of causing grievous bodily harm. The difference between the various forms of assault is beyond the scope of this discussion, but common assault warrants some attention. Common assault normally requires the victim, rather than the police, to initiate proceedings. It has been established at common law, however, that elderly and infirm people are to be treated as exceptions to this rule.

7.20.6 In *Pickering v. Willoughby (1907)*, an elderly woman who had suffered a number of strokes was assaulted by the niece who had moved to live with her. The court held that a great-nephew could institute proceedings on behalf of the victim on the grounds that 'if the person assaulted is so feeble, old and infirm as to be incapable of instituting proceedings, and is not a free agent but under the control of the person committing the assault, the information may be laid by a third person.' Many elderly victims of abuse may fall within this exception to the rule, in which case the police could initiate action on their behalf. This might assist those who are themselves reluctant to use the criminal law. Such actions might also overcome the problem that Legal Aid is not available for private prosecutions. Indeed, given these difficulties, there appears to be no good reason why the police should not shoulder the burden completely in the majority of cases and prosecute for assault occasioning actual bodily harm, particularly since such harm need not be serious. It could include, for example, an hysterical or nervous condition arising as the result of an assault (Maidment 1978). Those found guilty of common assault can be required to enter into recognisance to be bound over to be of good behaviour. It should also be noted in passing that the police could, sometimes, alternatively arrest for a breach of the peace. A common law breach of the peace can take place on private premises (*McConnell v. Chief Constable of Greater Manchester Police (1990)*).

7.20.7 Some commentators have questioned the value of using the criminal courts for alleged cases of elderly abuse. It has been suggested that the police should be involved only where abuse is blatant and mercenary. It has also been suggested that involving the police may be futile because many victims will be reluctant to become associated with criminal proceedings. These are dubious arguments since, as indicated above, the police can shoulder much of the responsibility for bringing cases to court. Similar arguments were put forward in the context of domestic violence, but research has shown that the problem of getting victims to co-operate had been exaggerated (Dawson and Faragher 1979).

7.20.8 An advantage of using civil proceedings is that the burden of proof in criminal prosecutions is heavier than in civil actions since an offence has to be proved beyond all reasonable doubt. Substantial damages can also be awarded in a civil action. For this and other reasons, it has been suggested that civil actions for assault, battery, and false imprisonment may provide better remedies than criminal proceedings. There are precedents, however, which could prove helpful in criminal proceedings. In *R v. Reigate Justices, ex parte Counsel (1983)*, for instance, it was held sufficient, in order for the court to infer actual bodily harm, for the victim of an assault to have suffered great pain, tenderness, and soreness even though no physical injury was discernible at the time of the hearing.

There remains one compelling argument against an increased use of the criminal courts, however, in that many of the abusers are carers, themselves the victims of the general apathy of the community and, in particular, of the welfare services towards them. Many of those looking after the very old are themselves elderly and under considerable stress because of the responsibilities they shoulder (Nolan 1993).

7.20.9 The Criminal Injuries Compensation Board can make *ex-gratia* payments to those who have suffered personal injury directly attributable to a crime of violence.

7.21.1 THE MENTALLY INCAPABLE

As the numbers in the population of those aged seventy-five and over increase, so, proportionately, does the incidence of mental infirmity. Individuals who have become mentally incapable of dealing with their personal affairs may need to have their interests safeguarded. Two different legal procedures exist to protect the affairs of the mentally incapable. The first provides for the transfer of responsibility for the management of the infirm individual's affairs to another person, known as an attorney. Under the second procedure, an application can be made on behalf of a mentally incapable person for responsibility to be transferred to a specialised court.

7.21.2 ENDURING POWERS OF ATTORNEY

An ordinary power of attorney is a document by which one person (the donor) authorises another (the donee) to act on his/her behalf. To be effective it must be signed by the donor, witnessed, and must be made under seal. It can then be produced to bodies such as banks and commercial firms as evidence of authority to act on the donor's behalf. A power of attorney of this kind, although useful in many circumstances, has the disadvantage of being automatically revoked should the donor become mentally incapable. Since 1986, it has been possible to make use of a new statutory power which overcomes many of the difficulties created by this rule. Under the Enduring Powers of Attorney Act 1985 (EPAA 1985), an enduring power of attorney (EPA) can be created. This has the advantage of not being affected by subsequent incapacity in the donor, as long as certain statutory procedures are followed should that occur. A detailed explanation is to be found elsewhere (Cretney 1991).

It is much better to execute a power of attorney when fit and in the prime of life. If it is never used, all well and good, but it is better to be prepared.

7.21.3 CREATING AN EPA AND CHOICE OF ATTORNEY

An EPA can be validly created only by a donor with sufficient mental capacity to do so. In *Re K.; Re F. (1988)*, however, it was held that a valid and proper EPA could be created by a person who was already incapable of managing his/her affairs by reason of mental disorder. The test is whether the donor, at the time when the EPA was executed, had the mental capacity to understand the nature and effect of creating the power, despite the existence of mental disorder.

An EPA must also conform in its form with the Enduring Powers of Attorney (Prescribed Form) Regulations, 1987. The regulations provide, among other things, that the EPA must be executed by both the donor and the donee (although not necessarily at the same time) in the presence of a witness. Only individuals (other than minors and bankrupts) and trust corporations (such as the Public Trustee) can be appointed to act as attorney.

The donor of an EPA has complete freedom of choice and may

appoint one, two or more attorneys. If more than one, then it is necessary to decide whether they are to act jointly, or jointly and severally, in which case the attorney can act either on his/her own or with another. A discussion of the advantages and disadvantages of joint or several appointments is available elsewhere (Francis 1993).

7.21.4 ONSET OF MENTAL INCAPACITY

If the donee has reason to suspect that the donor has become, or is becoming, mentally incapable, he/she must, as soon as practicable, take certain steps as prescribed by the Act if the EPA is to remain valid. 'Mental incapacity' is defined in the EPAA 1985 as inability in a person to manage his/her property or affairs by reason of mental disorder, as defined in the Mental Health Act 1983 (MHA 1983). It may not always be easy to determine a person's mental state. Since the donor's incapacity will, however, restrict the powers of the attorney should no action be taken, it can become important to act as swiftly as possible.

7.21.5 The first step is for the donee to inform the donor and certain of his/her relatives of the intention to apply to the Court of Protection for registration of the EPA. The relatives to be informed (in order of priority) are: husband or wife; children; parents; brothers and sisters, whether of the whole or half blood; the widow or widower of a child of the donor; grandchildren; children of the donor's brothers and sisters of the whole blood; children of the donor's brothers and sisters of the half blood; the donor's uncles and aunts of the whole blood; children of the donor's uncles and aunts of the whole blood. It is sufficient, in principle, to inform three relatives only, but, in practice, all relatives falling within a particular category must be included.

Entitlement to receive notice is waived where a person's name and address is not known and cannot reasonably be ascertained; or if he/she is believed to be under the age of eighteen, or mentally incapacitated; or where the Court has dispensed with the need to give notice; or where notice, in accordance with these rules, would otherwise need to be given to the donee him/herself. The purpose of giving notice in this way is to enable the relatives to object to the Court, if they so wish, against the registration of the EPA. It should be noted, however, that right of objection is not confined to the donor's relatives.

7.21.6 APPLYING TO REGISTER AN EPA

Application to the Court to register an EPA must be made in the prescribed form and must be accompanied by the document granting the original power of attorney, as well as the specified fee.

Generally, the Court will register all EPAs which comply in form with the statutory rules. In two instances, the Court may even allow an application where a prescribed relative who was entitled to receive notice, has not been informed. These are circumstances in which it is either undesirable or impracticable for the attorney to give him/her notice; or where no useful purpose is likely to be served by doing so (Sched. 1, paras. 3(2) and 4(2)).

There are circumstances, however, in which the Court will need to make further inquiries. They will be needed: (i) where a valid notice of objection has been received; (ii) where it appears that no relative of the donor was informed; and (iii) where the Court has reason to believe that inquiries might bring to light evidence sufficient to establish one of the grounds for objection set out in the Act (s.6(4)). The Court will then defer its decision until further inquiries can be made. Only if the Court is satisfied with the results of its inquiries will the EPA be registered.

7.21.7 EFFECT OF REGISTRATION

The effect of registering an EPA is that the Court of Protection has power to give directions on the management of property and the affairs of the donor, on the rendering of accounts, and on the keeping of records. It may also determine any question as to the meaning or effect of the EPA. Once registered, the EPA continues in existence until the powers of attorney are cancelled by the Court; or revoked, either automatically, or by an act of the donor or the Court; or by the attorney giving notice of disclaimer to the donor. It will be terminated automatically and by operation of law upon the death of the donor, and upon the death, mental incapacity or bankruptcy of the attorney.

7.21.8 DUTY OF ATTORNEY UNDER AN EPA

The duties of an attorney are confined to the conduct of financial and business affairs; the Act provides no authority for the attorney to engage in the management of welfare matters. Moreover, it is clear that the attorney need only have regard for business/finance considerations when executing his/her duties. In *Re R (Enduring Power of Attorney)*

(1990), a woman had been employed by R for a number of years. She was employed as a cook-housekeeper, but became more of a companion. She was transferred to a nursing home and subsequently made her nephew an attorney. The carer/companion was given notice terminating employment and seeking possession of her flat. The companion applied to the Court of Protection seeking provision from R's estate. Held, that she was not entitled because the court had no power to intervene on the basis of a moral obligation. An EPA's only legal responsibility is to ensure that the donor's finances and property are managed properly.

7.22.1 THE COURT OF PROTECTION

The second procedure for protecting the interests of a mentally incapable person is to invoke the powers of the Court of Protection. The Court of Protection has considerable powers to act in relation to the property and affairs of a person suffering from mental disorder as defined by the MHA 1983. The statutory provisions are now contained in Part VII of the 1983 Act and the jurisdiction of the Court can be invoked by making an application on the grounds set out in the Act.

7.22.2 APPLYING TO THE COURT

Any person can apply to the Court to have a patient's property and affairs placed under the Court's jurisdiction on the grounds that he/she is incapable of managing his/her property and affairs by reason of mental disorder (MHA 1983, s.95). The person who applies is often a relative, but the director of a social services department, acting on behalf of a local authority, or a creditor, adviser or friend could also make the application. Where the patient is married, the Court normally requires proof that his/her spouse has agreed to the application being made. The application must be accompanied by a medical certificate given by a doctor, who need not have particular expertise in the field of mental disorder. It must state that in the doctor's opinion, the patient is incapable by reason of mental disorder of managing his/her property and affairs. The grounds for that opinion must be given, as must the date upon which the patient was last examined; whether he/she is an informal patient or subject to detention under the MHA 1983; whether there is a previous history of mental disorder; whether he/she is dangerous to him/herself or to others; the state of his/her physical health and prospects for life; and the likelihood of his/her recovery.

7.22.3   An Affidavit of Kindred and Fortune must also accompany the application. This must set out prescribed details relating to the patient, such as his/her age, occupation or former occupation, nearest relative, and former residence. Other particulars must refer to the property owned by the patient and his/her income, present address and current commitments. Any debts incurred by the patient must be listed, including a statement whether or not the patient's income will be sufficient to meet them, and whether or not he/she is prepared, if necessary, to make use of capital for this purpose. The Affidavit must also state whether the patient has made a will, or executed a power of attorney. It should also propose the name of a receiver to act on behalf of the patient, and the name of a person to give a reference on the proposed receiver's suitability to act. A brief history of the patient should also be included.

7.22.4   Where the patient's assets are worth no more than £5,000, the Court can make a summary order without an application being made, and direct one of the Court's officers or some other suitable person to take particular action in relation to the assets. The Court can do this even where the estate is valued at more than £5,000 if it is considered that no receiver needs to be appointed (Court of Protection Rules 1984).

7.22.5   NOTICE TO THE PATIENT

Notice that an application has been made to the Court of Protection on his/her behalf must normally be given to the patient, but this requirement can be dispensed with if the Court is satisfied that the patient is incapable of understanding the notice, or that the notice would injure his/her health, or for any other reason (r. 23(2)).

If notice is given to the patient, he/she has seven days from its receipt, or up to the date of the hearing (whichever is later), within which to lodge an objection with the Court. The objection can be to the application as such, or to the recommendations and proposals which it contains. If the Court is satisfied that the patient is mentally incapable, the application is likely to be granted. If, however, the Court has doubts on this score, it may request one of its panel of Medical Visitors to visit the patient in order to examine him/her and prepare a confidential report on the patient's medical state. The Court will reach a decision on the basis of the report, and will inform the patient of its intention either to make an order (but giving him/her the opportunity to produce further evidence in support of his/her objection), or, if the report states that the patient is capable of acting on his/her own behalf, it will set the application aside.

7.22.6 THE EFFECT OF AN ORDER

An order by the Court of Protection invests it with power to manage and administer the property and affairs of the patient. It may then do all that is necessary or expedient under s.95(1) of the MHA 1983: (i) for the maintenance or other benefit of the patient; (ii) for the maintenance or other benefit of members of the patient's family; (iii) for making provision for other persons or purposes for whom or which the patient might be expected to provide if he/she were not mentally disordered; or (iv) for otherwise administering the patient's affairs. For this purpose, the Court is able to (i) control and manage the patient's property; (ii) sell, or deal or dispose of property; (iii) acquire property on the patient's behalf; (iv) make settlements or gifts to any persons mentioned in s.95(1)(b) and (c) of the Act; (v) make a will; (vi) carry on, by means of a suitable person, the profession, trade or business of the patient; (vii) dissolve a patient's partnership; (viii) carry out a contract entered into by the patient; (ix) conduct legal proceedings in the patient's name or on his/her behalf; (x) reimburse any person who has paid the patient's debts, or maintained the patient or members of his/her family, as well as providing for other persons or purposes for whom or for which the patient might have been expected to provide if he/she were not mentally disordered; and (xi) exercise any power vested in the patient for him/herself or as a trustee or guardian, or otherwise.

The powers are extensive. For instance, the Court has power to order the execution of a will on the assumption that the patient is a normal decent person who would act in accordance with contemporary standards of morality. In *Re C (Spinster and Mental Patient) (1991)*, the 75-year-old individual concerned was born with a severe mental disability and had been hospitalised since the age of ten. Her parents had left her a substantial estate. Held, that the Court could make provision for persons or purposes for whom the patient might have been expected to provide. The power extended to making immediate gifts out of property.

7.22.7 APPOINTMENT OF A RECEIVER

Under s.99 of the Act, the judge hearing the application can appoint a receiver to carry out the Court's instructions in relation to the patient's property and affairs. Usually the person appointed will be a close relative, but should there be no suitable or willing relative, the Court can appoint the Official Solicitor, or the director of social services for the area where the patient is living, if that person is willing to act. If the receiver needs to act outside the terms of authority which have been granted, he/she must return to the Court for further instructions.

7.22.8 There has been criticism of the way in which the Court of Protection works (Gostin 1983). In particular, it has been suggested that it is over-centralised in London, and that this leads to geographical remoteness from many of the patients with whom the Court is dealing. In addition, some patients who are under the protection of the Court may have been placed there inappropriately. To prevent this, stronger safeguards may be required. More flexible procedures are also advocated so as to enable patients, where appropriate, to retain a degree of control even when under the protection of the Court. The concerns have been addressed in a series of Consultation Papers by the Law Commission (see below at 7.23.1).

7.22.9 LITIGATION AND INCAPACITY

A mental patient who is incapable of managing or administering his/her property and affairs cannot bring or defend an action in the courts. If he/she is under the jurisdiction of the Court of Protection, only the Court can act. Otherwise, where the patient is the plaintiff, applicant, or petitioner, the action must be conducted on his/her behalf by a 'next friend', and where the patient is the defendant or respondent, a guardian *ad litem* must be appointed to act. Any suitable person may act in this capacity, but it is often the Official Solicitor who takes on this responsibility.

7.23.1 INCAPACITY AND LAW REFORM

As indicated above, the Law Commission, in a series of Consultative Papers (Law Commission 1991, 1993a, 1993b, 1993c) has recognised the need for comprehensive reform of private, public and medical law in the context of incapacity. The Reports highlight a number of weaknesses in the existing law, including the lack of any effective machinery in public law for protecting incapacitated or vulnerable people from abuse and neglect, and a similar deficiency in private law for resolving disputes about the care of incapacitated people.

The Reports recognise the need for more effective substitute decision-making in this context and make a number of specific recommendations, including, *inter alia*, the appointment of financial or personal managers in the context of private law, and the provision of emergency protective orders in the context of public law. Some proposals, particularly the retention of mental disorder within the definition of incapacity, have proved controversial (Carson 1993). Nevertheless, the need for overall rather than piecemeal reform is widely acknowledged.

Appendix I
Establishing entitlement to income support – a case study

1 Personal particulars

A married couple, both aged over sixty-five, were living in rented accommodation (private sector). Both are severely disabled. Owing to their increasing care needs, the couple wished to be rehoused nearer their immediate family.

2 Weekly income as at 19.7.93

Claimant's income:	retirement pension	£56.10
	graduated pension	4.47
	SERPS	12.60
	contracted out pension	12.60
	occupational pension	0.34
	mobility allowance	31.40
Spouse's income:	retirement pension	£33.70
	industrial disease	
	disablement benefit	25.28
	attendance allowance	
	(high rate)	44.90
Total joint income		£221.39

3 Income maintenance questions

The couple had been paying their own travel costs for regular visits to the hospital, following a heart attack and stroke suffered by the claimant the previous year. They could, however, claim for assistance with fares to hospital under the low income scheme. They were also paying a proportion of the rent and council tax from their own resources after housing benefit and council tax benefit. But, were they entitled to income support and therefore the passport benefits (namely, full housing benefit and council tax, full hospital fares and home removal grant under the Social Fund)?

Calculation of weekly income support applicable amount, as at 19.7.93:

Couple, personal allowance	£69.00
Higher pensioner premium	33.70
Income support applicable amount	£102.70

Their relevant income worked out as follows:

Total joint income	£221.39
Less claimant's mobility allowance	31.40
Less spouse's attendance allowance	44.90
Net income for income support purposes	£145.09

Thus, as their net income exceeded their income support applicable amount by £42.39, they were not entitled to any income support.

4 Proposed solution

Clearly, the only route by which the couple might come within the ambit of income support lay via an entitlement to the Severe Disability Premium (SDP). On 19.7.93, they satisfied all the conditions for SDP save for the fact that the claimant was not in receipt of attendance allowance (high rate) or DLA Care (middle or high rate) as well.

The claimant had previously been turned down for attendance allowance. On 19.7.93, the claimant applied for a review of the Adjudication Officer's (AO) decision on attendance allowance. However, on 6.9.93 the AO refused to revise the decision. At the end of October, the claimant suffered cardiac thrombosis and stroke. On 3.12.93, the claimant applied for a second review of the AO's decision, submitting detailed medical evidence from his consultants. On 23.1.94, the AO awarded the claimant attendance allowance at the high rate from 1.9.93 for an indefinite period.

On 17.2.94, the claimant learned that he had also succeeded in a separate claim for industrial injuries disablement benefit from 26.5.93 for life.

Clearly, from 1.9.93, the claimant had established a right to the income support severe disability premium by virtue of both of them being in receipt of attendance allowance at the high rate.

5 Revised calculation of income support applicable amount from 1.9.93:

Claimant's income:	retirement pension	£56.10
	graduated pension	4.47
	SERPS	12.60
	contracted out pension	12.60

	occupational pension	0.34
	industrial injury	
	disablement benefit	18.32
	mobility allowance	31.40
	attendance allowance	
	(high rate)	44.90
Spouse's income:	retirement pension	£33.70
	industrial disease	
	disablement benefit	25.28
	attendance allowance	
	(high rate)	44.90
Total joint income		£284.61

Calculation of weekly income support applicable amount, from 1.9.93:

Couple, personal allowance	£69.00
Higher pensioner premium	33.70
Severe disability premium	67.40
Income support applicable amount	£170.10

Their relevant weekly income from 1.9.93 worked out as follows:

Total joint income	£284.61
Less claimant's mobility allowance	31.40
Less claimant's attendance allowance	44.90
Less spouse's attendance allowance	44.90
Net income for income support purposes	£163.41

Thus, as their net weekly income fell below their income support applicable amount by £6.69, they had thus gained entitlement to income support for that amount, thereby gaining entitlement to the passport benefits identified in para.3 above as well.

6 A further complication

In December 1993, the claimant appealed separately on two outstanding claims for industrial diseases (attributable to his occupation as a miner). On 6.4.94, the claimant heard that he had succeeded in his claim for chronic bronchitis and emphysema and had been awarded disablement benefit at the rate of £46.92 per week. The question then arose: how did this affect his income support entitlement and all the other passport benefits?

6 Revised calculation of income support applicable amount from 6.4.94:

Claimant's income:	retirement pension	£56.10
	graduated pension	4.47
	SERPS	12.60
	contracted out pension	12.60
	occupational pension	0.34
	industrial injury	
	disablement benefit	18.32
	industrial disease	
	disablement benefit	46.92
	mobility allowance	31.40
	attendance allowance	
	(high rate)	44.90
Spouse's income:	retirement pension	£33.70
	industrial disease	
	disablement benefit	25.28
	attendance allowance	
	(high rate)	44.90
Total joint income		£331.53

Calculation of weekly income support applicable amount, from 6.4.94:

Couple, personal allowance	£69.00
Higher pensioner premium	33.70
Severe disability premium	67.40
Income support applicable amount	£170.10

Their relevant weekly income from 6.4.94 worked out as follows:

Total joint income	£331.53
Less claimant's mobility allowance	31.40
Less claimant's attendance allowance	44.90
Less spouse's attendance allowance	44.90
Net income for income support purposes	£210.33

Clearly, the couple's joint net weekly income now exceeded their income support applicable amount by £40.23. Thus they lost entitlement to income support altogether, as well as entitlement to the passport benefits identified in para. 3 above. In other words, they have gone full circle to the position they were in at the beginning, namely July 1993.

To summarise, the couple enjoyed the privilege of income support for a period of seven months in total.

Appendix II
The distribution of intestate estates

For deaths on or after 1 December 1993 in England and Wales.

Spouse and issue (children or grandchildren) survive

Spouse entitlement:
All personal chattels; £125,000 absolutely (or the entire estate where this is less);

Life interest in one half or residue (if any).

Issue entitlement:
One half of residue (if any) on statutory trusts plus the other half of residue on statutory trusts upon the death of the spouse.

Spouse survives without issue

Spouse entitlement:
All personal chattels; £200,000 absolutely (or the entire estate where this is less); one half share of residue (if any) absolutely.

Remainder distributable to:
(a) The deceased's parents. If no parent survives:
(b) on trust for the deceased's brother and sisters of the whole blood and the issue of any such deceased brother or sister.

Spouse survives but no issue, parents, brothers or sisters or their issue

Whole estate to surviving spouse.

No spouse survives

Estate held for the following in the order given with no class of beneficiaries participating unless all those in a prior class have predeceased. Statutory trusts may apply except under 2 and 5.

1 Issue of the deceased.
2 Parents.
3 Brothers and sisters and the issue of a deceased brother or sister.
4 Half-brothers and half-sisters and the issue of any deceased half-brother or half-sister.
5 Grandparents.
6 Uncles and aunts and the issue of any deceased uncle or aunt.
7 Half-brothers and half-sisters of the deceased's parents and the issue of any deceased half-uncle or half-aunt.
8 The Crown, the Duchy of Lancaster or the Duchy of Cornwall.

Bibliography

Acheson, D. (1981) *Primary Health Care in Inner London*, Report of a Study Group commissioned by the London Health Planning Consortium.

Adams, T. (1989) 'Growth of a Speciality', *Nursing Times*, 85(4), 30–2.

Ade, P. (1992) 'Why Keep War Pensioners?', *SSAFA News*, Summer, 6.

Adviser, no.39, September and October 1993, Shelter.

Age Concern (1991) *Raising Income or Capital from your Home* Fact Sheet no.12, 12 July.

Age Concern (1994) *Instructions for my Next of Kin and Executors upon by Death*, Age Concern England, London.

Alzheimer's Disease Society (ADS) (1993) *Deprivation and Dementia*, Report by the Alzheimer's Disease Society, London.

Arden, A. and Hunter, C. (1992) *Manual of Housing Law*, Sweet & Maxwell, London.

Ashton, G. (1993a) 'Decision Making and Mental Incapacity', *Eagle*, February/March, 11–13.

—— (1993b) 'Wills Containing Provision for a Mentally Handicapped Child', *New Law Journal*, 1190.

Association of Community Health Councils for England and Wales (ACHEW) (1989) *Homelessness: The Effects on Health*, ACHEW, London.

—— (1990a) *National Health Service Complaints Procedures*, ACHEW, London.

—— (1990b) *NHS Continuing Care of Elderly People*, ACHEW, London.

—— (1992) *Memorandum of Evidence for the Health Committee Inquiry 'into NHS Dental Services'*, ACHEW, London.

—— (1991) *From 'Citizen's Charter' to 'Patient's Charter'*, ACHEW, London.

Audit Commission (1992) *The Community Care Revolution: Personal Social Services and Community Care*, HMSO, London.

Baker, S. and Parry, M. (1983) *Housing for Sale to the Elderly*, Housing Research Foundation.

Barlow, A. (1993) 'Relationship Breakdown, The Co-habiting Owner', *Adviser*, March/April, 6–11.

Bergman, K. (1973) 'Psychogeriatrics', *Medicine* 9, 643–52.

Birch, S. (1988) 'Patient Charges Past and Present', *Health Care UK 1988*, Policy Journals, Newbury, Berkshire.

Blanchfield, K. (1992) 'Exploding the Pension Myths', *SSAFA News*, Summer, 7.

Bloomsbury Community Health Council (1982) *Finding a Doctor in Bloomsbury,* Bloomsbury CHC, London.

Bloomsbury Community Health Council (1991) *Services for Elderly Mentally Infirm People in South Camden*, Bloomsbury CHC.

Bolver, N. (1991) 'Avoid the Transfer Stampede', *Guardian*, 16 November.

Bookbinder, D. (1987) 'Housing Options for the Elderly', *Roof*, September/October, 39.

—— (1991) *Housing Options for Older People*, Age Concern, London.

Bourke, L. (1988) 'Employees Face Crucial Decisions on Pensions', *The Independent*, 9 April.

Bourn, C. (1988) 'Employment Protection Rights', *New Law Journal*, vol.138, 12 August, 581.

Braham, D. (1985) 'A Doctor's Justification for Withdrawing Treatment', *New Law Journal* 135, 48–9.

Bransbury, L. (1993) *Council Tax and Disability*, Disability Rights, Disability Alliance, London, 11.

Brazier, M. (1992) 'Personal Injury by Molestation – An Emergent or Established Tort', *Family Law*, 346–8.

Caldock, K. and Wenger, C. (1993) 'Sociological Aspects of Dependency and Disability', *Reviews in Clinical Gerontology*, 3, 85–6.

Carson, D. (1993) 'Disabling Progress: The Law Commission's Proposals on Mentally Incapacitated Adults' Decision Making', *Journal of Social and Welfare Law*, no.5, 304.

Casey, B., Lakey, J. and Fogarty, M. (1991) *Enquiring into the Third Age: The Experience and Attitudes of Older People to Work and Retirement*, Policy Studies Institute, London.

CBI (1989) *Workforce 2000: An Agenda for Action.*

Central Statistical Office (CSO) (1986) *Social Trends*, HMSO, London.

—— (1988) *Social Trends*, HMSO, London.

—— (1992) *Social Trends*, HMSO, London.

—— (1994) *Social Trends*, HMSO, London.

Centre for Policy on Ageing (1984) *Home Life: A Code of Practice for Residential Care*, CPA, London.

—— (1994) *The European Directory of Older Age*, CPA, London.

Chatterton, D. (1988) 'The Reform of Pensions into 21st Century: A Critique', *New Law Journal*, April 1988, 227.

Chatterton, D. (1993) 'Pension Rights on Divorce: The Implications of Brooks v. Brooks', *Family Law*, 423–4.

Cliff, D. (1991) 'Negotiating Flexible Retirement', *Ageing and Society*, vol.11, 319.

College of Law (1992) *Law and the Elderly Client*, College of Law, Guildford.

Common, R. and Flynn, N. (1992) *Contracting for Care*, Joseph Rowntree Foundation, York.

Cook, J. and Mitchell, P. (1982) *Putting Teeth in the Act*, RADAR, London.

Council on Tribunals (1990) *Annual Report for 1988–9*, HMSO, London.

Cretney, S. (1990) 'Comment', *Family Law*, 176.

—— (1991) *Enduring Powers of Attorney*, Jordans, Bristol.

Crook, H. (1994) 'Grandparents and the Children Act 1989', *Family Law*, 135–8.

Davenport, P. (1992) 'Pension Pitfalls Abroad', *Times*, 2 May.

Davies, B. (1993) 'Better Pensions for All', Institute for Public Policy Research, London.

Dawson, B. and Faragher, T. (1979) *Battered Women Project: Interim Report*, University of Keele.

Decalmer, P. and Glendenning, F. (eds) (1993) *The Mistreatment of Elderly People*, Sage, London.

Department of the Environment (DoE) (1988) *The English Housing Condition Survey*, HMSO, London.

—— (1990) *Mobile Homes*, HMSO, London.

—— (1992a) *Assured Tenancies*, HMSO, London.

—— (1992b) *Code of Guidance*, 3rd edn, HMSO, London.

Department of Health (DH) (1989a) *Working for Patients*, HMSO, London.

—— (1989b) *Practice Budgets for General Medical Practitioners*, Working Paper 3, HMSO, London.

—— (1989c) *Indicative Prescribing Budgets for General Medical Practitioners*, Working Paper 4, HMSO, London.

—— (1989d) *Caring for People, Community Care in the Next Decade and Beyond*, HMSO, London.

—— (1989e) *General Practice in the National Health Service. The 1990 Contract*, DH/WO.

—— (1990) *Community Care in the Next Decade and Beyond. Policy Guidance*, HMSO, London.

—— (1991a) *Care Management and Assessment. Manager's Guide*, HMSO, London, 89.

—— (1991b) *The Patient's Charter*, HMSO, London.

DH/Welsh Office (WO) (1993) *Code of Practice. Mental Health Act 1983*, HMSO, London.

Department of Health and Social Security (DHSS) (1977) *Nursing in Primary Health Care*, Circular CNO(77)8.

—— (1981) *Growing Older*, Cmnd. 8173, HMSO, London, 64.

—— (1986) *Neighbourhood Nursing – A Focus for Care* (The Cumberlege Report), HMSO, London.

—— (1987) *Promoting Better Health*, HMSO, London.

Department of Social Security (DSS) (1990) *The Way Ahead – Benefits for Disabled People*, Cmnd. 917, HMSO, London.

—— (1993a) *Equality in State Pension Age*, Cmnd. 2420, HMSO, London.

—— (1993b) *The Social Security Departmental Report: The Government's Expenditure Plans 1993/94 to 1995/96*, HMSO, London.

Diamond, A. and McGrath, S. (1993) 'New Rights for Long Leaseholders', *Legal Action*, November.

Dibben, J. (1991) 'Don't Defer a State Pension', *Sunday Times*, 17 January.

Dibben, J. and Hibbett, A. (1993) 'Older Workers – An Overview of Recent Research', *Employment Gazette*, 237–50.

Disability Alliance (1992) *The Way Around*, Disability Alliance.

Dunham, R. (1994) 'Planning for a Year's Prosperity', *Accountancy*, February, 48–9.

Eastman, M. (1984) *Old Age Abuse*, Age Concern, Mitcham.

Edwards, N. (1992) 'Hobson's Choice', *Social Work Today*, 30 April.

Ekherdt, D. (1983) 'Claims that Retirement Improves Health', *Gerontologist*, vol.38, 231–7.

Employment Policy Institute (1992) 'Disabled in the Labour Market', *Economic Report*, July/August, vol.7, no.15.

Family Law (1993) 'Pensions and Divorce', *Family Law*, April, 240.

Family Practitioner Services, vol.9, no.5, 1982.

Family Practitioner Services, vol.12, no.5, 1985.

Francis, J. A. (1993) 'Enduring Powers of Attorney', *Eagle*, February/March, 4–7.

Fricker, N. (1992) 'Personal Molestation and Harassment', *Family Law*, 158–62.

General Medical Council (GMC) (1992) *Annual Report of the General Medical Council*, General Medical Council, London.

General Medical Council (GMC) (1993) *Professional Conduct and Discipline: Fitness to Practice*, General Medical Council, London.

Goodwin, J. (1992) 'The Waiting Game', *Adviser*, no.34, November/December.

Gordon, R. (1993) *Community Care Assessments: A Practical Legal Framework*, Longman, Harlow.

Gostin, L. (1983) 'The Court of Protection: A Legal and Policy Analysis of the Guardianship of the State', *MIND*, London.

Green, H. (1988) *Informal Carers*. A study carried out on the behalf of DHSS as part of the General Household Survey 1985, HMSO, London.

Griffiths, A. and Bhowmick, B. K. (1978) 'Sick Role Status and the Elderly Discharged from Hospital', *The Practitioner*, vol.221, December, 926.

Griffiths, A., Roberts, G. and Williams, J. (1993) 'Elder Abuse and the Law', in P. Decalmer and F. Glendenning (eds) *The Mistreatment of Elderly People*, Sage, London.

Griffiths, R. (1988) *Community Care: Agenda for Action*, HMSO, London.

Gunn, M., Newth, J. and De Saram, R. (1992) 'Tolley's Conference', *Taxation*, 10 December, 262–8.

Hailstone, E. (1993) 'Carers and Wills', *Family Law*, 415.

Ham, C. (1992) *Handbook for Community Health Council Members*, ACHEW, London, 28.

Health Advisory Service (1982) *The Rising Tide*, HMSO, London.

Health Committee (HC) – *see* House of Commons Health Committee.

Health Service Commissioner (HSC), *Annual Report for Session 1989–90*, HMSO, London.

—— *Second Report for Session 1993–4, Failure to Provide Long-term NHS Care for a Brain-damaged Patient*, HMSO, London.

—— (1990) *Annual Report for Session 1989–90*, p. 8, HMSO, London.

—— (1992) *Annual Report for Session 1991–2*, p. 18, HMSO, London.

Henwood, M. (1992) *Through a Glass Darkly. Community Care and Elderly People*, King's Fund Institute, London, 30.

Hoggett, B. (1990) *Mental Health Law* (3rd edn), Sweet & Maxwell, London.

House of Commons Health Committee Debate (1966) vol. 754, col. 51. The Crossman Catalogue.

House of Commons Health Committee Sixth Report. *Community Care: The Way Forward*, volume I, Session 1992–3, HMSO, London.

Hughes, D. and McGuire, A. (1992) 'Legislating for Health: The Nature of

Regulation in the NHS', in R. Dingwall and P. Fenn (eds), *Quality and Regulation in Health Care.*

Hughes, M. and Hunter, T. (1993) 'Government Blamed for Disaster over Pensions', *Guardian*, 10 December.

Hunt, M. and Miller, D. (1994) 'After the Wages Councils', *Adviser*, no.41, January/February, 29–30.

Hunter, C. and McGrath, S. (1992) *Homeless Persons*, Legal Action Group, London.

Hunter, M. (1992) 'Pensions Fiasco', *Guardian*, 29 February.

Jackson, J. (1990) 'People who Live Together should Put their Affairs in Order', *Family Law*, 439–41.

Johnson, M. (1972) 'Self-perception of need among the elderly', *Sociological Review*.

Katz, F. (1994) 'New Lease of Life', *Gazette*, vol. 91/319, January.

Keady, J. and Nolan, M. (1994) (in press) 'The Carer-Led Assessment Process (CLASP): A Framework for the Assessment of Need in Dementia Caregivers', *Journal of Clinical Nursing.*

Keeling, D. (1992) 'Moving in with Children', in *Law and the Elderly Client*, College of Law, Guildford, 27–33.

Kirby, R. and Liddington, J. (1993) 'What a Relief', *Taxation*, 583–4.

Laing, W. (1993) *'The Independent Sector' NHS Handbook*, (8th edn), NAHAT/JMH Publishing.

Law Commission (1991) *Mentally Incapacitated Adults and Decision-Making: An Overview*, Consultation Paper no.119, HMSO, London.

—— (1993a) *Looking to the Future: Mediation and the Ground for Divorce*, Cmnd. 2424, HMSO, London.

—— (1993b) *Mentally Incapacitated Adults and Decision-Making: Medical Treatment and Research*, Consultation Paper no.129, HMSO, London.

—— (1993c) *Mentally Incapacitated and other Vulnerable Adults: Public Law Protection*, Consultation Paper no.130, HMSO, London.

Leat, D. (1993) *The Development of Community Care by the Independent Sector*, Policy Studies Institute, London.

Leigh, A. (1987) 'A Better Way of Life', *Community Care*, 4 June.

Liddington, J. (1993) 'Interest-Free but not Tax-Free', *Taxation*, 16 September, 565–6.

Luba, J. (1991) *Repairs: Tenants' Rights*, Legal Action Group, London.

Luba, J. and Madge, N. (1988) 'Recent Developments in Housing Law', *Legal Action*, March.

Luba, J. and Madge, N. (1993a) 'Recent Developments in Housing Law', *Legal Action*, March.

Luba, J. and Madge, N. (1993b) 'Recent Developments in Housing Law', *Legal Action*, September.

Luba, J., Madge, N. and McConnell, D. (1993) *Defending Possession Proceedings*, Legal Action Group, London.

McColdrick, A. (1984) *Equal Treatment in Occupational Pension Schemes: A Research Project*, Equal Opportunities Commission, London.

McFarlane, S. (1984) 'Control of Anatomy: Anatomy Act', *Solicitors' Journal*, vol. 128, 507.

McIntosh, I. B. (1990) 'The Right to Independence no matter How Illusory', *Geriatric Medicine*, May, 67–8.

Mackay, R. D. (1983) 'Statutory Reform and the Law of Wills', *New Law Journal*, 861.

Maidment, S. (1978) 'The Law's Response to Marital Violence: A Comparison Between England and the USA', in *Family Violence*, ed. Katz and Katz, Butterworths, Canada.

Masson, J. (1993) 'Pensions – A Scheme for Divorcing Couples', *Family Law*, 479–81.

Matthew, L. (1990) 'A Role for the CPN in Supporting the Carer of Clients with Dementia', in C. Brooker, (ed.), *Community Psychiatric Nursing Research*, Chapman & Hall, London.

Mental Health Act Commission (MHAC) (1985) *First Biennial Report of the Mental Health Act Commission 1983–5*, HMSO, London.

—— (1987) *Second Biennial Report of the Mental Health Act Commission 1985–7*, HMSO, London.

—— (1989) *Third Biennial Report of the Mental Health Act Commission 1987–9*, HMSO, London.

—— (1991) *Fourth Biennial Report of the Mental Health Act Commission 1989–91*, HMSO, London.

—— (1993) *Fifth Biennial Report of the Mental Health Act Commission 1991–93*, HMSO, London.

Midwinter, E. (1992) *Comes Safely Home,* Elderly Accommodation Council, London.

Mitchell, B. (1987) *Landlord and Tenant Law*, BSP Professional Books.

Moroney, L. (1993) 'Relationship Breakdown, and the Co-habiting Tenant', *Adviser*, May/June, 11–13.

Moroney, L. with Goodwin, J. (1992) *Homelessness and Good Practice Guide*, Shelter.

Morton, D. (1992) *Community Care*, SITRA Bulletin, Issue 38, March.

Nolan, M. (1993) 'Carer-Dependant Relationships and the Prevention of Elder Abuse', in *The Mistreament of Elderly People*, ed. P. Decalmer and F. Glendenning, Sage, London, 148–58.

Norman, A. (1985) *Triple Jeopardy. Growing Old in a Second Homeland*, Centre for Policy on Ageing, London.

Norman, A. (1987) 'Down and Out in Britain', *Community Care*, 12 November.

Nuffield Foundation (1986) *Pharmacy: The Report of a Committee of Inquiry.*

Office of Population and Census Studies (OPCS) (1986) *General Household Survey*, HMSO, London.

—— (1988) *General Household Survey*, HMSO, London.

—— (1990) *General Household Survey*, HMSO, London.

—— (1992) *Labour Force Survey – Great Britain*, Employment Department, HMSO, London.

Oughton, R. D. (1984) *Tyler's Family Provision*, Professional Books.

Pampel, F.C. (1981) *Social Change and the Aged – Recent Trends in the United States*, Lexington Books, Lexington, Mass.

Pension Law Review Committee (1993) *Pension Law Reform*, HMSO, London.

Poynter, R. and Martin, C. (1993) '*Rights Guide to Non-Means Tested Benefits*', CPAG, London.

Royal Association for Disability and Rehabilitation (RADAR) (1981).

Rae, M. (1994) 'Divorce a Better Way', *Family Law*, 9.

Raphael, A. (1992) 'Daylight Robbery – A Standard Business Practice', *Observer*, 3 May.

Ray, R. (1993) 'Washing Out Gains', *Taxation*, 15 April, 59.

Reardon, T. (1988) *Planning your Pension*, Longman, London

Reker, G. and Wong, P. (1988) 'Ageing as an individual process: Towards a theory of personal meaning', in Birren, J. and Bengston, V. (eds), *Emergent theories of Ageing*, Springer Publishing, New York, 214–46.

Richards, D. (1993) 'Screening the Over–75s: 1' *British Journal of Nursing*, 2, 16.

Robertson, S. (1993) *Disability Rights Handbook*, Disability Alliance, Colchester.

Royal College of General Practitioners (RCGP) (1986) *Morbidity Statistics for General Practice, 1981–2*, 3rd Survey, HMSO, London.

Royal Commission on the National Health Service (RCNHS) (1979), Cmnd. 7615, 150.

Samuels, A. (1983) 'Medical Negligence Today – An Appraisal', *Social Science and Medicine* 23, 1, 31.

Samuels, A. (1993a) 'Making a Will', *Eagle*, February/March, 18–20.

Samuels, A. (1993b) 'Grandparents and the Grandchild: The Legal Position', *Eagle*, October/November, 14–16.

Scheuer, M. A., Black, M., Victor, C., Benseval, M., Gill, M. and Judge, K. (1991) *Homelessness and the Utilisation of Acute Hospital Services in London*, King's Fund Institute, London.

Schweitzer, P. (1991) 'A Place to Stay: Growing Old Away from Home', in Squires, A. J. (ed.), *Multicultural Health Care and Rehabilitation*, Edward Arnold/Age Concern, London.

Securities Investment Board (1993) *Pension Transfers*, London.

Selwyn, N. (1993) *Law of Employment*, 8th edn, Chatham, Kent.

Shiner, P. (1993) 'Affordable Housing and Development Plans', *Legal Action*, May.

Silvey, J. (1991) *Co-operation in Community Care; Inter-Professional Issues in the Assessment of Older People*, Centre for Inter-Professional Studies, University of Nottingham, Nottingham.

Smith, A. (1994) 'N & P Make £2m Provision for Personal Pensions Claim', *Financial Times*, 15 February.

Smith, P. (1988) 'Meeting the Housing Needs of Elderly Asian People', *Social Work Today*, 4 February.

Solicitors' Journal (1993) vol. 137, no. 42, 5 November.

Social Services Inspectorate (SSI) (1992) *Implementing Care for People: Assessment CI(92)34, 14 December 1992* (often referred to as the Laming Letter).

—— (1994) *Discretionary Charges for Adult Social Services*. Advice note for use by Social Services Inspectorate, January, attached to Department of Health Circular 1AC(94)1.

Stacey (1974) 'Consumer Complaints Procedure in the British National Health Service', *Social Science and Medicine*, x, 429.

Taylor, R. C. and Buckley, E. G. (eds) (1987) *Preventive Care and the Elderly*, Occasional Paper No. 35, Royal College of General Practitioners, London.

The Economist (1993) 'The Welfare State – What Crisis?', 13 November, 35–8.

Therapy Weekly, 8 September 1988, 'Disabled miss out on Home Adaptations'.

Tinker, A. (1992) *Elderly People in Modern Society*, 2nd edn, Longman, Harlow.

Tinker, A. (1993) 'When Does Old Age Start?', *International Journal of Geriatric Medicine*, 8, 712.

Tomlinson, F. (1992) *Report of the Inquiry into London's Health Service, Medical Education and Research*, HMSO, London.

Traynor, J. and Haslip, J. (1984) 'Sometimes She Makes Me Want to Hit Her', *Community Care*, 2 August, 20.

Trinder, C. (1990) *'How Much Employment after 55?'*, Social Policy Research Findings, no.4, Joseph Rowntree Memorial Trust, York.

Trinder, C., Hulme, G. and McCarthy, U. (1992) *Employment: The Role of Work in the Third Age*, The Carnegie United Kingdom Trust.

Tulloch, A. J. and Moore, V. (1979) 'A Randomised Controlled Trial of Geriatric Screening and Surveillance in General Practice', *Journal of the Royal College of General Practitioners*, 29, 730–42.

Victor, C. (1991) *Health and Health Care in Later Life*, Open University Press, Milton Keynes.

Walker, A. (1991) 'The Social Construction of Dependency in Old Age', in Loney, M., Bocock, R., Clarke, J., Cochrane, A., Pegotty, G. and Wilson, M., (eds), *The State of the Market – Politics and Welfare in Contemporary Britain*, 2nd edn, Open University, Milton Keynes, 41–56.

Walker, A. (1993) 'Poverty and Inequality in Old Age', in Bond, J., Coleman, P. and Pierce, S. (eds), *Ageing and Society*, Sage and Open University Press.

Walker, A. and Taylor, P. (1992) 'Ageism v. Productive Ageing', in Bass, S., Carol, F. and Chen, Y., (eds), *Achieving a Productive Ageing Society*, Westport, Greenwood.

Walkington, L. and Scott, M. (1993) 'Fear Grows for State Pensions', *The Observer*, 5 December.

Warburton, J. (1993) *Sharing Residential Property*, Sweet & Maxwell, London.

Webster, L., Tate, G., Simmons, D., Vaux, G., Barnes, M., Knights, E., Read, J. and Gurney, J. (1994) *National Welfare Benefits Handbook*, 24th edn, CPAG, London.

Webster, L. and Wood, P. (1993) *National Welfare Benefit Handbook*, CPAG, London.

Welfare Rights Bulletin (1992a) 'Delays Swamp Agency Targets', October, no.110, 9.

Welfare Rights Bulletin (1992b) 'Social Fund Budget Update', October, no.110, 11–12.

Welsh Office (1991) *Managing Care: Guidance on Assessment and the Provision of Social and Community Care*, Welsh Office.

Welstead, M. (1990) 'Mistresses in Law', *Family Law*, 72–4.

Wenger, C. (1988) *Old People's Health and Experience of the Caring Services*, Occasional Paper no.4, The Institute of Human Ageing, Liverpool University Press, Liverpool.

Widdecombe, A. (1993) 'Pensioners' Deal', Letters Page, *The Times*, 1 December.

Widdowfield, G. and Coles, S. (1994) 'Community Care and the Homeless', *Adviser*, March/April, no.42, 7.

Wikeley, N. (1992) 'Disability Living Allowance', *Legal Action*, 16 January, 11.

Williamson, J. (1987) *Prevention Screening and Casefinding – An Overview*, Occasional Paper no.35, Royal College of General Practitioners, London.

Wright, D. (1988) 'Beware of Early Pensions', *Sunday Times*, 21 August.

Index